ALBERT SHAW LECTURES ON
DIPLOMATIC HISTORY

Under the Auspices of the

WALTER HINES PAGE SCHOOL OF
INTERNATIONAL RELATIONS

The liberality of Albert Shaw, Ph. D. 1884, has made it possible for The Johns Hopkins University to provide an annual course of lectures on diplomatic history. The lectures, while still included in the regular work of the Department of History, have since the establishment of the Page School of International Relations, in 1930, been placed under its auspices.

ALBERT SHAW LECTURES ON DIPLOMATIC HISTORY

1899. JOHN H. LATANÉ. The Diplomatic Relations of the United States and Spanish America. 1900. (Out of print.)

1900. JAMES MORTON CALLAHAN. The Diplomatic History of the Southern Confederacy. 1901. (Out of print.)

1906. JESSE SIDDALL REEVES. American Diplomacy under Tyler and Polk. 1907. (Out of print.)

1907. ELBERT JAY BENTON. International Law and Diplomacy of the Spanish-American War. 1908. $1.75.

1909. EPHRAIM DOUGLASS ADAMS. British Interests and Activities in Texas, 1838-1846. 1910. (Out of print.)

1911. CHARLES OSCAR PAULLIN. Diplomatic Negotiations of American Naval Officers, 1778-1883. 1912. $2.25.

1912. ISAAC J. COX. The West Florida Controversy, 1798-1813. 1918. $3.00.

1913. WILLIAM R. MANNING. Early Diplomatic Relations between the United States and Mexico. 1916. $2.50.

1914. FRANK A. UPDYKE. The Diplomacy of the War of 1812. 1915. (Out of print.)

1917. PAYSON JACKSON TREAT. The Early Diplomatic Relations between the United States and Japan, 1853-1865. 1917. $2.75.

1921. PERCY ALVIN MARTIN. Latin America and the War. 1925. $3.50.

1923. HENRY MERRITT WRISTON. Executive Agents in American Foreign Relations. 1929. $5.00.

1926. SAMUEL FLAGG BEMIS. Pinckney's Treaty: A Study of America's Advantage from Europe's Distress, 1783-1800. 1926. Second printing 1941. $3.00.

1927. BRUCE WILLIAMS. State Security and the League of Nations. 1927. $2.75.

1928. J. FRED RIPPY. Rivalry of the United States and Great Britain over Latin America, 1808-1830. 1929. $2.75.

1930. VÍCTOR ANDRÉS BELAUNDE. Bolivar and the Political Thought of the Spanish American Revolution. 1938. $3.50.

1931. CHARLES CALLAN TANSILL. The Purchase of the Danish West Indies. 1932. $3.50.

1932. DEXTER PERKINS. The Monroe Doctrine, 1826-1867. 1933. $3.50.

1933. CHARLES SEYMOUR. American Diplomacy during the World War. 1934. Second printing 1942. $3.00.

1935. FRANK H. SIMONDS. American Foreign Policy in the Post-war Years. 1935. $2.00.

1936. JULIUS W. PRATT. Expansionists of 1898. The Acquisition of Hawaii and the Spanish Islands. 1936. $3.00.

1937. DEXTER PERKINS. The Monroe Doctrine, 1867-1907. 1937. $3.50.

1938. ARTHUR PRESTON WHITAKER. The United States and the Independence of Latin America, 1800-1830. 1941. $3.75.

1939. WILLIAM SPENCE ROBERTSON. France and Latin-American Independence. 1939. $3.75.

1941. THOMAS A. BAILEY. The Policy of the United States toward the Neutrals, 1917-1918. 1942. $3.50.

1942. WILFRID HARDY CALLCOTT. The Caribbean Policy of the United States, 1890-1920. 1942. $3.50.

THE POLICY OF THE UNITED STATES TOWARD THE NEUTRALS,
1917–1918

LONDON: HUMPHREY MILFORD
OXFORD UNIVERSITY PRESS

THE ALBERT SHAW LECTURES ON DIPLOMATIC HISTORY, 1941
THE WALTER HINES PAGE SCHOOL OF INTERNATIONAL RELATIONS

THE POLICY OF THE UNITED STATES TOWARD THE NEUTRALS, 1917-1918

BY

THOMAS A. BAILEY

Stanford University

BALTIMORE

THE JOHNS HOPKINS PRESS

1942

COPYRIGHT 1942, THE JOHNS HOPKINS PRESS

PRINTED IN THE UNITED STATES OF AMERICA
BY J. H. FURST COMPANY, BALTIMORE, MARYLAND

PREFACE

For reasons that I present at length in the first chapter, I have made this study primarily one of policy. Considerable attention is devoted to both diplomacy and public opinion, but no more than seemed necessary for a reasonably adequate background.

At the cost of some repetition, I have given brief summaries at the end of each chapter, and an extended summary in the concluding chapter. These are concessions to the technical nature of the subject, which involves the inevitably dull analyses of a number of lengthy policy documents. The summaries are also designed to guide the reader who is interested only in special phases, or who does not have time to read the entire book.

I have proceeded on the assumption that there was international law in 1914, and that the relations of the belligerents toward the neutrals must, from a legalistic view at least, be judged in the light of that law. I have also assumed that the neutrals, under both law and treaty, had certain rights. Recent history has given a considerable degree of unreality to these assumptions; but they seemed very real in the years 1914-1918.

In preparing these pages I was constantly tempted to refer at length to analogous developments during the war that broke out in 1939, but for various reasons I decided against such a practice. In ordinary circumstances historical parallels must be used with great caution; they are doubly dangerous when they involve events that have not yet run their course.

Preface

Of the group of American officials who were most actively involved in formulating American policy toward the neutrals during this period, only two are dead: President Wilson and Secretary of State Lansing. Both of these men, aside from the voluminous official record, left private collections which I was privileged to consult. All of the principal survivors, without exception, have graciously provided me with valuable material from their files or their recollections, and all except two of them (whom I did not ask) found it possible to read and comment on all or substantial portions of the manuscript. Many of their remarks I quote at length in footnotes. In order to spare embarrassment, I have reproduced these observations in a few instances without indicating their authorship.

The participants to whom I refer and to whom I am profoundly indebted are herewith listed alphabetically.

Lawrence Bennett, of New York City, Secretary to the War Trade Board, who was present at the deliberations of that body, and who prepared and signed the official minutes.

George Creel, of San Francisco, Chairman of the Committee on Public Information, which had charge of propaganda in the neutral countries.

John Foster Dulles, of New York City, Assistant to the Chairman of the War Trade Board. (Aside from reading a portion of the manuscript, Mr. Dulles graciously provided me with photostatic copies of certain valuable documents in his possession.)

Paul Fuller, Jr., of New York City, Director of the Bureau of War Trade Intelligence of the War Trade Board July, 1917 to December, 1918; Acting Director of the Bureau of Enemy Trade, 1917-1919; member of the Censorship Board, 1917-1918.

Preface

Herbert C. Hoover, of Stanford University, Chairman of the Commission for Relief in Belgium, 1914-1919; United States Food Administrator, May, 1917 to July 1, 1919; member of the Exports Council and represented on the Exports Administrative Board and the War Trade Board.

Vance C. McCormick, of Harrisburg, Pennsylvania, Chairman of the War Trade Board, 1917-1919, and member of the war mission to Great Britain and France, 1917. (In addition to reading the entire manuscript, Mr. McCormick graciously provided me with copies of certain valuable materials in his possession.)

Hunter Miller, who was appointed special assistant to the Department of State, June, 1917, and who is better known for his work in connection with the drafting of the covenant of the League of Nations, and with the editing of the treaties of the United States.

William Phillips, of Boston, Massachusetts, Assistant Secretary of State, January 24, 1917 to March 25, 1920.

Frank L. Polk, of New York City, Counselor for the Department of State, August 30, 1915 to July 1, 1919; at various times Acting Secretary of State, and probably more intimately concerned with the problem of the neutrals than Secretary of State Lansing.

Alonzo E. Taylor, of Minneapolis, Minnesota, member of the War Trade Board from 1917 to 1919 as the representative of the Secretary of Agriculture; member of the war mission to Great Britain and France, 1917.

Charles Warren, of Washington, D. C., Assistant Attorney General of the United States, May, 1914 to April, 1918, who was actively engaged in legal matters relating to the neutrals.

Lester H. Woolsey, of Washington, D. C., Law Adviser,

Department of State, July 1, 1916 to June 27, 1917; Solicitor, Department of State, June 27, 1917 to March, 1920; probably more intimately concerned with the problem of the neutrals than any other official in the Department.

None of the persons named above saw the final draft of my manuscript; and the listing of their names in no wise implies responsibility for my shortcomings or agreement with my views. I merely wish to acknowledge my own debt and that of the scholarly world to a group of distinguished men, most of whom are still very busy, who gave generously of their time and energy.

I owe no less a debt to a number of scholars who most graciously consented to read and criticize all or considerable portions of the manuscript. Listed alphabetically they are: John Gange, of Stanford University, now with the Division of Cultural Relations, Department of State; Charles H. Hunter, of the University of Hawaii, whose doctoral dissertation on Anglo-American co-ordination first opened to me the possibilities of the present study; James R. Mock, of the National Archives, whose volumes on censorship and on the Committee on Public Information also proved most helpful; Alice Morrissey McDiarmid (nee Alice M. Morrissey), whose book and articles on this general subject were of substantial value; and Carlton Savage, of the Department of State, whose work on *Maritime Commerce* provided an invaluable introduction to the subject.

What I have already said about assuming responsibility for my own shortcomings applies to these scholars as well as to surviving participants.

Other persons most generously assisted by correspondence in providing information relating to fact and to international law. They are: Mr. Green H. Hackworth, Legal Adviser, Department of State; Captain Dudley W. Knox, in charge of the Office of Naval Records and Library, Navy Department, who during 1917-1918 was stationed at London; Professor Norman J. Padelford, of the Fletcher School of Law and Diplomacy; and Professor Vernon Van Dyke, of De Pauw University.

In connection with the use of the documents, I incurred special obligations to the following persons: E. Wilder Spaulding, George Verne Blue, Milford A. Shipley, and Merrill S. Potts, all of the Department of State; to Mrs. Woodrow Wilson, for permission to use the Wilson Papers; to President Charles Seymour, of Yale University, for permission to examine the House Collection, and to Russell G. Pruden for locating such of these papers as I needed; to St. George L. Sioussat, Thomas P. Martin, and Miss Katharine E. Brand, for courtesies in connection with using the materials of the Division of Manuscripts, Library of Congress; and to Miss Suda L. Bane, of the Hoover Library on War, Revolution, and Peace, who rendered the extraordinary service of collating all references to the Hoover documents with the original manuscripts in her custody. Those in charge of the Princeton University Library and the Stanford University Libraries cheerfully extended the usual courtesies.

Most of the materials used in this study were gathered while I was holding a fellowship of the Rockefeller Foundation, for which I wish to express my gratitude.

I am obligated to Professor Edward Mead Earle for his interest in my project, and for the privilege of participating in his seminar at the Institute for Advanced Study in Princeton.

Robert P. Browder and William R. Hitchcock, students at Stanford University, capably relieved me of much of the drudgery of routine checking.

The passages from volume VIII of *Woodrow Wilson: Life and Letters*, by Ray Stannard Baker, copyright, 1939, by Doubleday, Doran and Company, Inc., are quoted by special permission of the publisher.

THOMAS A. BAILEY

Stanford University

TABLE OF CONTENTS

	PAGE
PREFACE	v

CHAPTER

I. THE TRANSITION FROM NEUTRALITY TO BELLIGERENCY 1

(i) General assumption that belligerent America flagrantly violated neutral rights—(ii) Importance of present subject—Why it has not been investigated earlier—(iii) Timeliness of general subject—Emphasis in this book not on diplomatic history but on policy—(iv) Neutral America the leader and champion of neutrals—(v) Belligerent America turns back on neutrals—The question of what is a violation of international law—(vi) The question of which nations were neutral—(vii) Wilson's invitation to neutrals to follow America in breaking relations—Reactions of Europe; Liberia; Siam—(viii) Response of China—(ix) Replies from Latin America—(x) Pressures and inducements from Washington to bring neutrals into war—(xi) Conclusions.

II. THE BEGINNINGS OF A POLICY TOWARD THE NEUTRALS 34

(i) Agitation against indirect shipment of American foodstuffs and materials to Germany—(ii) Demand for export control—(iii) American misunderstanding of neutral problems—Charges of inconsistency in America—(iv) Neutral defense of position in trading with Germany—(v) Neutral accusations of American inconsistency—Possible neutral countermeasures against proposed American export restrictions—(vi) British desire for American co-operation in neutral control measures—Balfour Mission and its objectives—(vii) Discussions in Washington with British Embassy—British suggestions as to forcing neutral shipping into service—(viii) Report of British-American Joint Subcommittee on Export Licenses; Report of Subcommittee on Statistics and Sources of Information—(ix) Woolsey memorandum on extent of American willingness to co-operate with the British—(x) Observations on work of Balfour Commission.

TABLE OF CONTENTS

PAGE

III. THE ESTABLISHMENT OF EXPORT AND IMPORT CONTROL 64

(i) Debate over export control bill in Congress—(ii) Exports control established by Espionage Act—(iii) Executive order of June 22, 1917, creating Exports Council—First exports licensing proclamation (July 9, 1917)—Reactions—(iv) Legality of exports embargoes—(v) Policy toward neutrals outlined in memorandum of Exports Council, July 24, 1917—(vi) British seek more satisfactory export control—(vii) British refute danger of forcing neutrals into arms of enemy—(viii) State Department seeks fuller data as to British neutral commitments—(ix) Wilson's proclamation of August 21, 1917, creating Exports Administrative Board and new Exports Council—Wilson's second exports control proclamation (August 27, 1917)—(x) Executive order of October 12, 1917, replacing Exports Administrative Board with War Trade Board—(xi) Imports control authorized by Trading with the Enemy Act of October 6, 1917—Wilson's proclamation of November 28, 1917, establishing import control by license—Third export control proclamation of November 28, 1917—Wilson's proclamation of February 14, 1918, placing all exports and imports under license—(xii) Christmas concessions to Northern Neutrals—(xiii) Relaxation of embargo on non-essentials to Northern Neutrals.

IV. THE RATIONING AGREEMENT WITH NORWAY   102

(i) General position of Norway—(ii) Sending of Nansen Commission to United States, July, 1917—(iii) Norwegian-American grain agreement, August, 1917—(iv) Delay of Norway in presenting proposals—(v) Reasons for American delay in negotiations—Wilson's idealistic position—(vi) Nansen's first comprehensive proposal, November 16, 1917—Norwegian and American proposals and counterproposals—War Trade Board publishes its terms to bring pressure to bear on Norwegian government, January, 1918—(vii) Christiania's publication of position—(viii) German threats and Norway's declaration of neutrality, March, 1918—War Trade Board's ultimatum to Nansen, April, 1918—Nansen signs general agreement, April 30, 1918—(ix) Summary of the agreement—(x) General observations on the agreement—(xi) United States drives a hard bargain.

Table of Contents

PAGE

V. THE SWEDISH RATIONING AND TONNAGE NEGOTIATIONS 136

(i) General position of Sweden and her strength—(ii) Weaknesses—(iii) Sending of special commission to the United States, May, 1917—(iv) American grain deal with Sweden, August, 1917—Opposition and final consent of British—(v) British mail-pouch controversy with Sweden—Good offices of United States result in amicable settlement, October, 1917—(vi) Iron ore problem and early Allied suggestions of purchasing part of surplus going to Germany—(vii) Transfer of Swedish-American negotiations to London—(viii) Conclusion of *modus vivendi* on tonnage and embargo easement, January 29, 1918—(ix) Negotiations for general agreement in London—American opposition to requisitioning of Swedish tonnage—United States reluctantly assumes share of ore purchase—(x) War Trade Board's objections to final agreement—(xi) Summary of general agreement of May 29, 1918—(xii) Dissatisfaction with workings of agreement—More favorable attitude of Sweden toward the Allies—(xiii) General observations and conclusions.

VI. THE RATIONING AND TONNAGE AGREEMENT WITH DENMARK 165

(i) General position of Denmark—(ii) Problems confronting the Allies—(iii) Danish reaction to American criticisms—(iv) Initial steps in the Danish-American negotiations—Wilson vetoes Hoover's suggestion of drastic measures—(v) Negotiations in the autumn of 1917—British attempts to place onus on the United States—(vi) Policy of purposeful delay in negotiations ended by Wilson's intervention—(vii) General problems of rationing and tonnage—Denmark's allegations of distress—(viii) American ultimatum on danger-zone tonnage—Partial Danish capitulation—Fear of requisitioning—(ix) German pressure on Copenhagen—(x) Terms of Danish-American rationing and tonnage agreement of September 18, 1918—Earlier agreement with Iceland—(xi) General observations on agreement—Danish reaction.

VII. THE RATIONING AND TONNAGE NEGOTIATIONS WITH HOLLAND.................. 194

(i) General position of Holland—(ii) Instruments of coercion possessed by Allies—(iii) Dutch reaction to embargo—Breakdown of grain negotiations—Sending of commission—(iv) Protracted negotiations in Washington—Increasing bitterness in Holland—(v) Transfer of negotiations to London—Conclusion of *modus vivendi*—Dutch delay in carrying it out—(vi) Early steps toward requisitioning Dutch tonnage—Wilson's general requisitioning order of March 20, 1918—(vii) Reaction of the Dutch—(viii) Unofficial and official Dutch protests—Unofficial and official American replies—Legal position of United States—(ix) Dutch attempts to secure assurances against further requisitioning—German steps in direction of reprisals—More favorable auguries for continued negotiations with Dutch—(x) Reopening of negotiations in London—(xi) Tonnage and rationing agreement of November 25, 1918—Implementing Allied agreement with N. O. T. of December 17, 1918—Adherence to this agreement by War Trade Board, December 30, 1918—Reservations of United States—(xii) General observations and conclusions.

VIII. THE RATIONING NEGOTIATIONS WITH SWITZERLAND 239

(i) General position of Switzerland—(ii) American sympathy—Importance of tiny republic—(iii) Swiss concern over embargo on grain—Sending of commission to the United States—(iv) Silk agreement—Problems involving Switzerland and Italy—(v) Shift of negotiations to Paris—Connection between the grain and military situation—American declaration to respect Swiss neutrality—Signing of rationing agreement of December 5, 1917—(vi) Analysis of agreement—Swiss satisfaction—(vii) British-American misunderstanding as to obligation to deliver grain—(viii) Critical situation in Switzerland—American promise to send grain—(ix) Washington's decision to convoy grain ships to Switzerland—(x) Unsuccessful attempt to secure German and Austrian tonnage in Spain for Swiss grain—(xi) General observations and conclusions.

IX. THE RATIONING AND TONNAGE NEGOTIATIONS WITH SPAIN 272

(i) The general position of Spain—(ii) Pressures suggested by the Balfour Commission—

PAGE

Lansing's statement to Madrid—(iii) Gradual imposition of embargo on Spain—Cotton problem—(iv) U-boats in Spanish waters—Washington declines British invitation to protest jointly—Sinkings of merchantmen in Spanish waters—United States representations over escape of U 293 from Cadiz—(v) Washington joins with Associates in urging internment of German crews in Spain—(vi) Negotiations in Madrid for commercial agreement—Impossibility of securing tonnage—Difficulty over bunkering pressure—(vii) Summary of commercial agreement of March 7, 1918—(viii) Delay of Spain in carrying out agreement—Breakdown of tonnage negotiations—(ix) Spanish-American financial agreement of August 28, 1918—Negotiations for mules for A. E. F.—(x) Washington declines to urge Spain to enter war—(xi) General observations and conclusions.

X. THE UNITED STATES AND THE LATIN AMERICA NEUTRALS 305

(i) Absence of hemispheric solidarity—The belligerents; quasi-belligerents; neutrals—(ii) General observations on the group that remained neutral—(iii) The abortive conference of neutrals—United States opposition to—(iv) Unique position of Mexico—(v) Difficulty between United States and Mexico over twenty-four hour rule—Three-ship rule—(vi) Questions of hovering; violating Mexican territorial waters—(vii) The sisal problem in Yucatán—America refrains from drastic action—(viii) Problems involving Argentina—Washington's refusal to press for internment of German submarines—Allied grain agreement—Case of the *Bahia Blanca*—(ix) Chilean seizure of interned German ships—Similar action by Uruguay and Peru—(x) Latin America agrees to receive United States armed merchantmen and requisitioned Dutch ships—(xi) General observations and conclusions.

XI. BUNKERS AND BLACKLISTS 339

(i) British bunker control and attempts to persuade America to adopt it—(ii) Adoption of bunker control by the United States and its objectives—(iii) General conclusions on bunker control and neutral rights—(iv) British blacklist and its nature—(v) American protest against British blacklist (July 26, 1916)—Grey's reply—(vi)

TABLE OF CONTENTS

PAGE

British pressure on America to adopt blacklist in 1917—Blacklist authorized by Trading with Enemy Act of October 6, 1917—Four categories of the American blacklist—(vii) The three comprehensive United States blacklists—Extension of blacklist after Armistice—(viii) Inter-Allied coordination problems—Effectiveness of American blacklists—(ix) British proposal of a financial blockade of neutrals—Refusal of the United States to join—(x) General conclusions.

XII. PROBLEMS INVOLVING FREEDOM OF THE SEAS   380

(i) Declaration of London, 1909—Refusal of Britain to subscribe to—(ii) Lansing's protest against British blockade (October 21, 1915)—(iii) Embargo by belligerent America complements blockade—Washington's refusal to exchange prizes reciprocally with British; to participate in British blockade—(iv) Postwar discussions of American practices—(v) Was America a *particeps criminis* in helping enforce blockade?—(vi) Washington's neutral position on contraband—(vii) American belligerent attitude on contraband and continuous voyage—(viii) United States declines to seize reservists on high seas; to engage in mandatory routing of neutral ships—(ix) Elimination of Halifax call—Abortive scheme for mandatory routing—(x) American position on safe-conducts—(xi) Prebelligerent attitude on mining open sea—Laying the North Sea mine barrage—(xii) Washington declines to take strong measures to force Norway to close the barrage gap—(xiii) Observations on dealings with Norway—(xiv) Conclusions.

XIII. PROBLEMS OF INTERNATIONAL LAW AND NEUTRAL TREATY RIGHTS.............   421

(i) Early American protests against British postal censorship—(ii) Belligerent America adopts postal censorship of neutral mails—(iii) Questionable or inconsistent practices—(iv) Early American protests against British cable censorship; later adoption of—Questionable practices—(v) Drafting of neutral aliens contrary to treaty guarantees—(vi) Protests of neutral diplomats—Wilson's discharge order—(vii) Amendment of Selective Service Act—Injustices to aliens—(viii) Requisitioning of neutral shipping building in

United States—Hague Court (1922) finds against United States in Norwegian claims—(ix) Special arbitrator (1932) finds for United States in case of two detained Swedish ships—(x) Court of Claims (1927) finds against United States in case of detained Dutch ship *Zeelandia*—(xi) American refusal to violate neutrality of Panama Canal—(xii) Neutral protest against eliciting submarine information from neutral captains—(xiii) American propaganda in neutral countries; high tone of—(xiv) Summary and conclusions.

XIV. THE BALANCE SHEET 469

(i) Practices protested against by the United States as a neutral but adopted as a belligerent—(ii) Practices adopted as a belligerent after reserving rights as a neutral—(iii) Arguable violations of international law—(iv) Pressures brought to bear on the neutrals—(v) Practices protested against as a neutral and not employed as a belligerent—(vi) Unquestionable violations of treaty rights and international law—(vii) Practices not protested against as a neutral and not employed while a belligerent—(viii) Wilsonian idealism and the generosity of the United States toward the neutrals—(ix) General conclusions and observations—The record of the United States on the whole creditable.

SELECT BIBLIOGRAPHY 493

INDEX 505

TABLES

Population and Area of European Neutrals	16
Gross Steam Tonnage of the World, 1916-1917	104
Status of Latin America, 1917-1918	306
Enemy Trading Lists of the United States	364

MAPS

European Neutrals, April, 1917	17
Latin America, 1917-1918	307

Chapter I

THE TRANSITION FROM NEUTRALITY TO BELLIGERENCY

i

Burton J. Hendrick, in his widely read *Life and Letters of Walter Hines Page*, records an interesting conversation which allegedly took place in 1917, shortly after America entered the war, between Frank L. Polk, Counselor for the Department of State, and Arthur James Balfour, head of the British mission to Washington. Keenly aware of the recent controversy between the two countries over neutral rights, Balfour began to suggest, hesitatingly, that it might be desirable for the United States to adopt the British blacklist, against which the Department of State had strongly protested, and apply it to the remaining neutrals of the world. " Mr. Balfour," broke in Polk, " it took Great Britain three years to reach a point where it was prepared to violate all the laws of blockade. You will find that it will take us only two months to become as great criminals as you are! "[1]

What Polk actually said, according to his later recollection, was that since the British had taken several years to evolve their extreme policy, they ought to be willing to give the Americans several months in which to consider the problem.[2] But the important point is that the apocryphal

[1] B. J. Hendrick, *The Life and Letters of Walter H. Page* (Garden City, N. Y., 1922), II, 265.

[2] On January 3, 1941, Polk wrote the author: "This story has been told in various ways, and I have always wondered where

version was widely circulated, and has set the tone for much of the discussion of America's conduct after entering the war. It is commonly believed that the hypocritical Uncle Sam promptly became as great a "criminal" as Britain, and that he not only turned his back on the rights he had so eloquently upheld, but proceeded to mistreat the small neutrals in a thoroughly ruthless fashion.

This is one of those easy assumptions, so frequently encountered in history, that is not generally challenged because it is taken for granted. It is supported by our textbooks—that is, where the textbooks mention the subject at all; and it is repeated, with cynical embroidery, in countless classrooms. The present study is an attempt to get at the truth, and specifically to describe in some detail the policies actually adopted by the United States toward the neutrals

---

Mr. Page got his version as I have no recollection of having written it to him.

"Of course, it is a long time ago and I cannot find any notes on this particular conversation. However, as I recall it, when Mr. Balfour was in Washington in April and May, 1917, he took up with the Department of State various questions that had been the subject of debate between the two countries. He and two of his experts were in my office discussing, as I recall, the blockade and how we could cooperate in making it effective. Our relations were extremely pleasant and I could talk matters over with him quite frankly.

"After we had disposed of practically all the questions, he hesitated and then remarked that there was one more question we should discuss. I knew it was probably in regard to the blacklist, and as that was a question we did not wish to take up at that time, I remarked jokingly that it had taken Great Britain several years to reach the point it had reached in straining international law and I felt that they should be willing to concede us a few months for consideration and not expect us to reach immediately the limits that they had finally reached. He laughed and the matter was dropped."

The Transition from Neutrality

after it entered the war. We shall be particularly concerned with those acts of the Washington government which flew in the face of the precedents it had recently established, and with violations—or alleged violations—of neutral rights, whether based on international law or international morals. It may be that when all this is done we shall still hold that the United States was just as great a "criminal" as Great Britain; but in any event an effort will be made to substitute proof for assumption.

ii

The importance of the topic we are about to consider will not command unanimity of judgment. The extreme point of view—and one held by some of the men intimately connected with the problem at the time—is that the policy adopted by the United States toward the neutrals actually won the war. One may indeed argue with considerable plausibility that if Washington had not forced the neutrals to curtail their shipments of foodstuffs and other important commodities to the Central Powers;[3] if it had not seized or otherwise forced neutral shipping into the service of the Associated Powers; and if it had not used the economic

---

[3] The term Central Powers (derived from their central position in Europe) refers to Germany and Austria-Hungary, as well as to their allies, Bulgaria and Turkey. The Allies consisted originally of Great Britain, France, and Russia (the Triple Entente), together with Serbia, Belgium, Montenegro, and Japan. They were later joined by Italy, Portugal, Rumania, Greece, the United States, and fifteen other countries. When the United States, with its traditional antipathy for formal alliances, entered the war, the nations combined against the Central Powers were called the Allied and Associated Powers. In brief, the United States was an Associate rather than an Ally in the common enterprise.

club to extort other concessions and services, Germany and her allies would have emerged victorious.[4]

This extreme view, no matter how convincingly presented, can never be proved. A safer interpretation—and one generally accepted by those who were in a position to know—is that America's restrictions upon the neutrals shortened the war by a number of months. If we agree with this opinion, which is strongly supported by the evidence herein presented, and keep in mind the enormous losses in money and man power during every day of the war, and remember that Europe was teetering on the brink of social and economic chaos when the guns grew cold in November, 1918, we may not unreasonably conclude that the present subject is of some little importance. And when we note further that there have been neutrals since 1918, and that the methods perfected by the United States from 1917 to 1918 have been widely copied, this project takes on something more than the proportions of just another academic exercise.

Indeed, it is puzzling to determine why someone has not already undertaken a full-length investigation of the problem. The period of American neutrality—with its invasion of Belgium, its *Lusitania*, its sabotage agents, its propaganda campaigns—has inspired a considerable number

---

[4] American restrictions on the neutrals unquestionably hurt German morale while improving that of the Allies. A full exposition of the influence of American pressures on Germany's collapse may be found in an eighteen-page report (December 8, 1918) submitted by S. B. Conger, Foreign Adviser of the War Trade Board, to Vance C. McCormick, Chairman of the War Trade Board. Hereafter cited as "Conger Report." Mr. McCormick graciously sent the author a copy, which is now deposited with the Hoover Library on War, Revolution, and Peace, Stanford University, California.

of books, which, on the whole, are a credit to American scholarship. But the period during which America parted with her former neutral associates has been largely ignored.[5]

Perhaps the assumption that the United States took as many liberties with neutral rights as Great Britain is so generally accepted that prospective students have seen no particular point in a detailed elaboration of the obvious. Perhaps others have felt that such an investigation would prove to be a most unsavory chapter in American history; and since the flag waver is usually in better repute than the debunker, they decided to turn to more popular pastures. Others may have been repelled by the lack of drama. Here were no *Lusitanias* or spy plots—merely the dull, drab story of economic pressures and embargoes; and only the exceptional students find such material exciting. And still others probably avoided the subject because they regarded it as of secondary or even tertiary importance. Nor is this feeling difficult to understand. In checking through the contemporary newspapers one is struck with the fact that on only a few occasions did matters concerning America's treatment of the neutrals appear on the first page; more often, if mentioned at all, they were printed on page six or ten. This whole story, important though it may now seem to be, was pushed aside during the preoccupation with

---

[5] Only two works have broken the ground. The first is Carlton Savage, *Policy of the United States toward Maritime Commerce in War* (Washington, 1936), II, 3-160, which is primarily an abstract of many of the essential documents; the second is Alice M. Morrissey, "The United States and the Rights of Neutrals, 1917-1918," *Amer. Jour. of Int. Law,* XXXI (1937), 17-30, which is necessarily sketchy. Edgar Turlington's *Neutrality: The World War Period* (New York, 1936), is much broader in scope and discusses the United States as a neutral and as a belligerent, as well as its relations with the other neutrals and belligerents.

problems nearer home; it was lost in the almost hysterical efforts to raise an army and float Liberty Loans.[6]

But perhaps the strongest deterrent to a study of America's relations with the neutrals was the relative unavailability, up to the present time, of the manuscript records. It is true that from 1931 to 1933 the Department of State published several volumes of *Foreign Relations of the United States* which contained about 2,000 pages of documents bearing upon the present subject. Yet prospective students of the problem may have felt that the printed records were not reasonably complete; that the editors had carefully culled out all material discreditable to the United States; and that a scholar should not waste his time in preparing a monograph which could not, in the nature of things, be " definitive."

This situation was definitely altered when, in 1939, the Department of State issued an order making its records up to 1919 available to certain classes of scholars. Shortly thereafter the present writer applied for and secured permission to examine the papers concerning the neutrals. Every file that he asked for was turned over to him without

[6] Comment of Vance C. McCormick (November 4, 1941): " I notice . . . that you refer to the few occasions that matters relating to the American treatment of the neutrals appeared on the front page of our newspapers. I think the explanation of this is that the War Trade Board was, I believe, the only active war agency that did not have a publicity bureau attempting to give to the public the achievements of our Board, and, therefore, the administration's opponents in Congress did not disturb us as we were not considered important enough politically. As Chairman of the Board, I was never called before an investigation committee of Congress and it was not until the Armistice, when I was in Paris, that Clarence Woolley, Vice-Chairman of the Board acting as Chairman in my absence, was called to explain certain action of the Board before a Congressional Committee."

reservation; and during the course of his researches he made the gratifying discovery that few, if any, policy documents of primary importance had been omitted from the published record. He took notes on a large amount of material of a somewhat supplementary nature, and found some new items that were of considerable importance from the rather restricted point of view of this study.[7] But he can testify, after an exacting comparison, that the editing of the official documents was done with intelligence, discrimination, and care; and he can further testify that he found no evidence whatever that any important document had been withheld from publication because it would reflect unfavorably upon the government of the United States. And when his notes were submitted to the authorities of the Department of State for inspection, nothing was taken away and not a single mark of the blue pencil appeared. From all this it seems reasonable to conclude that the United States government is not ashamed of what was done from 1917 to 1918, and that it is perfectly willing to have the whole truth made known.

iii

During most of the two decades following the Armistice in 1918, neutrality and neutral rights were not regarded as

[7] The present writer was happy to note that, considering the limitations of space, the editors of *Foreign Relations* included a remarkably complete selection of materials of secondary importance. Omissions are indicated in some of the published documents in accordance with the principles announced in *Foreign Relations of the United States, 1914, Supplement*, pp. iii-iv (hereafter cited as *For. Rel., 1914, Supp.*). "Nothing," it is here stipulated, "should be omitted with a view to concealing or glossing over what might be regarded by some as a defect of policy." In comparing omissions in the printed record with the original documents, no instance was found of a violation of these regulations.

particularly vital subjects. President Wilson believed that when the League of Nations was established there would be universal peace. And if, perchance, a conflict should break out, there would no longer be neutrals because all the world would be united against the aggressor.[8] Even as late as 1928 the more ardent supporters of the Kellogg-Briand Pact believed, or professed to believe, that war had been abolished from the world, and that, as a consequence, neutrality was a dead issue. But whatever illusions remained by 1939 were completely shattered by the outbreak of hostilities in Europe. The old belligerent pressures on neutrals were revived and increased; and once more we heard of long-range blockades; contraband stations; seizures and detentions; the searching of mails; embargoes and rationing agreements; blacklists and financial blockades; and the requisitioning of tonnage. The synchronizing of renewed interest in this general subject with the availability of the manuscript records suggested the desirability of telling the story of America's treatment of the neutrals from 1917 to 1918.

The present investigation is a study of the policy of the United States toward the neutral countries after it became a belligerent. Where the policy adopted was the normal peacetime procedure, involving no question of rights and protests, the problem is touched on only lightly, if at all. The major emphasis is on those types of coercion, whether legal or illegal, whether in co-operation with the Allies or alone, which the United States brought to bear upon the neutrals for the purpose of winning the war.

This, it must be repeated, is a study of policy. It is not a study of the machinery for carrying out that policy.

[8] Savage, *Maritime Commerce*, II, 868, n.

The machinery of the War Trade Board, for example, was extensive and extremely complicated; and even if space permitted a thorough presentation of this phase of the subject, which it does not, the introduction of such material would only confuse our understanding of a problem which is already sufficiently complex. We are interested in knowing why the United States forced Norway to sign a rationing agreement, and in the methods that were used to attain that end. We are not interested in the subsequent procedure by which Firm A in the United States shipped a cargo of cottonseed cake to Firm B in Norway.

Nor are we concerned with a full-length diplomatic history of all the relations of the United States with all the neutrals of the world during the period of belligerency. This is something that obviously cannot be done adequately within the space available.[9] Besides, it is important to note that a good share of the negotiations between the United States and the neutrals, particularly those of Latin America,

[9] A detailed investigation of the diplomatic relations between the United States and any one of a half dozen or so of the neutrals would provide ample material for a monograph. Other possible subjects are: the United States and the Latin American neutrals during the war; the development of co-ordination with the Allies; friction between the United States and its Associates over the treatment of the neutrals; the establishment, operation, and effect of control machinery, particularly the War Trade Board; public opinion in the United States or in the neutral countries, especially the latter, regarding Washington's policy; American propaganda in neutral lands; and the post-Armistice liquidation of policies and machinery. The present study makes no attempt to go beyond November, 1918. The pre-Armistice period is an entity in itself; no new policies of fundamental importance as regards the neutrals seem to have been developed following November, 1918; the materials for the post-Armistice months are voluminous; and these later records were not open to scholars when the present writer was carrying on his researches in Washington, D. C.

was merely routine and involved no fundamental question of rights. This was notably true of the lengthy discussions with Mexico over the oil question. And when we come to problems that did relate to neutral rights, we shall be more concerned with the policy involved than with a detailed description of each of the various steps in the negotiation.

Other considerations also preclude a study of the diplomatic relations of the United States with all the neutrals. The chief obstacle is that the essential foreign archives are not open to investigators—and may not be for generations to come, if ever. A diplomatic history of this subject cannot be definitive until the story can also be told from the point of view of the other countries; and this cannot be done without access to their official unpublished records. But a study of policy is something different. As a sovereign state, the United States determined its own course of action. In some cases, this was done after consultation with the British and the other Allies; but the final decision was made in America. And since all of the official policy-making documents in Washington are available, and many others as well, it would seem as though a reasonably satisfactory study of policy could now be made.

iv

Throughout the thirty-two months—that is, nearly three years—from the outbreak of the World War until April, 1917, the United States enjoyed the distinction of being the most powerful of the neutrals. With the exception of Italy, which took the plunge in May, 1915, America was the only major power to remain outside the conflict for any length of time. And during the two years from May, 1915, to April, 1917, she had the field to herself.

America was not only the most powerful, actually or potentially, of those nations not engaged in the conflict, but she alone of the remaining neutrals raised up a great world leader in the person of Woodrow Wilson. Endowed with an extraordinary faculty of expressing his ideas in inspirational language, and radiating a spiritual fervor of righteousness which gave him the appeal of a major prophet, Wilson stood out as the champion of justice and international decency in a world that had seemingly gone mad. "Some of these days," he told a St. Louis audience in 1916, " we shall be able to call the statesmen of the older nations to witness that it was we who kept the quiet flame of international principle burning upon its altars while the winds of passion were sweeping every other altar in the world." [10]

But besides being the champion of international justice in a general sense, Wilson conceived of the United States as the leader of the other neutrals in the common battle for neutral rights. In his message to Congress of April 19, 1916, less than a month after the torpedoing of the *Sussex*, he solemnly declared:

> But we cannot forget that we are in some sort and by the force of circumstances the responsible spokesmen of the rights of humanity, and that we cannot remain silent while those rights seem in process of being swept utterly away in the maelstrom of this terrible war. We owe it to a due regard for our own rights as a nation, to our sense of duty as a representative of the rights of neutrals the world over, and to a just conception of the rights of mankind to take this stand now with the utmost solemnity and firmness.[11]

This point of view was even more emphatically stated in

---

[10] R. S. Baker and W. E. Dodd, eds., *The New Democracy* (New York, 1926), II, 110 (speech of February 3, 1916).

[11] *Ibid.*, II, 158.

Secretary of State Robert Lansing's memorable protest to London, dated October 21, 1915, in which the grievances of the United States against British maritime practices were summarized.

> This task of championing the integrity of neutral rights, which have received the sanction of the civilized world, against the lawless conduct of belligerents arising out of the bitterness of the great conflict which is now wasting the countries of Europe, the United States unhesitatingly assumes, and to the accomplishment of that task it will devote its energies, exercising always that impartiality which from the outbreak of the war it has sought to exercise in its relations with the warring nations.[12]

And when the United States broke with Germany, it avowedly did so for the purpose of upholding its rights as a neutral, and incidentally those of all the other neutrals.[13]

It is not surprising that these weaker nations gladly accepted Wilson as the self-appointed champion of their rights. Nor was this acceptance without warrant. There can be little doubt that the strong protests of the United States against British blockade practices resulted in a less stringent application of such measures to all neutrals than otherwise would have been the case. The record also reveals that the unyielding position of Wilson actually forced the Imperial German government to emasculate its submarine warfare on two different occasions. And the other neutrals were the direct beneficiaries of these concessions, because the bel-

---

[12] *For. Rel., 1915, Supp.*, p. 589.

[13] On April 24, 1917, the United States minister in Switzerland reminded Secretary Lansing that "The United States has entered into this war to defend the rights of neutrals unjustly infringed by illegal submarine warfare as conducted by Germany." *Ibid., 1917, Supp. 2,* II, p. 1159.

ligerents could not, with very good grace, apply one standard to one neutral, America, and another standard to the others. All this does not necessarily imply that the United States was thinking primarily of the neutrals and only secondarily of itself. The reverse was certainly true, as it is true of almost every situation involving national self-interest. Yet it no doubt gave great satisfaction to President Wilson to know that in upholding the rights of the United States he was making more tolerable the position of the weaker neutrals, who were less able to protest effectively.

v

America's championship of neutral rights, resolute though it was, probably would have been more vigorous if it had not been for at least one restraining factor. What would happen if the United States, despite its undeniable determination to stay out of the conflict, should eventually be drawn in? Would not the Washington government, in the interests of winning the war, then find it necessary to do a number of things against which it had protested as a neutral? Robert Lansing, in his revealing *Memoirs*, confesses that while he was Secretary of State he made it a policy to phrase his official protests in such a way that they would tie the hands of America to the least possible extent, should the nation ultimately be forced into the struggle.[14]

---

[14] Lansing wrote: ". . . It was of the highest importance that we should not become a belligerent with our hands too tightly tied by what we had written. We would presumably wish to adopt some of the policies and practices, which the British had adopted, though certainly not all of them. . . . If we went too far in insisting that Great Britain must cease certain practices as violative of our neutral rights, our utterances would certainly be cited against us by other neutrals if we, as belligerents, attempted

What Lansing suspected might eventually happen actually did happen. When the United States became a belligerent its point of view became that of a belligerent. It was no longer primarily interested in neutral rights; its major concern was the winning of the war. Freedom of trade, freedom of the seas, and those other grievances that had once loomed so large, now seemed academic. And although the point of view of America changed radically, that of the other neutrals remained the same. They were disheartened by the loss of their champion and spokesman; for henceforth they could scarcely be heard above the din of conflict. But more disillusioning than being left to their fate was the fact that their erstwhile defender vigorously adopted some of the practices, such as the blacklist, against which it had formerly protested with great bitterness; and more than this it began to apply these practices without mercy to its former neutral associates.

At this point it is necessary to correct a general misconception. It is true that the United States, after becoming a belligerent, proceeded to do some of the very things that it had protested against as a neutral. The general inference is that these things must have been violations of international law. This, however, does not necessarily follow. If a neutral, by alleging a violation of international law, can induce a belligerent to abandon an objectionable practice, it is clearly to the advantage of the neutral to protest. Sometimes such action has nothing to do with diplomacy but is taken for purely political purposes—to quiet the clamor of

---

to do the same thing. While our conduct might be illegal, we would not be flagrantly inconsistent." *War Memoirs of Robert Lansing* (Indianapolis, 1935), p. 128. For a similar statement see Savage, *Maritime Commerce*, II, 528.

an outraged populace or to win some advantage on the eve of an election, as was notably the case with the blacklist.[15] In short, a protest on the basis of international law does not of itself mean that international law has been violated.

This leads us to one other consideration. Who is to judge whether international law has been violated or not? In a few isolated cases involving the United States as a belligerent the questions at issue were referred to arbitral tribunals or courts. But in a great majority of instances from 1914 to 1918 one side would insist that international law had been flouted; the other would deny it. There the matter would rest, with the partisans of each side confident that they had the better of the argument. Where the principles of international law clearly supported one party to a dispute, the other could invoke (and frequently did) the principles of reprisal, retortion, retaliation, or some other weapon that rendered international law meaningless. In fact, there were very few, if any, legal controversies during the entire war in which each side could not make out a case. The case might have been good or bad; it might have been rejected by a competent judicial body; but the case was made out. One should be very sure of one's ground indeed before asserting that any particular belligerent was definitely guilty of a breach of international law.

vi

We must next turn our attention to another preliminary question: Who were the neutrals? The most important ones—or at least those with which the United States was involved in the most diplomatic discussion—were the

[15] Thomas A. Bailey, "The United States and the Blacklist during the Great War," *Jour. of Mod. Hist.*, VI (1934), 25.

countries easily accessible to Germany by land or water; namely, Norway, Sweden, Denmark, Holland, and Switzerland.[16] Spain, which was the sixth important European neutral, belongs in a different category. Though the largest and by far the most populous of the group, she was almost completely cut off from Germany, and consequently did not raise serious problems regarding the inflow of goods to the Central Powers.

POPULATION AND AREA OF EUROPEAN NEUTRALS *

Country	Population	Area (square miles)
Denmark	2,921,000	15,047
Holland	6,583,000	13,199
Norway	2,509,000	124,675
Spain	20,730,000	195,057
Sweden	5,758,000	173,008
Switzerland	3,880,000	15,945

* *Statistical Abstract of the United States, 1918* (Washington, 1919), pp. 842-43. Population as of 1918 or nearest available date.

In a technical sense, of course, there were other neutrals in Europe. Some nations dropped out of the war after the United States entered, notably Russia; others were in the process of formation, such as Finland and Poland; and still others, like Monaco and Liechtenstein, were too tiny to figure at all in the discussions of neutral rights.[17] And

[16] The Northern Neutrals were generally thought of as those in this group, except Switzerland.

[17] Little Luxemburg was occupied by American troops following the Armistice. Charles C. Hyde, *International Law Chiefly as Interpreted and Applied by the United States* (Boston, 1922), II, 790-91. There was also some correspondence over the refusal of Washington to grant licenses to Finnish sailing vessels for the removal of certain products from the United States in 1918. Green H. Hackworth, *Digest of International Law* (Washington, 1941), II, 8-9.

The Transition from Neutrality

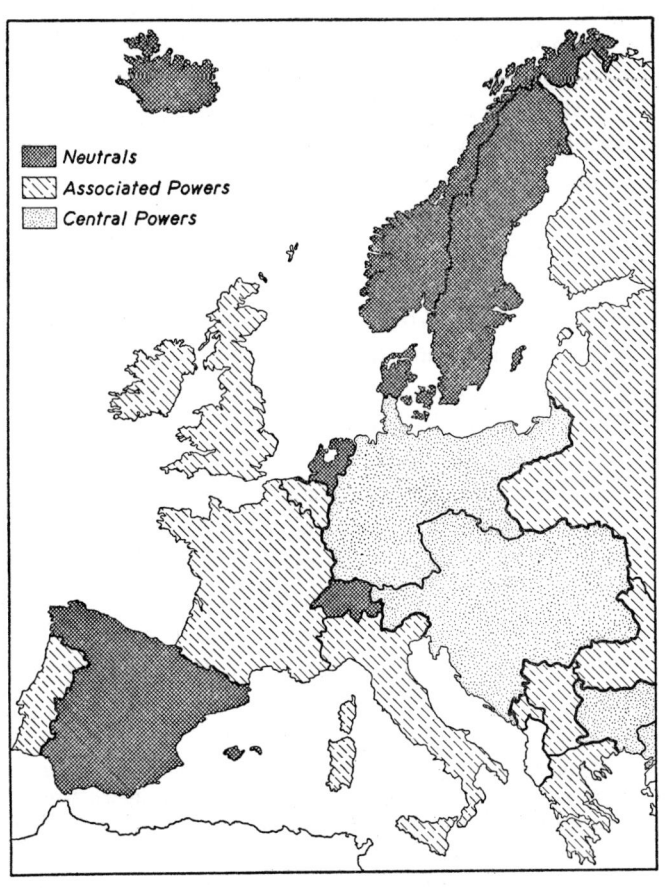

EUROPEAN NEUTRALS, APRIL 1917

Greece, by one way of calculating, was neutral for a time because she entered the war after the United States did.[18] There were also landlocked and secluded nations in Africa and Asia, such as Abyssinia and Persia, which preserved their neutrality but which played no role at all in our story. For all of these states, wherever they were, one rule has been followed: if they were technically neutral and became involved with the United States in any problem of consequence affecting neutral rights or objectionable pressures, they have been included. If not, they have been ignored.[19]

There were only two independent states in Eastern Asia that still maintained their neutrality when America declared war: China and Siam. Both entered the conflict before the end of 1917, and neither of them was concerned with the United States in an important way during this relatively brief period of indecision.[20]

The twenty republics of Latin America present several unique problems. Eight of them declared war on Germany, five severed diplomatic relations, and seven remained neutral. Concerning the eight that became belligerents there is no question of neutrality, except for the period before they made the plunge. In the case of Cuba and Panama, the declaration of war followed that of the United States by

---

[18] On November 25, 1916, the Venizelist provisional government proclaimed war against the Central Powers, in the face of opposition from the king's government. On July 2, 1917, when Venizelos, with Allied support, had the situation in hand, war was formally declared on the Central Powers.

[19] The kingdom of Albania, though independent when the war began, was fought over by the contending armies in such a way as to preclude any consideration of neutrality as here defined.

[20] Siam declared war on July 22, 1917; China, on August 14, 1917, after severing relations on March 14, 1917.

The Transition from Neutrality

one day. This is not surprising when we consider that the two republics were closely bound to the United States by treaty and other ties. Brazil was somewhat slower to go in, but she finally did so in October, 1917. The remaining five entered the war in 1918. (See map and table on pp. 306-07.)

Five of the Latin American states severed diplomatic relations with Germany but did not declare war. Technically their status was that of a neutral. But when we consider that three of the five extended harbor facilities to the United States contrary to their neutral obligations, and that a fourth, the Dominican Republic, had been occupied by American marines since 1916 and was largely under the domination of Washington, it would seem as though these five could hardly be regarded as neutrals. In any event, we shall here consider them as virtual belligerents, except where they occasionally became involved in problems affecting neutral rights.

Of the seven republics that neither severed relations nor declared war there can be little question. This category embraces Mexico, Chile, and Argentina—three of the most important states of Latin America; and they will ultimately engage most of our attention. We should note, however, that of the entire group of seven only one, Mexico, was conspicuously unfriendly to the United States and the Allied cause, largely as a result of the long-standing differences between President Carranza and President Wilson. The Argentine Congress actually voted to suspend relations with Germany, but President Irigoyen doggedly pursued his policy of neutrality. And Salvador, though neutral, went so far as to offer the United States unneutral use of her harbors. So even the neutrals that did not sever relations were, with the exception of Mexico, benevolently disposed.

vii

One of the most interesting features of America's transition from a neutral to a belligerent status is that she made a noteworthy attempt to induce the remaining neutrals of the world to follow her course. This aspect of the story deserves some little attention.

On February 3, 1917, the very same day that Washington formally severed diplomatic relations with Berlin, Secretary Lansing sent a remarkable circular telegram to all American diplomatic representatives in neutral countries.[21] Announcing that the United States had broken with Germany, Lansing went on to say that the President believed " it will make for the peace of the world if the other neutral powers can find it possible to take similar action to that taken by this Government." Lansing concluded by instructing the diplomatic representatives to report in full on the response to Wilson's invitation.[22]

It is not altogether clear from this striking circular instruction precisely what the President had in mind. At first glance it is somewhat difficult to understand how a severance of diplomatic relations by all neutrals—that is, the usual preliminary to a declaration of war—could make for " peace." [23] Wilson apparently felt that if all the neutrals of the world should immediately break with Berlin and present a solid front, Germany would be so taken aback by

[21] This appeal was sent at Wilson's request against the advice of Secretary Lansing, who felt that it would not be favorably received and that as a consequence the United States would expose itself to an unnecessary rebuff. Lansing, *Memoirs,* p. 307.

[22] *For. Rel., 1917, Supp. 1,* p. 108.

[23] The Swedish Foreign Office noted in its reply (February 8, 1917) that the method proposed by the United States was " absolutely contrary " to the policy pursued by Stockholm. *Ibid.,* p. 124.

this concerted action that she would not dare go through with her unrestricted submarine warfare. In this way an overt act would be avoided and the United States would be spared the curse of war.[24]

Even though Wilson hoped to aid the cause of "peace" by a world-wide break in diplomatic relations with Germany, the neutrals in question certainly did not interpret such action as other than jeopardizing their status. There were no favorable responses whatsoever from the nations of Europe. The Scandinavian countries—Sweden, Norway, and Denmark—promptly replied that all three were engaged in joint representations regarding Germany's conduct, and that they did not care to act separately in following the lead of Washington.[25] Specifically, the Norwegian govern-

[24] The United States minister in China, Paul S. Reinsch, later wrote: "I therefore considered it to be the policy of the Government to assure a common demonstration on the part of all neutral powers, strong enough to bring Germany to a halt." Paul S. Reinsch, *An American Diplomat in China* (Garden City, N. Y., 1922), p. 241. Lansing supported this view when he telegraphed (March 12, 1917): "All other important neutrals having declined that invitation, the adherence of China without other powers would be insufficient for purpose originally intended." *For. Rel., 1917, Supp. 1*, p. 419. Wilson later wrote to Roy Howard (January 16, 1918): ". . . certainly I never had anything in mind in regard to cooperation among neutrals which would be particularly advantageous to the United States. My thought was only to unite the opinion of the world so far as I could in protesting against the flagrant violations of right and of international justice which had been committed." Ray Stannard Baker, *Woodrow Wilson: Life and Letters* (New York, 1939), VII, 474.

[25] *For. Rel., 1917, Supp. 1*, pp. 118-19, 124, 116-17. The three Scandinavian countries made a joint protest to Germany on February 12, 1917. Eli F. Heckscher, *et al., Sweden, Norway, Denmark, and Iceland in the World War* (New Haven, 1930), p. 90. Hereafter cited as Heckscher, *Sweden, etc.*

ment answered that it would limit its action to a joint Scandinavian protest to Berlin; while Denmark pointed out that her situation was so fundamentally different from that of the United States that no analogy was possible.

Similarly, the Dutch Foreign Office declined the American invitation, and declared that the position of the United States, unlike that of the Netherlands, resulted logically from specific commitments on the part of the Wilson administration as to what it would do if Germany reopened her submarine warfare. Holland would therefore content herself with the " energetic protest " she had just addressed to Berlin. Likewise the Swiss government reaffirmed its determination to preserve its neutrality at all hazards, and pointed to the " unusual geographic situation of Switzerland," which was surrounded by belligerents and would, if it made a false step, immediately become " the theater of the general war." [26]

The government of Greece shared Wilson's zeal for " world peace," but because of a " peculiar situation " at home could not co-operate with the United States.[27] Spain, the only other important neutral in Europe, not only declined the American overture, but expressed an unalterable determination to stay out of the war. The King told the American minister, with perhaps pardonable exaggeration, that since Spain was the " sole remaining neutral nation of influence and power," she ought to use her position to soften the asperities of war.[28] Evidently there was some disposition on the part of Alphonso XIII to regard himself as the logical successor to Woodrow Wilson as leader of the neutrals.

[26] *For. Rel., 1917, Supp. 1*, pp. 123, 127-28.
[27] *Ibid.*, pp. 126-27.   [28] *Ibid.*, pp. 117-18, 120-21.

The republic of Liberia, which enjoys a peculiarly close relationship with the United States, was the only non-American nation to respond with any degree of enthusiasm to the invitation from Washington. It promised to sever relations, but only in the event that Germany actually carried out her threatened submarine warfare. The Liberian government recognized its inability to contribute military or naval aid to the Allies or even to defend itself; but rather than bargain for assurances of support, it threw itself upon the United States "for the protection of its vital interests against all eventualities." [29]

The Siamese government replied with a sympathetic refusal. It noted that Siam was geographically removed from the center of the conflict, and that its vital interests had not been so directly involved as those of the other neutral powers. It therefore preferred to watch further developments until its own welfare should demand similar action.[30]

viii

The United States minister in China, Paul S. Reinsch, regarded the State Department's invitation to sever relations as more than a "pious wish," and he felt that it obliged him to bring active pressure on the Chinese government to break with Germany. He plunged into this task with more than ordinary zeal, because he was exceedingly distrustful of Japan and therefore desirous of rescuing China from Tokyo's clutches by associating her closely with the United States. The Peking government, which likewise feared Japanese aggression, welcomed the American overture, but before following the lead of Washington endeavored to

[29] *Ibid.*, p. 458.   [30] *Ibid.*, p. 410.

secure certain inducements, among them assurances regarding the protection of Chinese arsenals. Because of the rapidly changing situation, Reinsch felt that he could not afford to wait for the reply of the State Department, so he made certain informal commitments on his own responsibility. Partially as a result of this action, the Chinese government sent a protest to Berlin, on February 9, 1917, and served notice that if Germany persisted in her announced policy there could be no alternative but a rupture of relations.[31]

The Department of State was naturally somewhat embarrassed by the unauthorized activity of its representative. On February 10, 1917, Secretary Lansing cabled Reinsch to make no further promises pending specific instructions, and he further pointed out that the United States, which was in no position to give assurances, did not wish to lead China " into danger." [32] A week later the American Secretary of State added that the circular cablegram suggesting a world-wide severance of relations " did not contemplate the offer to any neutral power of special inducements to take action similar to that of the United States. . . ." [33] In subsequent cabled instructions, during February and March of 1917, Lansing made it emphatically clear that even if

---

[31] This story appears in *ibid.*, pp. 400-20. See also Reinsch, *American Diplomat in China*, pp. 241-59; Thomas E. La Fargue, *China and the World War* (Stanford University, 1937), pp. 86-113.

[32] *For. Rel.*, 1917, Supp. 1, p. 408.

[33] *Ibid.*, pp. 410-11. Lansing also said: " You will be most particular to suggest . . . that it is the opinion of this Government that China should not, unless compelled by extraordinary circumstances, do more than break off diplomatic relations with Germany until the definite decision of this Government in the premises is communicated to it."

the United States should enter upon hostilities it was not disposed " to urge China to declare war also on Germany." Lansing also expressed the hope that Peking would not become " involved in difficulties from which we shall be unable to extricate it." [34] Nevertheless, even without American support, and with only certain rather unsatisfactory assurances from the Allies, China broke with Germany on March 14, 1917.

ix

Although Liberia was the only nation outside the Western Hemisphere to accept, even conditionally, Wilson's invitation to sever relations, the countries of Latin America, on the whole, responded with greater cordiality. The Cuban government promptly agreed to co-operate whenever Washington deemed it advisable.[35] Also favorable was the response of Brazil, whose President told the American chargé that " in any event " his country " would support the action of the United States." [36] The government of Guatemala also accepted, with the reservation that at " the right time " it would follow a course similar to that of Washington.[37] Two other nations, Panama and Bolivia, though not replying directly to the American overture, indicated by the general nature of their answers that they would

---

[34] *Ibid.*, pp. 411, 412, 420. In this telegram of March 2, 1917, Lansing declared: " There is nothing in the situation to hasten China's entrance into war under the Entente leadership. . . . China will lose nothing by waiting." In that of March 13 he said: ". . . the American Government is disposed to regard as inadvisable a declaration of war by China upon Germany at this time, if such declaration would mean the control of China's military resources by a foreign power."

[35] *Ibid.*, p. 221.
[36] *Ibid.*, p. 222.   [37] *Ibid.*, p. 223.

co-operate satisfactorily with the United States.³⁸ All of these countries ultimately declared war on Germany, except Bolivia, which merely severed relations.

The rest of Latin America may be disposed of in a few words. Paraguay and Uruguay (Uruguay later severed relations with Germany) were sympathetic but noncommittal.³⁹ Seven others were polite but completely evasive: Venezuela and Chile (both of which remained neutral), Ecuador and Peru (both of which later severed relations), and Haiti, Honduras, and Nicaragua (all of which ultimately declared war).⁴⁰ Honduras showed some interest at first, but cooled off when the United States declined to guarantee protection against the consequences of a break with Germany.⁴¹ Three other states that remained neutral throughout the war responded as follows: Colombia merely acknowledged receipt of the invitation; Argentina returned a sympathetic and polite declination; and Salvador bluntly refused the overture.⁴²

By the time most of these replies were received, some of them several weeks after the original invitation, it was evident that Wilson's purpose had been defeated. Only by a prompt and reasonably unanimous show of unity could anything have been accomplished, if then; and when Liberia alone of the non-American powers fell into line, and when not more than one fourth of the Latin American republics

[38] *Ibid.*, pp. 225, 230.
[39] *Ibid.*, pp. 227, 228-29.
[40] *Ibid.*, pp. 222, 223-24, 229, 230-31, 231-32, 237-38, 239-40.
[41] *Ibid.*, pp. 224, 237.
[42] *Ibid.*, pp. 225-26, 229-30, 235. See Frederic J. Stimson, *My United States* (New York, 1931), pp. 367-69, for the recollections of the United States ambassador in Buenos Aires. Mexico, Costa Rica, and the Dominican Republic appear not to have replied.

responded favorably, the scheme had to be abandoned. It is significant for our purposes, however, as revealing that the United States, in a perfectly proper diplomatic overture, was willing to invite the neutrals to approach the brink of war in order to preserve peace.

x

It was one thing for Wilson to ask the neutrals to break relations with Germany in order to bring about peace; it was another to induce them to enter the war after the United States had taken the momentous plunge itself. The republics of Panama and Cuba, quite in line with their sympathetic response to Washington's invitation to sever relations, promptly declared war on April 7, 1917.[43] The

[43] For pressure on Cuba and Panama, see Lansing, *Memoirs*, p. 314. In March, 1917, Secretary Lansing sent John Foster Dulles on a confidential mission to Panama for the purpose of making arrangements for her prompt entrance into the war. Mr. Dulles writes (January 12, 1942): "It was not necessary to bring to bear any particular coercion. Panama seemed to realize that her economic dependence upon the United States was such that it would be impracticable and give rise to very bad friction if she attempted to maintain a neutrality which might threaten to impair our ability to protect adequately the Panama Canal. At the time I went down, there was a controversy between the Panama government and the United States government with respect to the tax status of certain important investments of the Panama government in the United States. I was authorized by Mr. Lansing and Mr. McAdoo to intimate that if Panama were a co-belligerent this question would be settled in a way which would exempt Panama income from United States federal taxes. I did so intimate and the matter was in fact subsequently arranged to the satisfaction of Panama. I would hardly say, however, that this had any material bearing upon the outcome." Letter to author.

After Congress declared war on Austria-Hungary, on December 7, 1917, the United States minister in Panama communicated this

only other Latin American state to enter the conflict in 1917 was Brazil, which took action on October 26, 1917. She, too, had replied favorably to the earlier suggestion of a break with Berlin.

Other Latin American nations were more hesitant about following the great northern republic into the war, and they required either urging or guarantees of assistance. On April 18, 1917, the Guatemalan minister offered to cooperate fully with the United States and sought assurances of protection against the consequences of such action. On the same day Lansing replied that Guatemala would be given " full support " in the event that she entered the conflict, provided, however, that she placed herself at the disposal of the United States.[44] Two days later, April 20, the tiny republic accepted his proposal, and a week after that broke with Germany.[45] And although Guatemala did not actually declare war until a year later, she promptly offered her port and other facilities to the Washington government, which cordially accepted them.[46] Inasmuch as Guatemala was technically a neutral, the State Department, in accepting these favors, was responsible for encouraging

---

information to the " Panaman Government with the suggestion informally made that they declare war also." On December 10, the National Assembly unanimously passed a war resolution. Although this suggestion by the American representative was unauthorized, it was approved by the Department of State after the proper explanations had been made. *For. Rel., 1917, Supp. 1*, pp. 385, 389-90, 392.

[44] *Ibid.*, pp. 257-59, 261. Lansing was in favor of having Guatemala enter the war, and possibly Honduras, as a check on Mexico should the latter take action in the interests of Germany. Wilson agreed with him. *Papers Relating to the Foreign Relations of the United States: The Lansing Papers, 1914-1920* (Washington, 1940), II, 5-6. Hereafter cited as *Lansing Papers*.

[45] *For. Rel., 1917, Supp. 1*, p. 264.   [46] *Ibid.*, p. 272.

her to compromise her neutrality; yet the record reveals that in spirit if not in actuality the Central American republic was a belligerent.

Nicaragua severed relations with Germany on May 18, 1917, apparently without undue pressure from Washington; yet a week earlier the Department of State had gone so far as to assert that it would "view with gratification" an invitation on the part of the Nicaraguan government to use the facilities of the republic.[47] Although Nicaragua did not actually declare war until a year later, she co-operated satisfactorily with the United States. Thus, as in the case of Guatemala,[48] Washington encouraged a state that was technically neutral to compromise its neutrality.

[47] *Ibid.*, pp. 278-79. On April 12, 1917, the *de facto* government of Costa Rica offered the use of its harbors for the prosecution of the war, but Washington took no action on the grounds that it did not recognize the Tinoco regime, which had come into power through force. The Tinoco government felt that it would be undignified to break with Germany without recognition from the United States, but finally, on September 21, 1917, severed relations without having been recognized. *Ibid.*, pp. 274, 287, 328, 329; Naval War College, *International Law Documents, 1917* (Washington, 1918), p. 77. As in the case of Mexico, Costa Rica became an important test case in establishing Wilson's new policy of not recognizing governments established by revolution. See Lansing, *Memoirs*, p. 309; Baker, *Wilson*, VIII, 13, 15, 291; *Lansing Papers*, II, 518-22.

[48] In response to an inquiry as to whether or not the United States actually used the facilities of both Guatemala and Nicaragua during the year when they had severed relations and had not declared war, Captain Dudley W. Knox, of the Office of Naval Records and Library, Navy Department, writes (February 21, 1942): "Our records indicate that vessels of the U. S. Navy called at ports of Guatemala and Nicaragua during the time in question on such missions as courtesy calls, to search for enemy submarine bases, to offer assistance to Guatemala after the earthquake, to observe internal conditions and to embark and disembark Marines."

The commander of the American forces occupying Haiti suggested to the President of that country that it would be advisable to enter the struggle against Germany; but the Haitian Chief Executive, in view of possible opposition, wished to be assured in advance of armed support. On April 21, 1917, the Washington government pledged to Haiti "all proper assistance" should she declare war.[49] Two weeks later Acting Secretary of State Polk adopted a stronger tone when he insisted that Haiti "must decide promptly" to align herself with the Associated Powers, because her action had to be taken "immediately in order to be beneficial and to be appreciated by the other nations." "Further delay on the part of Haiti," concluded Polk, "would tend to place her in a difficult position as neutral countries must depend upon their own resources in time of war."[50] This thinly veiled threat of economic coercion probably would not have been employed if the United States marines had not had the situation well under control. In any event, the little republic waited until June 17, 1917, approximately six weeks, before actually severing relations. When Haiti finally declared war, on July 12, 1918, she did so under the active guidance and encouragement of the United States.[51]

The republic of Honduras broke with Germany on May 17, 1917, apparently without any pressure from Washington. In the spring of 1918, however, the Department of State went to considerable pains to point out to the Honduran Foreign Office the advantages that would accrue from a belligerent status, particularly in the matter of subsequent

[49] *For. Rel., 1917, Supp. 1*, pp. 266-68.
[50] *Ibid.*, p. 276.
[51] *Ibid., 1918, Supp. 1*, I, pp. 661-62, 688-89, 708-09.

The Transition from Neutrality

claims by Germany. Presumably in part as a result of these representations, Honduras officially declared war on July 19, 1918, and was warmly commended by Washington for its action.[52]

xi

It is quite understandable that the United States, once a belligerent, should have sought to weaken its enemy by inducing as many other nations as possible to enter the conflict. It is also understandable that Washington should have shown particular anxiety about Nicaragua, Guatemala, Honduras, Panama, Cuba, and Haiti, all of which were important in relation to the Panama Canal and the Caribbean defense zone. Elsewhere in the world the United States showed less interest in persuading other nations to declare war. There appears, in fact, to have been no attempt whatever to approach the European neutrals, and this is not strange in the light of their uniform rebuff to Wilson's invitation to sever relations. Three other countries, however, present problems of some little interest.

It will be remembered that Liberia responded with warm enthusiasm to Washington's suggestion that she break with Germany. But after the United States entered the war and the African republic showed a strong willingness to follow suit, Lansing declined to advise Liberia to sever relations with Berlin until the Allies had provided adequate protection against German intrigue.[53] After a British warship had arrived at Monrovia, the Liberian government broke with Germany, on May 8, 1917. The British and French

---

[52] See *ibid.*, pp. 689, 690, 693, 695-96, 710-11.
[53] *Ibid., 1917, Supp. 1*, p. 461. This episode appears in pp. 459-76.

were eager to have the small country forsake halfway measures and declare war; but the United States would not encourage the Liberians, who relied upon Washington for guidance, to take this step until Great Britain had removed certain trade restrictions. When this was done, and other guarantees were offered, the Department of State informed Liberia, on July 18, 1917, that it saw " no objection to that Government taking the contemplated steps with regard to Germany." [54] Two weeks later, on August 4, 1917, the negro republic declared war.

The United States did not play a particularly active role in inducing China to enter upon hostilities. The severance of relations with Germany by the Peking government, on March 14, 1917, was more the result of Allied suasion and promises than American influence. On April 23, however, Lansing reported having advised the Chinese minister in Washington that if China plunged into the war " she might have some reason to expect . . . financial assistance." [55] Early in June the State Department showed scant enthusiasm for Chinese participation when it declared that China's entrance into the conflict was a " secondary consideration "—a detached attitude that caused something of a furor in Allied chancelleries.[56] When China finally came to the point of declaring war, on August 14, 1917, Washington joined the Allies in giving her certain prearranged but meaningless assurances.[57]

Altogether, it can hardly be said that the United States brought strong pressure to bear on the remaining neutrals

---

[54] *Ibid.*, p. 475.

[55] *Ibid.*, p. 432. Such assistance was not forthcoming to the satisfaction of the Chinese.

[56] *Ibid.*, 1917, p. 49.   [57] *Ibid.*, 1917, *Supp. 1*, p. 455.

to enter the struggle. Although Washington did bargain to some extent with Guatemala and Nicaragua, although it did extend some encouragement to Honduras and Liberia, and although it did join half-heartedly with the Allies in holding out inducements to China, only in marine-occupied Haiti does the Wilson administration appear to have used anything suggesting coercion to bring about a rupture with Germany. It is bootless to say that any other great power similarly situated probably would have done as much, if not more; the fact is that this was done, and on the whole it is not a discreditable chapter in the relations of the United States with the neutrals.

CHAPTER II

THE BEGINNINGS OF A POLICY TOWARD THE NEUTRALS

i

During the weeks immediately following the declaration of war on April 6, 1917, the American people were primarily occupied with the gigantic task of raising an army and creating the other machinery necessary for active participation in the conflict. Only secondarily, if to that degree, did the plight of the neutrals attract attention. The position of these countries, in fact, presented no important new problems to observers in the United States who had been following the course of the struggle with anything more than superficial attention. It was a matter of common knowledge that the neutrals of Europe had long been serving as conduit pipes through which large quantities of food and other supplies had poured and were pouring into Germany. Many Americans had reaped handsome profits from participation in this indirect trade with the Central Powers, and the increasingly onerous restrictions of the British blockade had served to bring home to them the general nature of the problem.

But the entrance of the United States into the conflict created a new situation. Shortly before the declaration of war on Germany, several of the European neutrals, notably Holland, had begun to purchase huge supplies of grain in the American market—a course dictated primarily by the prospect of an embargo on foodstuffs. An almost immediate consequence of these purchases was a sharp rise in prices

The Beginnings of a Policy

at a time when the high cost of living was a grim reality to millions of Americans. The question was widely asked—and with good reason, as events were to prove—what the people of the United States would eat if enormous shipments of food went abroad and the nation should then be confronted with crop failures.[1] Besides, were not the Allies, who were fighting shoulder to shoulder with America in the war for democracy, more deserving of such foodstuffs than the profiteering neutrals? And what was the ultimate destination of all this grain? Were the neutrals going to consume it themselves, or were they going to send it to the Central Powers directly, or were they going to eat it themselves and then export their own food products to the Central Powers?

It is not surprising that the American newspapers, which were encouraged by their British and French contemporaries to support the blockade, began to devote increasing space to various aspects of the problem. Figures were published to prove that an abnormally large quantity of cotton was moving from the United States to the Northern Neutrals, whence it was presumably being transshipped to Germany for use in the manufacture of munitions.[2] Pig iron was

---

[1] Later in the year the Wilson administration was concerned not only with grain but also with hog and cotton shortages. "Minutes of the Exports Council," p. 59 (August 24, 1917); "Minutes of the War Trade Board," I, 37 (October 24, 1917), State Department.

[2] New York *Times*, June 4, July 13, 1917. The Office of the Foreign Trade Adviser, Department of State, concluded that some of the agitation against transshipment of cotton to Germany was being supported by American exporters who hoped for an embargo lest they be ruined by having to fill their old contracts at the unprecedentedly high current prices. Memorandum of June 25, 1917, State Dept., 600. 118/131a.

allegedly being exported from America to Sweden, which in turn sent its own iron products to Germany. Petroleum was going to Norway for fishing vessels, which brought home enormous catches for the German market. More disconcerting to the people of the United States were the figures showing that those nations which were buying grain, notably Holland and Denmark, were selling large quantities of their own butter, eggs, and meat to Germany. Official British statistics revealed that an annual fat ration sufficient to supply 7,700,000 soldiers was being shipped to Germany from the Northern Neutrals.[3] Not only was fat one of the most serious dietary deficiencies of the blockaded Central Powers, but the very cows that produced the butter were in large measure fed with feedstuffs produced in the United States. Indeed, it was reported on what seemed to be good authority that the German Supreme Command was counting heavily on receiving food supplies from America by way of the neutrals.[4]

[3] New York *Times*, July 2, 1917. See also the French official estimates, *For. Rel., 1917, Supp. 2*, II, pp. 822-25, which concluded that in 1916 Germany received 2,300,000 tons of foodstuffs from Holland and Scandinavia, enough to feed nearly the entire German army for a year. Further French statistics appear in *ibid.*, pp. 888-91.

[4] New York *Times*, July 24, 1917. See also " Conger Report." Conger asserts that the Germans postponed their final declaration of unrestricted submarine warfare for fear that American embargo measures would cut off the supply of fats that Germany was receiving through the neutrals. The German officials did recognize that American entry into the war would bring about an embargo on shipments to the Northern Neutrals, with perhaps complete stoppage to Germany; and they weighed this probability carefully before undertaking their final submarine campaign. *Stenographische Berichte über die öffentlichen Verhandlungen des 15. Untersuchungsausschusses der Verfassunggebenden Nationalversammlung nebst Beilagen* (Berlin, 1920), II; " Beilagen . . . 2. Unterausschuss," Beilage 1, p. 270.

ii

The figures, facts, and rumors about neutral exports formed the basis of a campaign in the editorial and letter columns of the American press urging that the government do something, through export control or absolute embargo, to keep American foodstuffs and materials from aiding the enemy.[5] This seemed all the more imperative in view of the reports that were coming from Germany of distressing crop shortages, and in view of the fact that the Allies were relying heavily on their food blockade to bring the Kaiser to his knees. Among the newspaper leaders in this agitation against the neutrals were the Washington *Post*, which condemned "pseudo-neutrality,'" and the New York *Times*, which published numerous editorials under the theme, or variations of the theme, "We Must Not Help Our Foes." [6]

The consensus of this chorus of demands was that the United States government was obligated to its own people and to its Associates to use every legitimate means to bring the war to a speedy and successful conclusion. There was no law—human or divine—which bound America to give aid and comfort to the enemy by providing the neutrals with food, with the materials (such as feedstuffs) for the production of food, or with any other products that would benefit the Central Powers, directly or indirectly.[7] On the

---

[5] A number of letters urging a severe policy toward the neutrals were sent to the Department of State. (File 600. 119.)

[6] See particularly the New York *Times*, June 10, 1917. Figures showing American exports to the Northern Neutrals were in part exaggerated, because considerable quantities were held up by the British navy, and because these exports were sometimes estimated in inflated wartime prices rather than in actual quantities.

[7] See editorial in *ibid.*, June 7, 1917.

contrary, as Herbert Hoover pointed out, when he accepted the post of chairman of the food committee of the Council of National Defense, the United States should conserve its none too bountiful supply of foodstuffs and other materials for itself and the common cause.[8]

At this early stage of the discussion, it was commonly felt that Washington had neither the intention nor power to stop the ordinary flow of trade between the neutrals and Germany. But there was also a general feeling that the United States ought to insist that its own products should not be used against it. If the neutrals wanted American food, they would have to take it on American terms; otherwise, they could do without. And the terms, which could be laid down in friendly agreements such as Great Britain had concluded with the neutrals, should stipulate that the country in question use no imports from the United States to feed Germany, either directly or indirectly.

The possibilities of using American foodstuffs as a club were explored as the discussion continued. Hundreds of thousands of tons of neutral shipping were tied up in neutral ports through fear of German mines and submarines; and this shipping was desperately needed by the Allies. An increasing number of Americans, conspicuous among whom was Herbert Hoover, urged that the neutrals be forced to render an equivalent service in the employment of their tonnage for any food provided them.[9] The vitally

[8] *Ibid.*, April 12, 1917.

[9] On April 11, 1917, Hoover declared: " If we are to divert our man and woman power to furnish foodstuffs to neutrals, they must be compelled to give some equivalent service to our allies. They can furnish shipping or commodities or manufactures which our allies need in return for food from us." *Ibid.*, April 12, 1917. On June 7, 1917, Hoover wrote Lansing: " It appears to me that it

The Beginnings of a Policy 39

important shipment of iron ore from Sweden to Germany was a normal and legitimate business; but could not the United States insist that this traffic be voluntarily stopped if the Swedes were to obtain American foodstuffs? A few extremists even suggested that America use her food club to force the neutrals into the war on the side of the Allies.[10]

iii

One can hardly avoid the conclusion, after reading the various comments in the press and in Congress, that in general the United States did not appreciate the difficult position of the neutrals. Few Americans seemed to realize that prior to 1914 these countries had supplied Germany with enormous quantities of fish, eggs, meat, and dairy products in exchange for coal and other German commodities; and that the complete cessation of this trade would bring about a serious economic dislocation, if not actual prostration.[11] So close were the ties of commerce that Norway continued to send the nickel to Germany from

---

is necessary for this Government to food ration the whole neutral world. This is an obligation to humanity, but, as this country and the Allies are fighting for the freedom of the world, we must ask the neutral world for much larger services than the mere payment in cash for this rationing, and only upon this basis could we justify the appeals we are making to our people to labor overtime and to self-denial in their own supply." Food Adminisination Records (hereafter cited as F. A. R.), Hoover Library (State Dept., Lansing).

[10] See *Cong. Record,* 65 Cong., 1 sess., pp. 4273-74.

[11] In reply to the argument that Holland had to exchange her goods in order to get German coal, the New York *Times* stated editorially that the Dutch could use their idle tonnage to transport coal from the United States or England. July 26, 1917. This did not, however, take into consideration the difficulties that such a shift would have entailed.

which were made the torpedoes that sank Norwegian merchantmen.[12] Nor was there adequate appreciation of the fact that the neutrals could not remain neutral if they ceased trading with one side, Germany, and traded solely with the other. Berlin would not have tolerated such a course; and the Northern Neutrals were so vulnerable to German invasion that they dared not provoke their powerful neighbor beyond a certain point.

In the clash of arms consistency and legality cease to be virtues; and it is worthy of note that only a few voices were raised in America against beating the neutrals into line with the economic bludgeon. As was to be expected, immigrants in the United States from Holland, Switzerland, and the Scandinavian nations warmly defended the good faith of the " old country." [13] There was also a scattering of protest from those Americans, chiefly " intellectuals," who were troubled by uneasy consciences. " We are no longer neutral," declared a feature writer in the New York *Times*; " but as a belligerent it is particularly becoming to us to remember that the rights of neutrals have always found us their foremost defender." [14] More vigorous was the ex-

[12] The New York *Times* was particularly distressed by this fact. " If she [Norway] had shown evidence of manliness and decent self-respect, and had become a war ally of her friends here and in Europe, she might reasonably ask for a part of the food we can spare." June 18, 1917.

[13] Some of this hyphenate opinion resulted in pressure on Congressional representatives and in direct communications to the Department of State. (File 600. 119.) Among the latter, Swiss and Swedish groups were perhaps most conspicuous. This is interesting in revealing that hyphenate opinion was at work during the periods of both American neutrality and belligerency.

[14] E. A. Bradford, in the New York *Times,* April 29, 1917.

hortation of Albert Bushnell Hart, the well-known member of the Harvard University faculty, who wrote:

> The United States is at war because Germany was determined that we shall not remain neutral and thus preserve our privilege of trade and commerce and freedom of the sea. We cannot fight, however, for those precious principles and at the same time deny the right of Switzerland, Holland, and the Scandinavian powers to trade with their immediate neighbor, Germany. To refuse supplies to Switzerland because that country exchanges products with Germany for coal and other necessities of life, to embargo Denmark because that country sells butter and cheese both to Great Britain and to Germany would be to cut out the ground from under our feet.
> Face the music.
> We are the great world defender of the right of neutrals to trade with either or both belligerents during a war. We must either stand by that or else accept the German contention that we have gone into the war simply to save the Allies from destruction.[15]

iv

The European neutrals were naturally much disturbed by the agitation in America for imposing an embargo on them. Each one of these countries had a Germanophile press of greater or less strength, and its columns painted an insincere and ruthless Uncle Sam in the most unflattering colors. Significantly, in each case the degree of anxiety was roughly in direct proportion to dependence upon the United States for food supplies.[16]

---

[15] *Ibid.,* May 20, 1917. W. B. Kahn, the author of several letters to the New York *Times* in favor of an embargo on the neutrals, reported that he had received "innumerable" communications from persons who declared that America, as a former neutral, could not consistently turn against its former companions in neutrality. *Ibid.,* June 8, 1917.

[16] This explains why the press of Switzerland was perhaps the

The case built up by the neutrals in defense of their position was not without elements of strength. Though none of these countries, except perhaps Spain, could deny that it was sending foodstuffs and other commodities to the enemy, they were unanimous in asserting that such trade did not directly involve American imports. Perhaps their strongest argument in support of this contention was the existence of the Allied blockade. Through letters of assurance (more commonly known as navicerts),[17] through control stations, and through rationing agreements, as well as through arrangements with the various neutral import associations, the British had satisfied themselves that few products from America were passing through neutral hands into Germany. Widely quoted were the statements of Lord Milner, member of the British War Cabinet, and of Lord Robert Cecil, British Minister of Blockade, both of whom gave the

---

most disturbed, and why that of Denmark and Spain was the least concerned. The President of the Swiss Confederation referred to the embargo as "a declaration of war on the neutrals." See *Daily Review of the Foreign Press, Neutral Supplement* (London), II, 3, 58, 62. Hereafter cited as *Neut. Press Supp.* For additional complaints against America's "hunger policy," see *Nachrichten der Auslandpresse,* May 16, 1917, p. 2; May 21, 1917, p. 4; July 7, 1917, p. 3; July 18, 1917, p. 8 (Switzerland); *ibid.,* July 14, 1917, p. 6; July 19, 1917, p. 7 (Denmark); *ibid.,* July 17, 1917, p. 7; July 22, 1917, p. 3 (Sweden); *ibid.,* October 16, 1917, p. 7; December 16, 1917, p. 3 (Norway); *Bulletin Périodique de la Presse Hollandaise,* September 29, 1917, p. 4; October 28, 1917, p. 3; *Bulletin Périodique de la Presse Scandinave,* August 9, 1917, pp. 1-2; September 8, 1917, p. 3.

[17] The navicert or letter of assurance was a document issued by the British Embassy in Washington certifying that a cargo had been found unobjectionable and thus facilitating its passage through the British blockade. H. Ritchie, *The "Navicert" System during the World War* (Washington, 1938), p. 7.

The Beginnings of a Policy

Northern Neutrals a relatively clean bill of health. Cecil declared that these countries " have not sold any appreciable quantity of imported goods to Germany." " Certainly," he continued, " they have imported fodder and sold pigs, but it is difficult to stretch the doctrine of enemy destination to cover this point." [18] In short, if Britain was satisfied with the conduct of the neutrals, what basis was there for the widespread American charges that these nations were transmitting great quantities of food to the enemy?

The border neutrals, of course, had ready explanations for this traffic with their neighbor. It was insignificant, they claimed, in view of the 70,000,000 Germans; it was normal, because in time of peace there had always been a mutually profitable interchange; and it was necessary, because if imports and exports were suddenly cut off, serious economic distress would result, with possible bankruptcy and political and social revolution. Moreover, Germany would strongly oppose such a cessation of commerce at the behest of the Allies, and if a stoppage actually occurred the German hosts would overrun the neighboring neutrals and use them to the disadvantage of the United States and its Associates. Nor was this trade in native products exclusively with Germany. Denmark, Holland, and Norway all sent much more butter, eggs, fish, and similar products to the United Kingdom than to Germany, in some cases, it was claimed, at less advantageous prices. And if these small nations were starved out by an American embargo, or driven

---

[18] Though noting that there was the inevitable petty smuggling, Cecil said that the neutrals had not even replaced their own exports with imported goods, except indirectly. New York Times, July 7, 1917.

into the arms of Germany by other drastic measures, Britain would be deprived of this valuable larder. The British could, of course, obtain substitute products elsewhere, but at a much higher price and at a much larger cost in tonnage, at a time when tonnage was perilously scarce.[19]

Forcible though these arguments may have been to the beleaguered British, to the average American they were largely academic. The indisputable fact remained that the neutrals were buying vastly more foodstuffs from the United States than they had imported before the war. Their populations had not increased appreciably, and their appetites were presumably about the same. Then where was the food going, if not to Germany, which needed it desperately?

The neutrals had a ready answer. Some of them, notably Holland and Switzerland, had received a considerable increase in population through the presence of hordes of hungry refugees and tens of thousands of interned or invalided soldiers. Both of these nations were sending some food to Allied prisoners in Germany and both were contributing substantially—this was especially true of Holland—to the relief of Belgium.[20] But the great increase in imported foodstuffs

---

[19] For a good official summary of Denmark's position, see the statement of her minister in Washington, Constantin Brun, on June 26, 1917. *For. Rel., 1917, Supp. 2*, II, pp. 1024-27. The Dutch minister in the United States issued a statement to the press in which he declared that Holland sent only 25 per cent of her exports to Germany, and 75 per cent to England. *New York Times*, July 3, 1917. See also the letter of J. E. Boggild, commercial adviser to the Danish legation, in which he said that the Danes had actually sold to the British at a loss when they might have sold to Germany. *Ibid.*, July 14, 1917.

[20] On April 17, 1918, Minister Garrett, in the Netherlands, reported to Lansing that there were about 150,000 refugees and interned prisoners in Holland. State Dept., 656. 119/461.

The Beginnings of a Policy

could be explained by other and more obvious causes. Before the war, the Northern Neutrals had relied in large part on the wheat fields of Rumania and Russia for their grain supply. This source, as Washington itself had earlier pointed out to Great Britain, was now cut off.[21] The vacuum had to be filled from somewhere, and what was more natural than that the neutrals should turn to America? It was patently unfair to these small nations to concentrate only on the statistics showing imports from the United States. If the total from all countries was considered, it would be discovered that the neutrals—at least so they claimed—were not buying appreciably more foodstuffs than they had purchased before the war. And if they were importing somewhat more, this was due to a perfectly natural tendency to store up some little surplus at a time when all Europe might soon face famine.[22]

V

Not content with a purely defensive position, the newspapers of the neutral countries struck back at the United States. Uncle Sam, they said, was in no position to be pointing the pharisaical finger at those nations which wished to continue their normal trade with both Germany and the Allies. Had not America recently sold far larger quantities

---

[21] See particularly Lansing to Page, October 21, 1915, *For. Rel., 1915, Supp.*, pp. 578-79.

[22] This argument of dislocation of normal grain supplies was a sound one, and was supported by the testimony of American representatives abroad. See particularly the dispatch of Minister Stovall, in Switzerland, April 24, 1917. *Ibid., 1917, Supp. 2*, II, p. 1159. The British were well aware of this situation and made due allowance for it. See *ibid.*; New York *Times*, April 20, 1917.

of goods, in this case death-dealing munitions, to the Allies, while not selling them at all to the Germans? And this was not the normal trade in natural products, so necessary to the economic life of the neutrals, but a nefarious, profiteer-making traffic, which the wealthiest nation of the world did not need. Trade with just one side, especially in the materials of war, could hardly be called neutrality. Yet the United States, unmindful of consistency, was now demanding that the neutrals discontinue their peaceful commerce with both sets of belligerents, and traffic with only one.[23]

Nor did American inconsistencies end here. During the first thirty-two months of the war, as we have noted, the United States had been the most powerful neutral, the natural leader and defender of the weaker neutrals. The Wilson administration had vigorously insisted upon the right to trade without undue restrictions, and upon freedom of the seas.[24] The Americans, so the neutrals claimed, had never been truly neutral, yet now they were apparently

[23] The Danish press was particularly exercised over American inconsistency. The *Socialdemokraten* (April 20, 1917) declared: "To the last moment we shall decline to believe that America will really establish an economic blockade of the small Scandinavian countries. This would be too much at variance with the principles of the United States *before* her entry into the war. Then America was in uninterrupted trade connection with *one* of the belligerent groups, whom she supplied not only with foodstuffs, but with *mountains of ammunition and other contraband*.

"It was as a spokesman of the *freedom of the sea* and *the right of the neutral countries* that America came into conflict with Germany, and finally went to war. It would be a strange *début* for her to start by committing exactly the same kind of outrage which Mr. Wilson pretended to fight against in the interest of the neutrals." *Neut. Press Supp.*, II, 11-12.

[24] See the pointed reminder of Minister Brun, of Denmark, in *For. Rel., 1917, Supp. 2*, II, p. 1027 (June 26, 1917).

going to be more severe than the British had ever been. One prominent Danish newspaper declared that the United States intended to force Denmark to join Germany and starve, or join the British and share the fate of Belgium.[25] " America proclaimed to the world that she was coming into the war for the sake of right," reminded a Swiss journal. "Don't begin with an injustice." [26] All that the neutrals asked for was permission to remain neutral and avoid starvation.

The strong protestations of the neutrals that they would

[25] *Politiken,* quoted in New York *Times,* July 8, 1917. There was a disposition in the Dutch press to blame the unfriendly attitude of the Americans on the British, who did not want to antagonize their butter-and-egg producers. *Ibid.,* June 28, 1917.

[26] *Journal de Genève,* quoted in *ibid.,* April 23, 1917. America's inconsistent position was stressed in *Nachrichten der Auslandpresse,* July 8, 1917, p. 4; July 23, 1917, p. 4; July 31, 1917, p. 3 (Switzerland); September 19, 1917, p. 1 (Sweden); December 16, 1917, p. 3 (Norway); also in *Bulletin Périodique de la Presse Scandinave,* May 20, 1917, p. 6 (Denmark); *Bulletin Périodique de la Presse Hollandaise,* November 22, 1917, p. 5. A considerable body of neutral opinion was shocked by America's entrance into the war, especially that of the Dutch pacifists. *Neut. Press Supp.,* I, 234, 250, 264; II, 102. There was some applause for Wilson's position, but the press of Denmark particularly stressed the point that the neutral nations had lost the support of the only great power that could defend their rights and interests with any authority. *Ibid.,* pp. 234, 260. The Germanophile press, especially in Switzerland and Spain, was bitter. The fear was also expressed that instead of a stalemate peace, which many expected, the entrance of the United States would prolong hostilities until the Allies finally triumphed. See *ibid.,* p. 234. For other expressions of dissatisfaction over America's entry, see *Nachrichten der Auslandpresse,* July 16, 1917, p. 4 (Sweden); July 25, 1917, p. 1; December 5, 1917, p. 7 (Denmark). One Danish newspaper thought that America would shorten the war. *Ibid.,* July 14, 1917, p. 6.

not yield to America's economic weapons carried more weight than the apparent defenselessness of these small nations would suggest. The Danes and the Dutch were quick to point out that if their fodderstuffs were cut off, they would have to kill their cattle; and inasmuch as their people could not eat all the meat themselves, they would have to send large quantities of their surplus to the Germans. And if American feedstuffs were embargoed, where would England get her butter, bacon, and eggs? The Dutch plainly hinted that in the face of strong measures by the United States they would have to withdraw their support of Belgian relief, and thus force an additional burden on the Associated Powers.[27] During these early weeks, as well as throughout most of the rest of the war, neutral spokesmen insisted that an embargo by the United States would drive their countries into the fold of Germany, economically if not politically. The distasteful blockade by the British navy had aroused a vast amount of bitterness against Great Britain among the neutrals; and it was feared in American diplomatic circles that if Washington adopted too ruthless a policy, this ill feeling would be turned against the United States, with consequent discrimination in postwar trade.[28]

While the press of neutral Europe was venting its indignation and alarm, the foreign offices of these countries had been making persistent representations in Washington and taking other steps to prevent or soften the proposed embargo. Late in April, 1917, the Netherlands government

[27] See the prepared statement of F. E. Posthuma, Dutch Minister of Agriculture, Industry, and Commerce. New York *Times*, June 18, 1917.

[28] *For. Rel., 1917, Supp. 2*, II, p. 1015.

The Beginnings of a Policy 49

issued a reassuring communiqué in which President Wilson was reported as having personally promised the Dutch minister that only in case of utter necessity would the United States prohibit the export of commodities to Holland.[29] On May 2, 1917, the President of the Swiss Confederation appealed to Wilson not to embargo grain exports; and later in the month it was revealed that a Swiss mission was going to the United States for the purpose of discussing the problem.[30] At about the same time similar announcements were forthcoming from both Sweden and Norway.

vi

During the weeks that the American press was berating the European neutrals, and Congress was debating ways and means of putting economic screws on these small countries, behind the scenes the British were quietly making available to the Washington officials the rich fruit of their experience as a blockading nation. The United States had been the chief obstacle to a more rigorous enforcement of the Allied blockade,[31] and if the Wilson administration could be persuaded to acquiesce in certain British practices, or co-operate whole-heartedly in executing them, the strangulation of Germany would be measurably hastened.

On March 30, 1917, significantly a week before Congress passed the war resolution, the United States consul general at London, Robert P. Skinner, was invited to have a frank

---

[29] *Ibid.*, p. 1117.

[30] The appeal is printed in full in the *Cong. Record*, 65 Cong., 1 sess., app., p. 148.

[31] See M. W. W. P. Consett, *The Triumph of Unarmed Forces* (London, 1928), p. xi.

conference with two officials of the War Trade Intelligence Department. The object of the meeting was to discuss the effect of America's prospective entrance into the conflict upon the existing blockade organization. The British representatives expressed the hope that the Washington government would permit a continuance of letters of assurance; that it would allow scrutiny of cargoes in America in order to avoid the danger and delay of search at control stations en route; that it would take steps to examine transatlantic passengers and mail, presumably in co-operation with the British; and that it would accept confidential data from London regarding such matters as contraband and enemy firms. Great Britain was prepared to believe, so Skinner inferred in his report, that the Americans would still consider the blockade illegal, and that the State Department would still be unwilling to accept the blacklist. But the British officials hoped that the United States, while a co-belligerent, would assume toward these weapons, to use Skinner's own words, "an attitude of benevolent neutrality." [32]

This informal conference was but the forerunner of the Balfour Mission, which arrived in Washington on April 22, 1917, for the primary purpose of co-ordinating the war effort of the United States with that of Britain and the other Allies. Food, finance, shipping, and military and naval matters appear to have been the principal problems for discussion, but the tightening of the blockade against Germany

---

[32] *For. Rel., 1917, Supp. 2*, II, pp. 803-06. Even earlier, on March 24, 1917, Acting Secretary of State Polk cabled Ambassador Page in London that it would be desirable to initiate informal conversations with the Foreign Trade Bureau with a view to future co-operation. *Ibid.*, I, 6.

The Beginnings of a Policy

and the plugging of leaks through the neutrals were also an important part of the agenda.[33]

Before sailing for America, Balfour presented seven memoranda to the United States ambassador in London, in which he outlined the suggestions of the British government as to the treatment of neutrals in the fields of trade and transportation. In summary form these were: [34]

Memorandum I. The United States was to participate with the Allies in their financial measures, primarily in preventing enemy-tainted banks in neutral countries from utilizing American resources. (This, as we shall see, Washington refused to do, insofar as these measures applied to a financial blockade.)

Memorandum II. The United States was to license the export of all important commodities, and adopt a list of undesirable consignees in the neutral countries, such a list to be prepared in conjunction with the Allies so as to make it as uniform as possible. (This Washington finally did in the fullest measure.)

Memorandum III. The United States was to utilize the information collected by the Allies regarding enemy-connected firms in the neutral countries so that American measures would not conflict with the machinery already in operation. (This Washington did, particularly in perfecting the blacklist.)

---

[33] Of the twenty-two members of the Commission (exclusive of Balfour and the secretaries), five represented the Blockade Department. Mimeographed statement of Department of State in F. A. R., Hoover Library (Personnel of Foreign Missions). For the general work of Balfour Commission, see *For. Rel., 1917, Supp. 2*, I, pp. 8-10, *passim*.

[34] *Ibid.*, II, pp. 808-14.

Memorandum IV. The United States was to employ its shipping to the fullest extent in the common cause, and regulate its coal supplies so as to force neutral vessels into service useful to the Allies. (This Washington did.)

Memorandum V. The United States was to co-operate in not granting insurance to enemy-tainted neutral ships. (This Washington did.)

Memorandum VI. The United States was not to permit merchant ships under construction to pass into the hands of the neutrals, or prevent Allied firms from obtaining the vessels being built in America for Allied service. (Washington requisitioned both neutral and Allied tonnage in this category.)

Memorandum VII. The Allies were to have the first call on available food and feedstuffs nearest them; next, the neutrals whose tonnage was employed largely in Allied service. The remaining neutrals were to haul their supplies from such places as Australia, South America, and India. (Washington ultimately adopted this recommendation in principle.)

So much, then, for what London expected of the United States. Aside from these broad matters of policy, which were discussed at length by the Balfour Commission, the British officials hoped for prompt assistance in the solution of certain specific problems that had arisen in connection with several of the European neutrals. In each case the Commission outlined the position of the neutral in question, pointed out what was expected of it, and suggested what the United States could do in the way of exerting pressure to bring about the desired result. These specific recommendations will all be treated in later chapters when we come to a consideration of individual countries.

The Beginnings of a Policy

vii

Intimately connected with the deliberations of the Balfour Commission were the discussions that took place simultaneously between the officials of the State Department and those of the British Embassy in Washington. Of great interest and significance were the revelations that the British made of their practices regarding the control of neutral tonnage, and the recommendations that they laid before the American representatives as to co-operation in this type of work. These views were fully summarized in detailed memoranda submitted to the Department of State, under the date May 11, 1917, by the Commercial Adviser of the British Embassy, Richard Crawford.

In the judgment of the British authorities the tonnage problem had two important aspects. First, the neutrals' policy of using their shipping only in " safe trades," or even in commerce beneficial to the enemy, while withholding such vessels from employment useful to the Allies. Second, the neutrals' tendency to lay up their tonnage altogether, rather than submit to Allied control or run the risk of being sunk by German submarines. Accordingly, the British outlined the action they had taken in the past and proposed to take in the future in order " to induce neutral tonnage to render reasonable services to the Allies." Such measures, they pointed out, would be greatly increased in effectiveness if the United States should co-operate, for in this event the Associated Powers would " be in control of practically the whole coal supplies of the world and any conditions, short of compelling the neutral shipowner to run his ships at a loss, can be imposed as a *quid pro quo* for the supply of coal."

The British Embassy then presented a detailed exposition of the various means that might be employed to coerce recalcitrant neutral shippers by withholding essential bunker supplies of coal and oil until conditions laid down by the Allies were satisfactorily met.[35] (Washington, as we shall note, accepted fully the British suggestions regarding bunker control.) The more knotty problem of owners who willfully laid up their ships in home ports could not be solved by such devices but rather by denying necessary food supplies to the entire country concerned. (This the United States later did on a large scale.) In any event, the British believed that the first essential step was the adoption of a common policy, lest the neutrals try to play one Associated Power off against the other, as Spain was attempting to do in the matter of getting coal from the United States rather than from England. If, for instance, the neutral merchantmen in question were tied up in a port of the Allies, they could be requisitioned, as Britain had recently done in the case of certain Danish ships. This had been accomplished by collusion with the owners, but, declared the British memorandum, there was no reason why such action could not be justified under the law of angary.[36] (The United States later requisitioned all Dutch merchant shipping in its ports.)

---

[35] The same policy could also be pursued toward neutral ships that wanted to secure needed repairs in the ports of the Associated Powers.

[36] Angary may be generally defined as the right of a belligerent in case of necessity to seize, use, or destroy the property of neutrals. For the entire memorandum of Crawford see *For. Rel., 1917, Supp. 2,* II, pp. 838-41; also the material on coal pressure in the memorandum of the Joint Subcommittee on Export Licenses (May 14, 1917), *ibid.,* pp. 857-62.

viii

Another highly revealing product of the Balfour Commission was the Report of the Joint Subcommittee on Export Licenses, which was signed on May 14, 1917, by representatives of the American and British governments.[37] This significant document is a comprehensive statement of the alternatives that the Allied Powers and the United States might employ in bringing pressure to bear on the neutrals. It was a recommendation rather than a final statement of policy mutually agreed upon, and the American members significantly added that it did "not commit the United States to agreement with or acquiescence in such methods, practices, or arguments" as the British therein outlined or had theretofore used.[38] The joint report was obviously an attempt by the United States to avoid having to turn its back on the principles it had stood for as a neutral.

The report began with the assumption that Congress would pass pending legislation designed to exercise rigid control over American exports to the neutrals. It was pointed out that the Allied governments had "rationed" the Northern Neutrals, first, by using "maritime international law," and second, by securing voluntary rationing agreements. In these circumstances the Allies had not found it possible to demand services or shipping from the neutrals as a compensation. But as the United States itself owned large supplies of provisions, it was in a position to insist that in exchange for them the neutrals perform desired services, such as the employment of their merchant marine in certain trades. Thus, by the entrance of America into the

---

[37] The entire text is published in *ibid.*, pp. 846-65.
[38] *Ibid.*, p. 857.

war, the Allies would be able to control the neutrals more satisfactorily and completely than before.[39]

British experience, the joint report went on to say, had revealed that it was impossible, under normal conditions, to prevent inhabitants of the border neutrals from selling produce to the enemy, because commodities will naturally seek the highest prices. Only by a definite diplomatic agreement with the country concerned could reasonably satisfactory restrictions be placed on such exports. The United States, by its ownership and control of vital commodities, could exert powerful influence upon the governments of the Northern Neutrals to enter into such rationing agreements.

With reference to bunker control, the report suggested that neutral shippers be required to perform a fuller measure of service to the Allies, and that they be allowed to carry only approved cargoes. The Balfour Commission had recommended that the export of coal from the United States to the neutral countries be on the basis of approved consignees, and that none be allowed to receive supplies that was not on the " white list." The British representatives on the joint subcommittee particularly stressed the desirability of having the United States establish " black lists," or lists of enemy-connected firms or persons in neutral

[39] Cf. the statement of the French Minister of Blockade, Denys Cochin: " As far as the food and economic blockade is concerned, it would appear that, little by little, the Allied countries have taken all measures compatible with international law and political exigencies, short of coming into conflict with neutrals on military and naval grounds, so dangerous from a diplomatic point of view. The appearance on the scene of the United States will change this state of things." Sharp to Lansing, May 11, 1917, enclosing Cochin's report, *ibid.*, p. 821.

THE BEGINNINGS OF A POLICY 57

countries with which American citizens would be forbidden to trade. The British members also pointed to the proved effectiveness of such a device in stopping the flow of money and credit to the enemy. The remainder of the report was concerned primarily with a consideration of ways and means of putting these recommendations into effect; and the British representatives emphasized the advantage of employing machinery already erected in England.

On the same day that this lengthy report of the Joint Subcommittee on Export Licenses was submitted, a briefer and less important joint report was forthcoming from the Subcommittee on Statistics and Sources of Information. This document stressed the necessity of securing accurate data on exports to and from the neutral countries, and noted in what ways American consuls and other officials might co-operate in gathering such information. It was further suggested that Washington, as a condition precedent to beginning rationing negotiations with the neutrals, insist upon full statistical information regarding their exports to the enemy.[40] This recommendation, as we shall later note, was subsequently adopted.

ix

Up to this point we have discussed the suggestions of the Balfour Commission and the joint findings of the British and American subcommittees. Little has been said of the willingness or unwillingness of the Department of State to accept these recommendations as the official policy of the United States. A flood of light is thrown on this aspect of the problem by what may be regarded as the most

[40] *Ibid.*, pp. 863-65 (report of May 14, 1917).

important policy document of these early weeks, a memorandum written by Lester H. Woolsey, at that time Law Adviser of the Department of State, entitled, "Questions of Policy Relating to Export Control" and dated May 17, 1917.[41] This statement, although not formally approved by the Secretary of State as the definitive policy of Washington, nevertheless summarized the attitude taken by the American representatives in their various discussions with the British.[42]

At the very outset the Woolsey memorandum declared that the United States was willing to have representatives on the international commissions dealing with rationing the neutrals, but the Washington government reserved the right to determine its own policy by agreement, and declined to be bound by Allied commissions on which it might be outvoted. The basis of American co-operation was "not to assist in the blockade of neutral countries, nor to take part in other measures of the Allies which the United States has heretofore regarded as unfounded in international law. . . ." Rather, the United States would exercise its "right" to control exports to any country for three purposes: (1) to conserve supplies for itself and its Associates; (2) to prevent persons in the United States from trading in the interest of the enemy; (3) to conserve tonnage for American and Allied military necessities. (Although not openly avowing such a policy, Washington also used its control over exports to force the neutrals to charter tonnage to the Allies and perform other services.)

[41] The entire memorandum appears in *ibid.*, pp. 865-70.
[42] This was Woolsey's recollection, in March, 1929, twelve years after the event. Shortly thereafter, on May 27, 1929, Frank L. Polk confirmed Woolsey's impression. *Ibid.*, p. 865, n.

The Beginnings of a Policy

Woolsey further recorded that the Administration was willing to go so far as to refuse coal to Spain unless the latter continued her exports of iron ore to England, but in all such cases of coercion the United States would act " purely on the ground of conserving its supplies as a domestic measure " and as a means of " conserving tonnage." Washington was likewise willing to prevent its exports from reaching the enemy through the border neutrals, or from being used to replace products sold to the enemy, but the United States was " unwilling to carry this policy to the point where it might force neutrals into the arms of Germany." As for pressure to secure tonnage, the Wilson administration was " unwilling to force neutrals to send their ships through the danger zone in the service of the Allies or of the United States further than to insist that they should use their ships to carry their own supplies to and from the belligerents." (Washington later required neutral tonnage to ply in the danger zone.) While recognizing " Sweden's absolute right to control transit of goods over her territory," the United States would nevertheless exercise its equally indisputable right to withhold exports in order to secure an agreement satisfactory to the Allies regarding transit to Russia and the limitation of exports to Germany. In short, the Washington government, while still regarding " certain " of Britain's belligerent maritime measures as illegal, was willing, through its sovereign right of export control, to bargain with the neutrals for " many of the objects attained by Great Britain."

The Woolsey memorandum also declared that the United States was willing to issue export licenses to cover shipments of commodities to the neutral countries, provided the British naval patrol would accept these documents as equivalent to British letters of assurance, and provided further that steps should be taken ultimately to substitute export licenses for letters of assurance.[43] With reference to bunker control, the United States was willing to deny coal supplies to both neutral ships and shipping firms blacklisted by the British, but desired to have an equal voice in approving or disapproving the neutral vessels or firms in question. The American government could not agree to deny ships' fuel and stores to persons merely on the grounds of enemy nationality or association. There would have to be reasonable grounds for believing that the fuel was being used for the direct benefit of the Central Powers. (In this the United States consistently refused to go as far as the British.)

As for requiring neutral ships to call at British ports for examination, a sore point with the Department of State during the neutrality period, the Woolsey memorandum stated that the Washington officials still opposed such a policy. It added, however, that the issuance of an export license in the United States would make such examinations unnecessary. As a possible compromise, it might ultimately prove desirable to allot to the outgoing vessels just enough fuel and ships' stores so that they would have to stop at a British port of control. Neutral craft which might possibly supply enemy raiders or submarines would unquestionably be denied American bunkering privileges. The United States would also be willing to force neutral merchantmen to agree not to transport enemy agents or reservists in return

[43] Letters of assurance were issued by British officials in the United States; exports licenses by American authorities.

for the favor of securing fuel and ships' stores. Washington was likewise prepared to induce neutral ships to carry supplies to and from neutral countries, but not to force them into danger zones " in service for the Allies or the United States." (This, as we have seen, was later disregarded.)

The United States, the Woolsey memorandum went on to say, was prepared to agree with the Allies on a " coal white list," or a list of firms without enemy connection to which coal could properly be sold. As for limiting the bunkers of the neutral ships so that they would be forced to put into British control ports for fuel, the Administration preferred to reserve judgment so as to determine how such procedure would actually work. Nor was Washington willing to accept the British and French blacklists in their entirety. It was, however, ready to refuse exports to neutral countries when there was good reason to believe that the consignees would use them in the interest of the Central Powers.[44] Yet the United States was not prepared to prohibit imports from blacklisted firms unless such transactions actually benefited the enemy.[45] (It will be interesting to note how the Washington government ultimately changed its views on the blacklist.)

The Woolsey memorandum concluded by declaring that

[44] "One point that did not concern the Allies is of interest as illustrating the Administration's nonrecognition policy. The United States would deny exports to "persons who, for special reasons, are not, in the opinion of the United States, entitled to exports; e. g., revolutionists in Central America, etc." *For. Rel., 1917, Supp. 2,* II, p. 869.

[45] The United States was unwilling to issue a blanket blacklist covering persons in neutral countries engaged in enemy intrigue, but would consider each case on its merits. *Ibid.,* p. 870.

the Administration would appoint representatives on the various Allied commissions designed to control neutral commerce; but this was to be done with the " understanding that arrangements reached by the Allies are not to be concluded without the approval of the United States government." Washington desired to co-operate with the Associated Powers, " not in an advisory capacity, but upon the basis of equality and mutual agreement." The Administration was also prepared to lend its assistance in obtaining all possible information " for the enforcement of the measures upon which it is in agreement with the Allies and *for the enforcement of other measures upon which it is not in agreement*, upon the reservation that such action is not to be taken as committing it to those measures." [46] In any system of issuing licenses to control imports from or exports to the United States, the Department of State desired to exercise veto power, on account of the " delicate " political questions of an international nature involved in any such control over the neutrals.

X

On May 25, 1917, after nearly five weeks in the United States, the Balfour Commission left Washington for its return trip to England. In reviewing the various discussions and memoranda, one can hardly avoid the conclusion that, as far as the neutrals were concerned, the British representatives were at pains to avoid any appearance of dictating to America. Throughout the deliberations they made it clear that the United States was a free agent, fully capable of accepting or rejecting such suggestions and recommenda-

[46] Italics inserted.

The Beginnings of a Policy

tions as were made.[47] Beneath the surface of the discussions appeared evidence that the British fully realized the delicacy of their position: that is, suggesting to the Americans a number of courses over which there had only recently been heated words. The policy of the Balfour Commission seems to have been to place the facts completely and frankly before the Washington officials, in the hope that the United States would find it possible to act in close co-operation with the British.[48]

On their part, the American representatives were keenly aware of the embarrassments involved in reconciling their new role with that of former champion of neutral rights. They revealed a strong determination to pursue both a righteous and an independent course, and showed a becoming reluctance to accept policies that were inconsistent with their professions before entering the war. Nevertheless, the United States expressed a willingness to join with the Allies in restrictive measures of which it disapproved, provided it did not have to assume responsibility for them, and provided also that by such action it would not be regarded as having admitted the legality of those measures against which it had protested as a neutral.[49]

---

[47] See particularly *For. Rel., 1917, Supp. 2*, II, pp. 871-72.

[48] The French government supplemented the discussions of the Balfour Commission by separate negotiations. It invited the United States to be represented on the several control committees, and urged Washington to use the blacklist and enter into rationing agreements with the neutrals to prevent the transshipment of goods to Germany. The Minister of Blockade reported that the French ambassador in Norway had received an admission from the Norwegian government that "the intervention of America would place the North[ern Neutrals] at the mercy of the Allies." *Ibid.*, pp. 817-20, 821-28.

[49] See particularly *ibid.*, p. 876.

CHAPTER III

THE ESTABLISHMENT OF EXPORT AND IMPORT CONTROL

i

While the Balfour Commission was engaged in its discussions with the Washington officials, and while the neutrals were becoming increasingly alarmed over the prospect of an American embargo, Congress was considering the problem of exports control with its characteristic deliberation. Indicative of the turn that the debate would take was a resolution introduced by Senator King of Utah, on April 12, 1917, requesting the Secretary of Commerce to provide five-year statistics on American exports to the European neutrals, together with data on the percentage of these exports going to the Central Powers. The resolution was adopted without dissent, four days after its introduction, and on May 1, 1917, the Secretary of Commerce supplied the desired information.[1] This action naturally had a most disquieting effect on the neutrals.

Early in May, 1917, as a result of both prodding and guidance from the Administration, a bill was before the Senate designed to give the President authority to control exports.[2] The measure was approved by the White House,

[1] *Cong. Record,* 65 Cong., 1 sess., pp. 622-23, 723, 1661.

[2] See report of the War Trade Committee accompanying a draft exports control bill, *For. Rel., 1917, Supp. 2,* II, pp. 799-801. For assurances to the neutrals that exports control would be made no more burdensome than absolutely necessary, see *ibid.,* pp. 806-07, 1199; and New York *Times,* April 20, 1917 (President Wilson's interview with the Dutch minister).

by the Department of State, and by the Department of Justice; in fact, the Attorney General had written vouching for its constitutionality.[3] Advocates of the bill in the Senate stressed the necessity of conserving American products for home consumption and for the Allies, and of preventing such products from flowing into Germany. A considerable group went even further and urged that the powers conferred by the act be used to compel the neutrals to pursue policies favorable to Allied interests.[4]

On the other hand, senatorial opponents of the exports control bill expressed strong doubts as to its constitutionality, deplored any attempt to diminish or destroy the overseas market of the farmer (senators from the cotton states were particularly disturbed), and pointed to the danger of any step that would curtail the domestic production of food.[5] Senator Hoke Smith of Georgia (a cotton state) held that a general embargo was not necessary and that it would cause unfair discrimination among American ports. Accordingly, he offered a substitute proposal which was designed to authorize embargoes only when the produce in question was reaching the enemy, directly or indirectly,

---

[3] *Cong. Record*, 65 Cong., 1 sess., p. 1786. On April 13, 1917, it was agreed at a cabinet meeting to ask Congress for power to establish embargoes. Baker, *Wilson*, VII, 17. On the day before, Secretary of Commerce Redfield wrote Wilson urging the establishment of exports control (the shortage of tin plate was acute), and enclosing the draft of a bill drawn up by the War Trade Committee looking toward that end. Wilson Papers, Library of Congress.

[4] Senator Walsh of Montana, who was perhaps the ablest advocate of this point of view, was quite willing to clothe the President with discretionary power over exports for coercive purposes. *Cong. Record*, 65 Cong., 1 sess., p. 1784.

[5] *Ibid.*, pp. 1783, 1792.

through a neutral country.⁶ This restriction, if adopted, would have seriously affected the Administration's plans, by preventing it from using any other products as a means of clubbing the neutrals into making rationing and tonnage agreements. Nevertheless, on May 4, 1917, the Smith amendment was adopted by a vote of 40 to 30.⁷

Taken aback by this unexpected snag, the Administration moved energetically to bring about a reversal. On May 7, 1917, the debate was held in secret session, presumably to avoid giving offense to the neutrals; and after a prolonged discussion the Senate voted to reconsider its action, and Smith was permitted to withdraw his amendment.⁸ Most of the senators held that the United States had the sovereign right to control its own exports, that this control would not be a violation of international law, and that such a policy was far different from the British practice of stopping traffic from one neutral to another on the high seas. Nevertheless, several members of the Senate were deeply concerned over the inconsistency of America's position, and when open debate was resumed there were some eloquent and vehement outbursts on this subject. In particular, Senator Townsend of Michigan caused something of a sensation when he insisted that the proposed embargo was not designed to conserve food at all but to coerce " neutral countries into a participation in this war. . . ." ⁹ Although

⁶ This was on May 2, 1917. *Ibid.*, p. 1686.

⁷ *Ibid.*, p. 1797.

⁸ New York *Times,* May 6, 7, 8, 1917; *Cong. Record,* 65 Cong., 1 sess., p. 1896.

⁹ Declaring that he would not " copy any of the barbarous methods of Germany, which we have condemned and which have led up to this war," Townsend continued: " We ought to fight this war honorably. If we are going to use these unusual means

Senator Knox of Pennsylvania suggested somewhat later that such a course might be pursued,[10] no evidence was uncovered in the present study to show that this was the intent of the executive branch of the government.[11]

ii

Senator La Follette of Wisconsin was also one of those who feared that the unrestricted use of economic pressure by the United States might result in grave injustices to the neutrals. On May 9, 1917, therefore, he introduced an amendment designed to prohibit an embargo on two classes of goods: first, those that were not needed by the United States, and second, those that were intended solely for the consumption of the neutral country concerned. La Follette further stipulated that the powers conferred upon the President by the exports control act should not " be used to interfere with the neutral rights of any neutral nation or to coerce the Government of any such neutral nation, directly or indirectly, to engage or participate in the existing war." [12] If the United States, for example, had an ample

---

. . . let us not force upon neutral countries the methods which we have condemned in others, and because of the use of which by Germany we are now at war." *Ibid.*, p. 1898.

[10] On June 26, 1917, Knox said: " . . .. this power of embargo, wisely and boldly exercised, should also serve to hasten the day when many more peoples, still neutral through fear or indifference and not through conviction, shall join the powers arrayed for freedom and civilization in a death struggle with ruthless militarism and the lust for world dominion." *Ibid.*, p. 4273.

[11] Comment of Frank L. Polk (January, 1942): "I am quite sure this was not the purpose of the Administration."

[12] *Cong. Record*, 65 Cong., 1 sess., p. 1998. On May 8, 1917, Senator Cummins of Iowa had introduced an amendment similar in purport but less sweeping in nature. *Ibid.*, p. 1944.

supply of grain, and the neutral in question agreed not to transship it to the enemy, the Administration could not withhold that grain in an attempt to compel the neutral to employ its shipping for the benefit of the Associated Powers.

On May 14, 1917, La Follette forced this amendment to a decision, announcing that he desired no debate on it but merely a record vote in open session. His proposal was overwhelmingly rejected by a count of 68 to 9, three of the nine being senators who had voted against the war resolution on April 4, 1917, and who had otherwise shown a reluctance to participate in the conflict.[13] It seems reasonably clear that the La Follette amendment was defeated primarily because it was regarded as unnecessary and as likely to tie the President's hands in the prosecution of the war. By this vote the Senate put itself squarely on record as not opposing the fullest and most effective employment of the embargo club by the Executive in order to force the neutrals to do the economic will of the United States.

In its final form, the legislation conferring authority on the President to control exports appeared as Title Seven of the so-called Espionage Act. This part of the bill was inserted by the Senate in such a way that the House never debated it or voted on it as a separate measure.[14] Instead,

[13] *Ibid.*, p. 2270.
[14] The Espionage Bill (H. R. 291), without exports control, passed the House on May 4, 1917. At the same time the Senate was considering a similar proposal (S. 2), and after passing it took up the House measure. The Senate approved the latter bill by adopting it as an amendment to S. 2, and striking out of the House proposal everything after the enacting clause. The conferees worked out the points of difference. *House Reports*, 65 Cong., 1 sess., no. 65.

differences between the two bodies were threshed out in conference committee. It was not until June 7, 1917, that the House adopted the second conference report on the Espionage Act; and five days later the Senate gave its approval. On June 15, 1917, President Wilson signed the bill.[15]

It is a striking fact that ten weeks elapsed between the declaration of war and the final approval of an exports control measure; and during this time large quantities of foodstuffs and other materials were being sent to the European neutrals, whence some of these materials found their way to the enemy.[16] Part of the delay may be put down to the natural slowness of the legislative process in a democracy; part to the necessity of considering more pressing war legislation first. It should also be borne in mind that the export control chapter was but a relatively small part of the Espionage Bill, several features of which, particularly the proposed press censorship, produced a lengthy and acrimonious debate, both in Congress and throughout the country.[17]

iii

On June 22, 1917, a week after signing the Espionage Bill, the President issued an executive order creating a four-man Exports Council and charging it with the task of mak-

---

[15] At the same time, it was announced that the War Trade Committee regarded the export control chapter as the most important in the bill. New York *Times,* June 16, 1917.

[16] During this period neutral purchases in the United States forced up domestic prices. Hoover to Lansing, June 29, 1917, F. A. R., Hoover Library (State Dept., Lansing).

[17] For complete text see *U. S. Statutes at Large,* XL, pt. 1, pp. 217-31.

ing recommendations to him for carrying out the act in relation to exports control.[18] Three days later Wilson issued an explanatory statement designed to quiet the fears of those who anticipated a serious dislocation of trade. He was careful to point out that exports would not be prohibited but merely controlled in the interests of the United States and its Associates; that the normal course of business would be interfered with as little as possible; that abnormal trade would be intelligently directed; and that the neutrals would receive as generous a portion as the necessities of the Associated Powers would permit. In short, the object of the act was to direct exports to places where they were the most needed, and to withhold them from places where they were the least needed.[19]

On July 9, 1917, more than two weeks after creating the Exports Council, the President issued his first proclamation forbidding the export of specified commodities except under license.[20] The list was small, when compared with later

---

[18] *For. Rel., 1917, Supp. 2*, II, pp. 883-84. The Exports Council was to consist of the Secretary of State, the Secretary of Agriculture, the Secretary of Commerce, and the Food Administrator. The Secretary of Commerce was charged with the responsibility of carrying out all instructions and proclamations issued by the President under Title VII of the Espionage Act.

[19] Text in *Official Bulletin*, June 26, 1917, p. 1. On June 26, 1917, Hendrik Willem Van Loon, the well-known author of Dutch birth, telegraphed President Wilson's secretary conveying the "sincere gratitude of a large number of neutrals residing in America" that the "farsighted and very fair embargo policy" had at last put an "end to the attempts made by several newspapers to impugn the good faith of the neutrals of Europe in their dealings with the Allies." State Dept., 600. 119/167.

[20] The delay was due in part to neutral protests and to the necessity of perfecting the machinery.

Export and Import Control

ones, and embraced mainly foodstuffs (chiefly cereals, meats, and fats), fuels (including ships' bunkers), iron, steel, fertilizers, and munitions of war.[21] In a public statement accompanying the order, the President declared emphatically that his primary purpose was to conserve American raw materials and food supplies, of which a serious shortage was feared, in the interests of winning the war. In permitting the export of any surplus, the United States would necessarily give precedence to the needs of its Associates. Wilson continued:

> As to neutral nations, however, we also recognize our duty. The Government does not wish to hamper them. On the contrary, it wishes and intends, by all fair and equitable means, to cooperate with them in their difficult task of adding from our available surpluses to their own domestic supply and of meeting their pressing necessities or deficits. In considering the deficits of food supplies, the Government means only to fulfill its obvious obligation to assure itself that neutrals are husbanding their own resources and that our supplies will not become available, either directly or indirectly, to feed the enemy.[22]

It cannot be too strongly emphasized that the embargo established by the proclamation of July 9, 1917, was not an absolute one. Many important commodities were not even mentioned. As for those that were, the Secretary of Commerce would grant export licenses if the domestic supply was adequate, provided, of course, that the needs of the Allies were satisfied and provided also that proper guarantees were offered by the neutrals against re-export to the enemy. The American press generally assumed that the proclamation was designed to stop the heavy purchases

---

[21] *For. Rel., 1917, Supp. 2*, II, pp. 903-05.
[22] *Official Bulletin*, July 9, 1917, p. 3.

of grain and fodderstuffs by neutral agents in the United States;[23] that the control of exports to the neutrals had in view checking leakages to the enemy; and that bunker restrictions would be used to force neutral tonnage into trades essential to the Associated Powers.[24] On the whole, American public opinion seems to have responded favorably to the new policy.[25]

An immediate result of the embargo proclamation was a rush for export licenses which almost inundated the recently established licensing machinery. Eleven grain ships (ten Dutch and one Scandinavian) made a dash for sea two days before the new regulations went into effect, evidently preferring to take their chances with the British blockade, without letters of assurance, rather than run the risk of being denied licenses.[26] When the proclamation became effective, on July 15, 1917, an almost complete paralysis of

---

[23] In urging a prompt issuance of the embargo proclamation, Hoover reported that the price of feedstuffs had been driven up to over $7.00 a ton at a time when " our dairy cattle are going to the slaughter house because of the high price of feeding stuffs." Hoover to Lansing, June 29, 1917, F. A. R., Hoover Library (State Dept., Lansing).

[24] See New York *Times*, July 9, 13, 1917.

[25] The general feeling seems to have been that the embargo was unpleasant but necessary. Only one prominent newspaper, the New York *Evening Mail*, appears to have opposed it as an " unnecessary blow at neutrals." See *Literary Digest*, LIV, 1489-90 (May 19, 1917); LV, 12, 17-18 (July 21, 1917); LV, 7-9 (October 27, 1917). Dr. E. E. Pratt, of the Department of Commerce, estimated that every ton of food withheld from Germany would be equivalent to the withdrawal of ten men from her battle front and the saving of one American life. Some advocates of the embargo estimated that it was tantamount to sending a half million men to Europe. New York *Times*, July 28, 30, 1917.

[26] *Ibid.*, July 14, 1917.

the grain trade resulted. In New York harbor some sixty Dutch grain ships were detained, and in Baltimore eighteen more neutral vessels were held, all of them denied export licenses. Although such licenses were being granted freely to the Allies and to the non-border neutrals, only a few were being issued to the Swiss, and still fewer to the Dutch, while all applications for export to the Scandinavian countries were being refused pending the receipt of statistical data requested by the Department of State.[27] In this way, a virtual embargo was instituted against the Northern Neutrals.

News of these long-expected restrictions caused a renewed outburst in the press of the neutral countries concerned, and there was a loud repetition of the now familiar charges of American perfidy and double-dealing. Although some of the newspapers referred bitterly to the illegality of America's action and to the impossibility of completely severing commercial ties with Germany, others pointed to the necessity of co-operation with the United States if needed goods were to be imported.[28] The German-inspired press of the border neutrals was particularly vehement, as was that of Germany itself, which used such captions as: "Wilson's Brutal Methods"; "Starving the Little Neutrals"; "Neutrals in Wilson's Thumbscrews"; "How

[27] See *ibid.,* July 24, 27, 28.
[28] *Neut. Press Supp.,* II, 210, 230, 235, 239, 294, 298, 321, 330. The Dutch press dwelt on the difficulties involved in getting coal from England (*ibid.,* p. 199); the Swedish on the alleged breach of international law involved in trying to force shipping into Allied service (*ibid.,* p. 237); and the Danish on the fact that the United States had earlier made huge profits by using Denmark as a way station for shipping goods to Germany (*ibid.,* pp. 266, 277-78).

Wilson Assaults Neutrals." [29] But the United States could hardly have expected applause from its enemy.

iv

The export embargo was by all odds the most potent single weapon that America employed in forcing concessions from the neutrals. It is important to determine at the outset, therefore, whether this instrument violated international law or flew in the face of precedents recently established by the United States during its prebelligerency period.

It is a clearly recognized principle of international law that the employment of an export embargo, whether for purposes of conservation or coercion, is an undeniable sovereign right and, like the blacklist (which will be considered later), falls within the category of municipal or domestic legislation. A member of the family of nations is privileged to control the disposition of the commodities produced within its borders, provided, of course, that such regulation does not run counter to treaty obligations. While the United States was a neutral, some of the belligerents established export embargoes which worked considerable hardship on American business. But no protest, at least on the basis of international law, appears to have been lodged by Washington against such measures.[30]

---

[29] See quoted excerpts in New York *Times*, July 31, August 7, October 19, 1917. The *Kölnische Volkszeitung* declared: " And America dares to talk thus after wearing the hypocritical mask of neutrality to the advantage of Germany's enemies for years. . . . Perfidious Albion is outstripped in harshness toward neutrals by free America. Where England uses the economic cane, worthy Uncle Sam falls to with the whip of scorpions." Quoted in *ibid.,* July 22, 1917.

[30] James W. Garner, *International Law and the World War* (London, 1920), II, 347.

After the American export embargo became effective, a number of the neutral countries were forced to enter into rationing agreements with the United States for the purpose of securing the restricted commodities. In the cases of Norway, Sweden, Denmark, Holland, and Switzerland, official or quasi-official organizations within these countries undertook to guarantee that the articles imported from the United States would not be used for the advantage of the enemy. Contrary to certain accusations, these arrangements were not at variance with international law or American precedents, as an examination of the years from 1917 to 1918 will reveal.[31]

Early in the war Great Britain placed an embargo on the export of wool, a commodity which was urgently needed by factories in the United States. In order to obtain the necessary supplies, the American Textile Alliance (consisting of a large group of manufacturers) entered into an agreement with the London officials, in February, 1915, whereby it secured great quantities of British wool in return for a pledge not to export this product to the Germans in any form. At the same time it was stipulated that the importation of British wool was not to result in a corresponding export of American wool. Similar agreements were subscribed to by American concerns which needed British-

---

[31] See T. S. Woolsey, "The Rationing System," *Amer. Jour. of Int. Law*, XI (1917), 846. The writer concluded that rationing of neutrals was legal "provided we do not violate a treaty or unreasonably limit a trade which the friendship of years has established and sanctioned." He added that while a belligerent is under no obligation to supply the enemy through a neutral, friendship demands that the neutral be kept from starving. The line between the two, he felt, can be drawn by a careful study of trade statistics and by due consideration of all interests involved.

controlled jute, rubber, and other commodities. The reverse of this situation occurred in the case of a product of which the United States had a large exportable surplus, such as wheat or copper. The producers of copper, for example, in order to get their shipments through the British blockade, voluntarily entered into agreements with the London government by the terms of which they undertook to prevent their exports from falling into the hands of the Central Powers.[32]

A German-connected firm in the United States which was unable to secure British-manufactured burlap bags wrote to the Department of State, on July 28, 1916, demanding that the agreement between the Textile Alliance and London be denounced as an interference with American trade. Secretary Lansing replied:

This Government recognizes the right of the Government of Great Britain to prohibit the exportation of articles from British territory, and therefore has no ground to protest against arrangements of this character entered into by British authorities and exporters of this country, nor has the Department had any part in the negotiation of the arrangements referred to.[33]

---

[32] See Ethel C. Phillips, "American Participation in Belligerent Commercial Controls, 1914-1917," *ibid.*, XXVII (1933), 675-93.

[33] *Ibid.*, p. 687. The American complaint regarding the British rubber embargo, which Sir Edward Grey referred to in his note of January 7, 1915, appears not to have been official. *For. Rel., 1915, Supp.*, pp. 301-02. A recent writer agrees that "the United States never denied that Great Britain was justified in cutting off her own exports. . . ." Alice Morrissey McDiarmid, "American Civil War Precedents: Their Nature, Application, and Extension," *Amer. Jour. of Int. Law*, XXXIV (1940), 230. An American embargo on coal, in 1862, forced Canada into an arrangement whereby she agreed to place an export embargo on this commodity if the United States would supply her needs. *Ibid.*, p. 228.

It is clear, then, that the Washington government, in using the embargo to extort rationing agreements from the neutrals, was merely employing a weapon which it had earlier recognized as legal and against which it had declined to protest. The fact that the United States was never faced with a food embargo gives a somewhat different aspect to the problem, but apparently does not affect the legal issue involved.

v

In the last analysis the question of legality was largely academic; whether legal or illegal the embargo was bound to bring privation and possibly starvation. To quiet the fears of the neutrals and to outline in unmistakable terms the future course of the United States, the Exports Council submitted substantially identical memoranda to the Danish, Dutch, Norwegian, and Swedish legations in Washington, on July 24, 1917. As this is a policy document of primary importance, it is deserving of a careful analysis.[34]

The Allies, began the memorandum, were in need of more foodstuffs and materials than America, despite great sacrifices, could provide. If the United States was to supply the neutrals it would mean in many instances " alternatively either a deprivation of the Allies, further sacrifice upon the part of the American people, or a diversion of labor and productivity from the necessities of war." If the neutrals were to be assisted, it was only proper to ask that contributions from the United States should not be turned to the advantage of the enemy. Consequently, it was expected

[34] The text is in *For. Rel., 1917, Supp. 2,* II, pp. 908-10. This was undoubtedly drafted in collaboration with the Department of State.

that no American food would reach the Central Powers, directly or indirectly, and that American feedstuffs would not be used to raise cattle for German consumption. It was also expected that the neutrals would make every effort to stimulate production, restrict consumption, and utilize non-American (e. g., Australian) sources of supply. Price was only a secondary consideration; and if the people of the United States were to deprive themselves and their Associates of needed goods, the monetary compensation would have to be supplemented by some service of corresponding value, as, for example, the chartering of tonnage.

The Exports Council concluded by stating that in order to determine the needs of the neutral countries it would be " glad to have " information regarding the stocks of commodities they already had on hand, those they had purchased in America, and those they were actually shipping to the homeland. The Council also declared that if the neutrals continued their shipments of food to Germany, no shortages caused by such exports would ultimately be supplied by the United States. This pointed warning was later to take on an increasing significance.

vi

We have already noted that ten weeks elapsed between the declaration of war and the signing of the export control bill, on June 15, 1917, and nearly four weeks more before the issuance of the first embargo proclamation, on July 9. During this protracted period London had been watching with increasing impatience the apparently dilatory action of Congress and the Administration. More disturbing to the British, in some respects, were an apparent reluctance to

Export and Import Control

co-operate in enforcing the blockade, a disinclination to recognize the British blacklist in neutral countries, and an unwillingness to permit American diplomatic representatives to confer formally with those of the Allies in neutral capitals.[35] It is not difficult to see in all this hesitation a desire on the part of Washington to move with the utmost circumspection, lest the United States become involved in some precedent-creating action that might later embarrass the Department of State or prove inconsistent with America's professions as a neutral.

Upon the departure of the Balfour Commission, Lord Eustace Percy had remained in Washington for the purpose of advising with the American officials on the subject of exports to the neutrals.[36] On June 27, 1917, after a wait of more than a month, he confidentially unbosomed himself to Herbert Hoover, a member of the Exports Council, when he wrote that "the decision on policy, as distinct from legislative action and the setting up of administrative machinery, is proceeding at present so slowly here that I have felt a doubt whether it was worth while for me to remain." He further pointed out that much of Britain's policy toward the neutrals, which involved curtailing supplies to the enemy, was being thwarted by delays in

---

[35] Informal conferences and the collection of information were sanctioned by Washington. *Ibid.*, pp. 878, 882-83, 915. On June 23, 1917, however, Lansing inquired if London, in accordance with the discussions with the Balfour Commission, was then willing to accept one or more American representatives in the War Trade Intelligence and War Trade Statistics Departments of the Foreign Office. *Ibid.*, p. 885.

[36] Lord Percy had been the head of the five blockade representatives on the Balfour Commission, and he had remained at the specific request of the United States government. "Minutes of Exports Council," p. 4 (June 26, 1917).

Washington, and that unless these matters were " energetically taken up" the war " will be most seriously prolonged. . . ."[37]

Lord Percy's confidential complaint was seconded on the same day, June 27, 1917, by a formal note from the British ambassador in Washington, Sir Cecil Spring Rice. This communication began by referring to the serious embarrassment which London was experiencing in regard to placing restrictions on the neutrals " pending the announcement of the policy which the United States Government intend to adopt in this matter." Spring Rice further reminded Lansing of the necessity of America's doing something about the shipment of coal to Spain and about the Swedish-Russian transit problem.[38] He also pointed out that Norway was driving the British government into disadvantageous bargains in the purchase of Norwegian molybdenite and fish, and that unless the United States quickly brought pressure to bear on Christiania through exports restrictions, London would either have to accept onerous terms or allow these products to go to Germany. Spring Rice concluded by saying that he was under " urgent instructions " from the Foreign Office " to express the earnest hope " that America would recognize the " urgency " of this matter and come to a " speedy decision " on the issues that had been mutually discussed. The British government was " firmly convinced " that upon the " immediate decision of these problems " hinged the question of " whether the war shall be shortened

---

[37] Percy to Hoover, June 27, 1917, F. A. R., Hoover Library (Washington Embassy, Great Britain). Percy also made oral representations to the Exports Administrative Board. "Minutes of the Exports Administrative Board," p. 2 (June 27, 1917).

[38] On the transit problem, see *post*, p. 138.

by a drastic restriction of German supplies, or whether it is to be seriously prolonged by the absence of such restrictions." [39]

The French ambassador in Washington, J. J. Jusserand, supplemented these proddings—probably at the suggestion of the British—by a lengthy note to Secretary Lansing, dated June 29, 1917. Under instructions from Paris he emphasized the " great importance and urgency" of limiting supplies to the enemy, particularly at a time when the new harvest was being awaited and when American controls ought to prove unusually effective. Such devices, he held, would expedite the return of peace by cutting off enormous shipments of foodstuffs to Germany. Jusserand concluded by saying that American export control would not threaten the neutrals with starvation, because they could not have a serious food shortage while they were sending so much to the enemy.[40]

Another British embarrassment resulted from applications of the neutrals for letters of assurance to cover shipments of grain through the blockade. Pending Wilson's proclamation prohibiting exports, Britain had been holding up such applications; and, as a consequence, representations from the neutral diplomats in London were becoming increasingly numerous and insistent. " Frankly," wrote Lord Percy to Herbert Hoover, on July 1, 1917, " at the present moment we are holding a fort which you alone can defend, and unless you can take command in a few days we shall be obliged to let up and issue letters of assurance for all the

---

[39] *For. Rel., 1917, Supp. 2,* II, pp. 886-88. Spring Rice also pointed out that the necessities of Belgian relief required that the United States use its exports control club to force Dutch and Spanish shipping into that work.

[40] *Ibid.,* pp. 888-91.

floods of foodstuffs which some of these neutrals are attempting to export in anticipation of your embargo." The British government feared, Percy concluded, that it would be accused of violating its own rationing agreements with the neutrals unless it could throw the responsibility for export restrictions on America.[41]

vii

One important reason for the reluctance of the United States to proclaim an embargo, even though a limited one, was the argument advanced by the neutrals that a drastic curtailment of their supplies would "throw them into the arms of the enemy." During the years 1917 and 1918 this allegation might almost be regarded as the neutrals' first line of defense, whether used against the Associated Powers or the Central Powers. In response to inquiries from the Department of State as to the weight of this argument, the British Embassy prepared a memorandum, dated July 5, 1917, in which it discussed the problem at great length.

The document began by saying that the neutrals had given every evidence during the past three years of the "supreme value" that they placed upon their neutral status.[42] On the whole, their sympathy was with the Allied

[41] Percy to Hoover, July 1, 1917, F. A. R., Hoover Library (Washington Embassy, Great Britain). The British were much concerned about these rationing agreements, which served to tie their hands, and they begged the United States not to hinder particular arrangements with some of the neutrals. Polk to Lansing, July 28, 1917, Lansing Papers, Library of Congress.

[42] In fact, neutrality was the only possible course for most of these small countries. In some of them, notably Switzerland, sympathies were so strongly divided that active participation would have invited civil war. In the case of the Scandinavian nations,

Export and Import Control

cause, and in the judgment of the British there was little prospect of their voluntarily joining Germany at a time when the Central Powers had the entire world arrayed against them and faced disaster. The situation would be different, however, if the Associated Powers should place such restrictions upon the neutrals as would " imperil their honor or the livelihood of their people." But such restrictions neither the United States nor Great Britain had ever advocated. Nor could the neutrals ignore the fact that if they entered the war on the side of Germany they would at once lose all of their vital supplies from the Allies and the United States, some of which were irreplaceable. The situation, therefore, was such as to give " no cause whatever to apprehend any rupture of any kind."

This British memorandum next dealt with the argument that if the neutral countries, under American pressure, refused to sell their butter, meat, and other products to the enemy, they would be invaded and overrun by the German armies. The British military authorities had come to the conclusion that Germany was in no position to undertake a series of invasions, and presented evidence that even vulnerable Denmark entertained no serious fear of such action. As for the argument that the neutrals could not stop their exports to Germany because they needed coal and other necessities in exchange, and that if they had to choose sides they would be forced by economic necessity to join the Central Powers, it was pointed out that many of the really necessary supplies that the Germans were then pro-

---

there probably would have been an inter-Scandinavian conflict, for it was unlikely that all three would have been found in the same camp. See letter from Norwegian prime minister in McCormick to Wilson, September 28, 1917, Wilson Papers, *ibid.*

viding, such as coal, could be obtained in substantial quantities from England, though, owing to tonnage difficulties, at perhaps a higher cost.[43] And even if shipments from the border neutrals to Germany were completely cut off, the Germans would continue to export commodities to them in order to maintain markets, establish credits, and serve other essential purposes.

The British argument concluded by asserting that, far from being driven into the arms of the enemy, in a very real sense the neutrals had already thrown themselves into those arms. Norway and Sweden, particularly Sweden, had provided such enormous quantities of minerals for making munitions as virtually to constitute a base of supplies for Germany. The conclusion to be drawn from all this was that the neutrals were already helping the enemy about all they could, and that there was much to be gained and little to be risked by imposing drastic export restrictions on them in the hope of reducing the flow of goods to the Central Empires.[44]

Whatever the effect of such arguments, President Wilson quieted British fears when, as we have seen, he issued his first embargo proclamation, on July 9, 1917. The newspapers of both England and France were delighted at this evidence of American readiness to take concrete steps in the direction of restricting trade with the enemy through the neutrals. These journals repeatedly asserted that before the United States entered the war the Central Powers had not been starved out, primarily because the British navy had not

[43] See *ante*, p. 39, n.
[44] Text of memorandum in *For. Rel., 1917, Supp. 2*, II, pp. 892-98. The case of Sweden is dealt with in Spring Rice to Polk, July 31, 1917, *ibid.*, pp. 1030-35.

been in a position to make its blockade devices completely effective. It had been hampered by international law and by fear of a retaliatory curtailment of butter, bacon, and eggs— a consideration which obviously did not concern the United States. But if it was contrary to international law for the British to seize American feedstuffs going to the neutrals, it was certainly not contrary to international law for the United States to embargo those feedstuffs and other commodities, whether on the grounds of conservation or on any other grounds that the Washington government cared to employ. If this was done, the blockade would become practically airtight, and Germany would presumably be compelled to surrender.[45]

The enthusiasm of Downing Street for Wilson's embargo proclamation of July 9, 1917, was far more restrained than that of the British press. While doubtless relieved at this positive, if belated, step in the direction of complete exports control, the Ministry of Blockade indicated to the American commercial attaché in London that the list was unsatisfactory because it was incomplete. In particular, it did not include such " vitally important articles as rubber, oleaginous seeds, animals, vegetables, waxes, chemicals, nonferrous metals, ores and alloys," the large-scale export of which enabled the four Northern Neutrals to continue to send their own products to Germany. The American attaché was convinced, after having received additional private information from the British Foreign Office, " that only a complete prohibition of all exports to these countries and Spain will cover the situation." [46]

---

[45] In Paris *Le Temps* spoke of Wilson's embargo proclamation as " one of the decisive acts of the war." Quoted in New York *Times,* July 12, 1917.

[46] *For. Rel., 1917, Supp. 2,* II, pp. 905-06.

viii

During the seven weeks that elapsed between the issuance of the first exports control proclamation, on July 9, 1917, and the second, on August 27, there was a good deal of discussion between the Department of State and the British officials on various aspects of the embargo. Despite the obvious need for prompt and decisive action, Washington was still determined to proceed with deliberation and examine the various implications of the problem before going to the length of imposing an embargo on all exports and demanding certain concessions from the neutrals in return for lifting it. During these anxious weeks the Department of State was positive in its assertions that it had as yet adopted no definite policy toward the neutrals.[47]

On July 31, 1917, Acting Secretary of State Polk had an interview with Ambassador Spring Rice, and after saying that the Department of State was hindered in its attempts to formulate a policy by the absence of full information from the Allies as to what they were doing or proposed to do, asked several pertinent questions. First, what were the complete texts of the various rationing and other agreements which Great Britain had negotiated with the Northern Neutrals and which France had drawn up with Switzerland—agreements which might be violated by the proposed American embargo? Second, did London wish to break these pacts? If so, the onus should not be placed upon Washington but shared jointly by the Associated Powers.

---

[47] On August 8, 1917, Secretary Lansing cabled the American ministers in the four Northern Neutrals that discussions were still being carried on with Allied and neutral representatives, but that "No definite policy has as yet been established." *Ibid.*, p. 919.

Third, were Britain, France, and Italy willing to forego the supplies which the neutrals might cut off as a reprisal for American export restrictions? Fourth, were the Allies prepared to resist the military occupation of the neutral countries by Germany, should such action be precipitated by an American embargo? Fifth, what demands did Britain and France wish Washington to make upon the neutrals? Were all exports to Germany to be stopped? Was neutral shipping to be demanded, and, if so, how much? Obviously, the United States could not proceed intelligently until it had answers to these questions.[48]

Within the next few days Spring Rice supplied most of the desired information. On July 31, 1917, he explained his position by saying that Downing Street had not purposely held anything back, but had been handicapped by not knowing exactly what Washington wanted. Some of the data that the Department of State had requested were in London and not immediately available. The British ambassador particularly emphasized the necessity of taking immediate steps to stop the heavy flow of iron ore from Sweden to Germany; and he gave assurances that Great Britain, having only minor agreements with Sweden, was free to join in any embargo policy, however drastic.[49] The next day Spring Rice supplied the Department of State

---

[48] Polk to Page, July 31, 1917, *ibid.*, pp. 912-13. This telegram sounded a new note in that the United States showed a most understandable desire to avoid the condemnation of the neutrals for taking the action suggested by the British and French, action for which the latter would not share the blame. Acting Secretary Polk pointed out in particular that America would appear in a most unfavorable light if she forbade shipments of wheat to Holland, while Britain continued to send grain under the existing agreement.

[49] *Ibid.*, pp. 1030-35.

with the most recent available copies of the rationing and similar agreements with Denmark, Holland, Norway, and Sweden, and two days later, on August 3, 1917, he provided full data regarding the status of British negotiations with the neutrals on the question of tonnage.[50]

A week later, on August 11, 1917, Ambassador Spring Rice further informed the Department of State that the British were willing to terminate any of their agreements with the Northern Neutrals in the interests of an adequate exports control policy, even to the extent of losing all of their food imports from Denmark and Holland, valued at £40,000,000 a year. London feared, however, that the Dutch would take retaliatory steps and send to Germany the margerine that was then going to England, especially if the British were to appear offensively conspicuous in presenting the initial demands to the neutrals. It was therefore delicately suggested that it might be wise for Washington to appear at the forefront in undertaking this unpleasant task. Nevertheless, London was prepared to share " full identity of policy and responsibility," and strongly urged " the importance of early action on the lines already discussed. . . ."[51]

ix

Late in August, 1917, Washington responded to the British pleadings for a more satisfactory exports control when President Wilson took two important steps. The first was the issuance of an executive order, dated August 21, 1917, which removed from the hands of the Secretary of Commerce and placed in those of a five-man Exports

[50] *Ibid.*, pp. 914-15, 916-18.
[51] *Ibid.*, pp. 920-22.

Administrative Board the carrying out of such instructions and proclamations regarding exports control as the President should promulgate. At the same time a new five-man Exports Council was created and charged with the responsibility of advising the Exports Administrative Board.[52]

Six days later, on August 27, 1917, President Wilson issued his second exports control proclamation. It divided the nations of the world into two categories: first, the enemy and the European neutrals, and second, the Allies and all remaining nations. To the former the export of practically every commodity of any importance was prohibited, except under license issued by the Exports Administrative Board. As regards the Allies and all other nations, including those of Latin America, the list of restricted commodities was much less inclusive and in essence constituted only a few additions to the first proclamation of July 9. In his explanatory statement, Wilson stressed the necessity of closer economic control over those neutral countries near the enemy. He further declared that the purpose of the proclamation was "not export prohibition but merely export control"; and he gave assurances that the needs of the neutral nations would be met, insofar as the necessities of the Associated Powers permitted. But, Wilson warned, such assistance to the neutrals would be subject to "the very

[52] *Ibid.*, p. 927. This order superseded that of June 22, 1917, which charged the Secretary of Commerce with the administration of exports control and created a four-man Exports Council to advise the President on exports policies. The new Exports Council was to be composed of the Secretary of State, the Secretary of Agriculture, the Secretary of Commerce, the Food Administrator, and the Chairman of the United States Shipping Board. The Exports Administrative Board was to consist of a representative of each of these officials.

proper qualification" that it should not be made to benefit the enemy "directly or indirectly." [53]

Despite renewed expressions of alarm, the government in Washington, in conformity with the new proclamation, took prompt steps to prevent practically all American goods from reaching the Northern Neutrals.[54] On August 30, 1917, the Exports Administrative Board voted to withhold all licenses for exporting controlled commodities to Norway, Holland, Denmark, and Sweden.[55] And on August 31 the Board gave instructions that no cargo ships destined for these countries should be given bunker supplies without its approval.[56]

These new measures did not mean, however, that Washington had adopted a definitive policy regarding the neu-

[53] *Ibid.*, pp. 933-38. No effort was made to indicate those commodities that were being restricted because of a domestic shortage, and those that were being withheld to bring pressure on the neutrals or to keep American products out of enemy hands. On September 17, 1917, the Exports Administrative Board issued its first export conservation list, which was supplemented from time to time, particularly by the War Trade Board. *Report of the War Trade Board* (Washington, 1920), pp. 63, 66. On September 7, 1917, the President issued a proclamation restricting the export of coin, bullion, and currency. *For. Rel., 1917, Supp. 2*, II, pp. 943-45.

[54] For the Swiss reaction see *Neut. Press Supp.*, II, 371.

[55] *For. Rel., 1917, Supp. 2*, II, p. 939. On September 29, 1917, Polk (Acting Secretary of State) cabled Page in London that, with a few very minor exceptions, "nothing is going to Scandinavian countries." *Ibid.*, p. 955. Some grain and fodderstuffs were, however, being licensed to Switzerland. War Trade Board, *Daily Record*, September 20, 1917. The British co-operated with the United States by refusing, with a few exceptions, to license to the Northern Neutrals the same goods refused licenses by the Exports Administrative Board. *For. Rel., 1917, Supp. 2*, II, pp. 950-52. For French co-operation see *ibid.*, p. 979.

[56] *Ibid.*, p. 939.

trals. In a circular instruction to the American ministers in the six European neutral countries, dated October 6, 1917, Secretary Lansing emphatically denied "that any final decision has been reached," and stated that the problem was still under discussion with the neutrals and with the Allies. Lansing was particularly distressed by press reports to the effect that the United States was the ringleader in urging a drastic policy upon Britain and France. He wanted it made perfectly clear that any action taken by these Allies would be the result of their own mature judgment, after consultation with the United States; and that Washington was not "dictating to England and France an embargo policy hostile to neutral countries." Indeed, "England has been urging us to adopt even a stricter control than we have been willing to sanction." Lansing was also at pains to emphasize the fact that America was concerned with keeping her products from the enemy and with securing needed commodities from the neutrals; and he denied the accusation that Washington aimed to interfere with the normal life of these small countries beyond the restrictions necessary for accomplishing such objects. But, Lansing concluded, the neutrals should know that the voluntary laying up of their ships in American ports complicated the situation and necessitated stricter measures than otherwise would be employed.[57]

X

A new stage in the development of export control was reached when, on October 12, 1917, President Wilson issued an executive order replacing the Exports Administrative Board with the War Trade Board, headed by Vance C.

[57] *Ibid.*, pp. 960-61. See also *ibid.*, pp. 974-76.

McCormick.[58] This powerful new organization, which functioned throughout the remainder of the war, was charged primarily with the task of issuing licenses to cover export and (later) import trade. Its personnel, both abroad and at home (in Washington and elsewhere in the United States) was numerous, and the volume of business transacted was enormous.[59] As far as the neutrals were concerned, the War Trade Board was not a policy-making organization but a policy-executing one. It did gather information from the various foreign representatives, and it did enter into detailed negotiations with them; but these matters concerned foreign policy and were therefore subject to the final approval or disapproval of the Department of State, although we must note that they did not always come to its notice.[60]

[58] The War Trade Board was composed of representatives of the Secretary of State, of the Secretary of the Treasury, of the Secretary of Agriculture, of the Secretary of Commerce, of the Food Administrator, and of the United States Shipping Board. *Report of War Trade Board*, p. 5.

[59] Indicative of the volume of business is the fact that the records of the War Trade Board in Washington fill over 800 four-drawer steel filing cases.

[60] All telegrams to the War Trade Board, and all telegrams from it to men in the field, were sent through the Department of State. A statement in the *Daily Record* of the War Trade Board reads: " Please bear in mind that matters of international policy are under the jurisdiction of, and handled solely by, the State Department." December 14, 1917. On March 27, 1940, Vance C. McCormick wrote to the author: " In answer to your first question, I should say that the major policies adopted by the War Trade Board with reference to the neutrals were approved or disapproved by the [State] Department although the negotiations originated and were carried on by the War Trade Board through its representatives and legal adviser, Thomas L. Chadbourne, Coun-

Export and Import Control

But once questions of policy were decided, the War Trade Board operated as a virtually autonomous body; and it was in an extraordinarily favorable position to do effective work. Created for the duration of the emergency, it had no past and no future. Unlike the Department of State, it did not have to worry about the precedents it had established; and unlike other agencies it did not have to worry about making enemies which might hamper its growth. As a consequence, the Board could apply itself to its task without fear or favor.[61]

The creation of the War Trade Board gave birth to a new crop of rumors as to the intentions of the Washington government. In order to counteract such distorted statements Secretary Lansing sent a circular telegram (October 17, 1917) to the ministers of the United States in each of the six European neutrals, and instructed them to make public the policy therein outlined. Lansing expressed regret that

---

selor of the Board. [Comment of Frank L. Polk (January, 1942): " It worked very well."]

" In answer to your second question, it is possible that certain minor decisions might have been reached without the knowledge or approval of the State Department but I should say generally such was not the case. The President was always willing to grant me an interview when it was needed and, as I had this direct contact, the State Department was willing that I, as their representative, relieve them of many matters which could thus be more expeditiously transacted." Dr. Alonzo E. Taylor, also a member of the War Trade Board, wrote the author on March 14, 1940: " It is not true that all of the policies or acts of the War Trade Board were specifically approved by the State Department. There was too much to do and too much hurry." Lester H. Woolsey commented (January, 1942) that some of these unauthorized acts " turned up later to surprise us."

[61] This was pointed out to the present writer by Vance C. McCormick, in an interview on March 23, 1941.

the neutrals, despite numerous requests, had as yet provided little information regarding their production, consumption, and other requirements; and despite earlier warnings were continuing " to send large quantities of vital supplies to the Central Empires. . . ." The newly created War Trade Board, Lansing went on to say, proposed to continue the policy of denying export licenses to the Northern Neutrals so long as the requested information was withheld, and so long as these countries continued to give aid, direct or indirect, to the enemy. Indeed, the United States might better send its own fodder and oil directly to Germany, for when they reached the enemy through neutral cattle or manufactured goods they represented the added contribution of equipment and labor. Lansing's concluding observation was an eloquent summation of a current American view:

> It is unreasonable to expect that our farmers shall raise foodstuffs and our people deny themselves the quantities they desire to consume in order that a surplus may be sent to the northern neutrals to render easier for them the help which they are extending to our enemies.
>
> The policy of this Government is in no way inspired by a desire to hamper or interfere with the normal life of neutrals. On the contrary we are willing to help these neutrals even at a sacrifice to ourselves in allowing export to them of commodities we can ill afford to spare, but in return for this friendly service we must demand some guarantee that these supplies will not be turned against us to kill our sons and prolong the war.
>
> The welfare of the northern neutrals is in their own hands.[62]

---

[62] *For. Rel., 1917, Supp. 2,* II, pp. 975-76. The food situation in America at this time was serious. Hoover to War Trade Board, November 8, 1917, F. A. R., Hoover Library (War Trade Board, McCormick).

xi

Up to this point we have considered only the subject of regulating exports from the United States, and have ignored restrictions upon imports. Import control, though far less important than export control from the point of view of the neutrals, was nevertheless an integral part of the work which fell within the jurisdiction of the War Trade Board.

Authority to control imports into the United States was granted to the President by the so-called Trading with the Enemy Act, which was not introduced into Congress until June 11, 1917. The failure to take any action earlier, or to move more rapidly when action was initiated, was doubtless due, as in the case of the Espionage Act, to the pressure of more important legislation and to the relative unimportance of this bill. The debate in Congress was not prolonged or particularly acrimonious, although there was some little discussion of censorship, enemy trade, and enemy property rights. Indeed, the legislators seem to have been not so much concerned with the control of neutral commerce as with the expropriation and administration of the valuable property assets that Germany had in the United States. The bill passed both houses of Congress without record vote, and on October 6, 1917, received the President's signature.[63]

It was not until November 28, 1917, nearly two months after the signing of the Trading with the Enemy Act, that President Wilson issued a proclamation forbidding the importation of a lengthy list of commodities, except under license from the War Trade Board. This proclamation limited imports to the more essential products, so that ship-

[63] The text is in the *U. S. Statutes at Large*, XL, pt. 1, pp. 411-26.

ping and foreign exchange might be used most advantageously for war purposes. Although import restriction did work some hardship on the neutral carrying trade and on neutral exports to the United States, particularly luxury articles, it appears never to have been used in an important way as a weapon against the neutrals, and as a consequence was of secondary significance from the standpoint of this study.[64]

On the same day that import restrictions were announced, November 28, 1917, the President issued his third exports control proclamation, this time placing a number of items, mostly of relatively minor importance, on the list of commodities which could be exported only under license.[65] Finally, on February 14, 1918, Wilson issued two additional proclamations under which *all* imports and exports became subject to licensing.[66] With these two instruments the widest possible basis was laid for commercial control.

xii

As the year 1917 neared its close, the temporary embargo on all shipments to the four Northern Neutrals was still effective. The War Trade Board estimated that the exports of foodstuffs by these nations to the Central Powers had consequently declined in amounts estimated at from 65 to 85 per cent, as compared with the previous year, and that there had been a corresponding decrease in the export of

---

[64] The text of the proclamation and the public explanation of it appear in *For. Rel., 1917, Supp. 2,* II, pp. 989-94.

[65] *Ibid.,* pp. 989-90. See also statement of War Trade Board in *Official Bulletin,* March 23, 1918, p. 1.

[66] *For. Rel., 1918, Supp. 1,* II, pp. 958-62. See statement of War Trade Board in *Official Bulletin,* March 23, 1918, p. 1.

many other commodities.[67] But this pressure from the United States to secure rationing agreements by which the neutrals would voluntarily restrict the outflow of their goods to Germany was without the desired effect. The negotiations in Washington with representatives of Norway, Sweden, Denmark, and Holland were languishing, and the resentment aroused against America was visibly increasing.

With this situation in mind, the War Trade Board proposed, early in December, 1917, that as a gesture of Christmas-time good will the United States license to the embargoed Northern Neutrals several cargoes of essential commodities, such as drugs, kerosene, and coffee. These last two items were regarded as particularly important because of the fondness of the Scandinavians for coffee, and because of the increased use of oil lamps during the long winter evenings. The War Trade Board was of the opinion that such a gesture would create a much better feeling in the nations concerned, facilitate the current negotiations in Washington, and offset the effect of German-inspired anti-American propaganda in the Scandinavian countries and Holland. It was expected, however, that the neutral nations so benefited would charter a sufficient amount of their own tonnage to the Associated Powers to compensate for the shipping diverted from war purposes by the Christmas cargoes.[68]

The British and the French, who opposed any whittling down of the blockade, were at first lukewarm, if not positively hostile, to the plan of Christmas concessions. But

[67] *For. Rel., 1917, Supp. 2,* II, p. 1011 (Report of War Trade Board for period ending December 31, 1917).

[68] *Ibid.,* pp. 1080, 1100-01; also "Minutes of the War Trade Board," I, 166-67 (December 14, 1917).

out of deference to Washington the London Foreign Office finally gave its rather grudging consent, together with suggestions designed to guarantee the most satisfactory compensatory tonnage arrangements.[69] The governments of the neutral countries accepted the American gesture of good will with effusive thanks, and although there was some bickering about the details of tonnage compensation, and about delays in the arrival of the cargoes, there can be little doubt that the objects of the scheme were at least partially attained.[70] The British, who were impressed with the success of the arrangement, finally came around to the belief that a larger amount of all commodities should be licensed to the Northern Neutrals for the purpose of improving good will and counteracting German propaganda.[71] It seems reasonable to conclude, especially in the light of comments that appeared in the Scandinavian and Dutch press, that the Christmas concessions took the edge off much of the bitterness that had been aroused by the American embargo.[72]

xiii

About the time that arrangements were completed for the Christmas cargoes, London began to move rapidly in

[69] *For. Rel., 1917, Supp. 2*, II, pp. 1102; *ibid., 1918, Supp. 1*, II, pp. 1387-88.

[70] For a survey of the final arrangements, see *ibid., 1917, Supp. 2*, II, pp. 1115-16. The War Trade Board representative in Copenhagen complained that the British promptly sent a Christmas cargo ship to Denmark, whereas the two American vessels were delayed and received little publicity when they arrived. Hurley to War Trade Board, April 11, 1918, *The Trade and Shipping Negotiations with Denmark* (Washington, 1919), pp. 66-69. See also Grant-Smith to Lansing, May 14, 1918, State Dept., 652. 119/282.

[71] *For. Rel., 1917, Supp. 2*, II, p. 1116.

[72] The press of Denmark was particularly grateful. See *Neut. Press Supp.*, III, 255-56.

the direction of relaxing the embargo. After some three months of a practically complete stoppage of exports to the four Northern Neutrals, a vacuum had been created in certain markets there, and German exporters were supplying this deficiency to the best of their ability. They were not only making handsome profits and improving their exchange in the border countries, but they were demanding and securing large quantities of foodstuffs and other commodities in return. In this respect the embargo had, in the short-run view, actually improved the position of Germany. The British, in particular, were distressed by the loss of their markets to the enemy and by the weakening of their foreign exchange; and late in December, 1917, they proposed that the embargo be lifted as regards certain nonessential (nonmilitary) items. The suggested list ran heavily to drugs and luxury articles (such as furs, wines, and pianos), and stressed those products which the Germans were exporting and of which the Associated Powers had a surplus.[73]

After mature consideration, Washington replied (January 23, 1918) that the surest way to expedite its negotiation of rationing agreements with the neutrals was " the continued maintenance" of " a complete embargo," and it felt that this consideration outweighed any effect of the capture of the Scandinavian and Dutch markets by Germany. But since the attempt of the War Trade Board to maintain a " strict embargo " against these countries had not been successful, and since the British blockade authorities were much more familiar with the situation than the United States, the final decision was left to them and to the War Trade Board representative in London.[74]

[73] *For. Rel., 1918, Supp. 1,* II, pp. 936-38, 938-39, 942.
[74] *Ibid.,* p. 950. In an earlier telegram the War Trade Board not only opposed the scheme but thought that certain items should be

The British persisted in their advocacy of relaxation, and on February 18, 1918, after the Italian government had come to the support of their view, the War Trade Board finally agreed to the export of nonessential commodities to Sweden and Holland. The United States still opposed such a concession to Norway and Denmark, primarily because of the state of its rationing negotiations with them.[75] But by April 16, 1918, the Board was in favor of including these two nations, because the negotiations with Denmark were regarded as almost hopeless, and because the agreement with Norway was on the point of ratification.[76] So in the end the policy of allowing the export of nonessentials to the four Northern Neutrals was adopted.[77]

Early in May, 1918, the British suggested the advisability of further relaxing the embargo by issuing licenses for trade with firms in the neutral countries that were known to be pro-Ally. The object was to offset the work of the Germans, who were making every effort to assist pro-German concerns, and thus further their propaganda.[78] Although the British did not offer this as a definite proposal, Washington opposed the scheme on two grounds. First, it would seriously weaken the blockade, which had already been relaxed by the concessions recently made on nonessentials. Secondly, such a list would be a white list rather than an embargo, and it might create commercial jealousy among the Associated Governments. In particular, it was pointed out that American merchants would feel that British trade

---

eliminated from the proposed list of nonessentials. War Trade Board to Sheldon, January 9, 1918, *ibid.*, p. 939.

[75] *Ibid.*, p. 972.
[76] *Ibid.*, p. 980.
[77] *Ibid.*, p. 984, n.   [78] *Ibid.*, pp. 984-85.

interests were being favored by any administrative agency of this nature set up in London.[79] Although nothing more seems to have come of the idea, it is significant as another manifestation of the latent friction over commercial matters that trembled beneath the surface during the joint prosecution of the war. It also indicates that on the whole the United States was more disposed to maintain a strict embargo, once it was established, than Great Britain.[80]

Now that we have considered at some length the gradual formulation of a definite policy by the Washington government, we may next turn to the series of negotiations with the individual European neutrals.

---

[79] *Ibid.*, pp. 985-86.

[80] S. B. Conger, Foreign Adviser of the War Trade Board, later testified that the influence of the War Trade Board was thrown on the side of strictness in enforcing the embargo and blockade. This policy was opposed in certain influential Allied quarters. " Conger Report."

Chapter IV

THE RATIONING AGREEMENT WITH NORWAY

i

The first of the trade or rationing agreements to be extorted from the Northern Neutrals was that with Norway. Since it illustrates our general problem remarkably well, it will provide a convenient introduction to the subject; and since the general pattern of these negotiations is roughly applicable to all the other neutrals, the various stages in the discussions will be developed somewhat more fully than otherwise would be the case.

Perhaps the most significant fact about Norway from our point of view is that she was the only one of the Northern Neutrals normally dependent upon the Allies and the United States for large quantities of essential foodstuffs. Although her population is small and her land area relatively large, only a small percentage of her acreage is arable. As a result, a large number of her people naturally turn to maritime pursuits, notably fishing and the carrying trade. During the course of the war enormous quantities of Norwegian fish and fish products were shipped to the Germans, who, because of the serious shortage of oils and fats, particularly welcomed fish oil. The Norwegians also exported to Germany considerable amounts of chemicals and mineral products for use in war industries, notably nickel, molybdenum, chrome, and pyrites (sulphur).[1] The

[1] This analysis of Norway's position has been drawn largely from a secret memorandum of the British Foreign Office, dated

The Agreement with Norway

Balfour Commission consequently urged the Washington government to use the economic weapons at its command for the purpose of forcing the Norwegians to reduce these shipments to the absolute minimum.[2]

But Norway by no means confined her export market to the Germans. She also sent important supplies of timber, ores, and other commodities to the British. Indeed, so closely was Norwegian economy integrated with that of England, and so dependent was Norway upon getting her necessities through the blockade, that the Norwegians, of all the Northern Neutrals, were probably most amenable to British influence and pressure.[3] This economic affinity was reinforced by a strong pro-Ally sentiment, for despite Teutonic blood and cultural heritage, the Norwegian masses were more sympathetic with the cause of the Allies than with that of the Central Powers.[4] Such sentiment was especially noticeable after the German submarine warfare began to take a heavy toll of Norwegian lives and tonnage.[5]

At the outbreak of the war in 1914, Norway had 2,559,000 gross tons of ocean-going shipping, the fourth largest

---

August 4, 1917, a printed copy of which is deposited with the Wiseman Papers in the Yale House Collection. See also Consett, *Triumph of Unarmed Forces*, pp. 86-88, 106-07.

[2] *For. Rel., 1917, Supp. 2*, II, pp. 833-34. The British admitted that if unduly strong demands were made the Norwegians might cut off milk and fish exports to England, or be overrun by the Germans. But at that time neither eventuality was thought likely.

[3] Secret British memorandum, August 4, 1917. The British found it necessary to facilitate the export of materials to those Norwegian firms that were manufacturing munitions for the Allies. *For. Rel., 1917, Supp. 2*, II, p. 952.

[4] Paul G. Vigness, *The Neutrality of Norway in the World War* (Stanford University, 1932), pp. 23-24.

[5] Heckscher, *Sweden, etc.*, p. 325.

GROSS STEAM TONNAGE OF THE WORLD, 1916-1917 *

(Neutral nations italicized)

Country	Ships (number)	Tonnage
Great Britain	10,030	20,463,881
United States	1,904	5,116,215
Germany	1,708	3,890,542
Norway	1,795	2,263,900
France	998	1,851,120
Japan	1,151	1,847,453
Italy	684	1,685,720
Holland	697	1,486,368
Sweden	1,037	926,650
Austria-Hungary	385	891,103
Russia	753	875,146
Spain	552	815,116
Denmark	589	797,371
Greece	361	717,045
Portugal	164	303,706
Brazil	377	290,637
Belgium	144	264,985
Argentina	238	181,929

* These figures include only steamers of over one hundred tons. All nations with a tonnage of 100,000 or more are included. The figures are based on *Lloyd's Register* for 1916-1917, and appear in the *Annual Report of the Commissioner of Navigation to the Secretary of Commerce for the Fiscal Year Ended June 30, 1918* (Washington, 1918), p. 81.

merchant marine in the world.[6] While the more cautious and the more economically self-sufficient Dutch and Danes tied up their tonnage rather than face the mine and submarine peril, the Norwegians kept virtually all of their ships on the high seas in trades, it so happened, that were generally of direct use to the Allies. Although the people of Norway probably would not have exposed themselves to

[6] Heckscher, *Sweden, etc.*, p. 347.

these dangers if they had not been so heavily dependent upon the sea for their livelihood, it is undeniable that their assistance was of great benefit to the British at a time when the U-boat warfare had caused a critical shortage of shipping. The Berlin government was naturally hostile to the policy pursued by Christiania, and Norwegian shipping suffered heavy losses from the German submarines, mines, and cruisers. By the time the United States entered the war, Norway had sacrificed about six hundred seamen and over four hundred of her merchant ships.[7] But since such losses were covered by insurance, and since the carrying rates were high, the Norwegians were experiencing, at least in certain quarters, a feverish blush of wartime prosperity.[8]

ii

The people of Norway were seriously disturbed by the entrance of the United States into the war and by the increasing rumors that a complete embargo would be laid on foodstuffs to the Northern Neutrals. This anxiety was perhaps most conspicuously reflected in the heavy purchases of American grain by Norwegian buyers prior to President Wilson's first embargo proclamation of July 9, 1917. The Norwegian minister in Washington, H. H. Bryn, made repeated oral and written representations in which he pro-

---

[7] *Pertes de guerre subies par la marine de commerce norvégienne, 1914-1918* (Christiania, c. 1919). By the end of the war Norway had lost over 800 ships of 1,180,316 gross tons. Of this amount 1,043,077 tons were sunk by submarines alone. See also C. Ernest Fayle, *Seaborne Trade* (London, 1924), III, 466.

[8] Report of Alexander V. Dye (War Trade Board representative in Norway), February 8, 1918, F. A. R., Hoover Library (Norway, General).

tested the innocence of his country in sending foodstuffs to Germany. In addition, he asserted that the rationing agreements with the British government were already working well, and he gave reasons why, in his judgment, Norway was entitled to preferential treatment by the United States.[9]

Meanwhile, the American minister in Christiania, Albert G. Schmedeman, had been reporting the results of several consultations with his Allied colleagues. It was their collective opinion that Norway, because of her special services to the Allies and because of political conditions, should be subjected to less severe restrictions than Sweden or Denmark. Schmedeman also sent figures which suggested that Norwegian trade with Germany had already been reduced to the barest minimum, and he observed that too severe a policy with Norway might react to the disadvantage of the Allies.[10] On the other hand, the British representatives in Washington drew up a memorandum in which they urged that the United States use its foodstuffs club promptly and effectively, particularly with the object of halting Norwegian exports of fish and molybdenum to Germany. "His Majesty's Government," read the document, "are firmly convinced that on the immediate decision of these problems depends the question whether the war shall be shortened by a drastic restriction of German supplies or whether it is to be seriously prolonged by the absence of such restrictions." [11]

Norwegian anxiety over the proposed American embargo

[9] See particularly Bryn to Lansing, April 23, 1917, *For. Rel., 1917, Supp. 2*, II, pp. 1016-17.

[10] Schmedeman to Lansing, July 11, 1917, *ibid.*, pp. 1028-29.

[11] Percy to Hoover, July 19, 1917, enclosing memorandum of July 17, F. A. R., Hoover Library (Great Britain, Washington Embassy).

ultimately found expression in a growing demand that a special commission be sent to the United States. Such a body could present the case of Norway as advantageously as possible, and at the same time endeavor to negotiate a trade agreement under which the most urgently needed foodstuffs and other commodities could be obtained. Responding to pressure from various quarters, including Norwegian-American shipping interests, Christiania finally appointed an eight-man commission. It was composed largely of representatives of the Norwegian economic interests, and was headed by Dr. Fridtjof Nansen, the distinguished Arctic explorer.[12] The entire group of negotiators sailed from Christiania on July 12 and arrived in New York on July 25, 1917.[13]

Whatever its expectations, the Norwegian commission received a most chilling reception at the hands of the American press. Editorial columns roundly condemned the Scandinavian kingdom for exporting various commodities to Germany, particularly enormous quantities of fish. Why, it was asked, should the United States send grain to a nation which was already supplying the enemy with vital foodstuffs, to say nothing of materials of war? An article by Carl W. Ackerman, entitled, "Black Sheep among the Neutrals," and published in a widely distributed American weekly magazine, caused Norway to appear in a most unfavorable light and created something of a stir, both in the

---

[12] Nansen was later prominent in postwar relief work and in the councils of the League of Nations. He was awarded the Nobel Peace Prize in 1923. Comment of Dr. Alonzo E. Taylor (November, 1941): "Nansen was fair, open minded and loyal—the best we had dealings with."

[13] Vigness, *Neutrality of Norway*, pp. 127-29; New York *Times*, July 13, 27, 1917

press and in diplomatic circles, on both sides of the Atlantic.[14]

Doubtless aware of the damage that was being done by these misleading accounts, Dr. Nansen gave out two statements to the press in which he attempted to make his nation's case appear to better advantage. He admitted that Norway was exporting fish to Germany, as she had done for many years past, but he pointed out that this was sanctioned by specific agreement with England. The Norwegians, he explained, did not think that it was true neutrality to supply only one belligerent while cutting off all exports to the other, and they feared a retaliatory attack from Germany if such trade was completely or even largely stopped. Nansen further emphasized the undoubted fact that Norway's shipping was being employed in the service of the Allies, and that most of her tonnage losses had been incurred in that service. As for the charges of supplying the enemy, he was prepared to give guarantees that no American imports would be re-exported to Germany, or even to Sweden and Denmark. "America," he concluded, "can starve us if she sees fit to do so but we hope and believe that she will decide not to." [15]

iii

An immediate concern of the Norwegian government was the detention of the large quantities of grain that had been purchased in America previous to the imposition of the embargo. These stocks, which were loaded on eleven Nor-

---

[14] *Saturday Evening Post,* July 28, 1917, p. 7, *passim*; also, New York *Times,* July 25, August 9, 1917; Vigness, *Neutrality of Norway,* pp. 131-32; *Neut. Press Supp.,* II, 397.

[15] New York *Times,* July 28, August 3, 1917.

THE AGREEMENT WITH NORWAY

wegian ships scattered from Galveston to Boston, had already suffered some deterioration, and it was feared that continued delays might result in complete spoilage. Minister Bryn therefore urged upon Herbert Hoover the prompt release of 50,000 tons of grain.[16]

Hoover was loath to grant the request, for, as he pointed out, Norway did not need the grain immediately, whereas the United States and its Associates did. As a compromise arrangement, he proposed that the Norwegians retain a part of the cereal themselves, and release the remainder for Belgian relief. He declared that this would not only be a notable act of humanity on the part of Norway, but would help conserve the American supply and relieve the United States of the necessity of going elsewhere to provide Belgium's needs.[17]

After considerable haggling, Hoover and Nansen finally came to an agreement, on August 20, 1917. In brief, the terms were as follows: (1) Norway would transfer 30,000 tons of her grain to the Belgian relief administration at contract prices; (2) Norwegian shippers would be granted licenses for 20,300 tons of cereals; and (3) Norway would provide seven of her own ships to transfer the Belgian grain to Europe.[18]

---

[16] Bryn to Hoover, July 23, 1917, F. A. R., Hoover Library (Norway, Legation); also, Schmedeman to Lansing, July 14, 1917, *ibid.*

[17] Hoover to Bryn, July 24, 1917, *ibid.* Hoover wrote: "I wish to repeat the emphatic desire of the American Government to divide its available exports among the various countries with justice and with full regard for the friendship which has so long existed."

[18] The text of the agreement is published in G. I. Gay and H. H. Fisher, eds., *Public Relations of the Commission for Relief in Belgium* (Stanford University, 1929), I, 369-70. The docu-

This settlement represented a compromise on both sides. The stocks of cereal were Norwegian property, and the American government might have found it somewhat embarrassing to confiscate them. But the grain was of no use to Norway unless Washington would issue the necessary export licenses. The arrangement finally agreed upon relieved Norway's immediate anxieties and benefited the Belgian relief, while at the same time easing the American grain shortage. The stipulation whereby Norwegian shipping was to be used was of particular significance, for otherwise the United States would have had to draw upon its own or desperately needed Allied tonnage to ship these supplies to Belgium. It will also be noted that this was one of the few instances of any importance during the strict American embargo when Washington permitted any quantity of foodstuffs to go to one of the Northern Neutrals.

iv

On July 24, 1917, as we have seen, the Exports Council outlined in general terms what its policy toward the neutrals was going to be pending the embargo. It is clear from this

---

ment was in the form of a letter signed by Hoover and countersigned by Nansen. It was evidently drawn up without reference to President Wilson, for, in communicating a copy to the State Department, Hoover wrote: "You will recollect the President's policy was to allow moderate food shipments to Norway, and, therefore, I do not see that he needs to be troubled in the matter." Hoover to Polk, August 20, 1917, Food Administration Archives, 1H A19, National Archives. (Hereafter cited as F. A. A.) Several of my informants who were in a position to know agree—and one of them puts it in these words—that "the general attitude of President Wilson was one of complete delegation of power and complete confidence in the men who headed the larger branches of administration."

The Agreement with Norway

statement, as well as from subsequent declarations, that the United States would undertake to supply, insofar as it could, the reasonable requirements of Norway, and in return would expect the Norwegians to stop or severely limit their shipments of commodities to Germany. But such exports were not to include American products, in their original or transformed state, nor substitutes for American products. The Department of State also made it clear that any shipments of foodstuffs to Germany during the embargo period would be subtracted from the supplies ultimately expected by Norway from the United States.[19]

Despite this unmistakable definition of policy, it was not until November 16, 1917, nearly four months after the arrival of the Nansen Commission, that Christiania advanced a proposition concrete enough so that the negotiators could actually come to grips with their problem.[20] Throughout these critical months the American embargo was in effect, Norwegian stocks were rapidly dwindling, and exports to Germany were continuing in large volume. Why this delay, which meant so much to the Allies in their attempt to strangle the enemy, and to Norway in her struggle for national existence?

On the Norwegian side, this anomalous situation may be explained in part by a number of factors. First, the food shortage had not as yet begun to be alarming, and the masses of the people, as distinguished from their govern-

---

[19] *For. Rel., 1917, Supp. 2,* II, pp. 908-10.

[20] The United States and the Allied governments were so much disturbed by the delay that they seriously considered shifting the negotiations either to Christiania or to London. The arrival of the definite Norwegian proposal of November 16, 1917, convinced the War Trade Board of the unwisdom of such a move. *Ibid.,* pp. 1059-60, 1069.

ment, were not fully aware of the ultimate seriousness of the situation.[21] Second, the prevalence of wartime prosperity in certain industries appears to have dulled the apprehensions of the rank and file. Third, the Norwegian government, which was keenly aware of political currents, revealed a quite understandable reluctance to come forward and voluntarily accept disagreeable restrictions on the economic life of the country. As a matter of fact, Christiania took the view that it was not acting in the role of a suppliant, but was requesting certain concessions from Washington as a right.[22] Fourth, throughout this period of delay, as later, there was abundant evidence that Norway was deliberately postponing the evil day of accepting unpalatable conditions in the hope that the war would suddenly come to an end, or that decisive German victories would weaken Allied and American demands.[23] Fifth, there was a strong reluctance in some Norwegian quarters to abandon a pan-Scandinavian policy of presenting a united front to both belligerents, and to substitute for it separate negotiations with the United States.[24] In fact, there was some effort on the part of Sweden to keep Norway from yielding to American terms.[25]

---

[21] On October 27, 1917, Beaver White, of the War Trade Board, estimated that Norway had foodstuffs on hand for eight or ten months. Memorandum of that date, State Dept., War Trade Board, American-Norwegian Agreement, vol. I.

[22] New York *Times*, November 12, 1917; also *Neut. Press Supp.*, III, 276.

[23] *The Rationing Agreement with Norway* (Washington, 1919), p. 24; Heckscher, *Sweden, etc.*, p. 297.

[24] Vigness, *Neutrality of Norway*, pp. 140-41.

[25] *For. Rel., 1917, Supp. 2,* II, pp. 1052-53, 1083, 1110-11. The Norwegian Foreign Minister told Schmedeman that if imports from the United States were stopped Norway probably would be forced to consult with the other Scandinavian countries with a view to arranging for an interchange of domestic products. Schmedeman to Lansing, September 4, 1917, State Dept., 657. 119/34.

A sixth factor in the Norwegian delay—and one of prime importance throughout the entire negotiation—was strong German pressure against concluding an agreement with the United States. This influence was exerted through German diplomatic channels as well as through the German newspapers, which indulged in dire threats of action against Norway if she should so far forsake her neutrality as to come to terms with Washington.[26] It should also be observed that a complicating element during these months was the attempt of Berlin to negotiate an agreement with Norway that would be disadvantageous to the Allies and to the United States.[27]

A seventh factor in the delay—and a corollary to the one just discussed—was the fact that Norway could not willingly consent to a complete or disproportionately unfair cessation of her exports to Germany. Aside from the possibility of strong German reprisals, including an attack upon their country, the Norwegian people would not permit the violent dislocation of their economy that such a course would entail. It must be constantly borne in mind that Norwegian-German trade flowed two ways: in return for exports of fish, minerals, and other commodities to Germany, Norway received large quantities of coal and other commodities necessary for the conduct of her economic life.

An eighth factor is to be found in the general character of the Christiania government. Partisan politics, which was strong, played a vital part in any important decision. The

---

[26] Vigness, *Neutrality of Norway,* p. 145; Schmedeman to Lansing, September 14, 1917, State Dept., 657. 119/46.

[27] *For. Rel., 1917, Supp. 2,* II, pp. 1069-70; *ibid., 1918, Supp. 1,* II, pp. 1112, 1126, 1127, 1151. The Norwegian-German agreement was finally signed on September 14, 1918. See Heckscher, *Sweden, etc.,* p. 371.

press, some of it inspired by pro-German sympathies if not by German money, was loud in its opposition to any concession, and the Minister for Foreign Affairs, Nils C. Ihlen, was generally regarded as pro-German.[28] In these circumstances, it is not surprising that the government, which normally displayed little vigor, was dilatory in sending definite instructions to Nansen.[29] Another aspect of this problem is that at first Christiania attempted to secure piecemeal concessions from the United States, rather than negotiate a sweeping agreement; and much valuable time was consequently lost in preliminary sparring.

v

The government in Washington, overwhelmed with the task of creating war machinery, was itself in some measure responsible for the delay in the negotiations. First of all, there was an understandable desire to wait for the embargo pinch to force the Nansen Commission to propose conditions.[30] There was also a natural unwillingness to lay down onerous terms and incur the opprobrium of being too severe on the neutrals. With each side reluctant to make the first overtures, and with each anxious for the other to take action,

[28] Vigness, *Neutrality of Norway*, p. 146; *Neut. Press Supp.*, III, 81, 128-30.

[29] The memorandum of July 24, 1917, which outlined the policy of the United States toward the neutrals, though presented to Minister Bryn on July 24, did not reach Christiania until October 19, 1917. A serious political controversy resulted. The embarrassment caused by this delay, however, probably put the government in a frame of mind for action. Vigness, *op. cit.*, pp. 135-36; *For. Rel., 1917, Supp. 2*, II, p. 1054; *Neut. Press Supp.*, III, 34-35, 58-59.

[30] *For. Rel., 1917, Supp. 2*, II, p. 1053.

it is not surprising that the Norwegians failed to come to close quarters with the problem. The situation was further complicated by the inability or unwillingness of Christiania to provide detailed statistics regarding exports, imports, and stocks on hand—preliminary data that the War Trade Board regarded as indispensable for any intelligent discussion of a trade agreement.[31]

During this stage of the negotiations, the United States was also handicapped by the necessity of keeping in close touch with the Allies and with its own representatives abroad, particularly those in London. A more serious difficulty was divided counsels in Washington, where definite policies had not yet been agreed upon, and where there was some misunderstanding between President Wilson and the War Trade Board as to what course should be pursued.[32] An incident of some importance will serve to illustrate this situation.

On November 15, 1917, Wilson met with Thomas D. Jones, Acting Chairman of the War Trade Board, in preparation for an appointment with Nansen at the White House. The two men discussed the existing negotiations with Norway, as well as the general shaping of American policy toward the neutrals. The President was emphatically of the opinion that the United States could not go beyond the principle of action already adopted; namely, that America should not supply anything to Norway except what the people there actually lacked, and should provide no

---

[31] *Ibid.*, p. 1058; Vigness, *Neutrality of Norway*, pp. 140, 142, 143.

[32] Much dissatisfaction was caused in Norway by the absence of a definite American policy. *For. Rel., 1917, Supp. 2,* II, p. 1043.

foodstuffs of which they deprived themselves by exportation to Germany. Jones understood Wilson to say that the Administration was not "willing to take part in insisting that there be no export from Norway to Germany," as such a restriction was "inconsistent with the principle upon which the United States has always insisted and the rights which she has always demanded for herself."[33] In an explanatory cablegram to Colonel House, his special representative in London, Wilson explained that such a course would also create practical difficulties.[34]

Later on that same day, November 15, 1917, Jones cabled an account of this interview to Vance C. McCormick, Chairman of the War Trade Board, who was then in London, and the latter expressed regret that there appeared to be some misunderstanding. McCormick pointed out that the proposed negotiations with Norway rested on the same principle as the Danish agreement, "which I understand [the]

[33] Jones to McCormick, November 15, 1917, *ibid.*, pp. 1065-66. As early as July 31, 1917, Frank L. Polk wrote to Vance C. McCormick: "I took up with the President today the question of the embargo against the Scandinavian countries. I had already submitted to him Mr. Hoover's recommendation with the memorandum. I think it is quite clear from his conversation that he is not prepared to go as far as the Council recommends. He feels that the neutrals have a legitimate right to trade with whom they please, and we have an obligation from the standpoint of humanity towards them. I think he is prepared to go some distance on these lines, but I think, from what he told me, he would be unwilling to accept our recommendation." War Trade Board Executive Files, State Dept.

[34] Wilson said (November 16, 1917): "I felt obliged on principle to take the position therein stated. It is based not only on principle but on the facts and advice contained in the confidential memorandum brought over by Reading and is all the more dictated by good sense in view of the present critical situation." Baker, *Wilson*, VII, 362.

THE AGREEMENT WITH NORWAY

President approved," the chief difference being that both the American minister in Christiania and his British and French colleagues wished to bring about a complete rather than a partial cessation of all Norwegian exports to Germany. These diplomats believed that such a scheme might be acceptable if the Associated Powers supplied all the needs of the Norwegian people, and at the same time guaranteed markets for their usual exports. McCormick doubted, however, whether Norway would ever consent to complete cessation of all sales to Germany.[35]

President Wilson, who had earlier expressed a strong desire to deal more leniently with Norway than with any of the other Northern Neutrals,[36] probably because of their shipping services to the Allies, promptly and vigorously vetoed drastic steps. In a cablegram to Colonel House, dated November 19, 1917, he strikingly revealed the golden-rule idealism which guided so much of his conduct during and after the war:

[35] *For. Rel., 1917, Supp. 2*, II, pp. 1069-70.

[36] On July 17, 1917, Secretary of Commerce Redfield appeared before the Exports Council and " stated that the President wished to treat Norway very liberally in the granting of licenses, and further, that while the President wished to work in accord with Great Britain and the other nations associated with us in the war, he drew a distinction between shipments to Norway and other neutral countries of Europe." On July 19, 1917, Frank L. Polk told the Exports Council that the President had informed him that morning " that he wished Norway given the most-favored-nation treatment. . . . " Polk stated further " that it was the President's wish that a liberal policy should be pursued towards Norway." " Minutes of Exports Council," pp. 25, 28 (July 17, 19, 1917). On July 17, 1917, Wilson gave instructions that all permits for shipments to Norway be granted at once. The British Embassy immediately remonstrated, for it felt that the character of all consignees should be investigated before licenses were granted. Polk to Wilson, July 18, 1917, Wilson Papers, Library of Congress.

Am distressed to differ with McCormick but inasmuch as we are fighting a war of principle I do not feel that I can consent to demand of Norway what we would not in similar circumstances allow any government to demand of us, namely, the cessation of exports of her own products to any place she can send them. I am convinced that our only legitimate position is that we will not supply the deficiencies which she thus creates for herself if the exports are to our enemies.[37]

In this concise statement Wilson clearly took the position that Washington could not properly insist upon the complete curtailment of exports from Norway to any other country, including Germany. He would not even demand that the Norwegians, as a condition for receiving American foodstuffs, stop sending iron, nickel, and other war materials to the enemy, provided, of course, that such materials did not create a deficiency that the United States would be expected to supply. In short, Wilson was unwilling to use the embargo club to its fullest possible extent. But since Norway was exporting fish to Germany while requesting foodstuffs of the United States, Wilson inferentially held that Washington would be justified in demanding a proportionate stoppage of such exports as a prerequisite to securing American supplies of grain and fodderstuffs.

Acting Chairman Jones pointed out to Wilson that his idealistic message would probably convey the misapprehension that the Administration was opposed to any limitation on exports from the Northern Neutrals to Germany, provided such exports had not originally come from the United States. The President thereupon directed Jones to cable McCormick that this was not his meaning; "that by cessation of exports he meant complete cessation and not limita-

[37] *For. Rel., 1917, Supp. 2,* II, p. 986.

tion." [38] Thus the suggestion of complete cessation was effectively vetoed by President Wilson.

vi

On November 16, 1917, nearly four months after the arrival of the Norwegian commission, negotiations for a trade agreement got seriously under way when Nansen presented a concrete and comprehensive proposal as the basis of discussion. Its principal points were these: (1) The United States would provide Norway with her necessary supplies, insofar as this was possible. (2) The Norwegians would reduce their annual exports of fish to Germany to 48,000 tons. (3) Norway would limit her sale of certain commodities to the Central Powers, such as calcium carbide, ferrosilicon, and calcium nitrate, all of which were important in war industries. (4) The Norwegians would completely stop the export of certain products to Germany, of which manganese and nickel were important. (5) Christiania would undertake to guarantee that there would be no direct or indirect transmittal of American goods to the Central Powers. (6) Norway would take the necessary steps to prevent her exports to Sweden and Denmark from reaching Germany contrary to any agreement with America. (7) Goods licensed by the United States to Norway were not to be seized in transit by the Allies.[39] After a delay of more than a week, the War Trade Board accepted this sweeping Norwegian proposition in principle as the basis for discussion, and the issue was at length joined.[40]

[38] Jones to McCormick, November 20, 1917, *ibid.*, pp. 986-87.
[39] *Ibid.*, pp. 1068-69.
[40] War Trade Board to McCormick, November 27, 1917, *ibid.*, pp. 1073-74.

The next period of the negotiation was the two and one-half months between November 16, 1917, when Nansen presented his first comprehensive proposal, and January 28, 1918, when the War Trade Board was driven to the expedient of publishing its own concessions to Norway. During these anxious weeks there was much delay, particularly on the part of the Norwegians, and the two parties to the negotiation made known their desires in a series of proposals and counterproposals.[41] Without analyzing in detail each succeeding interchange, it will suffice for our purposes to outline the main points of difference and the principal concessions made by both sides.

In brief, the United States and its Associates were contending for the following: (1) A reduction of Norwegian fish exports to Germany from the 48,000 tons proposed by Nansen to a maximum of 25,000 tons, with a proviso that no fish oil whatsoever be sold to the Central Powers, inasmuch as the United States was supplying the Northern Neutrals with fats. (2) A pledge by the Christiania government that no fuel oil or other supplies purchased from the Associated Powers were to be used in catching the Norwegian quota of fish for Germany. (3) A substantial reduction or complete cessation of the supplies of chemicals and minerals being exported to the Central Powers. (4) Assurances that Norway would keep up her important supplies of timber, minerals, and other commodities to the Allies. (5) An agreement on the part of Norway not to export goods to Germany which had been made available through the import of substitute products from Allied sources. (6) Inclusion of all the neutrals (not Sweden

[41] See particularly *ibid.*, pp. 1068-69, 1073-74, 1081-82, 1087-91, 1112-13.

and Denmark alone) in the group to which Norway would deny her exports unless she had assurances that they would not eventually reach the enemy. (7) An exemption of the Associated Powers from any absolute guarantee that they would have to provide all of Norway's necessities, in view of the fact that the United States and the Allies might not be able to supply even their own needs.

During these protracted ten weeks of proposal and counterproposal, the main preoccupations of the Norwegian government were: first, to keep exports of fish at the 48,000 ton maximum and to avoid burdensome restrictions on the kinds of fish that could be shipped to Germany; second, to insist on at least 300 tons of fish oil and train oil for German markets; third, to keep the exports of Norwegian minerals and chemicals at the highest possible figure; fourth, to secure positive guarantees from the United States that Norway's deficiencies in supplies would be filled, regardless of Allied shortages; and fifth, to gain permission to export freely to the Central Powers all commodities not specifically restricted by the proposed agreement.[42]

The Nansen Commission was willing, however, to make two concessions, or what appeared to be concessions. First, Norway was prepared to give guarantees that she would maintain her vital supplies to the Associated Powers. This, in fact, was not a concession at all, because Norwegian economic life was hardly less dependent on these exports than British. Second, Christiania was willing to agree that no foodstuffs should be shipped to the Germans, except fish and fish products. Again, this proposal was not of primary importance, because the amount of food sent from Norway to Germany, aside from this exception, was negligible.

[42] See *ibid.*, pp. 1081-82.

Nevertheless, these two gestures did contribute something to a final meeting of minds.

Throughout this period of diplomatic seesawing, public opinion in both Norway and the United States remained completely ignorant of what was going on behind the scenes. As supplies of grain, oil, and other necessities sank lower and lower, the Norwegian press began to show increasing concern over the outcome of the negotiations. The rumor even gained some currency that the United States was trying to force Norway into the war.[43] To quiet Norwegian apprehensions and put an end to such charges, the American minister in Christiania urged, on January 3, 1918, that the Washington officials give publicity to their proposals, for should this be done it would become clear that the United States was attempting to deal fairly.[44] Responding to this suggestion, the War Trade Board published its terms on January 28, 1918. (The counterproposals of Norway were not made public at that time, lest Christiania regard such an unauthorized disclosure as a grave discourtesy.[45]) This spectacular revelation of America's demands and offers deeply stirred the Norwegian populace. There was much division of opinion as to what should be done, and much criticism of the exacting terms of the United States. Yet so dark and uncertain was the future that there was considerable agitation in the press for acceptance.[46]

[43] *Ibid., 1918, Supp. 1,* II, pp. 1107, 1112-13.

[44] *Ibid.,* pp. 1107-08.

[45] *Ibid.,* pp. 1110, 1115-16. For the publication see *Official Bulletin,* January 28, 1918, pp. 13 ff. The War Trade Board privately stated that it regarded its proposals as "eminently fair and reasonable and must stand." Lansing to Schmedeman, January 5, 1918, *For. Rel., 1918, Supp. 1,* II, p. 1109.

[46] *Ibid.,* pp. 1116-17; *Neut. Press Supp.,* III, 406-07.

vii

The period from January 28, 1918, when the American proposals were published, to April 30, 1918, when the final agreement was signed, was marked by a number of interesting developments. Probably prodded into action by the "shirt-sleeve" publicity of Washington, and responding to the uproar in the Norwegian press, the Nansen Commission, on February 2, 1918, presented a detailed outline of its position to the War Trade Board.[47] This document was couched in such terms as to suggest that it was intended for publication and designed to placate the popular outburst at home. Such a surmise is supported by the fact that three days later, on February 5, the note was published in Christiania. One immediate result was the expression of strong support for Nansen by the Norwegian press, while that of the United States, insofar as it took any notice of the incident at all, seems to have reacted much less favorably.[48]

In summary, the declaration of the Nansen Commission asserted that the Norwegians could not be forced to give up their neutrality, and reminded the United States that Norway had rendered many valuable services to the Allies. Among these were listed the undeniable contribution of her merchant marine; the acceptance of Allied restrictions on her economy; the surrendering of prewar markets in some of the other neutral countries in order to supply the necessities of the Associated Powers; and the rendering of im-

---

[47] *For. Rel., 1918, Supp. 1,* II, pp. 1118-26. The War Trade Board felt that this publicity proved very effective. War Trade Board, *Daily Record,* May 4, 1918.

[48] Vigness, *Neutrality of Norway,* p. 158; New York *Times,* February 7, 18, 21, 1918.

portant banking and financial services. As for the American proposals, Norway would insist that her exports of mineral and chemical products to Germany be kept at a substantial figure, because the Norwegian people could not remain neutral while refusing such products to their neighbor. Furthermore, Norway would have to keep up a considerable trade in these items with the Germans in order to maintain a minimum exchange of essential goods. Christiania was unwilling to deny the export of all unstipulated articles to Germany, but it was willing, as compensation for receiving supplies from the Associated Powers, to keep such commodities at a small figure. Finally, the Nansen Commission sought to interpret the American proposals to read that the United States would guarantee Norway's essential imports, regardless of Allied needs.

viii

After further negotiations in Washington, and certain concessions on both sides that will be noted later, the final draft of the Norwegian-American agreement was being prepared for signature on February 21, 1918.[49] Apparently

---

[49] So the War Trade Board cabled Schmedeman, *For. Rel., 1918, Supp. 1*, II, p. 1134. The Committee on Public Information announced in the press on February 22 that full accord had been reached. New York *Times*, February 23, 1918. The imminence of an agreement was reflected in the disposition of the 10,000 ton Norwegian steamer *Kim*. This vessel was allowed to leave the United States for the Argentine, in September, 1917, on condition that she return. Upon arriving at Norfolk on December 12 with a large quantity of feedstuffs, she was denied an export license for her cargo pending the conclusion of the Norwegian-American agreement, and this detention cost over $200,000. After Nansen had vigorously protested against the unfairness of this procedure, Lansing announced on February 21 that the *Kim* had been allowed

the concluding steps were interrupted by the British, for on February 26 Blockade Minister Cecil made available to the American representatives in London a lengthy criticism of the proposed arrangements.[50] Although Cecil's comments were mainly concerned with phraseology and with the plugging of possible loopholes, some of his suggestions raised questions of fundamental importance which further delayed the conclusion of the pact.

By March 6, 1918, the terms of the Norwegian-American agreement had been approved by the United States and by representatives of Great Britain, France, and Italy in both Washington and London.[51] Yet further delay was made necessary as a result of threats from Germany, where the press had been attacking Norway with increasing bitterness. Aside from the imminent agreement with the Associated Powers, the German authorities were acutely displeased by the pro-Ally sympathies of the Scandinavian kingdom and by rumors that the Allies were endeavoring to obtain a naval base in Norway. Berlin finally insisted on formal assurances that Christiania would not abandon its neutral course; and on March 9, 1918, the Norwegian Minister of Foreign Affairs handed a circular note to Schmedeman, in which he strongly reasserted the neutrality of his govern-

---

to sail. The reason given was that the cargo was covered by the quotas in the agreement which was about to be signed. This case is illustrative of one type of pressure that was brought to bear on the Norwegian government. In some respects the *Kim* affair resembles that of the Dutch steamer *Zeelandia,* which involved the United States in a damage suit. *Post,* pp. 453-55. *For. Rel., 1918, Supp. 1,* II, pp. 1128-29, 1134; War Trade Board, *Daily Record,* February 23, 1918.

[50] *For. Rel., 1918, Supp. 1,* II, pp. 1134-38.
[51] *Ibid.,* p. 1145.

ment, and categorically denied all allegations to the contrary.[52]

Secretary Lansing's reply to the Norwegian declaration, dated April 2, 1918, was not presented until after the British government had made suggestions as to its content.[53] Lansing expressed appreciation of Norway's desire to remain neutral; but, with obvious reference to German pressure on Christiania, reminded the Norwegian government that it had certain duties as a neutral, and one of those was to insist upon its right to negotiate without coercion from belligerent sources.[54]

Following the flurry of excitement over the declaration of neutrality, Norway seemed even more reluctant than before to come to an agreement.[55] Nansen was about to sail, and the patience of the War Trade Board was near an end, in part because it believed that Christiania was dragging out the negotiations for political or other reasons. Accordingly, the Board notified Nansen that if the agreement was not signed before his departure the members would not consider themselves bound by any of their proposed concessions in any future negotiation, but would insist that if the subject

---

[52] Heckscher, *Sweden, etc.*, p. 369; *For. Rel., 1918, Supp. 1*, II, p. 1150. Allegedly in retaliation for the approaching Norwegian-American trade agreement, the German Central Purchase Company annulled its trade contracts with Norway, as of March 16, 1918, and closed its office at Bergen. This was regarded as a part of the German policy of menace. New York *Times*, March 13, 1918.

[53] *For. Rel., 1918, Supp. 1*, II, pp. 1152-53. The British also made similar suggestions to the French and Italian governments. *Ibid.*, pp. 1153-54.

[54] *Ibid.*, pp. 1154-55.

[55] *Ibid.*, p. 1169.

was reopened " it shall be *de novo* and without commitment on our part." [56]

Such a warning was doubtless not without influence on Nansen, who was wearied by the protracted negotiations, eager to return home, and probably convinced that if he held out for better terms he might lose such gains as had already been made. In any event, he decided to exercise the authority with which he was clothed and, on April 30, 1918, signed the agreement on his own responsibility.[57] The Christiania government, which was then debating the advisability of abandoning the negotiations altogether, was surprised and somewhat taken aback by this unexpected act of its agent.[58] Upon arriving home, Nansen declared to a representative of the press: " Possibly it seems that I signed too soon? I had the authorization to sign. And we had the choice between concluding this agreement or none at all. More favorable conditions were offered to us than the Government knew of."[59]

ix

The Norwegian-American agreement of April 30, 1918, was a lengthy instrument covering twelve closely printed pages.[60] Unlike similar pacts drawn up during the war with

[56] War Trade Board to Sheldon, April 27, 1918, *ibid*.

[57] Heckscher, *Sweden, etc.*, p. 370.

[58] Vigness, *Neutrality of Norway*, p. 162; *Neut. Press Supp.*, III, 730; IV, 10. Throughout the negotiation, Nansen, who was a prominent member of the opposition party, adopted a somewhat independent attitude toward the home government. *For. Rel., 1918, Supp. 1*, II, p. 1115; *Rationing Agreement with Norway*, p. 43.

[59] Schmedeman to Lansing, May 27, 1918, State Dept., 657.119/558.

[60] *For. Rel., 1918, Supp. 1*, II, pp. 1170-81. Clarification of

Denmark, Holland, and Sweden, it did not include tonnage, primarily because this problem had been worked out satisfactorily elsewhere.[61] For our present purposes, it will be necessary to outline only the main provisions of the final agreement and compare them, where possible, with the original proposals of the Nansen Commission.

First of all, the pact assured Norway sufficient supplies to cover her estimated needs, insofar as these supplies could be provided without detriment to the necessities of the United States and its Associates.[62] Long lists were given of the precise quantities of foodstuffs, fodder, fertilizer, textiles, metals, minerals, and miscellaneous articles which the Norwegians were entitled to receive. As compensation for these rations, Christiania agreed to export freely and preferentially to the Associated Powers a large group of its own products. As further compensation, Norway voluntarily

---

some of the provisions of the agreement was accomplished by supplementary notes. See *ibid.*, pp. 1182-83.

[61] For reasons previously noted, when the United States entered the war Norwegian tonnage was generally being employed to the satisfaction of the Allies. The British already had an extensive chartering agreement for Norwegian ships, and they permitted the United States to share its benefits. *Report of War Trade Board*, pp. 115-16. An additional agreement was made between the United States Shipping Board and the Norwegian Shipping Commissioners on April 20, 1918. *For. Rel., 1918, Supp. 1*, II, pp. 1163-68. Under this agreement the United States secured 614,000 dead-weight tons of steamers, and about 275,000 dead-weight tons of sailers. *Second Annual Report of the United States Shipping Board* (Washington, 1918), p. 52. At no time during the war did tonnage become a problem involving important matters of policy as regards Norway. The requisitioning of Norwegian tonnage being built in the United States was another matter, which will be considered later. *Post*, pp. 446-50.

[62] It was expected, however, that Norway would supply her needs, so far as possible, from other legitimate sources.

THE AGREEMENT WITH NORWAY

consented to certain important restrictions on her trade with the Central Powers. She agreed to send no foodstuffs whatever, except fish and fish products, and these were limited to the 48,000 tons annually which Nansen had originally proposed. Norway bound herself, however, to include no fish oil or other marine oil. Of chemical and mineral products that were being sold to the Central Powers, the Norwegians consented to restrict the annual export substantially, in a few cases completely.[63]

Norway further bound herself that no article received under the agreement would be exported directly or in the form of a substitute to the Central Powers. No oil, machinery, or other facilities or products provided by the Associated Powers were to be used, in whole or in part, in making goods available to Germany and her allies. Norway also consented not to re-export American or Allied products to any other neutral until proper safeguards had been erected against their falling into the hands of the Central Powers.[64] On their part, the Allies and the United States,

[63] Annual figures were as follows: calcium carbide was limited to 10,000 tons, as compared with the 20,000 tons demanded (November 16, 1917); ferrosilicon to 2,000 tons, as compared with 5,000; calcium nitrate to 8,000 tons, as compared with 18,000; molybdenite to none at all, as compared with 100 tons. In addition, Norway might send to Germany 1,000 tons of zinc, 40 tons of aluminum, 40,000 tons of iron ore, and 200 tons of copper (to replace manufactured copper imported from Germany). Norway also bound herself not to ship to the Central Powers any antimony, bismuth, manganese, mica, nickel, tin, titanium, wolfram, chrome ore, and pyrites. The exports to Germany of such items as were not specifically listed or restricted were not to exceed the 1917 figure. Nansen's original demands of November 16, 1917, appear in *For. Rel., 1917, Supp. 2,* II, p. 1068.

[64] The agreement might be terminated by either party after one year, or thereafter by either party on three months' notice.

through granting bunkers and ships' stores, would expedite the transportation of all goods to Norway that could properly be imported under the agreement.

X

Certain general observations on the Norwegian-American trade agreement are pertinent. It has already been noted that throughout the entire negotiation the United States acted in close concert with its Associates: France, Italy, and particularly Great Britain.[65] The British made a number of important suggestions, but they were always deferential in doing so, and they consistently made it clear that they regarded the Washington government as a sovereign agent.[66] The American officials, on their part, revealed a willingness to accept such advice, most of which was the outgrowth of extensive experience with the blockade. Although the necessity of having to work with three different cobelligerents undoubtedly slowed up the negotiations, the intervention of London stiffened the terms and probably saved the United States from various difficulties in the execution of the agreement.

Any fair appreciation of the Norwegian point of view leads to the conclusion that the Christiania government was laboring under great difficulties. The political situation was extremely delicate and the ministry dared not yield too much to the United States.[67] The prospect of a food

[65] *Rationing Agreement with Norway*, pp. 24-25, 28-30, 32-34, 61; *For. Rel., 1918, Supp. 1*, II, pp. 1183, 1186, 1197.

[66] See *ibid., 1917, Supp. 2*, II, p. 1072.

[67] *Ibid., 1918, Supp. 1*, II, pp. 1151, 1152. Schmedeman cabled the State Department on April 24, 1918: ". . . The situation here at the present time is, moreover, obscure. Responsibility for this can without doubt be placed upon the fact of the approach-

shortage had become so disquieting that the government was reluctant to reveal how bad the situation actually was, and this reticence laid it open to the charge of not taking the people into its confidence.[68] During much of the period when the United States was demanding vital concessions, the German press was threatening drastic measures if Norway should so far abandon her neutrality as to accept such terms. Although Christiania doubtless used the German bogey in part as a convenient and plausible excuse for not yielding to the onerous demands of the War Trade Board,[69] there was undoubtedly a genuine fear among Norwegians that if the government voluntarily cut off too much from the Germans such action would invite invasion, or, at the very least, reprisals. Moreover, Norway found it necessary to keep up a certain amount of trade with the Central Powers, lest she suffer a serious disruption of her economic life; and there can be no doubt that she was sincerely desirous of remaining neutral.

---

ing general election in October, 1918, and the preparations therefor. Factors which should be given consideration in judging the situation are jealousy of Nansen as an opposition partisan and the possibility of his success being used to the detriment of the party in power. Besides, there is quite a lack of coherence in the Cabinet." *Rationing Agreement with Norway,* p. 101.

[68] Schmedeman reported on May 11, 1918: "Stocks of all commodities are becoming so low in Norway that everybody felt that there was no time to be lost in making some arrangement to replenish them and that, unless new supplies of foodstuffs and industrial commodities were forthcoming soon, the country would undoubtedly be faced with a very serious and even critical situation which, in all probability, would have resulted in violent disturbances and riots on the part of the unemployed." State Dept., 657. 119/516.

[69] *Rationing Agreement with Norway,* pp. 12, 14. See also *For. Rel., 1917, Supp. 2,* II, pp. 1052-53, 1039.

A review of the evidence presented in this chapter leads one to the conclusion that the American embargo actually forced the Norwegians into the agreement. There was naturally much resentment in Norway over the coercive measures employed by the former champion of neutral rights, but the more sober-minded recognized that the United States as a sovereign nation was at liberty to dispose of its surplus products as it saw fit.[70] The Norwegian press received the agreement with mixed emotions. At first there was considerable resentment, but as time passed the predominant note seems to have been relief over the solution of a vexatious problem and particularly over the guarantee of needed food supplies.[71] Bitterness was further assuaged by the generally satisfactory working of the agreement, and by the consequent revival of certain Norwegian industries.[72]

[70] *Tidens Tegn* said (August 22, 1917): "All arguments are useless in face of the fact that no State is bound to sell its goods to another unless it wishes to do so. . . . How much the neutrals will obtain will depend on how much each of them can offer; not in merchandise, which America does not need, but in tonnage, export prohibition, and other services which they have already performed or are willing to offer to the Allies." *Neut. Press Supp.*, II, 356.

[71] There was particular rejoicing over the abolition of the blacklist with respect to certain normal traffic with Germany, and Nansen was made something of a national hero. The stipulations as to the blacklist, however, were not carried out to the satisfaction of Norway. Gade to Lansing, September 30, 1918, with enclosure, F. A. R., Hoover Library (Norway: Exports and Imports). For the press in general see *Neut. Press Supp.*, III, 730, 744, 748, 771-72; IV, 10, 27, 38-39; also Schmedeman to Lansing, May 11, 1918, State Dept., 657. 119/516. Unfavorable comments from the Norwegian press, stressing the one-sidedness of the agreement and the surrender of sovereignty involved, appear in *Nachrichten der Auslandpresse*, June 1, 1918, p. 7; June 12, 1918, p. 6.

[72] *Neut. Press Supp.*, III, 438, 496; *Rationing Agreement with Norway*, p. 110.

The Agreement with Norway

Interestingly enough, the Christiania officials seem to have been much more enthusiastic in their expressions of satisfaction than the press. On July 23, 1918, nearly three months after the conclusion of the agreement, and after some of the soreness had been forgotten, Foreign Minister Ihlen requested Schmedeman to inform President Wilson and Secretary of State Lansing that he wished to thank them over and over again for the fairness with which the American government had treated Norway during the entire negotiation. He added that he was "joined in these expressions of thanks by the whole cabinet and that they were all more than pleased with the interpretation of the agreement and with the way in which it is working now." Schmedeman further quoted Ihlen as saying: "It is hardly necessary for me to tell you of the feeling of sympathy and admiration that almost every Norwegian has for America and that the relationship between Norway and the United States is better to-day than it has ever been." [73]

xi

The question naturally arises: Who got the better of the bargain? It must be evident from the preceding discussion that both parties received desired assurances and

---

[73] Schmedeman to Lansing, September 30, 1918, *ibid.*, p. 109. This letter was written in Washington, during Schmedeman's absence from Norway, at the request of the Secretary of State, who apparently wanted the minister's oral report put on record. Schmedeman gave similar testimony before the War Trade Board. "Minutes of the War Trade Board," III, 389 (August 13, 1918). His contemporary reports are in the same vein. See Schmedeman to Lansing, May 11, 1918, State Dept., 657. 119/516. It is possible, however, that the American minister overdrew the picture of Norwegian satisfaction in order to cause his own diplomacy to appear in a favorable light.

concessions, and that the final agreement was in the nature of a compromise. It would be difficult to balance both sides of the ledger with anything like precision, but when we bear in mind that Norway was reluctant to accept the final terms, and that considerable pressure was brought to bear on her to sign, it would seem as though the Associated Powers derived more benefit from the agreement than Norway. There can be no question whatever that the Christiania government was made to consent to extremely distasteful restrictions upon its sovereignty.

Even though the War Trade Board took the position that it had been forced to make most of the concessions, and that its own proposals were "fair," "reasonable," and "liberal," there is much to suggest that the United States drove a hard bargain.[74] In a very real sense Norway did not come voluntarily to the negotiation as a free agent, but was driven into it by the increasing stringency of the American embargo; and the Norwegian press bitterly criticized Washington for unfairness in applying coercion while the discussions were still under way. Minister Schmedeman was constantly recommending a firm course; and when negotiations seemed on the verge of collapse, the War Trade Board, at his suggestion, published its proposals and thus started a backfire among the people of Norway. Although the delays of the Norwegian government were unquestion-

[74] On April 27, 1918, the War Trade Board cabled its London representative: "We have submitted an exceptionally liberal agreement to Nansen having conceded practically every substantial point he has raised excepting Norwegian Government's right to take over import and distribution of all commodities which we feel might menace French and English supplies." *For. Rel., 1918, Supp. 1*, II, p. 1169. For similar expressions of liberality see *ibid.*, pp. 1109, 1114-15; *Official Bulletin*, May 4, 1918.

The Agreement with Norway

ably exasperating, it is doubtful if Washington would have adopted such a strong tone in dealing with a first-class power. Secretary Lansing was fully aware of the opprobrium that was being incurred, for at one stage of the negotiations (November 24, 1917) he confidentially instructed Schmedeman to make it clear to Christiania " that we are acting with the Allies and frequently we are compelled to yield to them and make terms more onerous on neutrals."[75] So far as it went, this was true; but it was also true that on certain points the United States held out for a more stringent course than its Associates. Lansing's apologetic explanation indicates that Washington was somewhat embarrassed by its strong demands, and that it was uncomfortably aware of the disparity between its idealistic position as a neutral and its realistic course as a belligerent.

When one considers that the United States held the upper hand, and that the alternative to Norway's signing was extreme hardship, if not actual starvation, the terms of the agreement can hardly be regarded as grossly unfair. Whether any other power would have driven a harder bargain cannot be said. But it is significant that such opposition as was expressed against the agreement quickly melted away, and that the Norwegian officials, as well as a considerable part of the press, joined in expressing friendly sentiments toward the United States.

---

[75] *For Rel., 1917, Supp. 2*, II, p. 1073.

CHAPTER V

THE SWEDISH RATIONING AND TONNAGE NEGOTIATIONS

i

In several respects the kingdom of Sweden was the most important of all the European neutrals. It was the largest and most populous of the Scandinavian countries. Its people were homogeneous, its tradition was deep-rooted, its history was glorious, and its national pride was highly developed.[1] By common consent Sweden was bound to have a conspicuous share in the leadership of any joint Scandinavian program.

Perhaps the most noteworthy fact about the Swedes from the point of view of the present study is that they were in some respects less amenable to blockade and embargo pressures than any of the other Northern Neutrals. This was primarily because of the nature of their economy. Sweden was normally capable of providing her own basic foodstuffs, although serious crop shortages in 1916 and 1917 rendered her far more dependent upon the Allies than otherwise would have been the case.[2] Unlike Norway,

[1] Ira Nelson Morris, *From an American Legation* (New York, 1923), p. 24. Morris was United States minister in Sweden during the war years. See also Lucien Maury, *Les problèmes scandinaves; le nationalisme suédois et la guerre, 1914-18* (Paris, 1918).

[2] *For. Rel., 1917, Supp. 2*, II, p. 1057; Heckscher, *Sweden, etc.*, pp. 104-05. Much of Sweden's food shortage was caused by the diversion of agricultural labor to mining and manufacturing. If the pinch had become severe enough, much more food could have been produced at the expense of these industries. Report of the Bureau of Research of the War Trade Board, August 31, 1918, F. A. R., Hoover Library (Sweden: Exports and Imports).

which was so largely concerned with fishing and maritime transportation, Sweden was primarily an agricultural, mining, and manufacturing nation; and in general she prospered greatly during the war.[3] Her merchant marine was considerable, approaching 1,000,000 gross tons; and when the loss from German torpedoes and mines became too great, she could afford to lay it up and, in fact, did lay it up—much to the annoyance of the British.[4]

But the chief grievance of the Allies against Sweden was that she shipped enormous quantities of raw materials to Germany across the Baltic. Although wood pulp, fish, meat, and miscellaneous mineral products figured in this traffic, by far the most important item was iron ore.[5] Not only was the product of the Swedish mines of the best quality but it was available in virtually unlimited quantities, amounting in 1917 to 4,900,000 tons.[6] German smelters had been built to accommodate the high-grade Swedish ore; and German war industry was vitally, not to say indispensably, dependent on this supply. The maddening thing from the point of view of the Allies was that their naval power was unable to penetrate the Baltic, and as a consequence

---

[3] During the war Sweden lost 201,276 gross tons of shipping to mines, torpedoes, and cruisers; 142,493 tons of this amount to German submarines alone. Fayle, *Seaborne Trade*, III, 466. See also report of W. H. Owens (War Trade Board representative for Scandinavia), August 29, 1918, in F. A. R., Hoover Library (Sweden: Finance).

[4] *For. Rel., 1917, Supp. 2*, II, p. 830. A considerable part of Sweden's merchant marine was tied up in foreign ports because Britain would not grant the owners the bunkers with which to carry the cargoes they insisted on handling. See *ibid.*, pp. 1020-21.

[5] *Ibid.*, pp. 829, 1029-30.

[6] Heckscher, *Sweden, etc.*, p. 111. The shipment of Swedish iron ore lightened the burden on German mines and transportation facilities.

they were powerless to interrupt this vast flow of iron ore by direct action. Only indirect economic pressures could be resorted to; and as a rule they are slow to take effect.

A proud nation, such as Sweden was, naturally resented any serious attempt to apply coercive measures. In addition, she had certain weapons with which to strike back, better weapons, on the whole, than those of any of the other European neutrals. First of all, the most serviceable land route to Russia then open to the Allies lay through Sweden; and as the Allies were desperately anxious to keep Russia in the war, it was of the greatest importance to them to continue the movement of supplies eastward.[7] Sweden, however, was in a position to place onerous restrictions upon such traffic, and in fact did so. But by November, 1917, when the Bolshevist revolution came and Russia could no longer be counted on, the Allies lost interest and the transit club consequently decreased in effectiveness. The second important weapon that Sweden possessed was the power to embargo certain exports to the Associated Powers, particularly those that were of vital importance in war industry. Among these we may note ball bearings, various other steel products, iron ore, zinc, wood pulp, and timber.[8] A third weapon, which was a club only in the negative sense, was the possibility of demanding relaxations of the British blockade in return for putting Sweden's voluntarily immobilized merchant marine back into service.

The already strong position of Stockholm in regard to Allied economic measures was further bolstered by the pro-

---

[7] *For. Rel., 1917, Supp. 2,* II, pp. 830-31, 879.

[8] *Ibid.,* p. 831. Timber was essential for pit props in mines and trenches.

German bias of a large percentage of the people, despite the depredations of the U-boats.[9] When America declared war, Sweden, with the possible exception of Spain, was more friendly to Germany than were any of the other European neutrals. This, of course, was natural. The Swedish people were of Teutonic blood; their proximity to Germany had created close economic and cultural ties; and German influence was strong in both the educational system and the army. In addition, powerful and aggressive Russia was the hereditary enemy; and Swedish sympathies would naturally gravitate to the Czar's foe, Germany. When the United States entered the conflict, public opinion in Sweden seems to have been rather evenly divided between the Allies and the Central Powers, but the upper classes were predominantly pro-German and confidently expected Germany to win.[10] In these circumstances, the Stockholm government had little choice but to attempt to preserve a rigid official neutrality.

ii

It would be a mistake to assume, however, that the Swedish position was without elements of weakness. Crop failures, together with the absence of proper restrictions on the export of foodstuffs, had brought about a serious food shortage and the consequent introduction of rationing

---

[9] Morris, *American Legation*, pp. 81 ff. For an unfriendly summation of the various ways in which Sweden helped Germany, see Maury, *Les problèmes scandinaves*, pp. 315-17.

[10] Memorandum dated November 6, 1917, in F. A. R., Hoover Library (Sweden: General). See also Andreas Elviken, "Sweden and Finland, 1914-18," in Jesse D. Clarkson and Thomas C. Cochran, eds., *War as a Social Institution* (New York, 1941), p. 135.

in 1917.[11] Not only was the grain supply deficient, but such products as coffee, tea, rice, spices, and cocoa had to come through the British blockade. The Swedes also imported from England large quantities of other commodities, such as coal, coke, textiles, rubber, lead, and tin—coal and coke being especially important. Coal could, of course, be supplied by Germany, and in large measure was; but petroleum, which was of vital importance, lay at the mercy of the British.[12] In short, it was possible for the Allies to exert considerable pressure on Stockholm; but this had to be done with the utmost circumspection lest Sweden, already shot through with pro-German influence, be driven into the arms of Germany. On the other hand, there was little danger that Allied restrictions would impel the Germans to drastic measures, for this semi-isolated Scandinavian nation could not be invaded except across the Baltic; and she alone of the Northern Neutrals had a formidable army, consisting of from 500,000 to 800,000 reasonably well-trained men.[13] In fine, Sweden was perhaps the only neutral of Europe which the Allies could not directly coerce; except for Spain, she was the one best situated and prepared to

[11] Heckscher, *Sweden, etc.*, pp. 6-8, 96. Heckscher concludes (p. 8) that Sweden's shortage of food and other commodities was perhaps exceeded only by that of Russia and the Central Powers.

[12] *Report of War Trade Board*, p. 21. England hoped to cut off Germany from Swedish iron by buying the ore herself and shipping the necessary coal, but it was not satisfactorily demonstrated, in view of the tonnage shortage and other difficulties, that the British supply would be adequate. *For. Rel., 1917, Supp. 2*, II, pp. 1029-30, 1062.

[13] Secret British memorandum, August 4, 1917, Yale House Collection. This detailed and comprehensive memorandum has been drawn upon for many of the basic facts presented in the present analysis.

resist German invasion; and even though her normally strong position was considerably weakened by a shortage of foodstuffs, she was nevertheless able to pursue a relatively independent course.

iii

Shortly after America's entrance into the war the people of Sweden became deeply disturbed by rumors, some of them fantastically distorted, that Washington was going to lay an embargo on all shipments of foodstuffs to the Northern Neutrals. Prices were already high; the supply of food was running low; and anxiety as to the future caused the Swedish press to reveal its resentment in the usual charges of inconsistency and double-dealing. The more violent newspapers, some of them under pro-German influence, expressed their views below such captions as: "America's Thumbscrew Policy" and "Does the United States Plan a Starvation Blockade against the Neutrals?" Several journals insisted that the Swedish people would endure a complete stoppage of imports before they would surrender their neutrality by consenting to Allied restrictions.[14]

---

[14] Morris to Lansing, July 11, 1917, State Dept., 600. 119/246; also quoted excerpts in New York *Times,* July 13, 1917; *Neut. Press Supp.,* II, 317, 480. One pro-German paper declared that the United States had arrived at "a 'stupendous' emancipation from all conceptions of justice. The crime of the neutrals seems to consist merely in their venturing to continue to exist." The Russians were deeply concerned lest the Swedish government, in retaliation for the American embargo, should choke off the transit route completely. *For. Rel., 1917, Supp. 2,* II, pp. 961-62, 971. E. B. Trolle, former Minister for Foreign Affairs, denied that Sweden was a conduit for Germany. He also pointed out that much of the increase in Swedish trade with America was due to

The food situation was so ominous that the Swedish government, the first of the neutrals so to act, dispatched a special commission to America, which reached New York on May 18, 1917. It was headed by Herman Lagercrantz, an influential business man and former Swedish minister in Washington. The avowed objects of the commission were to enter into negotiations for the purpose of preventing or ameliorating the proposed embargo on goods to Sweden; to secure needed supplies of foodstuffs, petroleum, and other commodities; and to bring about the release of Swedish ships detained in the United States through a refusal on the part of the British to issue letters of assurance.[15]

On May 7, 1917, eleven days before Lagercrantz landed, and while the Balfour Commission was still in Washington, the British Embassy outlined to the Department of State what might be accomplished by the application of pressure of the strongest kind on Sweden.[16] The next month, after negotiations with the Swedish commission had got under way, the British Embassy clarified its suggestions when it pointed out that the American embargo club could be used on Sweden for the following objectives: (1) a complete cessation of all important Swedish exports to Germany; (2) the removal of all restrictions on transit to and from

---

European economic dislocations; that much of the material statistically shipped to Sweden had never arrived, being held up by the British; that the value of imports was illusory because based on inflated prices; and that the high figures on cotton imports were due to transit to Russia, at the request of the United States. New York *Times,* July 7, 1917.

[15] *Ibid.,* April 25, May 18, 1917; *For. Rel., 1917, Supp. 2,* II, pp. 1017-18, 1020-21.

[16] *Ibid.,* pp. 830-32, 1019-20.

Russia; (3) the maintenance of Swedish exports to the Associated Powers; and (4) the employment of Swedish shipping in services beneficial to the Allies.[17] As the British anticipated, this list of demands, particularly the complete cessation of exports to Germany, aroused strong opposition in Sweden; and the negotiations in Washington soon reached a deadlock. On August 7, 1917, Lagercrantz sailed for Stockholm to consult his government, leaving an assistant in charge.[18]

iv

When the American embargo went into effect, the Swedish government had already purchased and stored in the United States a large quantity of grain. Because of the urgency of the food situation in Sweden, and the danger of spoilage in America, the Swedish special commission earnestly besought Washington to release these stocks of cereal. After extended oral discussion, Food Administrator Hoover proposed that 552,000 tons of old wheat, which were owned by the Swedish government and stored in Baltimore and Philadelphia, be sold to the Commission for Relief in Belgium at cost, and that 271,000 bushels of rye already bought by the Stockholm authorities for September delivery be given a license to Sweden.[19] After further negotiations, the Swedish government accepted this offer, with the understanding that the United States would obtain

---

[17] *Ibid.*, p. 880 (June 14, 1917). This was a part of a larger memorandum embracing the other neutrals as well.

[18] New York *Times,* August 7, 1917; *For. Rel., 1917, Supp. 2,* II, pp. 1041-42.

[19] Hoover to Ekengren (Swedish minister), August 10, 1917; Nordvall to Hoover, August 14, 1917, F. A. R., Hoover Library (Sweden; Ekengren, Minister).

permission from the British for the passage of the rye through the blockade. Upon securing the consent of the State Department, Hoover approved these terms, on August 23, 1917, and four days later informed the Swedish commission that although the rye ships would have to stop at Halifax, he had assurances from the British Embassy that they would not be detained unreasonably.[20]

Apparently the British officials in Washington had given Hoover these assurances without proper authority, or perhaps under some misapprehension, for London declined to allow the rye ships to pass, despite the fact that the wheat covered by the agreement was already moving to Belgium. With evident embarrassment Secretary Lansing cabled Ambassador Page in London, on September 15, 1917, that if America was to maintain "even an appearance of good faith" the necessary permits would have to be granted by the British. Lansing emphatically added that in the existing "delicate situation" no excuse should be given for the belief that the United States was "putting pressure on the Swedish people."[21]

Upon taking up the matter at Downing Street, Page discovered that the London government not only did not know of the conclusion of the Swedish-American grain agreement, but had actually instructed the Embassy in

[20] Nordvall to Hoover, August 20, 1917, Hoover to Nordvall, August 23, 27, 1917, *ibid*. (Delegates of the Royal Swedish Government); Gordon Auchincloss (Assistant to the Counselor for the State Department) to Hoover, August 22, 1917, *ibid*. (State Department).

[21] *For. Rel., 1917, Supp. 2*, II, pp. 1042-43, 1049; also Hoover to Polk, October 1, 1917, State Dept., 658. 119/52; Polk to Hoover, October 3, 1917, F. A. R., Hoover Library (State Dept., Frank L. Polk).

The Swedish Negotiations

Washington to oppose it. The British felt that enough wheat cargoes had already been made available for Belgian relief, and they presumably did not favor the partial relaxation of the blockade in favor of the Swedish rye ships. But inasmuch as the American officials, through no fault of their own, had been misled into making embarrassing commitments, the British authorities agreed to permit the shipments of rye to reach Sweden.[22]

This relatively minor incident reveals that the United States, at least at this stage of its negotiations with Sweden, was less inclined than the British to establish a severe blockade and more inclined to deal liberally with the Commission for Relief in Belgium. Above all, the Washington government was jealous of its reputation for honorable dealing with the neutrals.[23]

v

Before the misunderstanding over the grain agreement was finally settled with the British, another and more serious controversy developed between Washington and London over the handling of Swedish affairs.

As a result of Britain's cable censorship, the Swedish legation in Buenos Aires had extended to the Germans the courtesy of cabling their dispatches in code to Stockholm, whence they were forwarded to Berlin. The British inter-

---

[22] *For. Rel., 1917, Supp. 2,* II, pp. 1044-45, 1052.

[23] It is probably true that Hoover's well-known solicitude for the Commission for Relief in Belgium was an important factor in this negotiation. On January 24, 1918, Hoover wrote in another connection: "As my department practically controls the despatch of foodstuffs from the United States, you may be assured that the Belgian Relief will have full priority in shipments." Gay and Fisher, *Public Relations of C. R. B.,* II, 175.

cepted these messages and discovered, among other things, that Count von Luxburg, the German minister in Argentina, had suggested to his government that in certain circumstances it might be advisable to sink Argentine merchantmen without a trace ("spurlos versenkt"). The London authorities turned these intercepted cablegrams over to the Department of State, which, on September 8, 1917, published the first of them.[24] The result was an immediate sensation both in America and in Europe. The Swedish people, who had already suffered heavily from German submarine depredations, were profoundly distressed by the fact that their diplomatic representative should have had a hand in this unpleasant business; and the resultant dissatisfaction not only reacted heavily against the government but measurably weakened pro-German influence.[25] Even in the United States so much animus was directed at the Swedes as to bode ill for the negotiations on rations and tonnage that were still going on in Washington.[26]

The involvement of Stockholm in this affair caused the British authorities to view Swedish telegrams and mail with redoubled suspicion. They stopped all communications by cable between Sweden and the United States, and in mid-September seized four bags of diplomatic correspondence and detained them at Halifax.[27] The Washington government was concerned about this incident for two reasons. First, the four pouches contained data from the Swedish Foreign Office which the legation in Washington needed in

---

[24] The story is told in Lansing, *Memoirs*, pp. 326-29.

[25] Morris, *American Legation*, pp. 81 ff. On Swedish submarine losses see Heckscher, *Sweden, etc.*, pp. 88, 100.

[26] New York *Times*, September 15, 1917.

[27] *For. Rel., 1917, Supp. 2*, II, p. 1048.

The Swedish Negotiations

its current negotiations with the American officials. Second, the United States feared that it would be falsely accused of having been responsible for this seizure. On September 20, 1917, therefore, Secretary Lansing cabled Ambassador Page instructing him to "suggest" to the British the "advisability" of releasing the pouches, "as the effect on the Swedish people in Sweden and here would be most unfortunate." [28]

The British finally offered to send the four mail pouches to their embassy in Washington, where they would be opened in the presence of Swedish and American officials. This was not agreeable to the Department of State, for it felt that Stockholm was "being pressed a little too hard." [29] By October 17, 1917, Lansing could instruct Page to inform Downing Street "unofficially" that "nothing is being gained by holding up delivery of these pouches," and that the negotiations with the Swedish commission in Washington were being "seriously hampered" by such action. Lansing added that American public opinion was beginning to feel that the Swedes had been punished enough, and that President Wilson, who was "taking a personal interest in the matter," favored more lenient treatment.[30]

The mail-pouch dispute was not finally settled until late in October, 1917. The British agreed to deliver the bags to

---

[28] *Ibid.,* p. 1241. For expressions by Polk and Morris that the British be lenient in dealing with Stockholm in the matter of mail and telegrams, see *ibid.,* pp. 1048, 1051.

[29] Lansing to Page, October 4, 1917, *ibid.,* p. 1242. The State Department felt that, because of the political situation in Sweden, it would be unwise to be too severe with the Stockholm government. Lansing to London Embassy, October 15, 1917, State Dept., 841.711/2178.

[30] *For. Rel., 1917, Supp. 2,* II, p. 1243.

the Swedish legation with the statement that they were making this concession primarily because they were unwilling to hamper the negotiations between Sweden and the United States, and not because they were satisfied with the innocent character of the correspondence. At the same time, London declined to give any assurances that other pouches would not be held up in the future.[31] Upon this settlement of the controversy, the Swedish minister called at the State Department to tender his thanks for the good offices of the United States government.[32]

This whole affair, while in itself of no fundamental importance, casts considerable light on the attitude of the Wilson administration in a matter affecting neutral rights. The United States found itself in the somewhat anomalous position of remonstrating with a cobelligerent in order to secure more lenient treatment of a neutral; of acting as a mediator between an Associate and a neutral; and of urging the Swedes to make a more satisfactory explanation of their case to London.[33] The controversy over Great Britain's search of American mails had flared up ominously in 1916; and the memory of this bitter experience may have played an important part in the attitude assumed by the Department of State and in the personal interest that Wilson took in the dispute. It is probable, however, that the more urgent matter of not interrupting the negotiations with the Swedish commission was as important a consideration. Throughout the affair Washington was deferential to the British in recognizing their sole jurisdiction both over the

[31] Polk's memorandum of a conversation with Barclay, of the British Embassy, October 23, 1917, *ibid.*, p. 1243.
[32] *Ibid.*, p. 1244.   [33] *Ibid.*, p. 1242.

pouches in question and over all other pouches similarly held; while the British were deferential to Washington in their desire not to interfere with the pending discussions. As in the grain agreement, the United States appeared to better advantage than Great Britain; and although this circumstance may have had no demonstrable effect on the outcome of the negotiations, it is clear that Stockholm was properly grateful.

vi

Meanwhile, the discussions between the Washington officials and the special Swedish commission had become virtually stalemated, primarily because of the obduracy of Stockholm in refusing to make acceptable concessions.[34] During these anxious weeks the chief bone of contention was the vitally important iron ore trade with Germany. The British, in particular, strongly urged the United States to take " strong and effective action at once " for the purpose of bringing about a complete cessation of the traffic.[35] But this was an impossible objective. Not only did iron ore occupy an important place in the economy of Sweden, but it was exchanged for indispensable supplies of German coal. The British expressed a willingness to make good the loss of German coal should the iron exports be stopped; but the problems involving tonnage, transportation, and labor were such that the Swedes were not disposed to have faith in such a promise. The Swedish officials stated bluntly that

---

[34] See *ibid.*, p. 1041. The United States sought to strengthen its embargo by protesting against the shipment of Russian oil cake to Sweden. The Russian government gave satisfactory assurances on this score. *Ibid.*, pp. 1040, 1041, 1042.

[35] *Ibid.*, pp. 1029-30.

rather than give up their iron ore trade with Germany they would abandon all negotiations for securing food and other imports from the United States.[36] So evident was the determination of Stockholm that the Allies feared to take drastic action lest Sweden be forced into the arms of Germany, with a consequent severance of the then-important transit route to Russia.[37]

Nor was the obduracy of the Swedes based solely on economic considerations. They feared, or professed to fear, that a complete or even substantial stoppage of the flow of iron ore would result in an armed German invasion for the purpose of getting the product by force.[38] The strength of this argument was vitiated by the simultaneous claim of Stockholm that Germany already had a large quantity of Swedish iron ore on hand, and that the continued shipments did not make nearly so much difference as the Allies thought.[39] This was undoubtedly true. In November, 1917, official American sources estimated that Germany had a supply of iron ore for seventeen months, or five months beyond the date of the Armistice that was finally signed.[40] But the Allies had no way of knowing when the war would end, and from a military point of view it was definitely to their advantage to try to sever this source of supply. And since the Swedes would not stop their export of iron ore in response to economic pressures from the United States,

---

[36] *Ibid.*, pp. 1047, 1050-51, 1085-86.   [37] *Ibid.*, pp. 1047-48.

[38] The German steel and iron industries were equipped to reduce high-grade ores such as Sweden produced, and they would have been seriously handicapped if they had been forced to use the low-grade product. *Ibid.*, pp. 1029-30.

[39] *Ibid.*, pp. 1047-48.

[40] Memorandum dated November 6, 1917, F. A. R., Hoover Library (Sweden: General).

the only practicable alternative seemed to be to outbid the Germans in buying up the surplus ore. In September, 1917, this scheme was discussed by Washington and the Allies, but action on it was deferred to a later date.[41]

vii

The auguries for a Swedish-American trade and tonnage agreement became distinctly more favorable when, in October, 1917, the Swartz ministry resigned and was succeeded by a cabinet more friendly to the Allies. The new Minister for Foreign Affairs, Justice Hellner, told Ira N. Morris, the American minister in Stockholm, that he was desirous of coming to an agreement. Specifically, he outlined certain concessions that his government was willing to make, and asked if the United States did not want the negotiations to be shifted to London. Morris came away from this interview with the impression that Stockholm regarded America as the Associated Power which was most anxious to stop Swedish trade with Germany. He also concluded that unless an attempt was made to press the negotiations at this favorable moment, Sweden would inevitably drift closer to Berlin.[42] In particular, Morris feared that unless the new Swedish government was able to conclude an agreement for the amelioration of the embargo, it ran a grave risk of being overthrown by its pro-German opponents, who were already subjecting it to a heavy cross fire of criticism.[43]

[41] For the Allied view see *For. Rel., 1917, Supp. 2,* II, p. 954. Late in September, 1917, the Exports Administrative Board made a tentative proposal to take over the entire Swedish iron ore output. *Ibid.,* p. 1047, n.

[42] *Ibid.,* pp. 1061-63.

[43] Morris to Lansing, November 30, 1917, State Dept., 658. 119/105.

The British were already urging the transfer of negotiations to London. They pointed out that the Swedish commission then in Washington did not represent the new Liberal-Socialist government; that this delegation was not competent to discuss all phases of the situation; and that accurate information on military aspects of the problem was readily available only in London.[44] The War Trade Board was at first opposed to the shift of negotiations, but the arguments of the British finally prevailed, and early in December, 1917, the Department of State consented to the change.[45]

The negotiations between the Swedish delegates and the representatives of the Associated Powers opened in London on December 13, 1917; and it soon became evident that much time would be consumed before there could be any final meeting of minds. In the first place, the subjects to be discussed were both numerous and complicated, particularly export stoppage, import control, rationing, iron ore shipments, Russian transit, and tonnage. In the second place, the negotiations were five-sided, involving representatives of Sweden, the United States, Great Britain, France, and Italy; and it is usually true in both the chancellery and the kitchen that the more cooks there are the longer it takes to prepare the broth.

The Swedish government, already keenly aware of the embargo pinch, was in no position to tolerate the delay that this negotiation would inevitably involve. The Parliament was scheduled to meet in Stockholm on January 15,

---

[44] The British also pointed out that Russia's interests, which were involved, had no representative in the United States, whereas there was one in London. *For. Rel., 1917, Supp. 2*, II, p. 1078.

[45] *Ibid.*, pp. 1067, 1071, 1080.

The Swedish Negotiations

1918; and unless the new administration did something to redeem its pre-election promises of getting relief from the blockade and embargo, it would be exposed to bitter attack, especially by the pro-German element. The Swedish government therefore favored a temporary agreement or *modus vivendi* to take care of some immediate needs, with the final arrangements to be concluded in a more leisurely fashion at a later date.[46] The British authorities fell in with this idea, primarily because they wanted to secure Swedish ships for the purpose of carrying coal to France, and particularly to Italy, where there was an acute shortage of fuel.[47]

viii

The negotiations for a *modus vivendi* revolved around two primary problems. First, the Associated Powers wanted to secure a large amount of Swedish shipping; and second, the Swedish government wished to obtain large quantities of grain, coffee, and other pressing necessities. Each party to the proposed agreement desired to win the largest possible concession with the least possible sacrifice; so there was naturally much haggling over details. There was also some disposition on the part of the Swedes to protract the discussion, in part because they felt that peace might soon come, and in part because the Germans were threatening Sweden with dire consequences should the *modus vivendi* be signed.[48] The negotiations were further delayed by the unwillingness of the War Trade Board to let down the embargo bars and relieve the cumulative pressure of the past months. The Board insisted that permitting the con-

---

[46] *Ibid.*, pp. 1086, 1091-92, 1093, 1111.
[47] *Ibid., 1918, Supp. 1,* II, pp. 1201-02.
[48] *Ibid.*, pp. 1200-01.

templated shipments of commodities to Sweden was "contrary to [the] policy approved by [the] British and continuously followed heretofore by this Board." It also felt that such concessions in favor of Sweden would evoke charges of discrimination from the other Northern Neutrals and make discussions with them even more difficult. But rather than disrupt the negotiations, the War Trade Board cabled its agent in London, on January 16, 1918, that if the Allied representatives, after weighing these disadvantages, decided to make such concessions, Washington would give its consent.[49]

Finally, all differences were ironed out, and the *modus vivendi* was signed, on January 29, 1918, by representatives of Sweden, Great Britain, and the United States. By its terms the Swedish people were to receive specific amounts of grain, oil cake, phosphates, oil, coffee, and other commodities, none of which could be re-exported, directly or indirectly, to Germany. In return, Stockholm would permit ships then tied up at home or in foreign ports to operate in the service of the Associated Powers. Altogether, the Swedes bound themselves to charter a minimum of 100,000 dead-weight tons for three months in the danger zone, in addition to such other vessels as might ply elsewhere in Allied service. All shipowners, of course, were to be properly compensated.[50]

In retrospect, this *modus vivendi* seems to have been an equitable and mutually profitable arrangement. The Asso-

---

[49] *Ibid.*, p. 1203; for other objections of the War Trade Board see *ibid., 1917, Supp. 2,* II, pp. 1095, 1113, 1114.

[50] For text of *modus vivendi* see *ibid., 1918, Supp. 1,* II, pp. 1204-07. One half of all charters under this agreement were to go to the United States and the other half to the British. *Report of War Trade Board,* p. 114.

ciated Powers were able to relieve their critical lack of tonnage by obtaining the use, even though part of it was on a three-months basis, of approximately 250,000 tons of shipping hitherto unavailable to them.[51] The Swedes secured some relief for their most urgent needs, and thus the government was able to strengthen its position against pro-German attacks.[52] All other problems were postponed to the final agreement with Sweden of May 29, 1918. Interestingly enough, the Washington government, quite in contrast with its stand on the deal involving grain for Belgian relief, was more disposed than the British to insist upon a rigid enforcement of the embargo. Probably the War Trade Board was not so keenly aware of the shipping shortage as the British. And although the partial lifting of the embargo doubtless did weaken its cumulative effect, as the War Trade Board predicted, it does not appear that this had any appreciable bearing on the satisfactory conclusion of the final agreement.

ix

Following the signing of the *modus vivendi*, the execution of which caused some minor disputes,[53] the general

[51] Estimate of War Trade Board. *For. Rel., 1917, Supp. 2*, II, p. 1012.

[52] For Swedish press criticisms see *Neut. Press Supp.*, III, 533, 567-68; *Nachrichten der Auslandpresse*, February 4, 1918, pp. 5, 6.

[53] These were largely concerned with bunkers. All of the disputes of this nature were resolved in Sweden's favor by the United States, and the promised commodities were allowed to go forward. See *For. Rel., 1918, Supp. 1*, II, pp. 1210-12, 1221-22. The Swedes proposed to send their grain ships in ballast to the Argentine; but Washington, in order to conserve tonnage, forced them to stop en route at United States ports for cargoes of coal. On this problem see *ibid.*, pp. 1218-19, 1221, 1229.

negotiations were inevitably protracted because of the conflicting demands of each party. Stockholm professed to fear that if it made a liberal tonnage agreement and cut off iron ore exports to the Central Powers, the Germans would seize or sink Swedish shipping.[54] As a consequence, the original five-sided negotiation in London broadened into a six-sided negotiation when the Swedish representatives in Germany sought to secure the consent of Berlin to the proposed concessions.[55]

The possibility that German warnings would prevent the signing of any general agreement prompted the British, French, and Italian ministers in Stockholm to suggest to their home governments the issuance of an ultimatum threatening the forcible requisitioning of all Swedish tonnage. In reporting this action of his colleagues, Minister Morris cabled, on March 28, 1918, that he, himself, did not favor so drastic a course.[56] Secretary Lansing agreed with him that it would be most unwise to seize Swedish shipping, especially in view of the bitter feeling that had just been aroused in Scandinavia by the American and British requisitioning of Dutch vessels. Lansing further pointed out

---

[54] For evidence that the Germans were threatening reprisals (including the stoppage of coal shipments), and that the Swedes feared drastic action from this quarter, see *The Rationing and Shipping Negotiations with Sweden* (Washington, 1919), pp. 28, 43, 55, 59, 63.

[55] *For. Rel., 1918, Supp. 1,* II, pp. 1213, 1222. Late in March, 1918, the Swedish Minister for Foreign Affairs told Morris that although Germany had a supply of low-phosphorous Swedish ores for two years, she would not, for reasons of prestige, permit a restriction of shipments. *Ibid.,* p. 1213. The Germans were naturally opposed to Sweden's tonnage concessions, for these weakened the effect of the submarine sinkings.

[56] *Ibid.,* pp. 1214-15.

that the Swedish and Dutch cases were not at all analogous, because the Dutch had been unable to carry out their *modus vivendi* in the face of German threats; while the Swedes were slowly complying with the terms of their agreement. Instead of requisitioning, Washington was in favor of permitting a certain amount of unofficial publicity as to the rations it would allow Sweden, presumably in the hope that this information would cause the Swedish people to demand favorable action by their government.[57] Downing Street likewise rejected the drastic proposal of its minister.[58]

During the discussions with the Swedish delegates in London it soon became evident that Sweden would never consent to a complete cessation of her iron ore exports to Germany. So profitable was this industry that the result probably would have been the same even if the Germans had not been threatening reprisals. Substantial curtailment seemed to be the best that the Associated Powers could hope for; and this curtailment was possible only if the Allies and the United States would themselves buy a substantial part of the huge quantity that was then going to Germany. This, to be even reasonably effective, would have to amount to between 2,000,000 and 2,500,000 tons of ore annually.

The Allies naturally looked to the financially fresh United States to assume its share of this obligation. But Washington frowned upon the scheme for two basic reasons. In the first place, the United States did not need and could not use the Swedish ore. Shipping was scarce; the cost of transportation was high; abundant supplies of first-grade iron ore lay at hand in America; plants in the United States were not equipped to reduce ores with the phosphorous content of the Swedish product; private concerns could not

[57] *Ibid.*, pp. 1215-16 (April 3, 1918). [58] *Ibid.*, p. 1216.

be forced to make the change; and only those near the seaboard could even consider it. In the second place, the plan seemed futile. It was estimated that Germany already had between a year and a half and two years' supply; and even if the Associated Powers purchased all of Sweden's output, this costly venture would pay dividends only if the war was protracted far beyond the calculations or hopes of many military experts.[59]

But by degrees the Allies were able to wear down American resistance. Early in April, 1918, Washington refused to purchase one third of the amount contemplated but offered to finance the British and French. Later in the month the United States expressed its willingness to go even further and bear one third of the ultimate loss, if any. But when legal objections were raised in Washington against assuming a problematical loss in the indefinite future, the Wilson administration reluctantly gave in, late in May, 1918, and agreed to pay $6,000,000 as its share of the purchase price.[60]

X

On May 17, 1918, when the general agreement with Sweden was practically completed, the War Trade Board

[59] *Ibid., 1917, Supp. 2,* II, pp. 1084-87. Late in March, 1918, President Wilson expressed a willingness to share the cost of the ore-purchase scheme, but believed that such a venture should be avoided, if possible. "Minutes of the War Trade Board," II, 72-73 (March 29, 1918).

[60] *For. Rel., 1918, Supp. 1,* II, pp. 1216-17, 1238. Formal consent of Washington to the plan seems to have followed the signing of the general agreement with Sweden on May 29, 1918. For the subsequent history of the joint purchase plan, which was a problem involving the Associated Powers rather than the neutrals, see *ibid.,* pp. 1291-92, 1293-95; *Official Bulletin,* July 16, 1918, p. 1.

threatened to disrupt the proceedings when it cabled serious objections to its London representative, L. P. Sheldon. It regarded the grain quota allotted to Sweden as too liberal, and the proposed preclusive purchase of iron ore shipments to Germany as so ineffective as to amount to virtually no restriction at all. In reply, Sheldon strongly defended the cereal ration and the iron clause, and noted particularly that great importance should be attached to the quality rather than the quantity of ore allowed Germany. He further declared that insistence by Washington on its position would wreck the entire agreement, the conclusion of which seemed imperative in view of the imminent renewal of the German offensive on the Western Front.[61]

Yielding to these arguments, the War Trade Board finally authorized Sheldon, on May 27, 1918, to consent to the agreement. He was to make sure, however, that there was no possibility of securing more tonnage and greater restrictions on exports to Germany, and that the shipping set aside for the Allies was definitely assured. Two days later, on May 29, the final draft was signed by the British, French, Italian, and Swedish delegates. The Washington government subscribed to it, not by a formal signature, but by a letter of the same date signed by Sheldon, who gave assurances that the United States would freely license the stipulated rations, provided they were not needed by the Associated Powers, and provided further that the goods in question would not be sent directly or indirectly to the enemy.[62] The refusal of the Wilson administration to be a party to the formal signing may have been in part due to the hereditary antipathy to foreign entanglements, par-

---

[61] *For. Rel., 1918, Supp. 1,* II, pp. 1230-33.
[62] *Ibid.,* pp. 1238, 1263.

ticularly those of a multilateral nature. The explanation given by the War Trade Board was that "certain technical considerations involving formalities in the execution and confirmation of agreements of the scope of the proposed arrangement" made it "impracticable for the Government of the United States to become a formal signatory party thereto." [63] It seems certain that fear of the Senate played no important part in this decision, because none of the series of trade and tonnage pacts concluded by the Washington officials during the war period was submitted to that body. They were all in the nature of executive agreements.

xi

The general trade and tonnage agreement of May 29, 1918, with Sweden was a comprehensive document, embracing twenty-four printed pages, together with ten additional pages devoted to explanatory or qualifying letters.[64] On their part, the Associated Powers agreed to provide certain stipulated rations of foodstuffs, fodderstuffs, manufactured goods, raw materials, coal, and other commodities, insofar as their own requirements would permit. In return, Sweden undertook certain obligations. First, she bound herself to keep these imports from benefiting the enemy, either directly, or through other neutrals, or in the

---

[63] *Ibid.*, p. 1225. The Swedish government ratified the agreement in mid-June, 1918. It attempted to secure a more formal adhesion from the United States but received only repetitions of the same assurances. *Ibid.*, pp. 1276-77, 1280; Ekengren to Lansing, June 15, 1918, F. A. R., Hoover Library (Sweden: Agreement with War Trade Board).

[64] *For. Rel., 1918, Supp. 1,* II, pp. 1240-73. The *modus vivendi* was to be kept in effect until the Swedish government ratified the general agreement.

form of substitute goods. Second, she agreed to prohibit completely the export to Germany of such commodities as foodstuffs, leather, and wool. Third, she undertook to terminate or restrict to specified maximum figures the export of certain mineral products to Germany, notably iron ore. In this category she bound herself to limit the output to 6,000,000 tons per annum, a maximum of 3,500,000 tons of which was to go to Germany, in certain categories of purity. (This latter figure represented a reduction of 1,400,000 tons, as compared with 1917). The Allies were to purchase 2,000,000 tons outright, with an option on an additional 500,000 tons. Fourth, Sweden was to make available to the Associated Powers 400,000 dead-weight tons of shipping. Of this, 200,000 tons were to be for service in the war zone, and 200,000 tons for the " safe " trades.[65] Moreover, 250,000 additional tons under Swedish control were to carry cargoes approved by the Associated Powers or to engage in runs sanctioned by them. Finally, Stockholm gave certain satisfactory assurances regarding the Russian transit question and agreed to keep up exports to the Associated Powers.

In essence, the major gain of Sweden was a lifting of the American embargo; the major gain of the Associated Powers was tonnage, of which they were in immediate need; while the cessation or diminution of exports to Germany was expected to count heavily in the long run. The iron ore purchase ultimately proved to be a liability to the Associated Powers; the Russian transit issue was dead; and the Swedes could be expected to continue their exports

---

[65] Of this amount the United States obtained 100,000 unrestricted tons, and the same quantity for use outside the war zone. *Second Annual Report of U. S. Shipping Board*, p. 52.

to the Allies anyhow. All things considered, the bargain was not essentially unfair. But there can be no doubt that the American embargo drove Stockholm into the negotiations and forced it to sign terms which it was reluctant to approve. This, of course, raises the same questions of ethics as were discussed in the case of Norway; but the answer again is that the bulk of the commodities involved belonged to America, and, from the point of view of Washington, they had to be used for the purpose of winning the war.

xii

The general trade and tonnage agreement was received with mixed emotions in Sweden.[66] The people were glad to obtain the hitherto embargoed foodstuffs and other commodities, but many persons, particularly those of pro-German persuasion, objected strongly to the restricting of exports to Germany and to the exposing of Swedish tonnage in the danger zone.[67] Considerable misunderstanding and friction developed between Stockholm and the Associated Powers when it was discovered that the Swedes were continuing to fulfill export contracts which they had entered into with German concerns prior to the signing of the pact. The position of Sweden was that she had made reservations on these points at London, and that a period of adjustment was necessary following the conclusion of the agreement. Nevertheless, the United States, together

[66] Morris to Lansing, June 22, 1918, State Dept., 658. 119/458; Heckscher, *Sweden, etc.*, p. 114; also *Neut. Press Supp.*, IV, 149-50. Some of the dissatisfaction resulted from the failure of the government to publish a full text of the agreement.

[67] The Swedish press reported that Germany had instituted commercial reprisals against Sweden. Morris to Lansing, July 10, 1918, State Dept., 658. 119/488.

with the other Associated Powers, became seriously disturbed by the fact that large quantities of forbidden commodities were still being shipped to Germany; but, before making drastic demands, Lansing requested specific information from Stockholm as to precisely what was happening. This, of course, took time; and before the matter could be properly investigated, the war was virtually over, and the delayed contracts had in considerable measure been filled.[68]

The conclusion of the general agreement and the inflow of American supplies through the British blockade unquestionably brought about a more friendly feeling for the Allies in Sweden. Already there had been a strong tendency in this direction as a result of Russia's withdrawal from the war, to say nothing of the submarine attacks on Swedish shipping and the painful Luxburg affair. In addition, Allied, especially American propaganda, grew in vigor and effectiveness, and finally was largely able to offset the efforts of German partisans, who formerly had had the field pretty much to themselves. By the end of the war it seems reasonably certain that the Swedish people, not even excepting the upper classes, were definitely pro-Ally. Nevertheless, the government continued in its persistent effort to pursue, so far as possible, a strictly neutral course.[69]

[68] For the printed documents on this subject, see *For. Rel., 1918, Supp. 1,* II, pp. 1281, 1284-91, 1293; also Whitehouse (chargé in Stockholm) to Lansing, September 11, 1918; Laughlin (chargé in London) to Lansing, November 25, 1918, State Dept., 658. 119/619, 704. There was some little trouble between the United States and Sweden over payments in kroner exchange. Polk (Acting Secretary) to London Embassy, July 18, 1918, State Dept., 658. 119/548a.

[69] Morris, *American Legation,* pp. 81 ff.

xiii

On the whole, the treatment of Sweden by the United States called for fewer apologies than was the case with Norway. In both the grain transaction and the mail-pouch controversy Washington appeared to good advantage, and intervened with its British Associate in order to secure justice for Stockholm. The general agreement was concluded, it would seem, with considerably less friction than accompanied the dealings with Norway. It is probable, however, that if the discussions had been bilateral, instead of multilateral, the United States would have held out for more severe terms; and if this had happened the negotiations would undoubtedly have been prolonged and much additional bitterness would have been created. As it was, the necessity of deferring to the Associated Powers and of counteracting political currents in Sweden caused the War Trade Board to consent to more lenient conditions than otherwise would have been acceptable.

The restrictions on Sweden's exports and the necessity of providing tonnage for the danger zone were, of course, onerous to Stockholm; but, on the other hand, the rationing terms were quite acceptable and the iron ore bargain was advantageous. When one considers the strong pro-German element in Sweden, and the relative immunity of the kingdom to direct action from either set of belligerents, it is remarkable that a general agreement was concluded so soon and with relatively so little animosity. The basic explanation appears to be that Sweden's abnormally low food supplies induced concessions that otherwise could not have been expected. And to this end the sweeping American embargo contributed powerfully.

Chapter VI

THE RATIONING AND TONNAGE AGREEMENT WITH DENMARK

i

The tiny kingdom of Denmark, although the smallest in area of the Scandinavian countries, exercised during the World War years an influence out of all proportion to its size. The only one of the three Scandinavian nations contiguous to Germany, it was geographically and economically almost a part of its powerful southern neighbor. Because of this situation, and because of strong racial and cultural ties, German influence and propaganda enjoyed at the outset certain signal advantages. But fortunately for the Allied propagandists, Germany had not always been the good neighbor. The seizure of the southern provinces of Schleswig and Holstein by Prussia and Austria in 1864 had left a bitter memory which a mere half century could not eradicate.[1] The fate of Belgium, coupled with the pitiable military weakness of Denmark, could not fail to arouse fear of Germany and a corresponding hope for the success of Allied arms. Nor did the ruthless attacks of German submarines, which took a toll of 200,000 gross tons of Danish shipping and several hundred Danish lives, lessen this disquietude.[2] Although, as a result of these

[1] American propaganda in Denmark held out to the Danes the hope of winning Schleswig back. *Complete Report of the Chairman of the Committee on Public Information* (Washington, 1920), p. 207.

[2] During the war Denmark lost 201,394 gross tons from submarines; 37,479 from mines; 4,834 from cruisers. Fayle, *Seaborne Trade*, III, 466.

and other developments, it would be hazardous to say that a majority of the Danes were pro-Ally, it seems undeniable that a large percentage of them were strongly anti-German.[3]

During the critical years of the World War, Denmark was the only one of the three Scandinavian countries that was self-sufficing in foodstuffs. More than that, she produced huge surpluses of such commodities as butter, eggs, bacon, milk, cheese, and fish, to say nothing of horses and cattle. Some of these items were exported in large quantity to Germany, which, because of the British blockade, was particularly eager to purchase foodstuffs with a fat content. The Danes, for their part, were dependent upon the Germans for coal and certain manufactured goods. So profitable and natural was this interchange that the exports of Denmark to Germany had increased by about twenty per cent since the outbreak of the war, and the British foresaw great difficulties in attempting to bring about a substantial diminution of this traffic.

Denmark also loomed large in the calculations of the Allies because of her merchant marine of some 800,000 gross tons. Although this ranked far below that of Norway and Holland, and somewhat below that of Sweden and Spain, it was nevertheless of vital importance to the Allies when the German submarine depredations reached a critical point. But the Danes, unlike the Swedes and the Dutch, were on the whole not loath to use their tonnage in traffic that was directly or indirectly beneficial to the Allies. In fact, Denmark was employing approximately one third of

[3] *For. Rel., 1917, Supp. 2,* II, pp. 1051-52; also the interview with United States Minister Maurice F. Egan published in New York *Times,* December 29, 1917, and his book, *Ten Years Near the German Frontier* (New York, 1919).

her shipping in Allied service before the tonnage agreement with the United States, which we shall discuss, brought about the addition of more. Thus, in the early stages of the negotiations with Washington the problem of Danish shipping did not rank in importance with that of preventing the export of essential commodities to Germany.

But the favorable statistics on food production must not blind us to the fact that Denmark was vulnerable to the weapons of blockade and embargo. In the first place, the Danes were heavily dependent upon overseas imports of petroleum products, fertilizer, coffee, and other essential commodities. In the second place, the highly important livestock industry of Denmark, from which came a large portion of her exportable food surpluses, could not subsist without feedstuffs from the United States. If this supply should be stopped by an embargo, as it was, the Danes would have no alternative but to slaughter a large percentage of their cattle and pigs.

ii

The apparently strong position of the Allies with reference to the blockade and an embargo was substantially weakened by the operation of four factors. In the first place, if Denmark, deprived of American fodder, was forced to slaughter much of her livestock, this large surplus of meat would inevitably find its way to the Germans, whose position, temporarily at least, would be bettered. In the second place, the Danes were shipping such huge quantities of food to England that a drastic embargo on feedstuffs would merely result in starving the goose that laid the golden eggs.[4] In the third place, there was the danger that too severe methods in dealing with Denmark would merely throw her into the embrace of Germany, economically if not politically. And finally, the Danes were so defenseless that the Germans could admittedly overrun their country in a short time without having to detach any additional troops from the fighting front. But Berlin was loath to do this, partly because such extreme action would offend the other Scandinavian countries, and partly because it would antagonize a large segment of liberal opinion at home.[5] Nevertheless, if the Allies had demanded that Denmark voluntarily cut off all or most of her exports to her powerful neighbor, the German Supreme Command could easily have justified strong measures.[6] In brief, the problem of the Associated Powers was to apply enough pressure to bring about a substantial curtailment of Danish exports to Germany, but not enough to force the Germans to take over the little kingdom bodily.

With such considerations as these in mind, the Balfour Commission, in May, 1917, made certain cautious recommendations to the American officials in Washington. First of all, it suggested that the United States permit feedstuffs to go to Denmark only on condition that the Danes supply the United Kingdom with bacon in prewar quantities, while at the same time keeping their exports of cattle and

---

[4] In 1916 Denmark exported 82,000 tons of bacon to the United Kingdom. On the other hand, if feedstuffs were denied Denmark, large quantities of tonnage would be released for direct British uses.

[5] Egan to Wilson, May 27, 1917, Wilson Papers, Library of Congress.

[6] An invasion of Denmark would have resulted in a German seizure of livestock and a more complete control of the Baltic.

beef to Germany at prewar figures. The British representatives also pointed out that it might prove desirable to embargo other commodities in addition to feedstuffs, particularly mineral oil.[7] These recommendations, as we have noted in an earlier chapter, finally bore fruit in the President's first embargo proclamation of July 9, 1917.

iii

During the months between the American declaration of war, in April, 1917, and Wilson's promulgation of the embargo, in July, 1917, Denmark was subjected to a very considerable amount of criticism in the United States. Editorial writers made much of the large exports of Danish foodstuffs to Germany, and of the huge profits resulting from this traffic. Indicative of American feeling was the action of the San Francisco Park Commission, which denied the Danish colony the use of Golden Gate Park for a national celebration, on the ostensible grounds that such demonstrations should be confined to American patriotic gatherings. This incident might have aroused no comment had not one member of the commission indiscreetly informed a newspaper reporter that Scandinavia had been "unfair to the United States," and that "through the back door of Denmark have gone American foods and supplies to help the Germans."[8] The resulting furor attracted attention even in faraway Denmark.

---

[7] These general observations are based principally on the secret British memorandum, August 4, 1917, Yale House Collection; *For. Rel., 1917, Supp. 2,* II, pp. 834-36; Heckscher, *Sweden, etc.,* pp. 411-558; Turlington, *Neutrality,* pp. 111-18; Consett, *Triumph of Unarmed Forces,* pp. 75-79, 93-97.

[8] The explanation of the commissioner in question, Curtis H. Lindley, appears in his letter to A. E. Taylor, November 1, 1917, F. A. R., Hoover Library (Denmark).

The Danes were naturally much disturbed by the prospect of an embargo and by the criticisms appearing in the American press, most of which, they felt, were based upon ignorance of the actual situation. From time to time editorial writers in Denmark urged that their government take active steps to arrange for the proper information of American public opinion.[9] Apologists for the Danes repeated the familiar argument that the normal economic life of their kingdom required trade with both sets of belligerents, and that the exports to Germany, while apparently large in quantity, were negligible when compared with the 70,000,000 Germans. Nor did the press of Denmark fail to remind America of her idealistic position as a neutral.[10] Such arguments were forcefully summarized in a statement by the Danish Minister for Foreign Affairs, who declared: " The extreme policy such as indicated would finally not be in conformity with the policy so splendidly advocated by the American Government when as a neutral power she defended the rights and duties of neutrals and thereby greatly supported the smaller neutral powers in their efforts to preserve the rights of neutrals according to international law." [11]

iv

Unlike the other two Scandinavian countries, Denmark did not at first send a commission to the United States to enter into negotiations for needed imports. Instead, Copenhagen announced, on May 16, 1917, that two special

[9] See *Neut. Press Supp.*, III, 605; IV, 440.
[10] Egan to Lansing, July 13, 1917, State Dept., 600. 119/254.
[11] Enclosure in Egan to Lansing, June 8, 1917, *ibid.*, 600. 119/111.

commercial advisers would be attached to the Washington legation for the purpose of looking after Denmark's interests. A year later, in May, 1918, Denmark took the additional step of sending five prominent experts to Washington to assist in the final negotiation of the rationing and tonnage agreement.[12]

It was not until July, 1917, shortly after President Wilson had issued the first exports control proclamation, that the Danish representatives in Washington appear to have come seriously to grips with the problem. Their principal complaints were the growing shortage of feedstuffs, the need for which would soon become critical, and the detention of Danish ships in the United States with cargoes approximating 75,000 tons of cottonseed cake. These supplies were not only deteriorating, but the demurrage charges ran to $17,000 a day.[13] The Copenhagen government supplemented the representations of its agents by a "very active one-sided propaganda" in the United States on the food situation in Denmark.[14]

The Food Administrator, Herbert Hoover, had been giving the European situation careful study, and he was not at all impressed by these protestations and complaints. On July 27, 1917, he read to the Exports Council a detailed memorandum in which he strongly urged restrictions upon the export of foodstuffs to the Danes. In particular, he pointed out that Denmark was more than self-sufficing

[12] New York *Times,* May 17, 1917; *For. Rel., 1918, Supp. 1,* II, p. 1330.

[13] J. E. Boggild (commercial adviser to Danish legation) to Hoover, July 23, 1917, F. A. R., Hoover Library (State Dept., Frank L. Polk).

[14] Egan to Lansing, August 7, 1917, State Dept., 659. 119/4.

without American imports; that she was supplying vast quantities of fat and protein to Germany, every pound of which contributed indirectly to the loss of American lives; and that the shipping of foodstuffs to the Danes meant depleting the scanty reserves of the Allies. Moreover, Hoover declared, American dairymen were slaughtering their needed milk cows because of the high price of fodder, a condition brought about in part by the heavy export of feedstuffs to Denmark; yet even if all such exports were stopped, the Danes could take care of their own essential needs by reducing the size of their herds correspondingly. Indeed, it was better in the long run for these people to kill their surplus cattle and send the meat to Germany rather than use American feedstuffs to supply milk to the Germans. Hoover concluded by protesting against the issuance of " any further permits to Denmark for foodstuffs from the United States." [15]

The Exports Council decided to submit the Hoover memorandum, with its drastic recommendation, to Wilson; and Counselor Polk informed the President of this decision in a strong letter, dated July 28, 1917. Among other things, Polk asserted: " It is the opinion of some members of the Council that the time has come when we should take an absolutely radical stand and state to the neutrals that we will not permit any exportations to Ger-

[15] " Minutes of Exports Council," p. 38 (July 27, 1917); Hoover to Exports Council, July 27, 1917, F. A. R., Hoover Library (Exports Council, 22 June—12 October, 1917). Hoover also concluded that Denmark could use her shipping to haul coal from England and the United States, and for this reason there was no justification for her complaint that she needed to keep up her exports to Germany in order to get coal in return.

many." But Wilson was by no means ready to retreat from the idealistic position to which he had so recently adhered during the prebelligerency period. At the bottom of Polk's letter to the President there appears an initialed memorandum by Polk (dated July 31, 1917): "President thinks Mr. Hoover goes too far. Said he had stood up for rights of neutrals in past and was not prepared to forbid them to trade with Germany." [16] Although the War Trade Board ultimately forced Denmark to restrict her exports to Germany, no real effort was ever made to bring about a complete cessation.

v

The Copenhagen government took full advantage of these early weeks of indecision in Washington to present its case as fully and as forcefully as possible. Specifically, the Danish Foreign Office asserted that during the three years of the war Denmark had sent 537,000 tons of butter, bacon, and eggs to England, while at the same time supplying Germany with only 206,000 tons of the same products. In addition, the Danes had already placed more than one third of their tonnage at the disposal of the Allies, and indirectly of the United States. Nor did the Copenhagen Foreign Office fail to make comparisons with America's position during the prebelligerency years:

While the United States were a neutral power the American Government came forward generously and powerfully as champion, not only of the neutrals' rights, but—what is mostly in the mind of the Danish Government—of the neutrals' obligations. The American Government will

---

[16] This is published in Baker, *Wilson*, VII, 197. The original is in State Dept., 659. 119/6a.

surely recognize, therefore, that, above all, it must be of moment for the Danish Government in their export policy to maintain an equal and impartial neutrality to both sides, and the American Government surely realizes that any deviation from the straight road of neutrality could involve fateful political consequences for Denmark.[17]

During the months of September and October, 1917, the period of indecision in the negotiations was prolonged by the failure of the United States to take a clear and unequivocal stand;[18] and this failure was attributable in part to the tardiness of the Danish government in providing the requested statistical data regarding food. By October, 1917, the Danes were responding more satisfactorily to American requests for information,[19] a development which appears to have been due primarily to the evident determination of Washington to continue the embargo, and specifically to the alarming shortage of petroleum in Denmark. Not only were the Danish fishing boats dependent upon oil from America, but, more important, the municipal electric and water works were equipped with Diesel engines, many of which had already stopped running by early October as a result of the cutting off of American

[17] Memorandum of Danish Legation, September 5, 1917, F. A. R., Hoover Library (Denmark, Agreements with U. S.). This was a reply from the Copenhagen government to the Export Council's circular memorandum of July 24, 1917.

[18] Lord Eustace Percy pointed out that mere restrictive action unaccompanied by a clear statement was ineffective, because the neutrals were living in the expectation that the United States would relax the embargo as soon as the pinch began to be felt. Percy to Hoover, September 5, 1917, F. A. R., Hoover Library (Great Britain, Washington Embassy).

[19] *For. Rel., 1917, Supp. 2,* II, pp. 1048, 1051; A. E. Taylor to Polk, October 3, 1917, State Dept., 659. 119/71.

fuel. The very real prospect of facing a long winter without even kerosene lights was a dismal one, and it was feared that the Danes would be driven to desperate lengths to get their minimum petroleum supplies from Germany.[20]

The continuance of this distressing situation was probably prolonged by the failure of the British and the Americans to present a united front. The impression had gained currency in Denmark that the United States and France were urging a stringent policy, while Britain was holding out for a lenient one. Whether or not, as alleged, these reports emanated from British sources, the Washington officials did not relish being blamed for policies that had been jointly determined upon.[21] When this awkward situation was brought to the attention of Lord Percy, of the British Embassy, he concluded that the neutrals were trying to improve their position by creating dissension in the ranks of the Associated Powers. Percy was willing to admit, however, that there is "no smoke without some fire"; and he implied that some of this misunderstanding

---

[20] *For. Rel., 1917, Supp. 2*, II, pp. 1051-52; Egan to Lansing, September 10, 1917, F. A. R., Hoover Library (Denmark); Egan to Lansing, October 3, 1917, State Dept., 659. 119/66. A Danish official told Egan that it might be possible to explain to the Danes why America was withholding foodstuffs, but petroleum for water and electric works was a different matter.

[21] Polk to Wilson, July 28, 1917, *ibid.*, 659. 119/6a. Polk revealed the dissatisfaction of the Exports Council over the attempts of the French and British to place the onus for stringent measures on the United States when he said that it was wise "to see to it that all the governments interested agree openly to such a course and share the responsibility. In other words, it is our view that the United States should not be used as the wicked partner and blamed by the Entente Powers for the suffering of the neutrals, particularly the Scandinavians."

had arisen from the difficulty which the British encountered in reconciling the differences between the United States and Denmark.[22] In any event, this was primarily a problem that concerned the United States and its Associates, rather than the United States and the neutrals.

vi

By early November, 1917, the negotiations between the War Trade Board and the Danish representatives had proceeded so satisfactorily that an agreement might have been arrived at then had it not been for the intervention of the British. First of all, the London officials suggested that extreme demands be made, including an absolute cessation of the export to Germany of horses, pork, dairy products, and eggs. Secondly, the British pointed out to the Americans the desirability of concluding the Norwegian agreement first, so that Christiania would not get embarrassing ideas from liberal concessions to the Danes; and with this end in view Downing Street proposed that the negotiations with Denmark in Washington be held up until the Norwegian agreement was closed.[23] In fact, so extreme were the British proposals as to Danish trade with Germany that one suspects London of having deliberately proposed them for the purpose of delaying the Danish negotiations.

The British were able to convince both Ambassador Page and the War Trade Board representatives in London

[22] *For. Rel., 1917, Supp. 2*, II, pp. 977-78; see also *ibid.*, pp. 976-77, 1051, 1053; Egan to Lansing, September 10, 1917, F. A. R., Hoover Library (Denmark); Egan to Lansing, September 25, October 13, 1917, State Dept., 659. 119/56, 77.

[23] *For. Rel., 1917, Supp. 2*, II, pp. 1056-58.

THE AGREEMENT WITH DENMARK

of the importance of prolonging the Danish discussions until the Norwegian agreement was signed, but the Department of State and the War Trade Board felt that such a course would place the United States in an equivocal position. The War Trade Board cabled to London that the negotiations could not be protracted much longer " without complete rupture," and that if they were to be transferred to London the Danes ought to be frankly informed of this step. Counselor Polk, of the Department of State, agreed that the Danish representatives should be told that the agreement was being delayed in compliance with the wishes of the French and British; otherwise, the United States would be subject to charges of "bad faith." In response to such remonstrances, the Chairman of the War Trade Board, Vance C. McCormick, who was then in London, cabled that a break in the negotiations with Denmark should be avoided, and that the delay in London was over questions which it was hoped could be adjusted satisfactorily.[24]

The policy of purposefully protracting the discussions in the interests of more favorable terms with Norway was finally brought to the attention of President Wilson by Thomas D. Jones, Acting Chairman of the War Trade Board, on November 15, 1917. Wilson's reaction was both prompt and unfavorable; and he authorized Jones to cable London that " in his judgment we cannot in good faith hold up the Danish agreement awaiting any other negotiations." [25] The President's intervention seems to

---

[24] *Ibid.*, pp. 1059-60, 1063, 1064-65.

[25] *Ibid.*, pp. 1065-66. In July, 1918, the matter of good faith came up again when the War Trade Board felt that if Denmark consented to the current tonnage proposals, the United States

have been decisive, for from this time on further references to deliberate delay disappear from the correspondence; and within two weeks (November 27, 1917) Jones presented to the Danish minister a comprehensive proposal which bore many resemblances to the final agreement that was signed nine months later.[26]

vii

It is not necessary for our present purposes to analyze in detail each of the proposals and counterproposals presented by the Danish and American representatives in Washington.[27] In general, this negotiation followed much the same pattern as the discussions with the Norwegian and Swedish commissions, whose representations to the War Trade Board were being made simultaneously.

The Danes, in common with the other neutrals, sought first of all to secure the largest possible quantities of needed commodities from the United States, and consequently much of the negotiation was concerned with the raising or lowering of these quotas. But in general this was a matter of detail that involved few if any serious problems of principle. On the whole, there was not so wide a gulf as one might expect between what the Danes

---

would have to conclude an agreement, unless fault could be fairly found with some other demand that Copenhagen was making. *Ibid., 1918, Supp. 1,* II, p. 1332.

[26] *Ibid., 1917, Supp. 2,* II, pp. 1074-77.

[27] See the British and American proposals of November 8, 1917, *ibid.,* pp. 1057-58; the Allied proposals of November 15, 1917, *ibid.,* p. 1066; and particularly the American letter of November 28, 1917, and the Danish counterproposal of December 24, 1917, *ibid.,* pp. 1074-77, 1102-07; and the American proposal of January 17, 1918, *ibid., 1918, Supp. 1,* II, pp. 1299-1305.

asked for and what the War Trade Board was finally willing to concede.

The second main phase of the discussions concerned limitations on the export of foodstuffs to Germany in return for the rations to be received from the United States. The Danes naturally sought to keep these figures at a high level, while the War Trade Board sought to force them down to an absolute minimum. But here again there were few disputes over fundamental principles, and most of the time was taken up with considerations of detail. It is significant that there was a surprisingly close similarity between what the Danes were finally permitted to ship to Germany and what they had exported during the prewar years.

The third aspect of the negotiation involved the employment of Danish tonnage by the United States and its Associates—a problem that raised the most serious questions of principle. The Danes strongly resisted Washington's demand that they charter a considerable percentage of their shipping for the danger zone, and they argued that they should retain for their own uses a larger percentage than the Allies approved.

As was also true of the other agreements, the embargo on Denmark was kept in force throughout the entire course of the discussions. With the passage of time the pinch, particularly in petroleum products, came to be increasingly painful. This distressing situation was partially and temporarily relieved by the two Christmas shipments that were sent to Denmark, among which was a quantity of oil. But the unfortunate delay attendant upon the arrival of the American cargoes did much to counteract the feeling of good will that had been created by the original announcement.[28]

Meanwhile, the Danish representatives in America were resorting to the usual strategy of painting their country's plight in the worst possible colors. The minister in Washington declared that "it is not too much to say that we are almost reduced to the misery and poverty of the Middle Ages." [29] On December 25, 1917, the most prominent charitable organization in Denmark, with a large membership of women, cabled Mrs. Carrie Chapman Catt, of the National American Woman Suffrage Association, asserting that the Freiland district was famine-stricken and pleading for immediate relief. Mrs. Catt sent the telegram with a covering letter to President Wilson's secretary, who in turn referred it to Dr. Alonzo E. Taylor of the War Trade Board. Dr. Taylor replied to Mrs. Catt that, according to official reports from Copenhagen, Denmark was exporting thousands of tons of foodstuffs to Norway, Sweden, Germany, and England. "If," he con-

---

[28] American Legation (Copenhagen) to War Trade Board, January 8, 1918, F. A. R., Hoover Library (Denmark); Grant-Smith to Lansing, May 14, 1918, State Dept., 659. 119/282. The War Trade Board representative in Denmark urged active propaganda to increase Danish good will for the United States. *For. Rel., 1918, Supp. 1*, II, pp. 1295-97. The War Trade Board, on April 12, 1918, approved the suggestion of the United States chargé in Copenhagen that a quantity of printer's ink be granted pro-Ally newspapers. Bennett (of War Trade Board) to Barton, April 13, 1918, State Dept., 659. 119/250.

[29] Brun to McCormick, January 16, 1918, *For. Rel., 1918, Supp. 1*, II, pp. 1298-99. On June 27, 1918, N. V. Boeg, one of the Danish negotiators, sent an article to Dr. Taylor which he had written for the New York *Evening Post* (June 20) on conditions in Denmark. F. A. R., Hoover Library (Denmark).

cluded, " the Danish government permits foodstuffs to be thus exported while citizens of a particular section of Denmark are suffering from lack of food, certainly the answer lies in Denmark and not in the United States. In view of our information as to the actual state of food supplies in Denmark, I cannot refrain from venturing the suggestion that the Danish women are being victimized by a clever piece of German propaganda." [30]

It was, of course, to the advantage of the Danes to represent themselves as being in serious straits; and it is not surprising that their accounts of conditions in Denmark differed widely from those reaching Washington from the representatives of the War Trade Board and of the diplomatic and consular service. As late as July 14, 1918, the American chargé in Copenhagen cabled that scarcely any other country in the world was suffering less from the war and was generally more prosperous.[31] Although it is undoubtedly true that there was much wartime prosperity, particularly in certain industries, it is also true that the embargo caused great distress in others. The official figures of the War Trade Board reveal that the stoppage of feedstuffs forced the Danes to slaughter much of their livestock and send it to Germany. By the autumn of 1917 the export of bacon and pork to the Germans had risen to seven and one-half times the prewar figure; but this level could not be maintained, and by the summer of 1918 it had dropped to one half the prewar rate. A similar trend was noticeable in the sale of cattle. By the summer of 1918 it

[30] Catt to Tumulty, December 28, 1917; Taylor to Catt, January 28, 1918, *ibid*.
[31] *The Trade and Shipping Negotiations with Denmark* (Washington, 1919), p. 81.

was clear that the purposes of the embargo had been almost completely achieved, for by that time the Danish exports of foodstuffs to Germany had dropped to but a small fraction of the normal prewar amount.[32]

viii

By the early spring of 1918 the negotiations between Denmark and the United States had moved into their critical stage. The chief bone of contention was tonnage: how much the Danes should be forced to charter to the Allies; for how long a period (six months or the duration of the war); and whether any of the vessels so chartered should be employed in the danger zone. This last issue aroused grave apprehensions, for the exposing of Danish shipping to the submarine hazard would mean the loss of precious seamen and the depletion of Danish merchant tonnage to a point where the nation would be seriously handicapped in postwar trade. In addition, Copenhagen insisted that the demands of the Associated Powers for ships were such that Denmark could not properly supply her own immediate needs with the remainder; and the government was fearful of arousing internal disturbances by too sweeping concessions in the matter of shipping. Nor did the Danish officials fail to point out that the chartering of a considerable portion of Denmark's merchant marine to the Allies, especially for service in the danger zone, would inevitably

[32] *Report of War Trade Board*, pp. 44-45. On May 22, 1918, the War Trade Board extended to Denmark the same relaxation of the embargo on nonessentials as had been granted to Holland and Sweden. Lansing to London Embassy, May 22, 1918, State Dept., 659. 119/292.

be regarded by Germany as an unfriendly act, with strong possibilities of reprisal.[33]

Impatient over the prolonged parley, and dissatisfied with Copenhagen's proposals, the War Trade Board finally delivered an ultimatum to Constantin Brun, the Danish minister in Washington, on March 1, 1918. Brun was flatly informed that the United States was interested only in tonnage, which was all that Denmark could offer as compensation for the rations she was seeking. Nor was the Board interested in any six-month time limit on the proposed charters; they would have to be for the duration of the war. And of this shipping "80,000 tons must go into the war zone." Until "Denmark saw fit to change its proposal respecting tonnage to meet these requirements" the Board "did not think anything would be gained by discussing balance of proposal." [34]

Nearly two weeks later, on March 13, 1918, Minister Brun replied to the American ultimatum. He reported that Copenhagen stood firm in its determination that none of the proposed tonnage should be permitted to operate in the danger zone, and in support of this position he referred to considerations of neutrality, economy, and politics (the general elections in Denmark were to be held the next month). But he did concede that on the question of time charter for the duration of the war, rather than for six months, the Danish government was "convinced that an agreement could be reached." [35]

---

[33] American Legation (Copenhagen) to Lansing, December 21, 1917, *Trade and Shipping Negotiations with Denmark*, pp. 24-25. See also the statement of the Danish Minister for Foreign Affairs, December 24, 1917, *For. Rel., 1917, Supp. 2*, II, pp. 1102-07.

[34] *Ibid., 1918, Supp. 1*, II, pp. 1319-20.

[35] *Ibid.*, pp. 1321-23. Brun added that the decision on the

Five days later, on March 18, 1918, and two days before Wilson's proclamation authorizing the seizure of the eighty-seven Dutch ships in American ports, Copenhagen conditionally capitulated on the danger-zone demands of the United States. Minister Brun expressed the earnest hope that Washington would not see fit to requisition Danish tonnage also (as was being rumored); and he gave a list of reasons why the shipping of Denmark was entitled to more favorable treatment than that of Holland. He concluded by saying that Copenhagen was prepared to offer one third of the tonnage under consideration for service in the danger zone, provided this concession was treated with "absolute secrecy" (this betrays fear of the Germans), and provided also that Washington accepted in principle the other counterproposals that Denmark had made on February 13, 1918.[36]

On April 11, 1918, some three weeks after Copenhagen's surrender, the Department of State rather belatedly assured Brun that the United States had "no present intention" of requisitioning Danish shipping.[37] Although direct evidence is lacking, the circumstances strongly suggest that Denmark's yielding to the American ultimatum was induced by the imminent seizure of the Dutch tonnage. Although this concession appears to have been the most important one made by the Danes, there were still other

---

danger zone had been reached "without consulting with any other nation [Germany]."

[36] *Ibid.*, pp. 1323-24.

[37] *Ibid.*, pp. 1326-27. As a result of protracted delays, the American chargé in Copenhagen reported, on May 22, 1918, that requisitioning seemed to be the only alternative. *Ibid.*, pp. 1320-30. This recommendation was disregarded.

The Agreement with Denmark

details to be threshed out before the final agreement could be concluded.

ix

The closing stages of the negotiations over rationing and shipping were complicated and delayed by some behind-the-scenes disagreements among the American and Allied representatives. For a time there was some doubt as to the wisdom of negotiating a tonnage agreement at all, inasmuch as the United States and Great Britain were already controlling more Danish shipping by unofficial or private arrangements than they could then hope to secure by an official pact; and informal arrangements were less likely to provoke German hostility than formal ones.[38] There was also some fear in Allied circles that the Danes, if pressed too hard, might follow the example of the Dutch and lay up their shipping; but for various reasons, economic and otherwise, this alternative was dismissed as improbable.[39]

Another important factor in delaying the negotiations—perhaps the most important factor—was the attempt of the Germans to prevent the Danes from limiting their exports to the Central Powers or chartering their shipping to the Associated Powers. This pressure took the form of threats in German newspapers, of inspired statements in pro-German Danish newspapers, of the work of undercover propaganda agents in Denmark, and of direct communica-

---

[38] *Ibid.*, p. 1388. In December, 1917, the War Trade Board learned that the British had taken certain steps advantageous to themselves regarding Danish tonnage without consulting Washington. The Board, on December 4, 1917, cabled its representative in Paris to "take up with British this failure to work frankly." State Dept., 659. 119/134a.

[39] *For. Rel., 1918, Supp. 1*, II, pp. 1331, 1332, 1336-37.

tions from Berlin. The most disquieting of the reports emanating from these sources was that the U-boats would sink all Danish shipping plying in the service of the Allies; and point was given to this rumor by the demand from Berlin that Danish shippers carry safe-conducts issued by the German government. Although threats of various kinds were unquestionably forthcoming from various German quarters, the American negotiators suspected that the Danish representatives were working the Berlin bogey overtime in order to moderate the demands of the War Trade Board.[40] The picture was further confused by the fact that while the Danes were negotiating in Washington the Germans were also negotiating in Copenhagen for an understanding involving an interchange of products. The latter discussions eventually resulted in a four-month agreement between Denmark and the Central Powers, signed August 1, 1918.[41]

Rather striking evidence of Copenhagen's fear of Berlin during the negotiations with America is found in the ratio of Danish tractability to German military success. During November, 1917, following the disastrous Italian defeat and the prospect of prolonged German ascendancy in Europe, the Danish representatives revealed little disposition to accede to the demands of the War Trade Board,

[40] American Legation (Copenhagen) to Lansing, January 30, 1918, State Dept., 659. 119/187; *For. Rel., 1917, Supp. 2*, II, pp. 1108-10; *ibid., 1918, Supp. 1*, II, pp. 1087-88; *Trade and Shipping Negotiations with Denmark*, pp. 24-25, 62, 65-66.

[41] *For. Rel., 1918, Supp. 1*, II, pp. 1330-31, 1335. The Danes were interested in German iron and steel products, and the War Trade Board agreed to license 2,000 tons of wrought iron tubing to Denmark in order to weaken Germany's bargaining power. *Ibid.*, p. 1331.

and in pursuance of a program of self-sufficiency they began to turn to the possibilities of an increasing interchange of goods among the three Scandinavian nations. By August, 1918, when the Germans had suffered severe reverses on the Western Front and the military complexion of the war was markedly changed, the Danish delegates showed a keen anxiety about coming to an agreement. Significantly, during the following month the definitive arrangements were perfected.[42]

X

The final agreement with Denmark was concluded on September 18, 1918, less than two months before the end of the war. The official documents were not signed by representatives of the Danish government at all but as follows. The rationing agreements were drawn up between the War Trade Board, on the one hand, and the Danish Chamber of Commerce and the Merchants' Guild of Copenhagen, on the other. Both of the latter organizations were semi-official agencies charged with the task of seeing to it that the rationing obligations of Denmark were faithfully fulfilled. The tonnage agreement was negotiated and signed by representatives of the War Trade Board and of the Danish Special Shipping Committee. These two documents were implemented by identic letters exchanged by Chairman McCormick, of the War Trade Board, and Minister Brun, representing Copenhagen, in which the restrictions that Denmark would place upon her exports were explicitly set

[42] *Ibid., 1917, Supp. 2,* II, p. 1064; *ibid., 1918, Supp. 1,* II, pp. 1336-37; report of Sheldon to War Trade Board, August 16, 1918, F. A. R., Hoover Library (War Trade Board; Foreign Agents and Reports Bureau).

forth.[43] It is interesting to observe that the American negotiators went to unusual lengths to draw up these agreements in such form as not to be offensive to the United States Senate, which is traditionally jealous of its share in the treaty-making process.[44]

The rationing agreement contained lengthy schedules stipulating the precise quantities of those commodities which the United States would license to Denmark, insofar as its own war effort would permit. These totaled about 352,000 tons annually, and fell under the following heads: foodstuffs (chiefly coffee, rice, fruits); fuels and nonedible oils (chiefly petroleum products); metals, machinery, and instruments (chiefly iron and steel products); fibres and their products (chiefly cotton and hemp); nonedible animal and vegetable products (chiefly tobacco and hides); wood, pulp, paper, plants, and seeds for sowing; chemicals, drugs, earth, minerals, and miscellaneous items.

The rationing agreement also contained various guarantees on the part of the United States designed to facilitate the shipment of the stipulated articles, and in turn Denmark agreed not to export any of these items (or substitutes for them) to the enemy, directly or indirectly. The Danes also bound themselves not to use the materials provided by the War Trade Board for the production of goods for Germany, although certain necessary exceptions were made with regard to the use of American petroleum products.[45]

---

[43] *For. Rel., 1918, Supp. 1,* II, pp. 1339-61.

[44] Lansing to McCormick, August 23, 1918; Chadbourne to McCormick, August 24, 1918, State Dept., War Trade Board, Danish Negotiations, vol. II.

[45] Petroleum was also involved in the much less important sepa-

The Agreement with Denmark

In the formal exchange of letters the Danes agreed to a substantial limitation on their exports to the Central Powers. Specifically, the sale of eggs, lard, cheese, milk, and various oils and fats was to be restricted to a maximum of 24,000 tons a year. A striking feature of the agreement was that Denmark had a prior obligation to export to Sweden and Norway at least thirty per cent of her total exportable surplus of butter, bacon, milk, and cheese; and at least twenty-five per cent of her total exportable surplus of eggs. This indicates the desire of the Associated Powers to relieve the necessities of the other Scandinavian coun-

---

rate negotiations for a rationing agreement with Iceland, which was then under Danish rule. The Associated Powers were primarily interested in this island because of its production of wool, which was being bought by three Danish firms with the object of sale to Germany after the war. In January, 1918, the Allies approached the United States for the purpose of seeking co-operation in working out a rationing agreement, and the War Trade Board promptly acceded to the extent of denying American purchasers import licenses for wool from Iceland. In the spring of 1918 representatives of the Allied governments met with those of Iceland and worked out an agreement (signed May 23, 1918, by the British, French, and Italian delegates) giving the Allies an option to purchase certain Icelandic commodities, principally wool, in return for which privilege the Allied Powers agreed to ration Iceland with stipulated supplies. Although the War Trade Board began to issue exports licenses for some of these, it delayed formal adherence to the agreement until September 11, 1918, primarily, it appears, because of a dispute between the Standard Oil Company of New Jersey and the originally designated British rival over a contract for supplying Iceland's petroleum requirements. The American company won out and signed the supplemental memorandum on September 9, 1918. On the subject of the Icelandic negotiations, see *For. Rel., 1918, Supp. 1,* II, pp. 1362-68; "Minutes of the War Trade Board," III, 5 (June 11, 1918); *Report of War Trade Board,* pp. 66-67; Heckscher, *Sweden, etc.,* p. 569.

tries without having to haul food products long distances. Provision was also made for permitting Great Britain to buy, should she elect to do so, quantities of Denmark's surplus foodstuffs equal to those purchased by the Central Powers. As regards fish, the Danes agreed to restrict their sales to Germany to 25,000 tons per annum, which was substantially what Copenhagen had contended for all along and which was approximately the prewar figure. The export of horses was to be kept at a maximum of 2,500 head each month, as compared with the average of more than 4,000 which the Danes had requested. The sale of cattle to Germany was to be held at a total of 226,000 head per annum at certain rates and in certain categories, as compared with the 416,000 figure which the Danish negotiators had asked for.

In addition to limiting her exports to Germany, Denmark bound herself to supply 265,000 dead-weight tons of shipping to the United States and 200,000 to Great Britain, a total of 465,000. This left Denmark with 340,000 tons for herself. Of the 265,000 tons for the United States, 80,000 were to be assigned to Belgian relief service, while one half of the balance (about 92,500 tons) would ply in the danger zone, and the other half outside the danger zone. The rates that were to be paid to the Danish owners were set, as well as an indemnification scale for those ships that might be destroyed by the Germans. Altogether, the Danes were required to charter somewhat more tonnage than they wished, and they were forced to yield on the very important principle of war-zone service.[46]

---

[46] Comment of Dr. Alonzo E. Taylor (November, 1941): "For us, shipping was the most important clause in [the] agreement."

xi

In retrospect, it seems clear that the rationing and tonnage agreement with Denmark caused, on the whole, less difficulty than any other drawn up with the Northern Neutrals during 1917-1918. If one may judge from the voluminous press digests collected by the British government, Danish newspapers were less interested in this problem than were those of any of the other important European neutrals.[47] Moreover, the materials collected for this study bulk much less large for Denmark than for any of the other five European neutrals. To be sure, the discussions were prolonged until the autumn of 1918; but, as we have seen, the War Trade Board could probably have closed them before the end of 1917, if a policy of protracted delay had not seemed necessary as a means of furthering other negotiations.

Despite certain harsh features of the agreement, Denmark, on the whole, came off rather well. Urgently needed supplies from the United States were guaranteed, while heavy exports to Germany were still permitted, though somewhat reduced in volume. It is true that nearly 100,000 tons of Danish shipping were to ply in the danger zone, but this represented only one eighth of Denmark's total merchant marine; and the United States might have insisted on more. Nor should we forget that satisfactory indemnification was provided for those ships lost.

---

[47] This was probably due to the fact that Denmark, as far as food was concerned, was less severely pinched than the other European neutrals, except Spain. See Oscar J. Falnes, "Denmark and Norway, 1914-40," in Clarkson and Cochran, eds., *War as a Social Institution*, p. 146.

Perhaps the best index to the liberality of these terms is the Danish press.[48] Although some little complaint arose over the disappointingly low quota of fertilizer, general satisfaction was expressed, not only by newspapers but by businessmen as well, over the conclusion of the agreement and the prospective relief of distressed industries. Particularly welcome were the schedules regarding petroleum, tobacco, and coffee—though the press made it clear that much would depend on the speedy arrival of the commodities promised. Indeed, it seems reasonably clear that this agreement was more generally popular than were any of the others negotiated with the Northern Neutrals. This may have been more a measure of Danish distress than of American generosity; it may even have reflected a growing pro-Ally sentiment and the imminence of Allied victory. Yet the fact must not be overlooked that the Danish press was conspicuously enthusiastic in its comments on American liberality.

The question of ethics that arises in connection with all the other agreements negotiated under the duress of an embargo again comes to the fore. There can be no doubt that the United States was taking extraordinary liberties with a sovereign nation like Denmark when it required that country, against its will, to send its ships and seamen into danger zones, and when it forced the Danes to restrict certain exports to Germany and sell others to Norway and Sweden. But the answer, repetitious though it may seem,

[48] *Neut. Press Supp.*, IV, 498-99. This source quotes eight prominent Danish newspapers. See also *For. Rel., 1918, Supp. 1,* II, pp. 1361-62; *Trade and Shipping Negotiations with Denmark,* p. 109; *Nachrichten der Auslandpresse,* September 10, 1918, p. 8; October 19, 1918, p. 7.

is the same. Denmark accepted these terms voluntarily. The alternative, of course, was continued deprivation; but she did have that alternative. The embargo was a legitimate and well-recognized weapon, albeit a disagreeable one, and the Americans would have been extremely naïve if they had refrained from using it in an attempt to weaken the enemy.

CHAPTER VII

THE RATIONING AND TONNAGE NEGOTIATIONS WITH HOLLAND

i

From several points of view the kingdom of the Netherlands occupied a place of the highest importance among the European neutrals. Though the smallest of the six in area, it had a larger population than any of the others, except Spain. It possessed a huge and immensely valuable colonial empire, which enabled its people to enjoy an unusually high per capita wealth. It controlled a merchant fleet of approximately 1,500,000 gross tons, which, in size, ranked next to that of Norway among the European neutrals. And of all the neutrals Holland had by far the longest border contiguous to Germany.

This factor of contiguity lay at the bottom of many of Holland's troubles. In time of peace the thrifty Dutch sold to the Germans great quantities of butter, cheese, eggs, meat, livestock, fruit, vegetables, and fish. Much as the Allies wished to choke off this traffic, they recognized that it would be no easy task to stop or even limit such a large and profitable outflow. Contiguity also created transit problems involving the railroads and rivers of Holland. Through the Netherlands to the Krupp works flowed enormous supplies of Swedish iron ore; through the Netherlands into Belgium and German-occupied Northern France flowed vast quantities of materials for military use, notably sand and gravel for construction work in the trenches. Naturally, the Allies were anxious to put an end to this traffic.

For a number of reasons the Dutch did not respond satisfactorily to Allied demands. First of all, the Netherlands boasted a splendid tradition, and this was manifested in a pride and stubbornness that had long been characteristic of the sturdy burgher.[1] Secondly, although it is probable that the masses of Holland were pro-Ally at heart,[2] there was nevertheless a strong pro-German element, and in this atmosphere a Germanophile press flourished and German propaganda agents schemed. Third, the Dutch were heavily dependent upon Germany for many commodities, such as fertilizers, shipbuilding materials, iron goods, and particularly coal.[3] Although it was theoretically possible for the British to substitute their own coal for that of the Germans, a satisfactory solution of the transportation and other problems involved was never convincingly demonstrated to the Dutch. It is not surprising, therefore, that Holland was unwilling to quarrel with her coal scuttle.

The Dutch also could employ, if forced to do so, a not inconsiderable embargo club. Their East Indies controlled

---

[1] For an excellent summary of the Dutch point of view, see Matthuys P. Rooseboom, "The Dutch Quandary," *Atlantic Monthly*, CXXII, 247-56 (August, 1918). The author denies that real prosperity resulted from the war. See also P. Geyl, "Holland and the War," *The Contemporary Review*, CXIII, 288-94 (March, 1918). A fuller account is Nicolaas Japikse, *Die Stellung Hollands im Weltkrieg politisch und wirtschaftlich* (tr. by K. Schwendemann, Gotha, 1921).

[2] The Dutch were deeply stirred by the invasion of Belgium and by the subsequent treatment of the civilian population.

[3] A discussion of the coal problem appears in Langhorne to Lansing, September 6, 1917, State Dept., 656. 119/22.

valuable quantities of tin and indispensable supplies of quinine, upon both of which the Netherlands government placed export restrictions.[4] Of perhaps more immediate concern to the British was the possibility that Holland, if hard pressed, would embargo the large and important shipments of foodstuffs to England, particularly margerine. Less important, but nevertheless not to be disregarded, was the fear that Holland would hamstring the work of Belgian relief by refusing the co-operation that was essential for its success.

In the background of all these problems, and sometimes overshadowing them, was the military situation. Quite in contrast with the Danes, the Dutch had enough troops and defenses, natural and otherwise, to be able to put up some semblance of resistance to a German attack. No one would deny that Germany could overrun the Netherlands if she chose to do so; but the effort would probably involve many more men than the Supreme Command was willing to detach from other and more pressing operations. Yet the invasion undoubtedly would have come had the Dutch accepted terms from the Allies that were sufficiently objectionable to Berlin. German control of Holland would have meant the complete cutting off of margerine and other food supplies to England; the consequent diversion of these and other products to Germany; and, most important, the establishment of submarine and other bases at the Dutch channel ports.[5] The strategy of the Allies was to press

[4] *Report of War Trade Board*, pp. 91 ff.

[5] As late as April, 1918, General Tasker H. Bliss, an American officer, concluded that Dutch participation in the war on the side of the Allies would prove a liability. *For. Rel., 1918, Supp. 1*, II, pp. 1800-02.

their demands with vigor, but not to the point where the Dutch would be forced into the camp of Germany, or to a point where the Germans would be forced to invade the Netherlands.[6]

ii

Unfavorable though this general picture may have been from the Allied point of view, it was by no means hopeless. First of all, Holland, like all the other Northern Neutrals, was vulnerable to an embargo, especially on grain, fertilizers, oil, and feedstuffs. In spite of the great quantities of bacon, butter, and other animal products that they shipped abroad, the Dutch were not self-sufficient in certain important foodstuffs, particularly cereals. And if feedstuffs had been cut off, the Hollanders, like the Danes, would have had to export much of their livestock to the Germans, or slaughter it and sell the surplus meat, which would have amounted to substantially the same thing.

It is true, as we have observed, that German coal and iron products were indispensable to the Dutch; yet, on the whole, the commodities obtainable only through the Allied blockade were more important. Besides, if it became necessary to do so, the British could provide a substantial portion of the supplies normally secured from Germany; whereas Germany could not provide in satisfactory quantity those products which the Associated Powers controlled.

The position of the Allies was also strengthened by the existence of two hostages. The first was the Dutch merchant fleet. Owing to German depredations (the total loss

---

[6] The British realized that they would again have serious trouble with the Dutch-descended Boers of South Africa should Great Britain and Holland become involved in war.

for the war was over 200,000 gross tons),[7] the cautious Dutch had immobilized about one third of their tonnage in American and British harbors, where it could, if necessary, be put under requisition. The second was the Netherlands East Indies. If the Dutch had thrown themselves into the arms of Germany, or had permitted themselves to be forced into those arms, the Associated Powers (Japan was commonly mentioned) would undoubtedly have taken over the Netherlands colonial empire, possibly on a permanent basis. In brief, a Dutch alliance with Germany would have invited disaster abroad and German domination at home; alliance with the Associated Powers would have invited German invasion. Hence the Dutch, with the horrible example of prostrate Belgium at their very door, were grimly and stubbornly determined to pursue a neutral course.[8]

It was with such considerations as these in mind that the Balfour Commission, in May, 1917, made its recommendations to the American officials. At this time the British

[7] The precise figures are: 131,948 gross tons by submarines, 5,584 by cruisers, and 74,310 by mines. Fayle, *Seaborne Trade*, III, 466.

[8] On this general background see the secret British memorandum, August 4, 1917, Yale House Collection; *For. Rel., 1917, Supp. 2*, II, pp. 836-38; memorandum of July 19, 1917, F. A. R., Hoover Library (Netherlands: Agriculture, Industry and Commerce Ministry); C. J. P. Zaalberg, *et al.*, *The Netherlands and the World War* (New Haven, 1928), vols. II, III, IV; Amry Vandenbosch, *The Neutrality of the Netherlands during the World War* (Grand Rapids, Mich., 1927); M. J. van der Flier, *War Finances in the Netherlands up to 1918* (Oxford, 1923); Blaine Free Moore, *Economic Aspects of the Commerce and Industry of the Netherlands, 1912-1918* (Washington, 1919); Turlington, *Neutrality*, pp. 123-32.

were primarily concerned with such problems as the smuggling of various overseas commodities across the Dutch border into Germany; the use of Netherlands soil for transit purposes by the Germans; and the continued refusal of the Dutch to employ their merchant marine in dangerous trades. But, for reasons that we have considered, the Balfour Commission was not prepared to urge stringent measures. Specifically, it advised that the Americans give The Hague a general statement of their policies regarding the conservation of shipping and supplies both for the Allies and for the home needs of the neutrals. Then Washington should add its support to the Allied protests against the use of Dutch soil for transit purposes by Germany. Next, the United States should adopt a policy of making continued exports to Holland " conditional on the proper employment of Dutch shipping." Finally, Washington should insist that the Netherlands take steps to prevent the smuggling of overseas products (including American) into Germany, and at the same time concert measures with the British by which Dutch importers of American oil would be kept from using this fuel in the manufacture or transportation of products destined for the enemy.[9]

iii

The prospect of an American embargo was no more pleasing to the Dutch than to the other Northern Neutrals, and the press of the Netherlands reiterated the usual charges of misunderstanding and hypocrisy. Nonetheless, President Wilson issued his first embargo proclamation on

[9] *For. Rel., 1917, Supp. 2*, II, pp. 836-38, 1118-19.

July 9, 1917.[10] The resulting predicament of the Dutch shippers was more distressing than that of the other neutrals, because at this time there were in American ports some sixty Netherlands freighters—an extraordinarily large number—laden with feedstuffs and various kinds of cereals. When Washington refused to issue export licenses for these cargoes, the owners were forced to tie up their ships indefinitely, at a heavy cost in demurrage charges; and when the grain began to spoil, as it did in a number of instances, there was no recourse but to unload and recondition the cargoes and put them in more satisfactory places. All this, of course, was most vexatious to the owners, to say nothing of the prospective purchasers in Holland, where the shortage of food and feedstuffs was already beginning to be felt.

Late in July, 1917, there seemed to be a good chance of freeing the delayed freighters, for at that time Hoover proposed that the Dutch be allowed to carry one third of their grain home, provided they would deliver two thirds of it, in good condition, to the Belgian relief administration, which would pay for it at cost. Negotiations were continued for about a month, when Hoover suddenly dropped them. By this time he discovered that the bulk of many of the cargoes consisted of feedstuffs and other products unfit for human consumption; and he revealed some pique over the fact that the Dutch negotiators should have taken up valuable time when it must have been clear that the Belgian relief administration and the American food

[10] At about this time there were serious riots in Amsterdam, involving some loss of life, because the already pinched citizenry objected to the shipment of potatoes to England under the existing agreement. New York *Times,* July 4, 6, 7, 1917.

authorities were not interested in the feeding of animals. The whole affair created an unfortunate atmosphere.[11]

Meanwhile, Dutch anxiety over the shipping and food problems had been reflected in the appointment of a commission of three, late in July, 1917, charged with the task of coming to America and presenting statistics and other information regarding Holland's needs. The head of the group told an American newspaper correspondent: " I hope the Americans will learn to appreciate that Holland is between the devil and the deep sea and that it is impossible to agree to all of America's demands." He added that he would attempt to dispel misunderstanding by presenting correct figures. The Dutch commission finally reached Norfolk, Virginia, on September 5, 1917, at almost the same time as the breakdown of negotiations over grain for Belgian relief.[12]

iv

Throughout the autumn of 1917 the negotiations with the Dutch commissioners in Washington languished. On September 10 the visitors made an attempt to solve the problem of detained tonnage and embargoed food and

[11] The Dutch claimed they never suspected that Hoover's proposal had to do with human food only. Hoover to Van Rappard, July 31, 1917; Van Rappard to Hoover, August 3, 1917; F. A. R., Hoover Library (Netherlands: Legation); *For. Rel., 1917, Supp. 2*, II, pp. 1129-34; Hoover to Woolsey, September 6, 1917, F. A. R., Hoover Library (Netherlands: Legation); *The Requisitioning of the Dutch Shipping* (Washington, 1919), pp. 10-11.

[12] New York *Times*, July 24, 26, August 19, September 6, 1917; *For. Rel., 1917, Supp. 2*, II, p. 1129; Van Rappard to Hoover, August 30, 1917, F. A. R., Hoover Library (Netherlands: Legation). The Dutch minister who had been conducting these negotiations was shortly thereafter recalled. New York *Times*, September 15, 16, 17, 1917.

feedstuffs when they revived the scheme for benefiting Belgian relief. Under the new proposal the Dutch ships would carry food (not feedstuffs) and share their cargoes with the Belgians. These overtures finally came to naught, primarily because the Netherlands officials would not provide Washington with the full information desired, and because they would not give satisfactory assurances that the commodities and facilities so released would not be used in behalf of the enemy. In addition, the Dutch consistently opposed any proposition that they employ their tonnage in the war zone, and they tenaciously adhered to the principle that they would not deviate in the slightest degree from the tightrope of neutrality between the Central Powers and the Allies.[13]

The negotiations in Washington were further complicated by a crisis between Britain and Holland over the sand-and-gravel transit question. In an effort to put a stop to this traffic the London government, in October, 1917, took the drastic step of denying the Dutch access to British cables for commercial transactions. Downing Street evidently desired to secure the co-operation of the United States in the support of such a course; but Washington seems to have avoided involvement. The Dutch, who were in mortal fear of provoking their powerful neighbor, refused to be beaten into line; and this policy of coercion ended in failure, after much bitterness had been aroused against both the British and the Americans.[14]

---

[13] *For. Rel., 1917, Supp. 2*, II, pp. 1133, 1134, 1136-38, 1138-39. Comment of Dr. Alonzo E. Taylor (November, 1941): " In matters of commerce the fault of the Dutch was offering too little and asking too much."

[14] New York *Times*, October 13, 15, 1917; *For. Rel., 1917*,

The possibility that the Dutch and the Associated Powers might come to an agreement on tonnage and rationing was lessened by the simultaneous negotiations between Holland and Germany. So alarming had the coal famine become that the Dutch, early in October, 1917, were forced to accede to an arrangement whereby they were to receive German coal and iron products in return for food.[15] This naturally had a disquieting effect upon the Associated Powers, and the news regarding the guarantee of foodstuffs to Germany was hardly calculated to inspire lenient treatment of the Netherlands on the part of the Washington officials.

Nor were the Dutch becoming more favorably disposed toward the United States as precious stocks of embargoed commodities dwindled away. A striking manifestation of this growing antipathy came late in October, 1917, when Mynheer Van Aalst, President of the Netherlands Overseas Trust, published a widely discussed open letter to President Wilson. The writer begged the United States not to take advantage of Holland's unhappy position; referred to the necessity of normal trade with Germany; recalled the friendliness of the Dutch for the United States during the days of the American Revolution; deplored the starvation

---

Supp. 2, II, pp. 1135-36, 1153-54, 1156; "Secret Memorandum on the Dutch Sand and Gravel Question," October 31, 1917, F. A. R., Hoover Library (Netherlands).

[15] *For. Rel., 1917, Supp. 2*, II, pp. 1145-47; Turlington, *Neutrality*, p. 130; New York *Times*, October 27, 1917. The problem of keeping exports from reaching the enemy through the neutrals confronted the Central Powers as well as the Allies. In the negotiations for the Dutch-German agreement Berlin sought to keep Netherlands ships built with German materials from plying in the service of the Associated Powers.

embargo of Washington; and besought the release of the detained ships. "Excuse me for saying," he declared, "that we have been feeling that your Government is standing on our neck in a most inconsiderate way, with a boot quite as heavy and painful as another jackboot [German] which has been severely denounced in your country."[16]

This was but one outward expression of a bitterness that had been increasing by leaps and bounds during the autumn of 1917. Among the many factors contributing to this exacerbation of feeling we may note the breakdown of the negotiations over the Belgian relief transaction; the failure of the Dutch commissioners in Washington to make progress on a new tack; the growing pressure of the embargo on foodstuffs; the necessity of slaughtering cattle (for which there were not adequate refrigeration facilities);[17] the evidence that the British were asking the United States to follow their lead in the sand-and-gravel controversy; and disquieting talk in America of the desirability of requisitioning the tied-up Dutch shipping.[18] At the same

[16] New York *Times*, October 21, 1917; *Neut. Press Supp.*, III, 53. See also *For. Rel., 1917, Supp. 2*, II, pp. 1143-44; New York *Times*, October 26, 1917; Alonzo E. Taylor memorandum of Paris negotiations, November 30, 1917, F. A. R., Hoover Library (Netherlands—Agreements). The Dutch referred repeatedly to their alleged friendliness during the American Revolution in regard to recognition and loans. See the letter of Professor C. H. Van Tyne which denied that Minister John Adams had been accorded a friendly reception. New York *Times*, October 27, 1917.

[17] For statistics and charts on the growing pinch of the embargo see *Report of War Trade Board*, pp. 34-35, 39-41. The cutting off of feedstuffs necessitated slaughtering of cattle and sending some surplus meat to Germany, but not an appreciable amount.

[18] See *Neut. Press Supp.*, II, 418; III, 29-30.

THE NEGOTIATIONS WITH HOLLAND

time, the Germans were relaxing their demands upon the Netherlands, possibly with the object of permitting the growing sentiment against the Allies to gain full headway. On October 16, 1917, the American consul in Amsterdam sent home a long dispatch in which he pointed out that the strong pro-Ally sentiment of a year ago was rapidly disappearing, and that there was even serious talk of severing relations with the United States.[19]

This thickening atmosphere of resentment proved to be ideal for German propagandists in Holland, and they took full advantage of their opportunity to turn sentiment against the United States. Inadequate news coverage from America naturally made their task much easier. The press in Germany was particularly bitter over the treatment of the Netherlands, and it published numerous editorials under such captions as: "The Neutrals' Worst Enemy"; "America's Thumbscrew"; "Wilson's Despotism."[20] With Dutch anger and stubbornness rapidly increasing, and with the Allied need for tonnage becoming more and more desperate, it was evident that vigorous measures of some kind were practically inevitable.

V

Early in December, 1917, the Washington government decided to transfer the negotiations for Dutch tonnage to London, where Vance C. McCormick and Dr. Alonzo E. Taylor, of the War Trade Board, were then staying as members of the House Mission. The discussions were continued

[19] *For. Rel., 1917, Supp. 2*, II, pp. 1147-50. See also *ibid.*, pp. 1140-41; *ibid., 1918, Supp. 1,* II, p. 1378; New York *Times*, October 10, 1917.

[20] *Ibid.*, October 18, 28, 1917.

in close co-operation with the British, French, and Italians, and a vital point of difference proved to be the unwillingness of the Dutch to consent to the chartering of their ships for war-zone service. Early in January a general agreement was finally drawn up, but when it was discovered that ratification by all parties would take much more time than the tonnage exigencies of the Allies would permit, it seemed best to arrange for a *modus vivendi* pending final adjustments. After much bickering over details, this arrangement was finally accepted by the Netherlands government, on January 25, 1918. By its terms the Dutch were to turn over to the United States, for periods up to ninety days, some 500,000 dead-weight tons of shipping which had been lying idle in American ports. This was not to be used in the danger zones, though up to 150,000 tons might be employed for Belgian relief or for safe-conduct transportation to Switzerland by way of France, assuming, of course, that Berlin would grant the safe-conducts.[21]

The conclusion of this *modus vivendi,* which was followed four days later (January 29, 1918) by a similar one with Sweden, was the occasion for much satisfaction in Washington; and the American officials began to make preparations for the employment of the ships in Allied service. As a token of its gratification, and also to forestall rapidly growing German traffic in such products, the War Trade Board announced, on February 20, 1918, that it would lift the embargo on nonessential commodities going to both Holland and Sweden.[22]

---

[21] *For. Rel., 1918, Supp. 1,* II, pp. 1377-81, 1392-93; see also *ibid., 1917, Supp. 2,* II, pp. 1011, 1151.

[22] *Official Bulletin,* February 20, 1918, p. 3; Page to Lansing, February 5, 1918, State Dept., 656. 119/160.

If the Associated Powers were pleased with the *modus vivendi,* the Germans definitely were not. It meant little to them that the 500,000 tons of Dutch shipping were not to ply in the danger zone; its employment by the Allies merely meant that other steamers would be freed for the dangerous routes. The German press denounced the unneutrality of the agreement, insisted that the owners of the vessels be put on the German blacklist, and even threatened to torpedo the Dutch ships.[23] The pressure from Berlin on the Netherlands grew increasingly strong, and before long it became evident that Holland, in the face of German threats, dared not carry out all the terms of the *modus vivendi,* at least not within an acceptable period of time. In particular, the Dutch found it impossible or impracticable to live up to that portion of the agreement whereby it was stipulated that for each ship sent to the Netherlands in the service of the Belgian relief, a corresponding vessel should leave Holland for the United States.[24]

When it finally became apparent that the *modus vivendi* had broken down, or that its execution would be unconscionably delayed, the Associated Powers found that they were where they had been before. Indeed, their position was worse, because much valuable time had already been lost in fruitless negotiation and delay. With Holland apparently afraid to execute the agreement as the Associated Powers had understood it, and with the tonnage

---

[23] Garrett to Lansing, January 24, 1918, *ibid.,* 656. 119/146; *Requisitioning of Dutch Shipping,* p. 40; *For. Rel., 1918, Supp. 1,* II, p. 1394; *Neut. Press Supp.,* III, 369, 561.

[24] Sheldon's confidential memorandum on the Dutch negotiations, March 4, 1918, F. A. R., Hoover Library (W. T. B.; Foreign Agents and Reports Bureau; London; L. P. Sheldon); New York *Times,* March 8, 1918.

situation still in a critical stage, the only practicable alternative seemed to be the drastic one of a wholesale requisitioning of all the idle Dutch tonnage within the grasp of the United States and Great Britain.

vi

Shortly after the United States entered the war, discussions had begun to appear from time to time in the American press to the effect that the rotting Dutch ships ought to be forcibly commandeered.[25] Legal justification for such an extreme step apparently could be found in the ancient law of angary, which had been used by belligerents to support the seizure of neutral property under stress of a national emergency; recent precedent could be found in the British requisitioning of a few neutral vessels in the spring of 1917.[26]

In May, 1917, during the visit of the Balfour Commission, the British Embassy had referred to the possibility of seizing idle neutral tonnage, as had recently been done in the case of certain Danish vessels.[27] This suggestion appears not to have resulted in any official action in Wash-

---

[25] *Ibid.*, April 26, September 2, 1917. On September 15, 1917, the *Times* declared that it was "almost a crime" that these ships should be laid up with rotting cargoes.

[26] In April, 1917, the British, with the consent of the owners, seized twenty-four Danish ships of 36,000 gross tons. In May, 1917, the British requisitioned eleven Dutch steamers of 40,000 gross tons. These ships, however, were owned by companies in which the controlling financial interest was British. Turlington, *Neutrality*, pp. 95-96. For the British requisitioning of certain Swedish and Norwegian ships under somewhat different circumstances see Heckscher, *Sweden, etc.*, pp. 106, 355.

[27] *For. Rel., 1917, Supp. 2*, II, p. 841.

ington until September 8, 1917, when the United States Shipping Board asked the Department of State whether it would sanction the drastic step of commandeering Dutch shipping. The Office of the Solicitor replied that there were no treaty provisions between the two nations relating to this problem, and that from a legal standpoint requisitioning might be effected. But, it was stated, political and diplomatic considerations were of the utmost importance. Secretary Lansing, at the same time, brought this question before the President, and, while seeking an opinion, pointed out that in his own judgment requisitioning would be unwise, not only because it would arouse extreme irritation in Holland but also because it would embarrass any negotiations taking place between Britain and Holland. Wilson's reply is most interesting, because it does not reveal the uncompromising adherence to idealism that had characterized his position in regard to several other drastic proposals affecting the neutrals. "I agree with you," he said, "that it would be unwise to do what the Shipping Board suggests about the Dutch vessels, at any rate at the present time, until the situation is more fully developed in its several elements." [28]

During September and October, 1917, Dutch public opinion was profoundly disturbed by the rumors of immi-

[28] Auchincloss to Lansing, September 8, 1917; Lansing to Wilson, September 10, 1917; Wilson to Lansing, September 18, 1917, State Dept., 656. 119/179, 180. When Frank L. Polk informed Hurley (of the Shipping Board) and McCormick and Chadbourne (of the War Trade Board) of Wilson's answer, they expressed disappointment and asked that news of this decision be withheld from the Dutch, presumably because it would strengthen their position. Polk memorandum, September 24, 1917, *ibid.*, 656. 119/180.

nent seizure, and the press made it clear that such a step would be regarded as a hostile act.[29] In November, the discussions of requisitioning shifted to London, where Colonel House, much to his surprise, found considerable Allied support for it.[30] Secretary Lansing cautioned House, however, to study the problem from all angles, and keep in mind " the possibility of Holland turning to Germany in case of the requisitioning of their ships." [31] The British discounted this possibility, particularly in view of the fact that the Dutch colonies would fall into Allied hands; but in part because of the ill success of Allied armies, Lord Robert Cecil thought it would be best to undertake a quiet and gradual requisitioning. This, he felt, would cause a minimum of irritation and humiliation.[32]

The negotiations drifted along for another month until December 22, 1917, when the War Trade Board formally voted in favor of requisitioning and authorized the Chairman to place its views before President Wilson and Secretary Lansing.[33] Two weeks later, on January 5, 1918,

[29] New York *Times*, October 13, 14, 1917; *Neut. Press Supp.*, II, 418, 500; III, 29-30.

[30] Charles Seymour, ed., *The Intimate Papers of Colonel House* (Boston, 1928), III, 227. McCormick, then in London, reported on November 15, 1917, that the Allied representatives had concluded that the time had come " to consider seriously requisition. . . ." *For. Rel., 1917, Supp. 2*, I, p. 637.

[31] Lansing to House, November 20, 1917, Yale House Collection; see also somewhat different version in *For. Rel., 1917, Supp. 2*, II, p. 1147. At this time Chairman Hurley of the Shipping Board strongly repeated his arguments for requisitioning. Hurley to Lansing, November 22, 1917, State Dept., 656. 119/183.

[32] *For. Rel., 1917, Supp. 2*, II, p. 1150; enclosure in Bertie of Thame to House, November 27, 1917, Yale House Collection.

[33] " Minutes of the War Trade Board," I, 190-91 (December 22, 1917).

Washington had made up its mind; two days later Lansing cabled the American minister at The Hague, John W. Garrett, as follows: "For your confidential information, but not to be used under any circumstances: This Government, in the event that reasonable propositions made by it are refused by the Dutch Government concerning tonnage, proposes to requisition Dutch boats under its control." [34] Three days later, on January 10, 1918, Garrett sent back a strong plea against seizure, and requested that his dispatch be shown to the President. He pointed out that the Dutch, with the terrifying example of Belgium before them, were paralyzed with fear of the Germans; that requisitioning would hurt the work of Belgian relief, much of which was carried on through Holland; and that while the great majority of the Dutch people were pro-Ally, they would be profoundly disillusioned by the departure from fair dealing which forcible measures would entail.[35]

The conclusion of the *modus vivendi* with the Dutch, on January 25, 1918, quieted further talk of commandeering for the moment; but when it seemed evident that the Germans would not permit Holland to carry out its terms, agitation for requisitioning was renewed in both British and American quarters. Secretary Lansing explained to Chairman McCormick of the War Trade Board, on February 27, 1918, that in a matter of such great importance the consent of the President would have to be obtained.[36] How Wilson was induced to approve a drastic act which might be interpreted as running counter to his idealistic profes-

[34] *For. Rel., 1918, Supp. 1*, II, p. 1383.
[35] *Ibid.*, pp. 1385-86.
[36] "Minutes of the War Trade Board," I, 423 (February 27, 1918).

sions the record does not reveal. Presumably the desperate need of tonnage and the patent helplessness of the Dutch brought him around to this position, apparently some time early in March, 1918,[37] for on March 20 he issued an executive order authorizing the requisitioning of all Dutch shipping in American ports—eighty-seven vessels totaling 527,746 dead-weight tons.[38] At the same time the British seized 124,000 dead-weight tons of Dutch ships, the combined action of the two governments accounting for more than one third of the entire Dutch merchant fleet.[39]

President Wilson stated in his proclamation that he was acting in conformity with international law, and under authority of an act of Congress of June 15, 1917, in taking this action to satisfy the "imperative military needs of the United States." In an accompanying explanation, Wilson traced the languishing of the general commercial negotiations, the substitution of the *modus vivendi* (which, being

[37] Comment of Vance C. McCormick (November 4, 1941): ". . . you raise the question as to how Wilson was induced to approve such a drastic act as taking over the Dutch ships. You were correct in stating it was the desperate need of tonnage and I remember several interviews with the President before we could get his consent to issue the Executive Order. When we were in London with the House Mission in the Fall of 1917 we realized it would be necessary to take over these ships but it took considerable arguing with the President to convince him to take this definite step. When the Dutch Minister Phillips, who had just recently arrived in Washington, was notified of the President's action, he was greatly shocked and came to my office to ask me if he could speak directly to the President on this matter. I arranged a hearing for him and the President stood by his department heads (as was his usual custom) and informed the Minister he would not retract his order."

[38] *For. Rel., 1918, Supp. 1*, II, pp. 1416-17.

[39] Fayle, *Seaborne Trade*, III, 299.

temporary, had to be acted upon promptly to be useful), and the failure of the Dutch government, after a two-month delay, to carry out the arrangement, admittedly because it feared retaliation on the part of the Germans. Wilson further explained:

But the events to which I have alluded had served to demonstrate conclusively that we have been attempting to negotiate where the essential basis for an agreement, namely, the meeting of free wills, is absent. Even were an agreement concluded, there is lacking that power of independent action which alone can assure performance. I say this not in criticism of the Dutch Government. I profoundly sympathize with the difficulty of her position under the menace of a military power which has in every way demonstrated its disdain of neutral rights. But, since coercion does in fact exist, no alternative is left to us but to accomplish, through the exercise of our indisputable rights as a sovereign, that which is so reasonable that in other circumstances we could be confident of accomplishing it by agreement.

The President went on to say that there was ample shipping left for Holland's necessities; that she might send ships to America for the purpose of obtaining needed grain (a maximum of 100,000 tons); that these vessels would be bunkered and guaranteed freedom from detention; that ample compensation would be paid the owners of the ships; and that suitable arrangements would be made to provide substitutes for those vessels (eventually six) destroyed by the enemy.[40] Altogether, the terms granted by the United

---

[40] A more detailed explanation of America's policy was cabled from Lansing to Minister Garrett by way of London, March 12, 1918, State Dept., 656.119/237; see also *For. Rel., 1918, Supp. 1*, II, pp. 1417-20, 1423-24. The British regretted the generous offer of 100,000 tons of grain. *Ibid.*, p. 1414. See the report of Chairman Hurley of the Shipping Board to President Wilson, *c.*

States were substantially as generous as those proposed before requisitioning.[41]

vii

This wholesale seizure of the Dutch ships could not have come as a surprise to the Netherlands. For weeks the Dutch newspapers had been anticipating and condemning such a measure, while those of Germany had been joining loudly in the chorus. When the long-discussed blow finally fell, the people of Holland were not in an amiable mood. The increasing shortage of breadstuffs had recently caused some alarming demonstrations and riots, several of which had actually resulted in bloodshed.[42] It is not surprising, therefore, that the immediate reaction to the requisitioning proclamation was an angry outcry. Minister Garrett reported from The Hague that an outraged group of students had gathered in front of the legation and had gone on their way only after whistling, jeering, hissing, and singing unflattering songs. A few newspapers and legislators even went so far as to suggest breaking diplomatic re-

---

September 26, 1918, for an excellent summary statement of how the problems of compensation and of handling the crews and the cargoes were all worked out. *Ibid.*, pp. 1536-43. There was also some dispute over the payment of compensation in florins rather than in dollars, in order to avoid losses through adverse exchange conditions. *Ibid.*, pp. 1499-1500. File 656.119, State Dept., especially vol. IV, contains much correspondence on such matters. The Chairman of the United States Shipping Board later pointed out that the Washington government went to great pains to treat the stranded crews fairly, and that President Wilson was much interested in this aspect of the problem. Edward N. Hurley, *The Bridge to France* (Philadelphia, 1927), pp. 116-17.

[41] See Fayle, *Seaborne Trade*, III, 300.

[42] Garrett to Lansing, April 17, 1918, State Dept., 656. 119/461.

lations with the United States, but such a dangerous move, so foreign to Holland's persistent policy of neutrality, seems never to have been seriously entertained by the government or the people.[43]

Almost without exception the Dutch newspapers ran the gamut from violent condemnation to aggrieved innocence. Favorite subjects for emphasis were the Prussian ruthlessness of the United States, Wilsonian hypocrisy, and the hollow sham of American idealism. In particular, Dutch opinion felt bitter over the fact that Washington had denied the Dutch ships licenses to sail with their cargoes of grain, and then had seized them because they were not engaged in useful occupations. The *Nieuwe Rotterdamsche*

---

[43] *For. Rel., 1918, Supp. 1*, II, pp. 1426-28; *Requisitioning of Dutch Shipping*, pp. 75-76; New York *Times*, March 16, 19, 23, 1918; press clippings sent by Garrett in State Dept., 656.119, vols. II, III. It is interesting to note that several Americans wrote to the State Department protesting against requisitioning and saying that if Washington were to carry on the war on this basis they would buy no more Liberty Bonds; others asked for data so that they could quiet the objections of their fellow citizens. On the whole, the press of the United States seems to have applauded or approved the wholesale seizure. See *Literary Digest*, LVI, 18-19 (March 30, 1918). One noteworthy exception was the New York *Nation*, which declared that "the whole transaction leaves an extremely unpleasant flavor in the mouth of a nation that is fighting 'for the rights and liberties of small nations.'" Comparing this seizure with the rape of Belgium, the *Nation* continued: "If we must win this war by adopting the principle that might is right, let us prate no more of moral justifications, let us weep no more tears for Belgium and Servia. Let us not allow ourselves to be held up before the neutral world as hypocrites who believe in principles when they work to our advantage, and who toss them into the scrap basket when they get in our way." CVI, 310 (March 21, 1918). This, however, was by no means a commonly accepted view in the American press.

Courant branded requisitioning as "a deed of robbery," and declared that "it will be a blot on the history of the United States not to be wiped out for decades." The *Volk* was even more bitter:

> It would have been more candid in President Wilson if he had followed the example of the late German Chancellor, Bethmann-Hollweg, speaking of the German invasion of Belgium, and had declared that necessity knows no law and that the rights of the neutrals are only scraps of paper to belligerents. For such is the real position.[44]

Members of the government were scarcely less outspoken than the press in their expressions of bitterness. Minister of Foreign Affairs John Loudon asserted in the Upper Chamber that the act was "without a shred of justice." In the same body, one senator said: "President Wilson calls himself our friend. Well, Heaven preserve us from our friends." A Socialist deputy was quoted as having declared: "The seizure of the Dutch fleet by President Wilson under the pretext of war necessity is as bad

---

[44] *Neut. Press Supp.*, III, 564, 682. A short time before this the *Nieuwe Rotterdamsche Courant* (March 17, 1918) had declared: "We are between hammer and anvil, between the pressure of hunger and the submarine. Our Government will do its best, but the prospect is not hopeful. We cannot reckon on the ideal[istic] aims of the Associated Powers. The American and English militarists are on precisely the same level as their German opponents." *Ibid.*, p. 562. See also excerpts from Dutch press printed in *Nachrichten der Auslandpresse*, March 19, 1918, p. 6; April 12, 1918, p. 4; April 13, 1918, p. 5; May 30, 1918, p. 6. The *Nieuwe Rotterdamsche Courant* was particularly exercised over Wilson's placing the odium of the seizure on the Dutch and Germans, instead of upon the Americans and British. *Nachrichten der Auslandpresse*, April 8, 1918, p. 3.

as the violation of Belgium by Germany on the same pretext." [45]

Minister Garrett was of the opinion that the chief offense of the United States was not so much the act of seizure as the brutal manner in which it was done, without adequate deference to Dutch sensibilities. The *Nieuwe Rotterdamsche Courant* was frank enough to admit that "the wound is rather to our pride than our pocket." [46] Much of the outburst was also based on a false conception of what had actually happened. Many Hollanders thought that the requisitioning was permanent and that the United States was trying to build up its own postwar merchant marine; others were not properly informed as to the terms of compensation that were being offered. In these circumstances, it is hardly surprising that the Dutch press should refer to the "piratical powers" and the "Associated robbers." There was also some feeling, which the State Department did its best to correct, that the United States was acting alone or as the ringleader in this enterprise; and at first not much emphasis was placed on the fact that the British had simultaneously requisitioned nearly one fourth as much Dutch shipping in their harbors.[47]

---

[45] Quoted in New York *Times*, March 24, 1918. Comment of Dr. Alonzo E. Taylor (November, 1941): "Several years after the war, a Dutch authority on international law told me we had destroyed the last vestige of international law."

[46] *Neut. Press Supp.*, III, 682.

[47] New York *Times*, March 15, 1918; Fayle, *Seaborne Trade*, III, 299. Fayle points out (*ibid.*, p. 300) that over a million tons of Dutch river-and-canal shipping were then employed in German trade; yet threats from Berlin denied the Associated Powers use of ocean-going Dutch ships.

But the passage of time finally dulled the edge of Dutch anger. At the outset a scattering of publicists and newspapers had suggested that the action of the United States might be justified on a legal basis; and as it became clear that Washington was offering generous terms of compensation, and as time permitted a careful study of the law of angary, there was far less disposition to challenge the action of America on legal grounds.[48] Moreover, events nearer home, notably the sand-and-gravel controversy with Britain and the giant German offensive, served to divert public attention from the wholesale requisitioning.

We have yet to note one of the most striking features of this entire incident. As soon as it became clear that the ships had been taken over on a temporary basis and that liberal compensation would be provided, the stocks of the principal shipping companies promptly rose from five to twenty-six points.[49] This was the most eloquent way possible of saying that the Dutch shippers were far better off while chartering their vessels at a profit than while paying wages to idle crews and incurring demurrage charges running into millions of dollars. There can be no question whatsoever that the seizure of the ships was a distinct pecuniary benefit to the owners.[50] Several of the Dutch

---

[48] One prominent journal (*Handelsblad*) had the grace to retract the words " theft " and " robbery," which it had first used. *Neut. Press Supp.*, III, 682.

[49] Garrett to Lansing, April 17, 1918, State Dept., 656. 119/461.

[50] One of my informants who prefers not to be referred to in this connection writes: " The Dutch shipowners wanted to get their ships back into profitable service. The Dutch Government, under pressure from the Germans, were opposed to transferring the ships or chartering them to the United States. I communicated to our agents in Holland the terms on which we would be prepared

newspapers were, in fact, candid enough to admit what the stock market was already advertising.

But does this all mean that the angry outcry of the Dutch was solely or primarily pretense? At the outset we must note that it was definitely to their advantage to pretend injury, even though they may not have felt it.[51] The Germans, in the last analysis, were the parties most aggrieved; and if they had had good grounds for suspecting, as they did suspect, that the Dutch had connived with the Associated Powers to get their shipping into service, the mailed fist would probably have fallen in some fashion. Obviously, the safety of the Netherlands depended in large measure on the loudness and bitterness of the complaint.[52] Nevertheless, a few of the more outspoken Dutch newspapers frankly admitted that the action of the Associated Powers had helped Holland preserve her neutrality. The tonnage arrangements with the Allies which The Hague had agreed

---

to charter the ships and suggested that one way out of the situation would be for us to seize the ships and pay these terms. I received assurances that if we made the kind of payment we proposed, there would be no more than nominal protest. We acted along this line, and my recollection is that the common stock of the Dutch shipping companies rose several hundred percent on their stock exchanges in a single day. They made a nominal protest, but long after expressed verbal gratitude for our action."

[51] Comment of Frank L. Polk (January 13, 1942): "As a matter of fact, while the Dutch protested very vigorously we always had a feeling that that was for the benefit of the Germans more than anything else. . . ."

[52] Also, the Associated Powers might be more willing to make concessions in other quarters if the Netherlands protested strenuously. One prominent Dutch newspaper noted that Germany, despite Dutch complaints, was treating Holland as if she had willingly given up her ships. *Nachrichten der Auslandpresse*, March 19, 1918, p. 6.

to make in the *modus vivendi* had elicited German charges of unneutrality. Now the same result could be accomplished with Holland, not Germany, the party directly injured.[53] Yet when all this has been said, there can still be no doubt that many, if not most, of the Dutch felt a deep and sincere resentment over what they regarded as an illegal and needlessly brutal act.[54]

viii

The immediate official reaction of the Dutch government to requisitioning took two forms: first, a published statement which appeared in the Dutch press on March 30, 1918; and second, a formal protest which was presented to the State Department on April 1 in the form of a memorandum. The published statement asserted emphatically that the seizure of the tonnage was both unfriendly and legally indefensible. The Allied dissatisfaction over the workings of the *modus vivendi* was discussed at length, and it was categorically denied that German threats had anything to do with the alleged breakdown. On the contrary, the agreement was actually being carried out, albeit somewhat slowly; but the blame for delay was placed squarely on the inexplicable holding up of Dutch telegrams by the Allied authorities, and by the British demand, contrary to the agreed terms, that some of the shipping be used in the war

---

[53] *Neut. Press Supp.*, III, 554, 682.

[54] Garrett to Lansing, April 10, 1918, State Dept., 656. 119/463. Chandler P. Anderson quotes Marshall Langhorne, the United States chargé at The Hague, then visiting America, as feeling that the attitude of the Dutch was largely brought about by fear of Germany. This does not, however, square with dispatches coming directly to the State Department from Holland. "Diary of Chandler P. Anderson," April 23, 1918, Library of Congress.

THE NEGOTIATIONS WITH HOLLAND

zone. The published statement further declared that the Netherlands government was merely " giving expression to the feeling of the whole of the Dutch people when it says that it sees in the seizure committed an act of violence against which it protests with all the force of its conviction and its injured national feeling." In conclusion, the familiar charge of inconsistency was touched upon:

> The American Government has always appealed to right and justice. It has always set itself up as the protector of small nations. That it now cooperates in a deed in diametrical opposition to these principles is a manner of acting which cannot be balanced by any expression of friendship or assurances of any mild application of the wrong committed.[55]

The formal protest lodged in Washington was about one third the length of the public protest, and was supplemental to it. The Netherlands government emphasized the fact that the seizure was most unfriendly, particularly in view of the fact that all the ships had been detained in American ports by the refusal of Washington to grant bunkers or licenses. Moreover, The Hague insisted that the hoary law of angary was not applicable in this case, because the ships involved were neutral, and because the law did not envisage such a wholesale requisitioning for the purpose of supplying a belligerent's lack of tonnage. The concluding paragraph was no less emphatic than that of the published statement:

> The seizure is an act of violence committed upon a friendly state whose flag the Government of the United States was bound to respect. To meet this abuse of force

---

[55] *For. Rel., 1918, Supp. 1*, II, pp. 1437-40. See also the Dutch rejoinder of May 13, 1918, which added nothing essentially new. *Ibid.*, pp. 1492-93.

the Netherland Government has no other weapon than that of a protest based on the justice of its cause. In the name of the people of the Netherlands the Queen's Government enters the most energetic protest against the seizure of which their merchant fleet is the victim. It reserves all its rights to full reparation for the injuries resulting from that act of violence.[56]

The official American reply to the Dutch protests was embodied in a formal note presented to the Dutch chargé in Washington on April 12, 1918, and in an explanation given to the press under date of April 13, the latter being a reply to the published statement of the Netherlands government. Secretary Lansing worked over both documents with care, and before putting them in final form sought the reactions of the White House. Wilson made several minor changes and deleted one paragraph out of deference to Dutch sensibilities. His explanation is characteristic.

This is a case of feeling, of hurt pride. Holland *is* helpless against her ruthless neighbour and I do not think that it is wise to rub that fact in or to call upon Holland for an explanation which would either be uncandid or deeply humiliating. I do not think that the note gains in strength by the addition of the passage I have eliminated. It is strong, dignified, and conclusive without it.

You will notice that all the changes I have made have been dictated by the same considerations: the desire to maintain our case without making the situation additionally trying to Holland's pride.[57]

---

[56] *Ibid.*, pp. 1445-46. A strong protest was also sent (March 30, 1918) to the British government for its simultaneous requisitioning of Dutch shipping in British ports. *Ibid.*, pp. 1440-44. There was some little friction between Washington and London over the alleged failure of the British to present a more solid front with the United States at the time of requisitioning. *Ibid.*, pp. 1447-48.

[57] Wilson to Lansing, April 11, 1918, State Dept., 656.119/355½.

The Negotiations with Holland

The official American reply to the Dutch protest invoked "the right of angary," and expressed regret that the Netherlands government should have regarded the action of the United States as so inconsistent with the traditional friendship between the two nations. But, Lansing alleged, the blame for the existing situation lay with Germany's ruthless disregard of neutral rights, which had resulted in the sinking or intimidation of neutral tonnage, and which had contributed to the existing shortage. Lansing further declared that Holland had unwittingly contributed to this situation by the position she had taken. The United States did not complain about Dutch helplessness in carrying out the *modus vivendi*, but the Department of State could not fail to express surprise that Holland should protest against action which had come about as a natural result of her own impotence.[58]

The explanation given to the press by the Department of State, on April 13, 1918, defended the requisitioning as legal;[59] pointed out that the prolonged detention of the

---

[58] *For. Rel., 1918, Supp. 1,* II, pp. 1458-60.

[59] Mr. John Foster Dulles, then Assistant to the Chairman of the War Trade Board, advises the present writer (letters of December 11, 1941, January 9, 1942) that he wanted to base the requisitioning on the "broad sovereign powers over property within our domain"; whereas the Solicitor's office in the State Department wanted to invoke the much narrower principle of angary. Mr. Dulles was called upon to prepare the original typescript drafts of the two statements that were made public defending the American position, those of March 21 and April 13, 1918 (*For. Rel., 1918, Supp. 1,* II, 1417-20, 1460-63), and he has graciously provided the present writer with photostatic copies of both. The first, signed by Wilson, has a number of minor verbal changes, several of them characteristically Wilsonian, in the President's own hand. The second document contains a number of alterations by Lansing, all of them relatively minor, except the

ships in America had been due to the Allied need for the fuel and foodstuffs involved; and sought, by referring to the statements of the Dutch leaders, to show that the *modus vivendi* had broken down under German threats. The public statement further noted that the United States could have requisitioned these ships earlier, but patiently negotiated for seven months until it was evident that no agreement was possible. The American explanation also observed that the Dutch owners were being properly taken care of and that arrangements were being made for sending 100,000 tons of grain to Holland. The concluding paragraph sought to meet the Dutch charges of unfriendliness:

The statement of the Netherlands Government explicitly recognizes the traditional friendship of the United States toward their country. It recognizes that we have heretofore sought to act in accordance with the dictates of right and justice and to champion the interests of smaller nations. It should not therefore hastily be presumed that we have now abruptly repudiated that friendship and been false to those ideals. It is in fact difficult to believe that such a conclusion could be drawn from this exercise of our rights in a manner which scrupulously safeguards and indeed promotes the national interests of the Netherlands.[60]

In retrospect, several features of this disagreeable episode

---

passage at the beginning where the Secretary changed "the right of a *sovereign* to control all private property" to "the right of a *belligerent* to utilize all private property. . . ." This reflects the point of view of the proponents of angary. Significantly, angary was not specifically mentioned in either of these public statements, although Lansing did refer to it in his formal reply to the Dutch protest, on April 12, 1918. Mr. Dulles has kindly agreed that the first of these two photostatic copies may be deposited with the Wilson papers in the Library of Congress; the second with the Food Administration Records in the Hoover Library.

[60] *For. Rel., 1918, Supp. 1,* II, pp. 1460-63.

stand out. Whatever the truth of the Dutch claim that the slow execution of the *modus vivendi* was due to the Associated Powers and not to German threats, the fact is that the ships in question were still unemployed, and that this situation played into Germany's hands. The legal basis of the requisitioning was the ancient right of angary, under which a sovereign could seize foreign property within his jurisdiction, provided due compensation was made. It is true that angary had not been exercised for many years prior to the War of 1914-18, and that it had never been extended to neutral shipping on such a large scale. Nevertheless, American and British publicists were able to make out a lengthy and not altogether unconvincing case in behalf of this practice.[61] As time went on Washington dropped

---

[61] See particularly the statement of William Howard Taft, *ibid.*, pp. 1425-26; also the lengthy memorandum of the British Foreign Office. *Ibid.*, pp. 1469-78. For a listing of the authorities pro and con (mostly pro) in connection with angary, see Vandenbosch, *Neutrality of Netherlands*, p. 306, n. An article published in 1919 analyzed the views of the various authorities in the field of international law on the question of angary. The table reads as follows:

	Before 1870	After 1870	Total
Favorable (provided just compensation)	8	42	50
Favorable (with qualifications)	1	7	8
Unfavorable	2	16	18
Noncommittal	0	3	3

J. Eugene Harley, "The Law of Angary," *Amer. Jour. of Int. Law,* XIII (1919), 275. For a more recent discussion of angary, see Lester H. Woolsey, "The Taking of Foreign Ships in American Ports," *ibid.*, XXXV (1941), 497-506. One writer points out that this right was founded on the same principles as the right of eminent domain; it inheres in the sovereignty of the state. He adds that angary is recognized by the great majority of publicists, and that belligerent control over neutral property is

its references to angary and spoke of requisition—the right of a sovereign to commandeer neutral property within its borders in time of urgent necessity, provided due compensation was paid.[62] This particular dispute was never adjudicated by an international tribunal, and it is therefore impossible to say what such a body would have decided had it been asked for a judgment. All that can be said— and this is all that can be said in most cases of this kind—is that the United States made out a strong case and that its compensation was liberal and satisfactory. Otherwise the Dutch government would undoubtedly have presented numerous claims to the Department of State with great vigor and persistence. The fact that such action was not taken is in itself prima facie evidence of the defensibility of the American position.[63]

ix

During the weeks immediately following the official interchanges over requisitioning, the United States sought to

---

not a transgression of international law, unless explicitly forbidden by treaty stipulations. Malbone W. Graham, Jr., "Neutrality and the World War," *ibid.*, XVII (1923), 704-23. The Dutch, of course, could argue that the need of the United States for the ships was not greater than their own; and they objected bitterly to the delays and various impositions prior to the actual seizure.

[62] George Grafton Wilson, "Taking Over and Return of Dutch Vessels, 1918-19," *ibid.*, XXIV (1930), 702. Another distinguished American international lawyer wrote that requisitioning in such circumstances was legal, provided just compensation was made. James Brown Scott, "Requisitioning of Dutch Ships by the United States," *ibid.*, XII (1918), 356.

[63] The Dutch steamer *Zeelandia*, which is discussed later, was among those requisitioned; but it is to be noted that the owners sought indemnification only for losses incurred during the period of detention prior to seizure. See *post*, pp. 453-55.

deal generously with the hard-pressed Dutch in the matter of provisions. On April 11, 1918, Lansing proposed that three cargoes of grain be consigned to the Netherlands in Dutch ships, and that in return three vessels be sent over to take their place. This offer involved a prolonged correspondence, and the American proposal was finally accepted.[64] At the same time, the Dutch repeatedly sought assurances that no additional shipping would be requisitioned by the United States. Such commitments the United States was unwilling to make, because at some time in the future the situation might become so desperate that further tonnage would have to be commandeered.[65]

The replies of Washington to the repeated Dutch requests for assurances against further requisitioning reveal a persistent attempt to avoid taking a positive stand. On April 26, 1918, Lansing informed the Netherlands chargé that the United States was bound by a pledge of the Associated Governments not to seize any more vessels leaving Netherlands harbors. The chargé was quick to point out that this guarantee did not cover ships coming to the United States from other than Dutch ports.[66] Finally, on May 9, 1918, Lansing came out with an unequivocal statement. He declared that from March 21, 1918, no Dutch vessel would be

[64] *For. Rel., 1918, Supp. 1*, II, pp. 1457, 1484. The British were annoyed that the offer of grain should have been made without consulting them. *Ibid.*, pp. 1463-64.

[65] *Ibid.*, pp. 1465 ff. The negotiations in Washington were complicated by a crisis with Germany late in April, 1918, when Berlin demanded transit across Holland of sand, gravel, and other war necessities. The Dutch Command cancelled army leaves and war seemed imminent; but the dispute was finally adjusted without resort to arms. *Ibid.*, pp. 1797-98 ff.; Turlington, *Neutrality*, p. 131.

[66] *For. Rel., 1918, Supp. 1*, II, pp. 1481, 1482.

requisitioned in a port of the United States, and that " at the present time the thought of such action against any ship flying the Netherlands flag is not even entertained by this Government."

None the less [Lansing concluded] the Government of the United States would be found wanting in candour towards the Netherlands Government should it fail to point out that, while such an eventuality is indeed difficult to imagine, it is yet conceivable that the United States might in the future be confronted by a military situation of such gravity as would compel this Government once more to exercise the undoubted right which pertains to its sovereign authority to requisition Netherlands vessels within its jurisdiction.[67]

The discussions with the Netherlands government over the further requisitioning of tonnage had meanwhile merged with another problem, and had become eclipsed by it. On April 27, 1918, presumably as a reprisal for the seizure of the Dutch vessels, Berlin issued a revised prize ordinance which stated that neutral nations with a " preponderating part " of their merchant marine in the service of the enemy were to have their shipping regarded as of enemy status. The assumption was that Dutch ships sailing without safe-conducts would be sunk.[68]

The significance of this order immediately becomes apparent. At the time of the general requisitioning, Washington had promised Holland 100,000 tons of foodstuffs, provided that vessels were supplied to transport them.[69]

---

[67] *Ibid.*, p. 1487.   [68] *Ibid.*, p. 1491.

[69] The War Trade Board did permit three Dutch ships in American waters to carry grain cargoes to Holland, and later allowed the three ships that had come over as replacement tonnage to do the same thing. Lansing to The Hague Legation, June 20, 1918, State Dept., 656. 119/571a.

Under the new decree of Berlin, the Dutch were afraid to send their tonnage through German-controlled waters. The result was that the people of Holland, whose food supplies were becoming distressingly low, complained bitterly against the American embargo. Yet at the same time the Dutch had some 400,000 tons of laid-up shipping, which, theoretically at least, could have been used to transport these foodstuffs. Washington was somewhat annoyed that Holland should be shifting the responsibility for the food shortage onto the American embargo instead of onto the German prize order; and with reference to Dutch ships within its control the War Trade Board steadfastly refused to issue bunker fuel or allow such vessels to abandon their work in Allied service so that they might transport grain to the Netherlands. President Wilson, for all of his sympathy with the plight of the neutrals, was not pleased by the attempts of Holland to blame the grain shortage on the American embargo rather than on the German submarine threat. He therefore had Lansing inform the Dutch chargé, on July 9, 1918, that the United States must withhold bunkers from the three unrequisitioned Dutch ships in American ports until he had convincing evidence that the Netherlands government had protested vigorously to Berlin against the recent prize order, and until The Hague had given effective publicity to such a protest.[70]

While this dispute was dragging on from May to September, 1918, other significant developments were taking place. In May and June, when the Dutch attempted to defy the British and send an armed convoy to the Dutch East Indies,

---

[70] *For. Rel., 1918, Supp. 1,* II, pp. 1510-11. Lansing and Wilson were not satisfied with subsequent Dutch assurances as to publicity. *Ibid.,* pp. 1517-18, 1518-20, 1530-32.

Washington refused to become involved in the quarrel.[71] Before this controversy was finally ironed out, a hopeful augury appeared when The Hague notified the British, about June 4, 1918, of its willingness to reopen negotiations for a general rationing agreement; the auguries became less hopeful, however, when London greatly displeased Washington by entering into secret discussions without first informing the American officials.[72] On the constructive side, a significant development occurred on June 21, 1918, when the War Trade Board announced its intention of entering into rationing negotiations with the Netherlands Oversea Trust (N. O. T.)—a highly important quasi-official organization set up in Holland for the purpose of guaranteeing the nonexport to Germany of imported commodities.[73] Then, on July 3, 1918, came the Dutch general

[71] *Ibid.*, p. 1504. The convoy was not permitted to sail until the Dutch had first given certain assurances to the British.

[72] *Ibid.*, pp. 1500, 1521-22; Lansing to The Hague Legation, June 28, August 13, 1918, State Dept., 656.119/573, 660. Washington was also displeased when the British opposed an American suggestion of offering the Dutch two months' rations in addition to the 100,000 tons of foodstuffs already promised. *For. Rel., 1918, Supp. 1,* II, pp. 1508-09.

[73] *Ibid.*, p. 1505. The N. O. T. did not receive the direct support or approval of the Netherlands government, as that would have meant approval of the Allied doctrine of continuous voyage. Malbone W. Graham, Jr., "Neutrality and the World War," *Amer. Jour. of Int. Law,* XVII (1923), 718. It appears, however, that in the early days of the N. O. T. the Dutch government recognized it to the extent of guaranteeing the good faith of those persons in charge of it. Maurice Parmelee, *Blockade and Sea Power* (New York, 1924), p. 136. See also Georg Brodnitz, *Das System des Wirtschaftskrieges* (Tübingen, 1920), pp. 44-60; I. Jastrow, *Völkerrecht und Wirtschaftskrieg: Bemerkungen und Aktenstücke zur Methode der englischen Wirtschaftskriegführung* (Breslau, 1917), pp. 23-27. An excellent summary of the N. O. T. and

election; and the subsequent cabinet reorganization gave promise of more satisfactory progress in the direction of a general agreement.[74] Another development of some significance came on August 15, 1918, when the War Trade Board relaxed its embargo on exports to the Netherlands East Indies, in part, it appears, as a means of securing the tin and quinine which Holland had restricted, and in part as a means of fulfilling America's promise, made at the time of the embargo, that efforts would be made to facilitate trade with the Dutch colonies.[75]

X

Throughout the months of September and October, 1918, events moved rapidly in the direction of a tonnage and rationing agreement with Holland—rapidly if we consider the slow progress up to this point. The change of ministry, the increasing distress caused by food shortage, the growing pervasiveness and persuasiveness of American propaganda,[76]

---

other neutral organizations of a similar character may be found in Philip C. Jessup, *American Neutrality and International Police* (Boston, 1928), pp. 50-56.

[74] William C. Bullitt was not optimistic: "In considering Dutchmen as pro-Ally or pro-German, it must be remembered that they are very fundamentally pro-Dutch and anti-everyone else, and that no vital change in the foreign policy of the country is to be expected because of a change of ministry." Memorandum for Gordon Auchincloss, July 9, 1918, State Dept., War Trade Board, Holland Negotiations, vol. IV.

[75] *For. Rel., 1918, Supp. 1,* II, p. 1522; see also *ibid.*, p. 1489.

[76] The growing strength of the American war effort greatly impressed the Dutch. An attaché of the American Legation in Holland overheard two Hollanders in a railway carriage discussing the great exploits of the United States.

"These Americans can do anything," said one of them. "They have brought an army of millions across the ocean in a few

and the turn of the tide in favor of the Allies—all these factors appear to have played a part in bringing the Dutch to terms. The most important of these, of course, was the imminence of an Allied victory and the growing impotence of the Germans to strike back at the Dutch should they make advantageous terms with the enemy. Moreover, the Allies could hardly be expected to increase the attractiveness of their terms to Holland after the German armies had been beaten.

On September 13, 1918, both the United States and Britain approached the Netherlands government with a proposition for reopening negotiations.[77] The Dutch responded rather favorably to the suggestion, and after some little discussion as to the meeting place (the Dutch wanted The Hague; the British, London; the Americans, Washington), it was decided to return to the British capital. As was so often the case during negotiations with the neutrals, the United States and its Associates did not see eye to eye on the question of how the existing problems should be solved. London favored effecting control over imports through the Netherlands Oversea Trust and by an identic agreement (not by separate arrangements) subscribed to by the Associated Powers. The British proposals were strongly objected to by the United States on the grounds that they would lay America open to the charge of having turned her back upon her professions as a neutral. In particular, Washington did not want to become a party to any general agree-

---

months; milliards of money mean nothing to them, and now they have launched a big merchant-vessel in 28 days."

"You are mistaken," replied his friend, perfectly seriously, "the ship was launched in 28 hours." Garrett to Lansing, August 13, 1918, State Dept., 656. 119/755.

[77] *For. Rel., 1918, Supp. 1*, II, pp. 1530-31.

ment which involved the joint application of pressures that it did not approve. As a consequence, the War Trade Board resolutely opposed accepting any type of control over neutral commerce, especially as between neutral countries, that was not brought about by the employment of American shipping, bunkering, or other facilities.[78] The Board was also insistent that the Dutch send their own idle ships to America for the purpose of lifting such commodities as were promised; and it became much provoked when the British, without consulting it, agreed to relax the embargo in anticipation of the imminent signing of a final agreement.[79]

In the closing stages of the negotiations in London, the War Trade Board took the view that it could secure better terms if it waited until the Dutch came to the Associated Powers in the attitude of a suppliant.[80] But the threat of grave disorders, or even of a Bolshevist revolution in Holland, contributed to greater haste than would otherwise have been necessary, and on November 16, 1918, the War Trade Board approved the draft of terms that had been drawn up between the Associated Powers and the Dutch.[81]

---

[78] *Ibid.*, pp. 1524, 1543-44.

[79] *Ibid.*, pp. 1559-61, 1561-63, 1564-65. For other evidence of working at cross-purposes with the British, see *ibid.*, pp. 1527-28. In mid-October the United States, with the reluctant acquiescence of the British, offered the Dutch 100,000 tons of coal a month, provided they stopped their export of foodstuffs to Germany and used their own tonnage to lift the coal. This offer finally merged with the general negotiations. *Ibid.*, pp. 1544 ff.

[80] *Ibid.*, p. 1548.

[81] *Ibid.*, pp. 1565-72. It is to be noted that there were serious troubles with Communists in Holland shortly after the Armistice. For a summary of general conditions see "European Neutrals and the Armistice," *Current History*, vol. IX, pt. 2, pp. 70-75 (January, 1919).

xi

The tonnage and rationing agreement between the Netherlands government and the Associated Powers was signed in London on November 25, 1918—two weeks after the Armistice—by representatives of Holland, Great Britain, France, Italy, and the War Trade Board. It was agreed that idle Dutch ships were to resume their voyages, and that the Associated Powers would provide them with bunker and other facilities for doing so. The Hague further bound itself to recognize the subsequent agreement that was to be entered into between the Netherlands Oversea Trust and the Associated Powers for the purpose of controlling the import of rations. In return for Holland's fulfilling these obligations, the Associated Powers promised to provide the Dutch with certain stipulated necessities, insofar as their own needs would permit. The schedules embodied in the agreement specified large amounts of cereals, feedstuffs, petroleum products, fertilizers, oils and fats, coffee, and other commodities. As compensation for these concessions, the Dutch agreed not only to utilize their shipping but to limit their exports to Germany to certain maximum figures, such as 4,400 tons of condensed milk and 15,000 head of cattle per year. Article 16 specifically relieved the United States of the responsibility of doing anything other than granting licenses and facilitating exports under the agreement. Here we should note that Washington did not want to become committed to a complicated multipartite arrangement that might interfere objectionably with the internal affairs of Holland.[82]

The joint agreement with the Netherlands Oversea Trust,

[82] *For. Rel., 1918, Supp. 1*, II, pp. 1574-83.

concluded December 17, 1918, and designed to implement the rationing arrangements of November 25, was approved by representatives of Britain, France, Italy, and the Netherlands Oversea Trust, but not by the War Trade Board. This was a complicated instrument drawn up for the purpose of guaranteeing that the Netherlands Oversea Trust would keep imports from the Associated Powers from falling into enemy or other objectionable hands. Proper guarantees were also exacted covering the exports of commodities to the three Scandinavian countries, and the Dutch were forbidden to re-export a long list of products, except under special permission from the Associated Governments.[83]

The qualified adherence of the United States to the agreement of December 17, 1918, with the Netherlands Oversea Trust, was effected on December 30 through a letter signed by the London representative of the War Trade Board. At the outset, the Board made it clear that its approval was individual, not joint, and it pointed specifically to certain portions of the agreement which it wished to modify. Article 1 stipulated that Dutch vessels sailing for home ports might be searched by the Associated Powers. The letter of the War Trade Board stated that as far as the United States was concerned such examination would take place only in American ports. Article 3 specified that the Trust would import no goods for consignment to firms on the Allied blacklists. The letter of the War Trade Board declared that as far as the United States was concerned this would apply only to the blacklists of the War Trade Board. Article 17 provided that in certain instances vessels sailing from Dutch ports with certified nonenemy

[83] *Ibid.,* pp. 1584-90.

goods would have to put into control stations, but they would not be delayed any longer than necessary for the examination and verification of their papers. The letter of the War Trade Board pointed out that as far as the United States was concerned this whole article was nonexistent.[84]

The unwillingness of Washington to become a joint subscriber to the Netherlands agreements reflects not only the traditional American antipathy toward entanglements but a desire not to become unduly involved in practices offensive to the neutrals. The qualified adherence of the War Trade Board to both documents, particularly that with the Netherlands Oversea Trust, reveals a determination to avoid anything that could be pointed to by the neutrals as a marked departure from America's position during her prebelligerency period. As we have already noted, Washington was especially concerned about becoming implicated in any practices involving the objectionable searching or rerouting of neutral shipping.[85]

xii

Any review of Holland's position as regards the Associated Powers, and particularly the United States, leads inevitably to the use of superlatives. The Dutch resisted demands for a rationing and tonnage agreement for a longer period and more stubbornly than any of the other neutrals. In fact, it was not until two weeks after the Armistice that the general agreement was signed, and not until three weeks later was that with the Netherlands Oversea Trust con-

[84] *Ibid.,* pp. 1591-92.

[85] It is difficult to assess Dutch public opinion regarding these agreements, because the terms were kept secret at the time, and interest was soon absorbed by problems of peace and reconstruction.

cluded. By this time the Associated Powers were deeply involved in their preparations for the peace conference. It would follow, therefore, that no voluntary agreement which Holland entered into with Washington had any bearing upon the pre-Armistice strangulation of the Central Powers, though it should be pointed out that the American embargo on feedstuffs and other commodities sharply reduced Dutch exports to Germany.

If the Dutch were the most stubborn of all the neutrals in resisting embargo and blockade pressure, it must be emphasized that they were in some ways in the most difficult position of all. For them it would have been suicidal to have gravitated into either camp; hence they remained neutral at all costs—and the cost was high. There can be little question, as bread riots and other disorders attested, that the Dutch, of all the Northern Neutrals, felt the shortage of foodstuffs most critically.

Nor does this exhaust the store of superlatives. Beyond question the requisitioning of eighty-seven Dutch ships was the most spectacular single act of force employed by the United States against the neutrals. This sensational move, together with the hardship produced by the embargo, aroused a degree of bitterness in Holland that apparently was not equaled by any of the other neutral countries. That requisitioning was a blessing in disguise, and that Wilson went to extraordinary lengths to defer to Dutch sensibilities, are facts that seem not to have been fully understood by the people of the Netherlands. We should also note that the United States appears to have had more difficulties with its British Associate in connection with the Dutch negotiations than it had during any of the other discussions with the neutrals. And in the agreements that were finally drawn up, Washington exercised great care to avoid entanglements and inconsistencies.

The Dutch were naturally not appreciative of these favors, if favors they were. They were pinched by the embargo, which was of undeniable legality; they were outraged by the requisitioning, which, from their point of view at least, was of debatable legality. Whether any other nation would have granted them such liberal terms for the ships that were finally seized, one cannot say. But it does seem clear that Wilson showed remarkable patience in waiting for the Dutch to put their tonnage into service, and considerable persistence in resisting the demands of his advisers for strong action. Perhaps the most striking thing about this whole episode is not that the ships were requisitioned at all but that they were not requisitioned sooner.

Chapter VIII

THE RATIONING NEGOTIATIONS WITH SWITZERLAND

i

The landlocked republic of Switzerland ranked fourth in both size and population among the neutrals of Europe. Perched high in the Alps between the two sets of belligerents, it succeeded in maintaining a precarious neutrality throughout the four years of the war. There were times, to be sure, when it appeared that Switzerland would be turned into a battleground, but the mountainous terrain and the efficient Swiss army of some 500,000 men were strong guarantees against having to share the fate of Belgium.

From our point of view several facts must be heavily underscored. First, and perhaps most important, Switzerland was the least self-sufficient, economically, of all the six European neutrals. The rugged mountains and the unfavorable climate militated against agriculture; and both manufacturing and stock raising were more important industries. Altogether, Switzerland relied on the Associated Powers for a large percentage of her foodstuffs; and her dependence on outside sources for grain, especially wheat, was so heavy that the stoppage of these supplies for a few months would literally have brought starvation.

If the Swiss people could not eat without outside assistance, neither could they work. Those who raised cattle relied to a considerable extent on imported oil cake and other feedstuffs. Those who engaged in manufacturing were almost completely dependent on both the Allies and the

Central Powers for raw materials, to say nothing of export markets. The country was so poor in mineral deposits and other basic natural resources that virtually all of the coal and iron products used by Switzerland came from Germany, while virtually all of the cotton fibre, raw silk, petroleum, and other materials of a similar nature came either from or through the Associated Powers. Neither set of belligerents was in a position to provide all the things that the Swiss needed. If either had completely embargoed all of its raw materials, the industry of Switzerland would have been prostrated. The Germans knew that their coal and iron were being used in part to manufacture goods that went to the Allies; the Allies knew that their raw materials were being used to manufacture goods that went to Germany. Yet both groups of belligerents drew such important manufactured goods, foodstuffs, and other commodities from Switzerland that neither could afford to see her collapse.[1] The problem of both the Central Powers and the Associated Powers was to keep Swiss exports to their enemies at a minimum figure, while securing for themselves the largest possible quantity of needed products. Before the United States entered the war both sets of belligerents had negotiated economic agreements with Switzerland looking to this end.[2]

[1] See Rudolf Pfenninger, *Die Handelsbeziehungen zwischen der Schweiz und Deutschland während des Kreiges, 1914-1918* (Zürich, 1928).

[2] See Turlington, *Neutrality*, pp. 132-43. Edward N. Hurley, Chairman of the Shipping Board, gives an interesting case of cross-purposes. Ambassador Jusserand, of France, urged the War Trade Board to license lard for Switzerland. This product was to be exchanged for the German coal which ran the electric power and other plants making war materials for France. The War Trade Board denied the request. Hurley, *Bridge to France*, p. 170.

Quite in contrast with the other neutrals, the problem of controlling Swiss economic life was relatively simple from the Allied point of view. In the first place, Switzerland was not only landlocked and completely surrounded by the belligerents, but as a result of the Allied blockade and the necessity of transporting materials to or from the outside world through either Italian or French territory, it was relatively easy for Rome and Paris to exercise a close scrutiny over Swiss imports and exports. The people of Switzerland could, of course, buy from or sell to Germany and Austria-Hungary, but both of these nations were within the blockade wall and could not readily be used as a conduit pipe to the outside world.[3] Both the Central and the Allied Powers established organizations designed to prevent their own products from passing through the hands of the Swiss to their enemies. That set up by the Allies was called the *Société Suisse de Surveillance Économique* (generally known

---

[3] The principal food products from Switzerland to Germany were cattle, milk, cheese, and chocolate. But as compared with Denmark or the Netherlands this traffic was not important. It was estimated by American experts that the food exports of Switzerland during 1916 fed the populations of the Central Empires for one hour and seven minutes. Other important exports from Switzerland to Germany were cotton cloth, embroidery, silk, clothing, ferrosilicon, calcium carbide, machinery, and watches. On the whole, these were more important than foodstuffs, as most of them could be used in the war effort. Memorandum of the Bureau of Research, War Trade Board (September 13, 1918), entitled "Analysis of the Trade of Switzerland during the year 1917"; also undated memorandum, "Balance of Trade in Alimentary Calories between Switzerland and the Central Powers," both of which are in F. A. R., Hoover Library (Switzerland: Exports and Imports); also confidential memorandum on Switzerland (dated July 12, 1917) from British Embassy, *ibid*. (Switzerland: S. S. S.).

as the S. S. S.), and it was actively participated in by the Berne government.[4]

Throughout the war the Allies received important commodities from the Swiss, notably chocolate, condensed milk, lumber, embroidery, silk, woolen yarn, machine tools, watches, and aniline dyes. After the American Expeditionary Forces (A. E. F.) reached Europe and found themselves in critical need of supplies (lumber, cloth, machinery, refrigerator cars, machine tools, watches), Switzerland assumed an increasingly vital importance.[5] Most of these articles could, of course, have been obtained from the United States, but that would have meant both delay and a drain on the resources of the Associated Powers. Most important of all, bulky articles like lumber would have placed a heavy burden on the already critically small tonnage reserves.[6] So if humanitarian reasons were not

[4] For details of this organization see Jastrow, *Völkerrecht und Wirtschaftskrieg,* pp. 27-37; Brodnitz, *Das System des Wirtschaftskrieges,* pp. 60-71. Much more complete studies are Jöhlinger, *Der britische Wirtschaftskrieg und seine Methoden;* and particularly Max Obrecht, *Die kriegswirtschaftlichen Überwachungsgesellschaften S. S. S. und S. T. S. und insbesondere ihre Syndikate* (Berne, 1920).

[5] Louis A. Rufener, *The Economic Position of Switzerland during the War* (Washington, 1919); also Jacob Ruchti, *Geschichte der Schweiz während des Weltkrieges 1914-1919* (2 vols., Berne, 1928). An exhaustive economic study is Traugott Geering, *Handel und Industrie der Schweiz unter dem Einfluss des Weltkrieges* (Basel, 1928).

[6] The Signal Corps of the A. E. F. alone placed orders for 21,000 Swiss wrist watches with illuminated dials. On October 3, 1918, General Pershing cabled that he needed 200,000 tons of Swiss lumber. McFadden to McCormick, September 10, 1918, F. A. R., Hoover Library (Switzerland: A. E. F.); "Minutes of the War Trade Board," IV, 202 (October 7, 1918).

sufficient, practical considerations pointed to the folly of driving the Swiss into the arms of Germany by too stringent embargo measures. And by the same token, the Germans perceived that it was unwise to drive the Swiss into the arms of the Allies. In short, Switzerland was nicely balanced between the two belligerents, and it was to the advantage of neither to force her into the camp of the other.

ii

In a military sense Switzerland did not become a battleground; but in an economic and ideological sense she did. The bulk of the population spoke German; the rest, French and, to some extent, Italian. Naturally, there were divided loyalties and strong pro-German sympathies among the German-speaking population, especially in the early stages of the war.[7] But the testimony of competent observers generally agreed that on the whole the Swiss were neither pro-German nor pro-Ally but pro-Swiss; and that they were fiercely determined to preserve their neutrality.[8] There can

---

[7] Pleasant A. Stovall, *Switzerland and the World War* (Savannah, Ga., 1939), pp. 50 ff. See also the interview with Professor William E. Rappard, head of the Swiss Commission to the United States, in *Outlook*, CXVII, 287-89 (October 24, 1917).

[8] For Swiss ordinances designed to control the press and propaganda in the interests of neutrality, see Francis Deák and Philip C. Jessup, eds., *A Collection of Neutrality Laws, Regulations and Treaties of Various Countries* (Washington, 1939), II, 1016, 1032. Minister Pleasant Stovall wrote that " Switzerland is playing the War game under difficult circumstances, with great fairness. So far as I could see when in Berne, the country is neutral and the people are very jealous of their neutrality and national integrity." Stovall to Wilson, December 7, 1917, Wilson Papers, Library of Congress. Mrs. Vira B. Whitehouse, head of the Committee on Public Information in Switzerland, wrote: "And, on the

be no doubt, either, that they did this amid great difficulties; for German agents swarmed into Switzerland and used their wiles to turn opinion against the Allies, and later against America. It is a striking fact that at one time the German consulate in Berne had approximately five hundred employees.[9]

We shall have occasion to note that the United States—and this was also true to a considerable extent of the other Associated Powers—treated Switzerland with greater consideration and sympathy than it did the other European neutrals. The gallant determination of the Swiss to preserve both their neutrality and their liberty; their helplessness in the face of blockade and embargo; their splendid tradition of freedom that went back to the legendary William Tell; their humanitarian treatment of invalided prisoners of

---

whole, they succeeded in maintaining a surprisingly just neutrality. I wonder what other country could have done so well with such perplexing problems both human and political." Vira B. Whitehouse, *A Year as a Government Agent* (New York, 1920), p. 193. See also Hugh R. Wilson, *Diplomat between Wars* (New York, 1941), pp. 7 ff. Unfriendly to the Swiss was a report of Commander Hugh Whittall, Chief of British Intelligence in Switzerland (October 14, 1918). He states that a great majority of the Swiss were pro-German at the beginning of the war; that sentiment began to change about the middle of 1915; and that America's prowess turned the tide in 1918. He insists that the attitude of the Swiss was dictated by pure materialism, and that they had in view postwar trade with the victorious Allies. Herron Papers, Hoover Library.

[9] Assistant Secretary of State Phillips to President Wilson, December 12, 1917, Wilson Papers, Library of Congress; Herron to Wilson, July 6, 1918, State Dept., 600.119/226; Wilson (chargé in Berne) to Lansing, April 8, 1918, enclosing a letter of April 5, written by "a prominent American residing in Switzerland." F. A. R., Hoover Library (Switzerland: Federal Food Office, Bread and Cereals).

war—these factors all touched American public opinion and had something to do with the general attitude of the Associated Powers.[10] But from the point of view of the United States one additional factor appears to have dominated all these others. Switzerland, alone among the European neutrals, was a republic—the oldest republic in the world. She was regarded by many Americans as the last stronghold of democracy in Europe, a veritable fortress behind which the troubled continent might be reorganized for democracy. Nor could one overlook the fact that Switzerland, the later home of the League of Nations, was a logical medium through which to approach the Central Powers for peace, and the possible nucleus of a movement for remaking Europe in conformity with the Wilsonian dream.[11]

But aside from these sentimental considerations, there can be no doubt that Switzerland was in several ways the most important of the European neutrals to the Allies.[12]

---

[10] Two Congressmen forwarded protests from their constituents against clamping down an embargo on Switzerland. See State Dept., 654.119, vol. I. On August 8, 1917, the Exports Administrative Board considered a letter (dated July 22, 1917) from the Boston Swiss Society, which had been originally sent to Representative Tinkham in protest against the embargo. "Minutes of the Exports Administrative Board," p. 79. William B. Southworth of Brookline, Massachusetts, wrote to President Wilson, on July 15, 1917, protesting against the embargo aimed at "our little sister Republic," and asserting that she had "a special claim to your consideration." "We Americans," he concluded, "believe ourselves the champions of neutral nations. Let us not begin our war by outraging one of the most helpless." State Dept., 600.119/249.

[11] Herron to Wilson, July 6, 1917, *ibid.*, 600.119/226.

[12] George McFadden, the War Trade Board representative in Paris, cabled: "The neutrality and friendship of Switzerland to the Associated Governments is probably more important from a military point of view than the neutrality of any other continental neu-

As an ideological battleground; as the "front door" of Germany; as a center for spreading American propaganda in Germany; [13] as the means through which information regarding the conditions in the enemy countries might be obtained; as the source of important food supplies and manufactured goods; and, above all, as a military bastion, Switzerland was of the first importance. Had the German armies been able to penetrate the tiny republic, they would have been able to threaten the flanks of both Italy and France. That they did not was due to the resolute determination of the Swiss, and also, in part, to the policy pursued by the United States.[14]

---

tral." See Sharp to Lansing, May 3, 1918, *ibid.*, 654. 119/225. A few days later he added: "No matter from what point of view you regard this subject, whether from political, military or economic, the value of the friendship and neutrality of Switzerland cannot be overestimated." McFadden to McCormick, May 8, 1918, F. A. R., Hoover Library (Switzerland: Federal Food Office, Bread and Cereals). Pierce C. Williams (visiting commercial attaché) wrote from Zurich: "Switzerland is the most important place in Europe, as far as the War Trade Board function is concerned, in my opinion." Williams to McFadden, September 10, 1918, *ibid.* (Switzerland: Exports and Imports). On November 27, 1917, Lansing sent a letter from the Swiss minister to President Wilson, adding that "the Swiss situation is so important that you should be familiar with the negotiations which have taken place because I am not at all satisfied that we are following a policy which will preserve the good-will of the Swiss people and Government." State Dept., 654. 119/64.

[13] The German press in Switzerland outnumbered the French six to one; and alone among the neutral countries newspapers from Switzerland in the German language had free access to readers in Germany. Whitehouse, *op. cit.*, p. 131. Mrs. Whitehouse also reported: "Getting our news into the German Swiss press was the best way of getting it into Germany." *Report of Committee on Public Information*, p. 185.

[14] The American minister in Switzerland, Pleasant Stovall, was

iii

For reasons that have been indicated, the rumors of an American embargo, particularly on foodstuffs, caused much alarm in Switzerland. The Swiss were not only disturbed by the prospect of going hungry but they resented the American misunderstanding of their position, and particularly the charges that they were importing abnormally large quantities of grain with the thought of sending the surplus to Germany. In the hope of correcting these misconceptions, President Schulthess, of the Swiss Confederation, gave to the press a statement, on May 2, 1917, designed to clarify the position of the little republic. He outlined the great dependence of Switzerland on both sets of belligerents, but stressed the fact that the control agencies set up in collaboration with the Allies prevented re-export to the Central Powers. It was true, he admitted, that the Swiss were seeking to import more grain from America than they had secured during the prewar years, but this was due primarily to the cutting off of the Russian and Rumanian supplies. Emphasizing that his people would be starved if the Americans should refuse help, Schulthess deprecated the

---

a boyhood friend of President Wilson. The State Department found that Berne had become the most important neutral capital in Europe from its point of view, and sought to have Stovall replaced by an abler man. But Wilson characteristically took no action in the matter. Phillips to Wilson, December 12, 1917; Wilson to Phillips, December 14, 1917, Wilson Papers, Library of Congress; also Phillips to author, February 25, 1942. Earlier, on July 30, 1917, President Wilson had written Stovall: "I read all your dispatches and so feel that I am in a way keeping in touch with you and you may be sure that my thoughts often turn to you. You are in the midst of a whispering gallery and it must be intensely interesting, though very puzzling what to believe." Baker, *Wilson,* VII, 200.

suggestion that the United States would embargo grain to Switzerland:

> It seems to me out of the question that so high-minded and just a man as President Wilson would lend his hand to a measure which would hit the oldest Republic in the world hard and place it in an extremely critical situation.
>
> We claim the right to live and work. We have done nothing to forfeit this right. He who thinks justly must admit this.
>
> Tell this to your big-hearted American people and carry to them an expression of my sympathy and the greeting of the Swiss people.[15]

A week later, on May 10, 1917, a no less extraordinary appeal was cabled by a group of distinguished Swiss citizens to President Wilson. The list of signers was headed by George D. Herron, a remarkable American idealist-journalist, then resident in Switzerland, who was an enthusiastic supporter of President Wilson's program for a new world order, and who later played a part of some importance at the Peace Conference.[16] The statement read:

> Unless reported decision regarding shipment to neutrals is modified in favor of Switzerland the Swiss people will be in a position of greatest peril. Switzerland is absolutely necessary to your program for a world democracy and is an enthusiastic supporter of that program. Switzerland is the European foothold for the democratic conquest of Europe. We pray you permit America to furnish Switzerland with the necessities of life[.] she deserves it from America.[17]

The British officials, during the discussions with the

---

[15] *Cong. Record*, 65 Cong., 1 sess., app., p. 148.

[16] See Mitchell P. Briggs, *George D. Herron and the European Settlement* (Stanford University, 1932).

[17] State Dept., 600. 119/69; see also Stovall to Lansing, May 12, 1917, *ibid.*, 600. 119/68.

Balfour Commission, were less concerned about taking drastic measures against Switzerland than they were against any of the other neutrals. This was not because of the Swiss appeals for mercy but because it was evident that both Allied supervision over transportation and the establishment of export control regulation by the S. S. S. were operating satisfactorily. The British did recommend, however, that the United States attach a representative to the Allied rationing committee in Paris (which set limits on the imports from the Associated Powers to Switzerland), and that Washington take no action without consulting this committee. The British also pointed out that they were proposing to join with the French in buying up surplus Swiss livestock so as to keep it out of German hands, and they indicated that they would appreciate financial support from the United States in carrying through this scheme.[18]

On June 7, 1917, the Swiss Minister for Foreign Affairs informed the American minister in Berne, Pleasant A. Stovall, that a special mission, consisting of a group of distinguished men, would go to the United States for the purpose of explaining the peculiar economic conditions of Switzerland.[19] Before the delegation arrived Lansing

[18] Memorandum of British Embassy, May 7, 1917, *For. Rel., 1917, Supp. 2,* II, p. 838; also Percy to Hoover, July 14, 1917, National Archives, F. A. A., 1H A19, enclosing memorandum of July 12, 1917. On May 12, 1917, a commercial agreement was signed in Paris by representatives of Switzerland, Britain, France, and Italy. Among other things it resulted in a reduction of cattle exported to Germany by 12,000 head. Stovall was informed that this reduction "was brought about by the threat of action on the part of the United States in grain shipments. . . ." *For. Rel., 1917, Supp. 2,* II, p. 1161.

[19] *Ibid.,* pp. 1167, 1176-77; Stovall, *Switzerland and the War,* pp. 133-34. Stovall stressed the fact that Switzerland was the

quieted the fears of Berne to some extent when he declared, on June 19, 1917, that it was not the intention of the United States " to interfere with the exportation of needed supplies to Switzerland or other neutral European countries where measures have been adopted to prevent the reshipment of such supplies to Germany and its allies, subject always, of course, to the paramount needs of this country and its allies in connection with the prosecution of the war." [20]

George D. Herron had something to do with the appointment of the Swiss commission, and on July 6, 1917, he sent a remarkable appeal from Geneva to President Wilson bespeaking for these men "a sympathetic reception," though he knew " well enough that no mission from this little mother of democracies can have any other than a hearty welcome at your hands." Herron explained that his representations seemed necessary because a systematic campaign of misrepresentation was being carried on in the American press—a campaign which cast doubts upon Switzerland's neutrality and which pictured her as an economic ally of Germany. Herron not only denied such charges with emphasis but placed some of the blame upon German agents. He also expressed his conviction that the Swiss " have been honest in their intentions and efforts to maintain, so far as economic and political favors go, their position as a meeting-place wherein all belligerents may discuss the terms of peace when the moment arrives for such discussion." Herron continued:

" good Samaritan of Europe," and fed large numbers of refugees and interned soldiers. See also Marie Widmer, " Switzerland, the Good Samaritan," *Review of Reviews*, LVI, 186-90 (July, 1917).

[20] *For. Rel., 1917, Supp. 2,* II, p. 1168.

... The whole heart of Switzerland is with America at this moment. There is not a German Swiss, any more than a French or Italian Swiss, who does not look to America to deliver Switzerland from the constant menace to her national being on the part of the Central Empires. There is no other place in the world, not in the deepest heart of America itself, where there is such devout and yearning faith in and support of your program for a world-democracy. It is supremely important to America that Switzerland shall not be left to starve, and she certainly will starve unless the [imminent] American embargo is somehow interpreted in her favor.[21]

iv

During the four months following the arrival of the Swiss commission, on August 15, 1917, to December 5, 1917, when the general commercial agreement with Switzerland was finally signed, the British, French, and American governments at times had more trouble with their Associate, Italy, than with the tiny neutral. The Allies were still permitting large quantities of thrown silk to go from Italy to Switzerland, and from Switzerland to Germany, because Rome was unwilling that one of its most important industries should suffer ruin through the loss of this market. After considerable discussion, the French, British, Italian, and American representatives at Paris signed an agreement by which Britain, France, and the United States were to buy up Italian silk at a minimum price and share the losses equally.[22] A not dissimilar problem was the large inflow of

---

[21] Herron to Wilson, July 6, 1917, State Dept., 600.119/226. While visiting in the United States, Minister Stovall wrote to Wilson (December 7, 1917) testifying strongly that the Swiss were maintaining their neutrality with great fairness. Wilson Papers, Library of Congress.

[22] *For. Rel., 1917, Supp. 2,* II, pp. 1162, 1166-67, 1184-85;

Italian oranges and lemons into Germany through Switzerland, a traffic which Rome was unwilling to stop and which was of importance dietetically to Germany. When the British proposed a similar scheme to buy up the Italian oranges and lemons, Food Administrator Hoover denounced it as "perfectly appalling," and nothing more seems to have been done with it.[23]

The Italians, of course, were more at fault than the Swiss in both of these matters, because it would have been a very simple matter, theoretically, to have stopped the supply at its source. Of more direct concern to Switzerland was the sale of manufactured Italian silks to Germany, for these had considerable military value. After some discussion, and without undue difficulty, an agreement was signed at Paris by representatives of Switzerland, Britain, France, Italy, and the United States, under the terms of which the Swiss agreed to limit their export of silk goods to Germany to 2,500 quintals per annum.[24]

V

Meanwhile the discussions with the Swiss commission in Washington had developed considerable divergence of opinion, and in mid-November, 1917, it was decided to

---

for text see *ibid.*, pp. 1169-70. The profits, if any, were to be shared equally by the four powers, including Italy. Later Italy agreed to share the losses as well. *Ibid.*, pp. 1197-98.

[23] Hoover to Polk, September 22, 1917, F. A. R., Hoover Library (State Dept., Frank L. Polk).

[24] *For. Rel., 1917, Supp. 2,* II, 1172-73. Switzerland later renounced this agreement, and on September 4, 1917, it was replaced with another, the terms of which were essentially the same, except that the Swiss ration was somewhat increased. See *ibid.*, pp. 1175-76; Savage, *Maritime Commerce,* II, 647, n.

NEGOTIATIONS WITH SWITZERLAND

shift the negotiations to Paris.[25] Vance C. McCormick and Dr. Alonzo E. Taylor happened to be there at the time, and it was felt that they, working in collaboration with the Allied representatives who were closely in touch with the situation in Switzerland, could bring the negotiations to a successful termination.[26]

A principal stumbling block in the way of an agreement was the critical shortage of food in the United States, and the consequent reluctance of Food Administrator Hoover to allow the Swiss to have the quantities of wheat they were requesting. Hoover was willing, however, to permit considerable shipments of barley, oats, and rye, although not wheat, which he advised the Swiss to get from the Argentine or elsewhere.[27] But the haul from South America would take twice as much tonnage (assuming that stocks of wheat were available), and that from Australia four times as much, at a time when the Swiss had no chance of getting adequate shipping facilities.[28]

Hoover's figures were doubtless correct, but the food situation could not be considered apart from the military. In late October and early November, 1917, came the collapse of the Italian front; and fear, amounting almost to panic, spread throughout Switzerland lest the Germans, who

---

[25] See Sulzer to Lansing, November 25, 1917, *The Rationing and Tonnage Negotiations with Switzerland* (Washington, 1919), pp. 5-17.

[26] *For. Rel., 1917, Supp. 2,* II, pp. 1177, 1178; T. D. Jones to Wilson, November 16, 1917, Wilson Papers, Library of Congress.

[27] Hoover to Lansing, November 22, 1917, F. A. R., Hoover Library (State Dept., Lansing); *For. Rel., 1917, Supp. 2,* II, pp. 1180-81, 1182.

[28] *Ibid.,* pp. 1180-81; Phillips to Hoover, December 4, 1917, F. A. R., Hoover Library (State Dept., William Phillips).

were reported to be massing troops for such a purpose, drive through the small republic in order to attack Italy on the flank. The United States chargé, Hugh R. Wilson, cabled an alarming description of conditions on November 22, 1917, and stated that he had been urged by the British and French representatives that "no unbearable demands should be made on Switzerland at the present time in view of the prevailing uneasiness." The American chargé urged that Washington take the occasion formally to announce that it would respect the neutrality of the Swiss as long as the Swiss maintained their existing policy. The Chief of the Political Department of Switzerland indicated to Chargé Wilson that such a declaration from the United States would " shut the mouths of the Germans," who were saying that the Americans would violate the territory of Switzerland when it served their purposes to do so.[29]

Secretary Lansing promptly sounded out London, Paris, and Rome as to whether there were any objections to such an American pronouncement. The French and the Italians had none; the British were not actively opposed to this course, though they thought it would look somewhat better if the four principal Associated Powers made a joint declaration. On November 30, 1917, therefore, Lansing instructed Chargé Wilson to present the following communication to the Swiss Minister of Foreign Affairs:

In view of the presence of American forces in Europe engaged in the prosecution of the war against the Imperial German Government, the Government of the United States deems it appropriate to announce for the assurance of the Swiss Confederation and in harmony with the attitude of the co-belligerents of the United States in Europe, that the

[29] *For. Rel., 1917, Supp. 2*, I, pp. 755-56; II, 1179-80; *Diaries of Vance C. McCormick*, November 27, 1917, p. 14.

United States will not fail to observe the principle of neutrality applicable to Switzerland and the inviolability of its territory, so long as the neutrality of Switzerland is maintained by the Confederation and respected by the enemy.

This declaration was communicated to the Berne government on December 3, 1917, and evoked the appropriate expressions of gratitude, as well as assurances that Switzerland would defend her territory at all hazards.[30] The American statement is noteworthy in that it was the only one of its kind given out by Washington during the course of the war.

The decision to issue a declaration regarding Swiss neutrality was not the only step taken by the United States during the last week in November to bolster the morale of Switzerland in the face of possible German attack. On November 26, 1917, Food Administrator Hoover, acting at the request of Secretary Lansing, informed Minister Sulzer in Washington that one third of the 15,000 tons of Swiss shipping then in New York would be loaded with wheat and the balance with other grains.[31] Two days later Dr. Alonzo E. Taylor cabled from Paris to Hoover stating that for military reasons he would "strongly urge" that Switzerland be given some kind of grain until that from the Argentine was ready.[32]

But the great achievement in the direction of strengthening Swiss morale and neutrality—and the high point of

---

[30] *For. Rel., 1917, Supp. 2,* I, pp. 756-59. The Swiss press, which had been somewhat concerned over the arrival of American troops in France, regarded this declaration as a friendly act. *Neut. Press Supp.,* III, 164.

[31] Hoover to Sulzer, November 26, 1917, F. A. R., Hoover Library (Switzerland: Hans Sulzer, Minister).

[32] *For. Rel., 1917, Supp. 2,* II, p. 1182.

Swiss-American relations during the war—was the signing of a rationing agreement at Paris on December 5, 1917. Even though this involved months of discussion, unlike similar pacts negotiated during the war it was completed without undue difficulty.[33] In view of the circumstances that have been outlined, there can be little doubt that the relatively speedy conclusion of the agreement (it was the first to be drawn up with any of the neutrals), as well as the generous terms granted by the United States, reflected in considerable measure the critical military situation.[34]

vi

The Swiss-American agreement of December 5, 1917, was signed by Vance C. McCormick, representing the War Trade Board, and by three representatives of the Berne government.[35] At the outset it was stipulated that Wash-

---

[33] *Ibid.*, I, 404-05.

[34] On November 23, 1917, Lansing cabled to Paris: " Quick action would seem to be necessary to reassure these people." *Ibid.*, II, 1180. McCormick recorded that he regarded the signing of the agreement " at this particular time a most important event due to the strenuous propaganda being carried on in Switzerland to turn that country against the Allies." *Diaries of Vance C. McCormick,* December 5, 1917, p. 20. For a similar statement by McCormick see *For. Rel., 1917, Supp. 2,* I, 405. An undated memorandum, presumably prepared by Dr. Alonzo E. Taylor, and entitled " Comment on British Proposal of Swiss Cereal Needs," states: " The action of the Paris Conference was based upon proposal by the British Minister in Berne as to the serious political and military results that would follow if Switzerland were unable to secure the minimum grain requirements and would be compelled to accede to the maximum German demands in order to avoid starvation." F. A. R., Hoover Library (Switzerland: Federal Food Office, Bread and Cereals).

[35] For text see *For. Rel., 1917, Supp. 2,* II, pp. 1185-96.

ington would furnish the commodities enumerated therein, provided they were not required by the Associated Powers, and provided, in general, that they would not be used to benefit any country or the ally of any country at war with the United States. It was also specifically stated that the sections relating to issuing licenses and to the allotment of certain commodities " shall not be held and construed to constitute an agreement or contract on the part of the United States with the Swiss Government; but shall be held, construed, and regarded as a declaration merely of the domestic or internal administrative action of the said board [War Trade Board] pertaining to the licensing of shipments from the United States." It was further agreed that " Said board does not assume the power or authority to make contracts or agreements binding upon the Government of the United States, nor does it assume to deal in regard to the policy of the United States relating to foreign affairs." This remarkable reservation, which does not appear in any of the other trade agreements made by the Washington government with the neutrals, was obviously designed to shield the War Trade Board from senatorial criticisms to the effect that it was usurping the treaty-making power. In brief, this instrument was a gentleman's agreement which the War Trade Board was honor bound, but not legally bound, to carry out.

The agreement further stipulated that Switzerland would have to fulfill certain conditions if she was to receive licenses for the enumerated commodities. She would have to operate under the rules and restrictions of the S. S. S.; she could not import greater quantities than could be accounted for by genuine Swiss consumption; she would give relevant information to accredited representatives of

Washington; she would transport at cost from the United States 1,000 tons of cargo each month for the Red Cross in Switzerland; she would guarantee that Swiss tonnage coming to America would be fully loaded; and she would agree that, with the exception of those manufactured goods which were free under the S. S. S., none of the items imported from the United States should be used directly or indirectly for the benefit of the enemy. Yet it was provided that, subject to certain safeguards, articles manufactured in Switzerland from American raw materials might be exported to the other neutrals of Europe.

There were then listed the quantities of metal and grain that might be licensed by the United States for shipment to the Swiss. Specifically, there were to be 300,000 metric tons of wheat and rye, 120,000 tons of oats, 140,000 tons of corn, and varying amounts of other cereals. It was definitely stated that from December 1, 1917, until September 1, 1918, the Swiss were to receive a guaranteed allotment of 240,000 tons of cereals for breadstuffs, three fourths to two thirds of which were to consist of wheat. Because of the existing shortage of grain in Switzerland, it was provided that 30,000 of the 240,000 tons should be shipped during December, 1917. (Both of these guarantees, as we shall later note, were to cause a good deal of trouble.) Then followed schedules setting forth the kinds and quantities of mineral oils, sugar, leather, cotton (none of which in any form was to go to the Central Powers), fats, and miscellaneous articles.

Certain general observations remain to be made on this interesting agreement. In comparison with those drawn up with the other neutral countries it was most generous, particularly when we consider the shortage of grain in the

United States. On the one hand, it made provision for liberal allotments of food and other commodities to Switzerland; on the other, it exacted no compensatory restrictions on Swiss exports to the enemy. It was, in fact, the only trade agreement negotiated by the Swiss with any of the belligerents that did not require such compensations; it was the only trade agreement entered into by the United States with either Switzerland or the four Northern Neutrals that did not do so. This was not due, however, to any idealistic impulse but to the fact that the restrictive agreements already drawn up by the Swiss with the Allies, including the S. S. S., were exercising satisfactory control over exports.[36]

Naturally, public opinion in Switzerland was much gratified by the conclusion of the agreement, and by the consequent laying of the specter of starvation. The press, in particular, pointed to the fact that the delivery of grain was guaranteed—this was no mere permission to purchase—and to the further fact that no compensations of any kind were demanded. *Der Bund* (December 19, 1917) was most enthusiastic:

> We never had any doubts of the noble sentiments entertained by the American people and their President with regard to Switzerland. Since the beginning of the war America has stretched out her hand to alleviate the misery and suffering in the belligerent countries, and she has not refused to come to the relief of the sister Republic. Her action is fully appreciated in Switzerland, and is to be numbered among the noble, high-souled deeds of this most unspeakable time.[37]

---

[36] The silk agreement of August 9, 1917, into which the United States had entered, placed restrictions on Swiss exports to Germany.

[37] *Neut. Press Supp.*, III, 245; see also *Nachrichten der Auslandpresse*, December 14, 1917, p. 8.

vii

The excellent impression created in Switzerland by the commercial agreement with America gradually changed to apprehension and even anger as weeks passed by without any considerable deliveries of the promised shipments of cereals.[38] Indeed, on February 25, 1918, nearly three months after the signing of the agreement, Secretary Lansing could declare that the United States had shipped only 2,500 tons, and was approximately 60,000 tons in arrears on its pledged supplies.[39]

Initially, one of the most important reasons for this delay was the unwillingness of the British, who were not parties to the agreement, to co-operate with the Americans in discharging their obligations. Although the British representatives had been present during the Paris discussions which had resulted in the Swiss-American agreement, London held that the United States had merely promised Switzerland the *right to purchase* 30,000 tons of grain a month. But since the Swiss had already been free to buy in various markets, and since the crucial problem was that of tonnage, Washington took the view that it was not only absurd but contrary to the agreement to guarantee supplies and then refuse to take steps to see that they got to their destination. As the War Trade Board cabled its London representative on January 15, 1918:

---

[38] For Swiss opinion see *Neut. Press Supp.*, III, 290, 297.

[39] Lansing to McCormick, February 25, 1918, State Dept., War Trade Board, American-Swiss Agreement, vol. I. For evidence that the Swiss were to some extent responsible for the delay in grain shipments, see McFadden to McCormick, May 8, 1918, F. A. R., Hoover Library (Switzerland: Federal Food Office, Bread and Cereals).

. . . Swiss inability to find the tonnage, under present conditions and control of tonnage, was the very reason why they appealed for relief. The Swiss appeal for relief was an appeal for tonnage; if they were promised relief at all, it could be only in the shape of tonnage, or of wheat in France; any other promise was mere words.[40]

London not only placed difficulties in the way of securing Allied tonnage for the Swiss, but proposed to Washington that Switzerland advance a substantial loan in return for receiving the promised grains. The War Trade Board officials found this suggestion highly objectionable, because it did not "seem to us to be in accordance with international equity to request a loan in performance of what we have already agreed to do." The Board therefore cabled emphatically to its representative in London (January 15, 1918):

The British representatives sat in on the negotiations with Switzerland in Paris and concurred with all the other Allies in the agreement and we feel we must insist upon the agreement being carried out in the greatest good faith. . . . But in any event, tonnage must be found to carry these foodstuffs to Switzerland in accordance with our promise and the promises of the Allies.[41]

---

[40] *For. Rel., 1918, Supp. 1*, II, p. 1595.

[41] *Ibid.*, pp. 1595-96. This instruction was evidently prepared from an earlier and more emphatic draft presumably written by Dr. Alonzo E. Taylor. It reads in part: "The British representatives sat in on the negotiations with Switzerland in Paris and never breathed a word about a loan at the time when it could have been incorporated in the original agreement. I am neither a banker nor a diplomat, but it seems to me that desperate as the war situation is it ought to be possible to carry it through without violation of agreements that have been made with our eyes open. If the Swiss are willing to give Great Britain a loan in return for Great Britain securing the ships which the Allies have promised implicitly to make available to Switzerland, it is from one point of view, of course, a satisfactory arrangement; but that the Swiss

In an effort to break this deadlock, the United States proposed to Great Britain that the Associated Powers provide the Swiss with a two-month supply (60,000 tons) out of their own stocks, with the expectation that this would tide Switzerland over until the Argentine crop was ready. When the British showed reluctance to fall in with this scheme, Acting Secretary Polk instructed Ambassador Page, on January 19, 1918, to threaten drastic measures. Polk's statement read in part:

We are unable to regard the suggested British interpretation . . . as anything else than an indefensible misconstruction of the clear meaning of Paris action [Swiss agreement] . . . . If fulfillment is deserted by Allies and left to us on the ground that this is purely an agreement between United States and Switzerland, we will be compelled to withdraw this grain from our allocations to Allies and take ships out of Allied service into Swiss-grain trade. Since undertaking must be carried out if Switzerland is not to be driven into arms of Germany, it is important to have Allies fulfill undertaking rather than to have United States fulfill it independently, since Switzerland will regard England and France as having turned back on them and passed responsibility to United States.[42]

No steps were taken immediately, however, to carry out this threat.

---

will regard it as sharp practice can not be doubted. It is, however, probable that they have submitted to so much sharp practice in the past that they will discount that if they get the tonnage." Undated memorandum, entitled "Comment on British Proposal of Swiss Cereal Needs," F. A. R., Hoover Library (Switzerland: Federal Food Office, Bread and Cereals). This memorandum was almost certainly written by Dr. Taylor. It reflects his style; indicates that it was written by one who took part in the Paris negotiations; and is in effect a summary of a shorter cablegram signed at about the same time by him.

[42] *For. Rel., 1918, Supp. 1*, II, pp. 1596-97; also pp. 1594-95.

viii

By early March, 1918, the Swiss grain situation had become critical. So little of the promised stocks had been moved that there was actual danger of starvation unless something could be done promptly and effectively.[43] The position of the United States by this time had come to be worse than a few weeks before, inasmuch as Washington had relied upon tonnage secured by the *modus vivendi* with Holland to help out the Swiss; and with the breakdown of this temporary agreement relief could no longer be expected from Dutch shipping.[44]

Growing Swiss anger against the United States had two ominous aspects. First, shipments of lumber and other commodities from Switzerland for the A. E. F. were becoming increasingly important, and the American military officials began to fear that Berne might retaliate by stopping such supplies. (The lumber problem was later solved by a formal agreement.) [45] Second, the Germans were holding out to the Swiss seductive promises of grain supplies from the Ukraine in return for closer economic co-operation. So

---

[43] See the long and bitter letter of the Swiss minister in Washington, Hans Sulzer, February 20, 1918, *ibid.*, pp. 1599-1603; also Sulzer to Lansing, April 1, 1918, F. A. R., Hoover Library (Switzerland: Hans Sulzer, Minister).

[44] On March 14, 1918, Dr. Taylor read a letter to the War Trade Board from General Pershing to the Chief of Staff, setting forth the need of adopting extraordinary measures to relieve the Swiss. "Minutes of War Trade Board," I, 496.

[45] On May 1, 1918, the Swiss government signed an agreement with representatives of Britain, France, Italy, and the War Trade Board, under the terms of which a considerable amount of lumber was to be prorated among the Associated Powers, including the United States. For text see *For. Rel., 1918, Supp. 1*, II, pp. 1613-18.

desperate was the plight of Switzerland that the prolonged nonfulfillment of American promises and the prospect of substantial deliveries through Germany were threatening to throw the Swiss into the arms of the Germans.[46] Such a development would not only have deprived the A. E. F. of the urgently needed supplies, but would have exposed the Italian and French flanks to direct German attack through Switzerland.

Recognizing fully the dangers inherent in this situation, Lansing cabled the legation in Berne on March 1, 1918: "The difficulties in the way are almost insuperable but there is full realization of the obligation of the United States in this regard and this obligation will be performed even though it becomes necessary to deprive the Allies and ourselves of foodstuffs which are imperatively required."[47] When Chargé Wilson conveyed this pledge to the Swiss President, the latter stated that "he was touched and thoroughly recognized America's noble attitude in the matter."[48] The assurances from Washington were promptly made public in Switzerland and created a favorable impression.[49]

ix

The United States took steps to translate its promises

---

[46] *Ibid.*, pp. 1604-05; Sharp to Lansing, March 13, 1918; Stovall to Lansing, March 7, 1918, State Dept., 654. 119/147, 144; enclosure from Skinner to Lansing, March 12, 1918, F. A. R., Hoover Library (Switzerland: Supplies from the Ukraine); Stovall to Lansing, April 1, 1918, State Dept., 654. 119/170; Pershing to Adjutant General, March 12, 1918, *Rationing and Tonnage Negotiations with Switzerland*, pp. 37-38.

[47] *For. Rel., 1918, Supp. 1*, II, p. 1603.

[48] *Ibid.*, p. 1604.   [49] See New York *Times*, March 11, 1918.

NEGOTIATIONS WITH SWITZERLAND

into action when, late in March, 1918, it proposed to make available for Swiss relief 64,000 tons of shipping, "despite the urgent need of utilizing all available tonnage in purely national service." The only condition attached to this offer was that Berlin provide satisfactory safe-conducts for the vessels engaged in Swiss service.[50] Prior to this time the Germans had granted immunity to neutral ships carrying cargoes to Cette, in France, for ultimate delivery to Switzerland;[51] but the extension of immunity to enemy vessels was another matter. After considerable negotiation Berlin agreed to issue safe-conducts to such shipping, with the reservation that this protection would not become completely effective for three months, because of the time needed to countermand existing orders issued to submarine commanders.[52]

An additional three-month delay would unquestionably have proved disastrous to Switzerland. German propaganda was making much of America's failure to deliver the grain that had been promised; Swiss apprehension of Germany was growing; labor unrest was on the increase; and revolu-

[50] *For. Rel., 1918, Supp. 1*, II, p. 1606.

[51] A total of 472 such safe trips had been made when, in March, 1918, a German submarine sank the Spanish steamer *Sardinero*, which was carrying American grain under Swiss charter and flying the Swiss flag, a large white cross on a red background. This unfortunate affair created a most unfavorable impression in Switzerland, where it was alleged, whether with foundation or not, that the Germans had attacked the ship because they mistook the Swiss flag for the Red Cross. New York *Times*, April 13, 1918; Haskell (U. S. consul at Geneva) to Lansing, March 8, 1918, F. A. R., Hoover Library (Switzerland: General).

[52] *For. Rel., 1918, Supp. 1*, II, pp. 1610, 1611-12; New York *Times*, April 26, 28, 1918; "Minutes of the War Trade Board," II, 246 (April 26, 1918).

tion was in prospect.⁵³ On April 30, 1918, the War Trade Board representative in Berne (his opinion was concurred in by Minister Stovall) cabled that if it was possible to follow definite assurances by a " prompt expedition of wheat ships, even at the cost of real sacrifices in other directions, [the] political and moral effect here would be almost incalculable. In my opinion the critical moment for decisive action has arrived." ⁵⁴

Three days later, on May 3, 1918, Acting Secretary of State William Phillips reported to Stovall that decisive action had been taken. Two grain ships for Switzerland, flying the American flag and escorted by units of the United States Navy, were en route to France. Phillips believed that this extraordinary step of diverting naval strength from operations against the enemy should be sufficient proof of Washington's determination to honor its obligations, par-

⁵³ On April 2, 1918, Sulzer, the Swiss minister, addressed a personal letter to Lansing: " May I appeal to you, Mr. Secretary, not to leave Switzerland in the lurch. Do not forget her unity and strength, both internal and external, are at stake." Lansing Papers, Library of Congress. Chargé Wilson sent to Lansing a long letter from an unnamed American in Switzerland who had interviewed a number of prominent Swiss. He noted that German propagandists were capitalizing on the grain delay, and concluded that the Swiss question might " indeed become, in certain eventualities, the pivot on which the whole cause of America and the Allies would swing." He added: " I find that throughout all the smaller nations lying between Switzerland and Constantinople, the action that America shall decide upon in this particular issue is being regarded as a kind of test of the new international morality, this super-morality, indeed, which the world is beginning to really expect of the United States of America." Wilson to Lansing, April 8, 1918, F. A. R., Hoover Library (Switzerland: Federal Food Office, Bread and Cereals).

⁵⁴ *For. Rel., 1918, Supp. 1*, II, pp. 1618-19.

ticularly in view of the fact that American exports to neutrals and cobelligerents had reduced the consumption of grain in the United States until it was "substantially below the per capita consumption of wheat in Switzerland." [55] As Phillips evidently expected, both Swiss official and public opinion was deeply and favorably impressed by this energetic action on the part of Washington.[56] The Swiss Chief Executive stated to Stovall that "he was deeply touched by this new evidence of America's good will of which he had never been in doubt." He added that "America was [the] only country on which [the] Swiss could rely at the present time and that without America they would be lost." [57]

By May 22, 1918, the United States had increased the number of ships en route to Switzerland under American convoy to five, with a total of over 30,000 dead-weight tons.[58] On May 31, the Swiss minister in Washington could express to Vance C. McCormick his deep satisfaction that since April the deliveries of grain tonnage had been "approximately the 60,000 tons agreed upon." He added:

---

[55] *Ibid.*, pp. 1619-20.

[56] *Neut. Press Supp.*, III, 768. There was some dissent on the part of the pro-German newspapers.

[57] *For. Rel., 1918, Supp. 1,* II, p. 1620. Dr. Herron and his Geneva advisers had suggested the convoy as early as April 6, 1918, stressing particularly the excellent moral effect that such a move would have. *Ibid.*, pp. 1607-08. See also Stovall to Herron, May 8, 1918, with an attached note written by Herron in 1924. At this date Herron remembered that Switzerland was in danger of being thrown into German arms; that Germany was prepared to furnish wheat if the United States failed; and that Germany hoped the United States would fail. Herron Papers, Hoover Library.

[58] *For. Rel., 1918, Supp. 1,* II, p. 1624.

I wish to express to you my heartfelt thanks for your untiring efforts in our behalf, which I appreciate all the more as I realize fully the great difficulties you have to overcome. I have more than once cabled my Government never to lose faith in the United States as Switzerland would not be left in the lurch no matter how great the difficulties to be contended with, and I am glad to see my assurances fully verified.[59]

By August 12, 1918, the Swiss government could report with satisfaction that the three-month period for notifying the German submarine commanders of the safe-conduct system had passed; and with this announcement it was evident that the tiny republic's shipping worries had been largely removed.[60]

There can be no doubt that the action of the United States in convoying grain that it needed in ships that it needed, in order to discharge its solemnly contracted obligations, had a salutary effect on Swiss opinion. The press was enthusiastic in its appreciation of the " noble action " of the United States; and American observers in Switzerland could report that this gesture had done more than anything else to counteract the pernicious effect of German propaganda.[61]

X

Closely connected with the Swiss grain problem, because it involved tonnage, was the proposal made by Berne that

[59] *Ibid.*, pp. 1625-27.   [60] *Ibid.*, pp. 1637-38.

[61] See the lengthy report of William P. Kent (U. S. consul at Berne) to Lansing, June 17, 1918, F. A. R., Hoover Library (Switzerland). Stovall cabled to Lansing on May 10, 1918: " Swiss papers German and French full of praise of noble action of United States in sending wheat ships for Swiss trade under convoy. Splendid example for Allies; splendid challenge to Germany. Such action worth all the propaganda that can be started

the considerable number of German and Austrian ships in Spanish waters, totalling some 130,000 dead-weight tons, be chartered or purchased by Switzerland for the purpose of transporting grain and other necessities. This scheme was seriously discussed for the first time early in May, 1918, and Washington promptly consented to it in principle. The French were not at all enthusiastic about the proposal, and they vigorously opposed that part of it which provided that the money realized by the enemy owners be deposited in Spanish banks. Paris feared that these funds would be employed to further the already active German propaganda in Spain. The British likewise raised numerous objections; and in September, 1918, the whole project fell through. Basically, the reason was that Germany would not consent to Allied terms, and the Allies would not consent to German terms. Each of the belligerents feared that the other would gain the more. The representative of the War Trade Board in Paris learned through a letter from the British Foreign Office that the London officials discouraged the whole transaction because they felt that it was wise to keep these German ships in an unseaworthy condition; otherwise they would be able to compete with the British immediately upon the close of the war. There were unquestionably other and perhaps more important objections from the British point of view; but this is an interesting case of neutral interests having suffered because of considerations involving after-the-war trade.[62]

---

here by amateurs." State Dept., 654. 119/246. This allusion was doubtless to Mrs. Whitehouse. *Post*, p. 463, n.

[62] *For. Rel., 1918, Supp. 1*, II, pp. 1622 ff.; Lansing to Paris Embassy, July 9, 1918; Acting Secretary Phillips to Paris Embassy, June 10, 1918, State Dept., 854. 85/12, 32a; "Minutes of War Trade Board," III, 195-96 (July 15, 1918).

The problem of tonnage for Switzerland, and consequently of the Swiss grain supply, was still an object of considerable concern to the very end of hostilities. There was much hunger and unrest in the Alpine republic; and the Swiss claimed that up to September 26, 1918, they had received only 157,000 tons of cereal from the United States, as compared with the 240,000 tons promised. The commercial agreement of December 5, 1917, expired by limitation on September 30, 1918, but certain important aspects of it were extended by Washington pending the negotiation of a new pact. Consideration was being given to a more general agreement, entered into by all the Associated Powers, when the fighting came to an end, and as a consequence the necessity of a close supervision of Swiss affairs was no longer so imperative.[63] It is true that the problems of continuing to feed Switzerland and of solving the critical economic conditions that confronted the republic were an important phase of the post-Armistice period, but they are not relevant to our present study.

xi

In surveying American relations with Switzerland during 1917 and 1918, we may safely conclude that the United States had less to apologize for than it had in its dealings with any of the other European neutrals, except possibly Spain. Throughout the Swiss negotiations Washington revealed a sympathy with the plight of Switzerland that did not extend to some of the other neutrals, notably to the Netherlands.[64] This was doubtless due in part to a com-

---

[63] *For. Rel., 1918, Supp. 1,* II, pp. 1647-59.

[64] For warm expressions of sympathy for Switzerland, see *ibid.,* p. 1627; Lansing to Sulzer, December 3, 1917, State Dept., 654.

munity of interest between the oldest democracy of the Old World and the oldest democracy of the New. But no less important, and probably more important, was the necessity of keeping Switzerland out of the embrace of the enemy, and of keeping the enemy from forcing its way into the small republic. There were other considerations as well, such as supplying the A. E. F.; and there can be no doubt that it was definitely to the advantage of the United States to keep Switzerland strong, flourishing, and neutral. In this particular situation generosity was the best policy.

We have already noted that the trade agreement with Switzerland embodied terms that were extraordinarily favorable to that republic; and the attractiveness of America's concessions doubtless explains in large part why this agreement was the first to be accepted by any of the neutrals. When the United States encountered difficulty in fulfilling its promises to supply grain, it refused to fall in line with the British suggestion of evading its obligations on a technicality. And when Washington found that it could carry out its pledges only by sending food that its own people needed, in ships that its own army needed, convoyed by naval vessels that the Associated Powers needed—it did so. It is true that the amount of material and effort thus diverted was not large when one considers the entire war effort, and it is also true that this diversion had no demonstrable bearing whatsoever on the prolongation of the war. Nevertheless, it is well worth emphasizing that America was so determined to fulfill her plighted word that she took energetic action counter to her own short-run interests and to those of her Associates.

119/64. In making concessions to the Swiss, Hoover wrote on December 1, 1917: "I have gone farther than I should have with anybody else." *For. Rel., 1917, Supp. 2*, II, p. 1183.

CHAPTER IX

THE RATIONING AND TONNAGE NEGOTIATIONS WITH SPAIN

i

The kingdom of Spain was by far the largest of the European neutrals both in territory and in population. Primarily an agricultural and grazing country, it was in many ways the most self-sufficient of the six, at least as regards foodstuffs. For this reason, the people could not be starved into submission by blockade or embargo; but, as was true of all the other neutrals, they could be seriously discommoded by the cutting off of certain necessary raw materials, particularly oil and cotton. At Barcelona, the Manchester of Spain, there was a flourishing textile industry, which employed, both directly and indirectly, some 300,000 workers. If this large group of men had been thrown out of work by a cotton famine, as at times seemed likely, the government would have been confronted with serious economic and political difficulties.

In spite of her size and population, Spain was in some respects the least important of the neutrals from our point of view. She was the only one not in a position to send considerable quantities of manufactured goods or foodstuffs to the Central Powers. There were, in fact, only two ways by which anything could be transported to Germany.[1] The

[1] Spain was of particular value to Germany as a means of maintaining wireless communication with the outside world. See Lansing, *Memoirs*, p. 329.

272

first was through other countries; and Allied surveillance or the British blockade took care of this problem. The second was by German submarines. Obviously not much could be sent through such media, though the Allies were constantly worried about the possibility that some quantities of oil, rubber, and other necessities were finding their way to Germany on U-boats. Yet if the Spaniards did not enjoy the advantage of trade with the Central Powers, they did enjoy the very great advantage of being the only one of the six neutrals completely invulnerable to German invasion. The only way that Berlin could strike back at Spain for close co-operation with the Associated Powers was to torpedo her ships, which the U-boats were already doing with distressing frequency. Throughout the war Spain lost nearly 170,000 gross tons of shipping to German ruthlessness, or about one fifth of her entire merchant marine.[2]

Two other general considerations must be mentioned. First, except for Denmark, Spain controlled the smallest merchant marine of all the maritime neutrals of Europe; and as she needed most of it for herself, the Allies did not exert such great pressure to secure it as they did on Holland, Denmark, and Sweden. Second, the Spaniards were generally regarded as pro-German, perhaps more so than any of the other neutrals, with the possible exception of Mexico.[3] The all-powerful clergy was reactionary and undemocratic, and hence disposed to sympathize with the autocratic methods of Germany. The army and the educational system,

---

[2] A total of 152,387 tons was sunk by submarines, 16,104 tons by mines. Fayle, *Seaborne Trade*, III, 466.

[3] George Creel found that German propaganda was strongest in Spain and Mexico. Creel, *How We Advertised America* (New York, 1920), p. 303.

especially the army, were pervaded with German influence. But it is necessary to add that a great deal of this feeling was anti-Ally rather than pro-German. For one thing, there was a long and well-founded tradition of hatred for both Great Britain and France. Moreover, the Spanish-American War of 1898 was not twenty years in the past when the United States entered upon hostilities with Germany; and one could hardly have expected the active participation of the Yankees to increase Spanish sympathy for Allied objectives.[4]

Although, as we have seen, much of the sentiment in favor of the Germans sprang from natural causes, a large amount of it was artificially cultivated. A veritable hotbed of espionage and propaganda activity was to be found in the some 75,000 Germans interned or refugeed in Spain. Throughout the war the country was turned into a battleground for ideological supremacy between the pro-German and pro-Ally factions; and although it would be unwarranted to say that at any time the German element controlled majority opinion, it seems clear that by the late summer of 1918, when Allied successes on the Western Front gave promise of a decisive victory, the tide of opinion in Spain had turned heavily in favor of the Associated Powers.[5]

---

[4] On this general background see T. H. Pardo de Tavera, "Spain and the Great War," *Century Magazine*, LXXIII, 360-65 (January, 1918); Luis A. Bolin, "Spain and the War," *Edinburgh Review*, CCXXVI, 134-52 (July, 1917); Sanford Griffith, "The German Myth in Spain," *Outlook*, CXVI, 364-65 (July 4, 1917). See also Creel, *op. cit.*, p. 336.

[5] George McFadden, War Trade Board representative, wrote from Paris (September 5, 1918): "The Spaniards are first pro-Spanish, and secondly, pro-winner, and with the improvement in the military situation, pro-Ally sentiment in the country is increasing." *The Trade and Shipping Negotiations with Spain* (Wash-

Nevertheless, Madrid appears to have made a genuine attempt to steer a neutral course throughout the conflict.[6] There was not, in fact, any reasonable alternative. To enter the war on the side of the Allies was unthinkable; to enter the war on the side of the Germans was useless, for Spain could render little direct aid, while at the same time she would be vulnerable to French and British attack.

Even though Spain was in some ways on the periphery of the conflict, the fact nevertheless remains that she was of vital importance to the Associated Powers. The Iberian peninsula was so located as to flank Atlantic shipping routes, and the Allies were repeatedly being disturbed by reports, some of them well-authenticated, that German submarines were getting fuel and valuable shipping information from Spain, either directly or by wireless.[7] Of positive and tangible importance were the commodities that Spain was in a position to sell to the Associated Powers. Iron ore was

---

ington, 1919), pp. 83-85. Will Irwin gives a good example of the ingenious anti-American propaganda of the Germans in *Propaganda and the News* (New York, 1936), p. 189. For the law of July 7, 1918, which was designed to suppress foreign propaganda and agitation that might involve Spain in trouble, see Deák and Jessup, *Neutrality Laws,* II, 929-30.

[6] The King, Alphonso XIII, was reliably reported as personally not liking the Germans and definitely favoring a neutral course. Wilson (Madrid chargé) to Lansing, November 23, 1917, State Dept., 763. 72111 Sp 1/110.

[7] Josephus Daniels to Vance C. McCormick, March 15, 1918, *ibid.,* 652. 119/2636. General Pershing gives definite data as to intercepted wireless messages regarding shipping which were sent from Spain to German quarters. John J. Pershing, *My Experiences in the World War* (New York, 1931), I, 122. Comment of Dr. Alonzo E. Taylor (November, 1941): "Admiral Sims told me in the summer of 1918 that he had no convincing proof that German submarines refueled in Spanish territorial waters."

indispensable to Britain and pyrites were required by the United States; while the A. E. F. was in urgent need of Spanish timber, mules, horses, and other supplies and provisions. Much of this material, to be sure, could have been secured from the United States, but with the tonnage situation in a critical state, the supply from Spain was doubly important. In short, the Spaniards needed British coal and American oil and cotton; while the Allies needed Spanish supplies of various kinds.[8] The basis therefore existed for a natural and a profitable exchange; and the possibilities of a satisfactory bargain were enhanced by the fact that (unlike the case of the other five neutrals) the Germans could not interfere by threatening armed invasion.

No understanding of the negotiations that will here be described would be complete without some reference to Spanish national characteristics. The mañana spirit is proverbial; the sensitiveness and out-at-the-elbows pride of the Castilian are traditional. Obviously we have here no stolid Scandinavians, but a people in a strong bargaining position who would have to be handled carefully.

ii

The Balfour Commission, during its visit to the United States in April and May of 1917, devoted some attention to the Spanish problem, though for reasons that have already been indicated it was more interested in the Northern Neutrals. The British were particularly anxious

[8] The Chief of the Bureau of Foreign and Domestic Commerce concluded in a letter to Frank L. Polk (June 18, 1917): " In the last analysis I think we can do without the supplies that we get from Spain much better than Spain can afford to do without our products." State Dept., 600. 119/266.

that the exports of oil from the United States to Spain should be carefully controlled, lest they be used for the refueling of German submarines. In general, the Commission concluded that the attitude of Madrid made it advisable to apply the " very strongest " embargo pressure if a continued flow of supplies from Spain to the Allies was to be assured.[9] Specifically, England needed Spanish iron ore, copper, and lead in her all-important munitions industry; Spain, in exchange, required British coal. But primarily because of the submarine hazard the Spaniards were refusing to employ their ships in this run and were insisting that Britain use her own dwindling tonnage. More than this, they were demanding that the British allocate twenty per cent of their cargo space for carrying Spanish oranges— a fruit which was not urgently needed in England.[10] The Spaniards held the whip hand because they threatened to embargo their own supplies of minerals and to transport the necessary coal from the United States in their own ships, in which case England would neither sell her coal nor get the desperately needed ores. This critical situation prompted the Balfour Commission to urge the United States to employ prompt pressure by withholding supplies of coal.[11]

Secretary Lansing fell in with British desires, at least in

[9] British memorandum of May 7, 1917, *For. Rel., 1917, Supp. 2*, II, pp. 832-33. This was preceded by a note from Balfour to Lansing (May 5, 1917), in which Balfour suggested that the United States make it clear that no American coal would be available to the Spaniards unless they co-operated satisfactorily with England. *Ibid.*, pp. 1199-1202.

[10] *Ibid.*, I, 594. Americans were complicating the problem by chartering Spanish tonnage for the safe trades.

[11] The British Embassy supported these recommendations, and pointed out that 40,000 tons of coal had recently been landed in Spain. *Ibid.*, II, 879, 881.

part, when he informed Madrid that because of the necessities of the Associated Powers it might prove necessary to restrict or prohibit the export of coal to the European neutrals. If, however, the Spaniards should continue to supply iron ore to England, " it may be possible to facilitate the exportation of limited amounts of coal to Spain." [12] This is noteworthy as being perhaps the earliest threat to use the American exports club for the purpose of forcing a neutral into co-operation with one of the Allies.

iii

The rumored imminence of an American embargo caused considerable disquietude in the cotton manufacturing center of Barcelona, but for reasons that we have noted the people of Spain seem to have been somewhat less concerned than those of the other five European neutrals.[13] Even following the issuance of Wilson's first embargo proclamation, no export restrictions were placed upon the Spaniards as rigid as those upon the Northern Neutrals. The War Trade Board adopted a policy of licensing shipments of various commodities to Spain, provided that the consignors and the consignees were unobjectionable. But the Board was particularly cautious about issuing permits for the export of oil, in view of the fact that the German submarines were allegedly refueling in Spanish ports, and in view of the further fact that there were no dependable means of determining the ultimate destination of the fuel.[14]

---

[12] Lansing to Willard, May 22, 1917, *ibid.*, pp. 1202-03.

[13] *Neut. Press Supp.*, II, 466. It was reported that Catalonia, which consumed 35,000 bales of cotton each month, had only 65,000 left. See also *ibid.*, III, 182; IV, 12.

[14] *For. Rel., 1917, Supp 2,* II, pp. 1209, 1210.

From July, 1917, when Wilson issued his first embargo proclamation, until early December, 1917, when the War Trade Board finally instituted a virtually complete embargo on exports to Spain, several interesting problems kept the wires busy between Madrid and Washington. During the late summer and early autumn of 1917, the chief concern of the United States was over the supply of Spanish pyrites, which were indispensable for the manufacture of an adequate supply of sulphuric acid. A plan was under discussion for the sending of several cargoes of pyrites to America in return for equivalent cargoes of oil to Spain, but much to the dissatisfaction of Madrid this scheme did not work out as anticipated.[15] During November, 1917, the problem of securing supplies from Spain for the A. E. F. came up conspicuously for the first time, and particular concern was shown for lumber, on which the Spanish government had placed an export embargo.[16]

Throughout the early months of these discussions, the United States ambassador in Madrid, Joseph E. Willard, suggested to his superiors the wisdom of following a liberal policy in the licensing of shipments of coal and oil to Spain. Among other things, he had in mind strengthening the hands of the existing ministry, which he regarded as distinctly favorable to the Allies.[17] He also felt that a liberal policy should be pursued regarding the shipment of cotton to Spain, a scarcity of which was already being felt in the textile centers. But the Department of State was less inclined to be generous than its representative in Spain; and

---

[15] *Ibid.*, pp. 1205-06, 1210-12.

[16] *Ibid.*, pp. 1212, 1213, 1214; *Diaries of Vance C. McCormick*, November 25, 1917, p. 12.

[17] *For. Rel., 1917, Supp. 2*, II, pp. 1206-09.

by December 1, 1917, Lansing could inform Willard that everything was being held up that could be without giving the impression of an absolute embargo.[18]

Interestingly enough, the embargo on cotton created problems at home as well as abroad. Not only did the Spanish manufacturers want the fiber but the Southern growers were also anxious to dispose of their product. Some of them had already contracted for tonnage, which was involving them in heavy losses; and they were bringing strong pressure to bear on Washington to secure the issuance of licenses.[19] On December 1, 1917, Lansing cabled Willard asking him whether in his opinion the shipment of 30,000 bales spread over a period of several weeks would be undesirable. The American ambassador, who already suspected that the Spanish manufacturers were trying to accumulate a comfortable reserve of raw cotton so as to protect themselves against an embargo, urged that no further licenses be granted until January 1, 1918, and not in any case until after a further exchange of views. He suggested that the refusal to issue such permits be based entirely on the grounds of American needs.[20] Presumably he felt that at this time the brazen employment of the cotton club would have an unfortunate effect on Spanish pride.

Evidently the pinch of the unannounced but nevertheless partially effective American embargo was beginning to have some result, for on December 4, 1917, the Spanish ambassador in Washington informed Lansing that Spain was prepared to examine proposals of the United States looking

[18] *Ibid.*, p. 1216.
[19] Lansing to Willard, November 26, 1917, State Dept., 652. 119/265b.
[20] Willard to Lansing, November 30, 1917, *ibid.*, 652. 119/267; *For. Rel., 1917, Supp. 2*, II, pp. 1216, 1217.

toward a general commercial agreement.[21] With this overture the discussions may be regarded as having entered upon a phase which gave definite promise of successful consummation.

iv

Paralleling these early negotiations for a commercial agreement, and to some extent affecting them, were several incidents involving the neutrality of Spain, particularly with regard to the activity of German submarines in her waters.

In June, 1917, the German submarine UC 52 put into the Spanish port of Cadiz for the purpose of securing necessary repairs. The British government, backed by the French, promptly sought the support of the United States in a joint representation designed to bring about an internment of the craft. Specifically, the Allies held that a submarine was not entitled to the same privileges as an ordinary man-of-war, and that it should not use a neutral port for purposes of repair and supply.[22]

The United States appears to have taken no action in response to this appeal for joint representations; and on June 29, 1917, the submarine, having completed its repairs, left Cadiz. The British Embassy in Washington then requested support of a protest against the departure of the vessel. After a delay of more than a month, the Department of State filed a reply under date of July 30, 1917. It pointed out that the submarine had been disabled by ordinary wear and not by enemy action; that only strictly necessary repairs had been made; that Madrid had secured a guarantee from the commander not to attack merchantmen while en

[21] *Ibid.*, p. 1217.
[22] *Ibid.*, pp. 1289-91; Jusserand to Lansing, June 28, 1917, State Dept., 763. 72111 Sp 1/27.

route to his home port (a promise that apparently was kept); and that nothing objectionable had either been brought or taken away by the U-boat. The Department of State concluded that

> ... while appreciating the gravity of the situation which might ensue from the indiscriminate use of a neutral port by an enemy submarine, it feels that from the full statement of the incident now given to the Department by the Spanish Government, which this Government has no other alternative than to accept, such treatment was accorded by the Spanish Government to the U. C. 52 as would have been properly given to any belligerent war vessel.[23]

This interesting reply suggests that while the temptation was probably strong to join with the Allies in seeking to put one more German submarine out of commission, Washington was so determined to deal justly with neutral Spain that it declined to take a position which it felt was not well-founded in international law.

The case of the UC 52 did, however, have one immediate aftermath of considerable importance. Apparently as a result of Allied representations, the King signed a royal decree on June 29, 1917, the day of the craft's departure, proclaiming that belligerent submarines were thereafter barred from Spanish territorial waters; that those entering for any reason whatsoever would be interned; and that neutral submersibles would have to operate on the surface.[24]

---

[23] Memorandum to British Embassy, July 30, 1917, *ibid.*, Sp 1/18. This document seems to have been based on an opinion of the Law Adviser, L. H. W[oolsey], to Sterling, June 20, 1917, *ibid.*, Sp 1/57.

[24] *For. Rel., 1917, Supp. 2*, II, p. 1292. In compliance with this decree a German submarine, the B-23, was promptly interned on July 29, 1917. *Ibid.*, p. 1293. The text of the decree may be found in Deák and Jessup, *Neutrality Laws*, II, 939-40.

THE NEGOTIATIONS WITH SPAIN

The controversy over interned submarines directed the attention of the Department of State to the rumor that some twenty neutral and belligerent ships had been sunk by German U-boats within Spanish territorial waters. Washington was much concerned over these reports, for it feared that American troop and supply ships might suffer; and with a view to securing the proper facts upon which to lodge a protest, it instructed Ambassador Willard to collect evidence on these cases and find out what preventive measures Spain was taking. Madrid replied that there was only one authenticated case of a vessel being sunk within Spanish territorial waters (a Norwegian freighter), and that a strong protest had been presented to Berlin, which had denied that the incident had occurred within the three-mile limit. Washington was not satisfied with this explanation, because the State Department had within its possession evidence that two other Norwegian ships had been similarly sunk. It also had under consideration another British memorandum (August 27, 1917) seeking diplomatic support at Madrid in protesting against such attacks, when a sensational case was forced upon its attention.[25]

In mid-September, 1917, the damaged German submarine U 293 put into Cadiz and was promptly interned. The wireless was removed, the munitions were unloaded, and the commanding officer gave his parole that he would not attempt to escape. On October 6, 1917, with the acquiescence, if not the active connivance, of the local Spanish officials, the U 293 fled from the harbor. Madrid expressed great chagrin over the carelessness or disloyalty of its sub-

[25] *For. Rel., 1917, Supp. 2,* II, pp. 1292-94; memorandum from British Embassy, August 27, 1917, State Dept., 763.72111 Sp 1/28; New York *Times,* July 22, 1917.

ordinates, and promptly announced that they would be properly disciplined. The Department of State instructed Ambassador Willard to follow the lead of his British and Italian colleagues, and express "profound regret" at the escape of the German submarine. The Department also asked that additional precautions be taken to prevent the departure of the interned B-23, but this request had already been anticipated by Madrid.[26]

V

The unfortunate affair of the escaped U 293 again focused attention upon the submarine hazard in Spanish waters. On October 25, 1917, the British Embassy urged the Washington government to instruct its representatives to make representations against the use of neutral territorial waters by enemy submarines or other ships.[27] Such a step seemed to be imperative because of the recurring rumors that the German crews of interned merchantmen in Spain were helping the U-boats in various ways.

The Department of State, in line with the nation's age-old policy, preferred to act independently. It did not think that the various acts of unneutrality were sufficiently proved to warrant formal action, and on November 10, 1917, it asked the American chargé in Madrid, Charles S. Wilson, for his advice as to what course to take. The Department's own suggestion was that informal representations might be made to the effect that these reports of unneutral acts, whether true or not, were being credited in the United

[26] *For. Rel., 1917, Supp. 2*, II, pp. 1294-96; Gracey (U. S. consul at Seville) to Lansing, October 7, 1917; Willard to Lansing, October 12, 1917, State Dept., 763. 72111 Sp 1/91, 96.

[27] *For. Rel., 1917, Supp. 2*, II, p. 1296.

States and were having an unfortunate effect.[28] Chargé Wilson replied, on November 14, 1917, that in his judgment independent action was likely to offend Madrid and give the Germans strong grounds for complaining that Washington was trying to exert undue pressure on the Spanish government. He therefore recommended that any proposed steps be taken in close co-operation with the Allies.[29]

The Department of State now found itself in an awkward position. If it took independent action it might offend Spain; if it took joint action it would run counter to its traditional policy, to say nothing of its immediate policy of not becoming any more entangled with its Associates than necessary. The problem seemed to be of sufficient importance to warrant the attention of President Wilson, and on November 16, 1917, Acting Secretary Polk outlined the situation to him and specifically asked if he approved of "joining the Allied ambassadors in similar representations to the Spanish government?" Three days later the President replied that the course proposed by the American representative in Madrid "seems to me wise and sensible

---

[28] Lansing to Madrid Embassy, November 10, 1917, State Dept., 763. 72111 Sp 1/106. Lansing referred to reports that German submarines were being supplied with munitions and fuel, and that they were the beneficiaries of signals flashed from Spanish soil.

[29] Wilson to Lansing, November 14, 1917, *ibid.* In Allied quarters, Wilson added, there was no doubt that these breaches of neutrality were occurring. He also suggested that if he were finally authorized to make separate and informal representations, it would be well to hint that the effect of these unneutral acts upon American public opinion might affect unfavorably the issuance of licenses for the export of fuel, cotton, and other commodities to Spain.

and I hope that you will authorize him to act upon it." [30]

While the Department of State and President Wilson were considering the course to be pursued, the British ambassador called an informal meeting of the Allied (and American) representatives in Madrid, on November 13, 1917, for the purpose of discussing the problem of the interned German merchantmen. Although definite proof was lacking, rumors were current that these ships were being used as bases from which German submarines were receiving supplies, information, and even crews. The assembled diplomats finally decided to request authorization from their governments to support the recent request of the French ambassador that the crews of these merchantmen be interned. Chargé Wilson was not hopeful of any immediate action, but he felt that it would be well to put the matter on record at the Spanish Foreign Office.[31]

Six days after the American representative in Madrid had sent this report to Washington, President Wilson gave his approval of co-operative action; and on that same day Acting Secretary Polk instructed the American chargé to join with the Allied ambassadors in similar representations urging the internment of the German crews. On November 21, 1917, the American representative presented his formal note. He pointed out that German merchantmen were allegedly flashing signals to German submarines, and giving information about the movements of Spanish and Allied vessels that might contribute to their destruction. Concluding that the existence of this situation endangered the neutrality of Spain, the chargé expressed the hope that

[30] Polk to Wilson, November 16, 1917; Wilson to Polk, November 19, 1917, *ibid.*

[31] *For. Rel., 1917, Supp. 2*, II, pp. 1297-98.

the crews in question would be interned in the interior of the country.[32]

The slow-moving Madrid government appears to have taken no immediate action in response to these representations, but the whole affair indicates that the United States was not adverse, even though the evidence of unneutrality was not indisputably established, to joining with its Associates for the purpose of protecting its vital interests. Co-operative action was reluctantly taken, but it was taken.[33]

---

[32] *Ibid.*, pp. 1298-99. File 763.72111 Sp 1 of the Department of State contains an impressive number of documents purporting to prove unneutral activity on the part of Germans and others in Spain. It is worth noting that a memorandum from the Office of the Solicitor (September 26, 1918) raised objections to demanding the internment of the German crews. It stated: "When the United States was still a neutral power it allowed complete liberty to the crews of refugee merchantmen as long as they did not disturb the tranquillity of this country. It would, therefore, seem inconsistent for us now to complain of Spain's treatment unless there was definite information of unlawful acts committed by the German crews." *Ibid.*, Sp 1/157.

[33] About this same time the War Trade Board was considering a proposal to check German propaganda in Spain by restricting the export of paper and other materials. But the British and French authorities felt that this would produce more irritation than benefit. Polk to Madrid Embassy, November 17, 1917; Wilson to Polk, November 22, 1917; Spring Rice to Polk, December 19, 1917, State Dept., 652.119/200, 240, 265. On June 11, 1918, Ambassador Jusserand communicated to the State Department a suggestion from the French consul at Las Palmas, Canary Islands, to the effect that an Allied submarine be stationed in the islands to combat enemy submarines. Belatedly, on September 4, 1918, Lansing replied that " in view of the fact that the stationing of a United States submarine boat within the territorial waters of the Canary Islands would be a violation of Spanish neutrality, this Government could not see its way clear to consider favorably the suggestion of the French Consul at Las Palmas. In addition, it does

vi

The attention of Washington next shifted to the negotiations for a commercial agreement with Spain. These had entered upon a more definite basis with the statement of the Spanish ambassador, on December 4, 1917, that his government would consider proposals. The discussions continued actively throughout the next three months until March 7, 1918, when the final terms were approved. With the exception of the Swiss agreement of December 5, 1917, this was the first to be signed with any of the neutrals.

Several unique features of the negotiation deserve special emphasis. Unlike all of the other agreements entered into by the United States with the neutrals, the formal discussions were not carried on by special commissioners or representatives in Washington, London, or Paris. Instead, the Department of State empowered Ambassador Willard, in Madrid, to conclude the negotiations with the help of two Americans then stationed in Spain, and in close collaboration with the Allied, particularly the French, representatives in the Spanish capital.[34]

It should also be noted that the Spanish-American pact was made contingent upon the simultaneous acceptance of a Franco-Spanish financial agreement. This was an arrange-

---

not deem that it would be practicable for a submarine to remain long in that locality without detection, unless it remained at sea, when the endurance of the crew would become the controlling factor in determining the length of its stay." It will be observed that both principle and expediency were here invoked. *Ibid.*, 763. 72111 Sp 1/46.

[34] *For. Rel., 1918, Supp. 1,* II, p. 1659. Chandler P. Anderson, who was intimate with the Spanish ambassador in Washington, made some acid comments on the disorganized state of the negotiation. "Diary of Chandler P. Anderson," February 1, 1918.

ment by which Spain was to extend to the French large credits for the purchase of needed supplies for their army. Since France was at the end of her financial tether (or at least claimed to be), since the supplying of the French forces was of vital importance to the joint cause, and since the United States probably would have had to advance the money itself had not the agreement been made, it is not surprising that the Washington government co-operated closely with its Associates in this phase of the negotiation.[35]

Unlike all of the other general agreements with all of the other maritime European neutrals, except Norway, no provision was included for the employment of Spanish tonnage. At one point in the discussions, the Department of State was prepared to insist that such arrangements be made or the whole matter be postponed. But for various reasons this view did not finally prevail. Ambassador Willard counseled strongly against it, and pointed to the pride of the Spaniards (who would have resented coercion), and to the reported statement of the King that he would never consent to a commercial agreement that forced the employment of Spanish tonnage. It seems clear, also, that the immediate necessities of the A. E. F. pointed strongly to the wisdom of speedily concluding a commercial agreement and of putting off the shipping negotiations to a later date.[36]

[35] *For. Rel., 1918, Supp. 1*, II, pp. 1664-65, 1666; Lansing to Madrid Embassy, January 29, 1918, State Dept., 652. 119/478b. Chandler P. Anderson reported the Spanish ambassador in Washington as saying that the Spanish government was embittered against the United States by this financial deal. The French collateral was not regarded as good, and it was felt that France was taking advantage of the shift of foreign exchange in Spain's favor. " Diary of Chandler P. Anderson," February 13, 1918.

[36] *For. Rel., 1918, Supp. 1*, II, pp. 1663-65, 1667. At the last

When one remembers the prevalence of the mañana spirit, perhaps the most striking feature of this agreement is that it was made so speedily. The Spaniards were in an unusually strong position, for the large requests of the A. E. F. were eloquent testimony as to the pressing needs of the American army. Moreover, as we have seen, Spain was less amenable to economic pressure than the other European neutrals; and the embargo, though causing some distress, had been made only partially effective. The War Trade Board had continued to issue licenses for export to Spain until a comparatively late date, and when it discontinued these, the sixty day expiration period still allowed a considerable outflow of goods. Even these partial restrictions seriously embarrassed relations with Madrid, and at one time Lansing suggested that the embargo be relaxed in favor of Spain. Willard, however, was strongly opposed to such a course, because he felt that this type of pressure was the only thing that would force the Spaniards to terms. But he did recommend that export permits be issued in return for similar privileges granted by the Spaniards, and that this arrangement be extended to help out pro-Ally firms, to create good will in Spain, and to counteract German propaganda. The suggested policy of reciprocal permits was adopted by Washington and was used with considerable success.[37]

Aside from granting reciprocal export permits, the War Trade Board exerted additional pressure through the refusal

---

minute the British threatened to disrupt the negotiation because it did not provide for tonnage, but they were persuaded to withdraw their objections. *Ibid.*, pp. 1670-71.

[37] *Ibid., 1917, Supp. 2,* II, pp. 1218, 1220-22, 1223, 1225-26, 1227, 1230; *ibid., 1918, Supp. 1,* II, pp. 1658-59; Willard to Lansing, December 27, 1917, State Dept., 652.119/473.

to grant bunker fuel to Spanish merchantmen, even though their cargoes were properly licensed. The practice of delaying these vessels caused much resentment in Spain, and Willard was told flatly by the Foreign Minister (the King was reported to have said the same thing) that no commercial agreement would be signed while Spanish ships were being arbitrarily detained. This situation was finally adjusted by assurances from Washington that freighters with properly licensed cargoes would be freely bunkered.[38]

vii

The Spanish-American commercial agreement of March 7, 1918, may be summarized as follows. Madrid agreed to permit the exportation (without restrictions as to destination or quantity) of pyrites, lead, zinc, copper, and "minerals of every kind," as well as manufactured wool. This relieved American anxiety over pyrites and British concern over iron ore. Spain also bound herself to export, insofar as her national requirements and international obligations would permit, rice, raisins, onions, olive oil; manufactures of cotton, hemp, jute; leather and leather products; and rolling stock of various kinds. As for the immediate future, Madrid promised to allow the exportation of the following necessities for the A. E. F.: 300,000 blankets (in addition to the 200,000 already purchased); 240,000 yards of canvas; 100,000 pounds of leather for various kinds of harness;

---

[38] *For. Rel., 1918, Supp. 1,* II, pp. 1660, 1666, 1669, 1670; *Trade and Shipping Negotiations with Spain,* p. 48 (Willard to Lansing, February 21, 1918); Lansing to Madrid Embassy, January 18, 1918; Polk (Acting) to Madrid Embassy, January 26, 1918; Willard to Lansing, February 17, 1918, State Dept., 652. 119/410, 452, 550.

20,000 bridle leather backs; 20,000 collar leather backs; 20,000 saddle blankets; 20,000 pounds of Castile soap; 20,000 gallons of olive oil; 4,000 tons of onions; 2,000 tons of raisins; and 2,000 tons of rice.[39] These figures not only attest the tremendous consuming capacity of the A. E. F. but also the great importance of Spain to the United States in procuring the neeeded supplies. Much to the disappointment of the American purchasing agents, it was impossible to secure mules for the army and lumber for the making of railroad ties.[40]

As compensation for these concessions, the United States agreed to allow the exportation to Spain of certain stipulated articles, but only insofar as American and Allied necessities would permit, and only insofar as the national needs of Spain required. This last proviso was specifically designed to prevent the accumulation of unnecessary reserves of cotton. Subject to these general conditions, the United States agreed to permit the export of 35,000 bales of cotton a month, as well as 4,000 tons of petroleum and its derivatives a month.[41] Subject also to these general conditions,

---

[39] The text is in *For. Rel., 1918, Supp. 1*, II, pp. 1671-74.

[40] The Spanish railroads, which were in bad condition, opposed the sale of lumber; and the scarcity of mules (the French had drained heavily on the Spanish supply) prevented further sale of the animals. *Ibid.*, pp. 1660-61. It is a striking fact that the figures here listed correspond exactly with those requested by the War Department several months earlier. The items not secured were 20,000 mules, 10,000,000 feet of lumber and lumber products, 10,000 tons of charcoal, and 100,000 pounds of grease. *Ibid., 1917, Supp. 2*, II, p. 1229.

[41] The export of cotton was to commence as of March 1, 1918, and that of petroleum as of May 1. These figures were not to include the 8,000 tons of petroleum already promised. Specific quantities of the petroleum products were earmarked for immediate export.

THE NEGOTIATIONS WITH SPAIN 293

Washington promised to allow the exportation of copper and iron products in various forms; certain chemicals and mechanical apparatus; aluminum; tobacco; and, most important, locomotives and railway material. This last item was designed to expedite the delivery of supplies to the A. E. F., for the Spanish railroads were in such wretched condition that, without help, it was doubted whether they could do the work.

Certain general conditions were laid down in the latter part of the agreement. Compliance by one party was contingent upon compliance by the other; each nation was to provide the water transportation for its own purchases at its own risk; re-exportation of articles was not to be permitted without the consent of the other party concerned; and each country would provide suitable railway facilities to move the products involved. When each party should have fulfilled its specific obligations, neither was to employ an embargo against the export to the other of additional quantities of the commodities listed in the agreement. This did not, however, relieve purchasers of the necessity of securing proper licenses, nor did it preclude an embargo should national need or international obligations require one. It was finally stipulated that, following the signing of the commercial agreement, negotiations would be commenced looking toward the conclusion of a satisfactory arrangement for the employment of Spanish shipping.

On the whole, the press of Spain appears to have commented favorably on the agreement. Even certain journals that had been prejudiced against the negotiations greeted the final terms with evidences of satisfaction. The pro-German newspapers, of course, kept up their opposition, but even this seems to have been appreciably weakened.[42]

[42] *Neut. Press Supp.*, III, 413.

viii

If the Spanish government showed a noteworthy absence of its traditional mañana spirit in the negotiations, it ran truer to form in the execution of the pact. Although the War Trade Board promptly began to issue hundreds of licenses covering the export of the stipulated commodities to Spain, five weeks after the signing of the agreement Willard could report that Madrid had not granted a single permit for the export of supplies for the A. E. F.[43] In American quarters it was assumed that this backwardness was due to direct pressure from Berlin and to the sensational German successes in the current drive on the Western Front.[44] Madrid also procrastinated in honoring its obligation to grant credits under the financial agreement with France. W. A. Chadbourne, the War Trade Board agent in Madrid, was so thoroughly disgusted with this whole performance, or lack of it, that he strongly urged Washington to denounce the pact and begin negotiations afresh. But Willard emphatically counseled against such a drastic course, on the grounds that it would be a most serious step and would also adversely affect the Franco-Spanish credit agreement. In this judgment he was supported by both the War Trade Board and the Department of State.[45]

There were, however, two clubs which Washington could use. The first was again to withhold bunkers from Spanish

---

[43] *For. Rel., 1918, Supp. 1,* II, pp. 1675-76. The Spanish government had a grievance in that the War Trade Board had agreed to license 8,000 barrels of oil, provided Spain secured barrels, which were then unobtainable. "Diary of Chandler P. Anderson," May 9, 1918.

[44] *For. Rel., 1918, Supp. 1,* II, pp. 1674-75.

[45] *Ibid.,* pp. 1678-79, 1681-82.

ships, after the two-month period stipulated in the commercial agreement had expired. The second was to refuse to issue further export permits to Spain until Madrid had lived up to its promises to supply the A. E. F. On April 16, 1918, the War Trade Board specifically instructed Chadbourne to inform the Spanish Foreign Office that the old bunker regulations would apply after May 7, 1918. In the face of such pressure, the Spanish authorities began to expedite the flow of supplies, and by mid-August they were actually ahead of the United States in fulfilling their contract.[46]

It will be remembered that the commercial agreement had provided for a reopening of negotiations looking toward the early employment of Spanish tonnage in Allied service. Late in April, 1918, the Minister for Foreign Affairs notified Willard that he was prepared to begin discussions, and Chadbourne was authorized by the War Trade Board to collaborate with his British colleague in taking the initial steps in Madrid. There was at first some thought in Washington of using the bunker club to force the Spaniards into a tonnage agreement, now that the two-month period had expired, but Willard advised strongly against such a course. He felt that the proud Spaniards, who were particularly sensitive on the question of shipping, would only be made more stubborn by such drastic methods. Willard's counsels finally prevailed. Bunker privileges were granted for an additional month, and thereafter were quietly extended without serious difficulty.[47]

[46] *Ibid.*, pp. 1675-76, 1701. For the comments in the Spanish press on the temporary detention of Spanish ships, see *Bulletin Périodique de la Presse Espagnole,* June 27, 1918, p. 2.

[47] *For. Rel., 1918, Supp. 1,* II, pp. 1677, 1679-82; Lansing to Madrid Embassy, June 26, 1918, State Dept., 652. 119/1027.

Late in June, 1918, Alfred G. Smith, a shipping expert from the United States, arrived in Madrid for the purpose of helping Chadbourne and the British representative with the negotiations. After working on the problem for several weeks, Smith came to the conclusion that the situation was hopeless. The records of the Spanish shipping companies were chaotic; tonnage was not being judiciously employed; the owners ignored the government; and some 85,000 tons had been sunk by the Germans since January, 1918. Smith also concluded that most, if not all, of the Spanish shipping was needed for Spain's requirements, and he felt that the amount which could be made available to the Associated Powers was not of great importance. His final judgment was that the tonnage negotiations should cease, and that the United States should be left free to apply bunker and other regulations.[48] Even Willard, who had consistently counseled deference to Spanish sensibilities, was prepared by July 22, 1918, to recommend a more vigorous policy. Specifically, he would inform Spain that the requirements of the Associated Powers were such that they could not spare needed commodities unless Spain took more vigorous steps to protect her neutrality.[49] The Washington government at first felt, as a result of its previous experience with

[48] *For. Rel., 1918, Supp. 1*, II, pp. 1686, 1687-88, 1691-92. Chadbourne, who was suffering from a disabled knee, did not get along well with Smith and was disposed to blame the British. "I couldn't do anything for or with Mr. Smith," he wrote to Thomas L. Chadbourne. "I can't even judge about his conclusions on shipping. The English did what they could to put any negotiations of ours on the bum." W. A. Chadbourne to T. L. Chadbourne, July 19, 1918, F. A. R., Hoover Library (War Trade Board; Foreign Agents and Reports: Madrid).

[49] Willard to Lansing, July 22, 1918, State Dept., 652. 119/1191.

the Northern Neutrals, that the amount of tonnage allegedly needed for Spanish necessities could be scaled down; but it, too, finally gave up, and on August 10, 1918, ordered Smith home for an oral report.[50] Thus ended the last serious efforts to secure a tonnage agreement with Spain.

ix

Before the tonnage negotiations were finally dropped, Norman H. Davis, of the United States Treasury Department, arrived in Spain for the purpose of arranging credits pursuant to the commercial agreement of March 7, 1918. He found the Spanish officials disposed to co-operate, perhaps because of the success of the Allied offensive in the summer of 1918, and perhaps also because Washington had shown more generosity than was specifically called for when it replaced certain oil shipments lost through fire and German submarines.[51]

The negotiations continued without serious difficulty, and resulted in the Spanish-American financial agreement of August 28, 1918, which was signed by Norman H. Davis and two Spanish representatives. It authorized the granting of credits, up to 250,000,000 pesetas, by Spanish banks or

[50] *For. Rel., 1918, Supp. 1,* II, pp. 1689-1696.

[51] *Ibid.,* pp. 1697-99. One cargo burned in New York harbor; another was reported to have been sunk by a German submarine. The War Trade Board announced publicly, for the purposes of cultivating Spanish good will, that these supplies would not be deducted from the allotments due Spain under the commercial agreement. Norman Davis did not favor this policy of liberality, and preferred to use these replacement cargoes for the purpose of forcing concessions in regard to credit and the lifting of the Spanish embargo on lumber for the A. E. F. New York *Times,* August 2, 1918; *For. Rel., 1918, Supp. 1,* II, pp. 1693-94, 1696-97, 1702-03.

bankers for the purchasing of the supplies listed in the commercial agreement of March 7, 1918. It was stipulated that the financial agreement was supplementary to the general commercial agreement and should be regarded as a part of it. It was further stated that both governments would grant export licenses without undue delay, and that they would permit the export of commodities over and above the maximum figures set forth in the general agreement, if such commodities could be conveniently spared. Altogether, the negotiation of this understanding was an achievement of no little importance, and it reflects creditably upon the relations subsisting between the two powers.[52]

Also closely connected with the general commercial pact, although not a part of it, was the attempt of American officials in Spain to obtain additional supplies for the A. E. F. It will be remembered that the negotiators of the general agreement had been unable to secure lumber and mules, primarily because of the existing shortages in Spain. In the late summer of 1918, as the operations on the Western Front went into their final stages, the American army found itself beset with an alarming shortage of draft animals. The Spanish government, although not bound to do so, finally agreed to permit the export of 6,000 horses and mules, as well as several thousand railroad ties. But

---

[52] The text is in *ibid.*, pp. 1707-11. The Germanophile press of Spain protested against the loan, but otherwise it appears to have been greeted with satisfaction, particularly in those sections that would be benefited by the American purchases. The amount borrowed was to be liquidated by the United States imports, and as a consequence the prospective recipients were pleased. Proof of the high regard for the loan in financial circles is seen in the protests of those banks that were not permitted to participate in the transaction. *Neut. Press Supp.*, IV, 444.

these supplies were all slow in coming, and were also entirely inadequate in quantity.[53]

In mid-October, 1918, the War Trade Board offered to license for Spanish consumption as much as 20,000 tons of ammonium sulphate, in exchange for the immediate sale of 50,000 mules to the A. E. F. The Board also expressed itself as ready to make other concessions or to exert economic pressure in order to secure the needed animals.[54] Early in November, 1918, an arrangement was concluded by which the American representative promised to recommend to the War Trade Board the licensing of 20,000 tons of ammonium sulphate in return for 47,500 mules. A week later the Armistice came, and with it a lessened demand for the animals. On November 22, 1918, the A. E. F. cancelled all outstanding contracts on undelivered mules, and advised Washington that the ammonium sulphate did not have to be licensed, because no definite promise regarding it had been made.[55] But the War Trade Board felt that such an evasion was open to serious criticism, and it authorized its representative in Madrid, W. A. Chadbourne,

[53] *For. Rel., 1918, Supp. 1*, II, pp. 1701-02. Some of the American divisions were reported as practically immobile because of the shortage of mules. There is considerable information on purchases of horses in Charles G. Dawes, *A Journal of the Great War* (2 vols., Boston, 1921).

[54] *For. Rel., 1918, Supp. 1*, II, pp. 1711, 1713. The War Trade Board representative in Paris cabled: " It is quite possible Spanish Government for one reason or another will again refuse to release mules, notwithstanding your offer of ammonia, and under such circumstances we venture to suggest most vigorous diplomatic representations and, if necessary, drastic blockade policy, if you think by such procedure the release of mules can be secured. We send this cable on the urgent solicitation of the military advisers of the A. E. F." *Ibid.*, p. 1712.

[55] *Ibid.*, pp. 1714, 1716.

to state that, irrespective of the cancellation of the contracts, and "as an expression of its appreciation of the friendly attitude of Spain in this matter," the Board would license to Spain the 20,000 tons of ammonium sulphate. With an eye to Spanish good will, Chadbourne was instructed to give such publicity to this concession as seemed suitable.[56] Although it is true that the war was now over, and that Washington could afford to be more generous with its own scanty store of ammonium sulphate, it would seem as though this act were prompted largely by a desire to protect the good name of the United States.

x

A month before the Armistice was signed, an issue came up in regard to Spain which again involved the policy of encouraging neutrals to enter the war and of lending them active assistance once they had taken the step. We have noted that from time to time German submarines sank Spanish ships laden with iron ore and other contraband for England. These sinkings not only depleted Spain's merchant marine and took a steady toll of lives, but they were galling to the pride of the Spaniards. Late in August and early in September, 1918, reports were published to the effect that two other Spanish ships had been sunk, in one case with a loss of six persons. Madrid announced its readiness to seize an equivalent interned German ship for every Spanish vessel torpedoed; while Berlin was reported as threatening war should such action be taken without full and frank discussion.[57]

[56] Lansing to Madrid Embassy, November 30, 1918, State Dept., 652.119/2209.
[57] *For. Rel., 1918, Supp. 1,* II, pp. 1718-21.

The French and British diplomatic representatives in Madrid had come to the conclusion that, because of heavy shipments of iron ore and other supplies, Spain was worth more as a neutral than as an ally.[58] Willard informally told the Spanish Minister for Foreign Affairs that in his judgment the United States did not wish to see Spain plunged into war, but in the event that she should be forced in he personally believed (though he was without instructions on the subject) that she could rely on the United States, insofar as possible, to supply " those things necessary for her national and economic life. . . ."[59]

Curiously enough, Willard's other dispatches to Washington did not reveal such a desire to keep Spain out of the war. On September 5, 1918, he advised that the bunker club be used as a means of encouraging Madrid to enter the conflict. Specifically, he asked for instructions to say to the Spanish Foreign Office that, because of the increasing demands of the Associated Powers, the War Trade Board might not be able to continue to exempt Spain from certain bunker restrictions; but that if Spain, " in defense of her rights, repeatedly disregarded by Germany, or for other reason feel justified in taking a position more definitely favorable towards the Allies," then " the United States would endeavor to continue to except Spain " from the operation of this bunker restriction.[60] In reply to Willard's

---

[58] *Ibid.*, p. 1725. On the other hand, General Pershing had written, on November 15, 1917, that Spain's entry into the war would materially strengthen the Western Front, guarantee supplies, assure a flow of ore to the Allies, and put an end to U-boat activity on the Spanish coast. Pershing, *My Experiences in the World War*, I, 237.

[59] *For. Rel., 1918, Supp. 1*, II, pp. 1717, 1722-24.

[60] *Ibid.*, p. 1722.

request for instructions, Lansing cabled that the Department of State doubted the wisdom of such a suggestion, and nothing more seems to have been done with it.[61] Perhaps the most surprising thing about this proposition is that it was not rejected with particular emphasis; and the grounds for making the decision may have been expediency rather than principle. But it was well for the good name of the United States that the proposal was dropped, for to have used bunker pressure as a means of getting Spain into the war would have been seriously out of line with the policy that Washington attempted to pursue throughout the belligerency period.

On September 23, 1918, the Spanish Minister for Foreign Affairs sounded out Willard (as he had previously sounded out the Allied ambassadors) as to the position of the United States if Spain should enter the conflict. Willard forwarded this inquiry to Washington with the following recommendation:

. . . I venture to suggest that assurances on part of United States, France and England that support will be given Spain in the event of conflict with Germany would have great effect here, first on those who are really pro-Ally and second on those who want to pick and support the winners; such assurances would correspondingly depress the pro-German element. Allied successes have had a great effect in Spain and the opportunity thus created should not be lost.

The reply from the State Department was prompt and decisive:

This Government will of course not exercise the slightest influence on the action of Spain. If Spain, however, decides to enter into a state of war with Germany, the United States

[61] *Ibid.*, pp. 1724-25.

The Negotiations with Spain

will naturally support and assist her in every practical way. The above is for your information and guidance and not for formal transmission to the Spanish Government.[62]

This, of course, did not preclude the conveying of Washington's general views in informal conversations with the Spanish Foreign Office. A week later, on October 5, 1918, Lansing cabled Willard further: "I desire to say for your personal and strictly confidential information that this Government is not anxious to have Spain enter into a state of war with Germany and considers that little would be gained thereby. You will be guided in your intercourse accordingly." [63] It would be difficult to declare more emphatically that the United States did not want Spain to enter the war, and would hold out no encouragement to her to participate, except the most obvious assurances of full co-operation.

The crisis over the sinking of Spanish ships, together with the possible seizure of German merchantmen, was amicably settled in mid-October, 1918, when, by friendly negotiation, Berlin arranged to transfer seven vessels to the Spanish flag as recompense for those that had been sunk. The temptation, if any existed in Washington, to bring Spain into the conflict passed away; and the war ended the next month with the United States not having compromised Spanish neutrality. If victory had not been in sight, and if Spain's active participation had been of vital importance, the story might have been different. But we are here concerned with what actually happened; and the record is distinctly creditable to the United States.

[62] *Ibid.*, p. 1726.
[63] *Ibid.*, p. 1727.

xi

Perhaps the most striking feature of Spanish-American relations during 1917-1918 is that there was, comparatively, so little friction, particularly when we bear in mind the strong pro-German element in Spain. The general commercial agreement was the second to be concluded, well ahead of those with Norway, Sweden, Denmark, and the Netherlands. This appears to have been primarily because Spain was largely immune from German threats, and to a lesser degree from Allied pressures. Unlike Switzerland and the four Northern Neutrals, she was more a free agent and at liberty to act in accordance with her best interests.

On the whole, the record of the United States in its dealings with Spain is free from serious criticism, more so, perhaps, than was the case with any of the other European neutrals, except Switzerland. Basically, this was no doubt due to the fact that the Spaniards were in no position to give substantial aid directly to the enemy. Although the United States used embargo and bunkering pressures to some extent, its restrictions in this regard were not so prompt or so airtight as they were in its treatment of the border neutrals. Washington was reluctant to lodge protests with Madrid, particularly those of a joint nature involving the Allies, and it refused outright to do so unless they were well-founded. It displayed generosity in replacing oil that had been destroyed; it showed jealousy for the good name of the United States in deciding to carry through its promised deliveries of ammonium sulphate. Above all, the United States declined to use pressure or persuasion, individual or joint, for the purpose of forcing Spain into the war. Some of these decisions may have been motivated in part by self-interest; but others were unquestionably influenced by a desire for fair and honorable dealing.

Chapter X

THE UNITED STATES AND
THE LATIN AMERICAN NEUTRALS

i

The republics of Latin America, contrary to the desires of the United States, failed to join wholeheartedly in presenting a solid front to the Central Powers, thus shattering the Allied hope of a united continent stretching from Patagonia to the Pole. There was, to be sure, a good deal of pro-Ally sentiment among those Latin Americans who were shocked by Germany's ruthless methods; who feared a Prussian-dominated world; and who wanted the full influence of Pan-Americanism to be exerted on the side of democracy. Yet it is important to remember that in general the pro-Ally sympathy of Latin America was pro-French, pro-British, and pro-Italian rather than pro-Yankee.[1]

On the other hand, there were forces at work which tended to weaken or offset pro-Ally sentiment. The presence of large German populations; German influence in the schools and in the army; the pervasiveness of German propaganda; resentment against the British blacklist and blockade; and the nursing of a number of grievances at the hands of the United States—all these factors produced doubt, indecision, or active pro-German sympathy. In addition, there were republics, like Paraguay and Salvador,

[1] For background material this chapter has relied heavily on Percy A. Martin's valuable *Latin America and the War* (Baltimore, 1925).

Status of Latin America, 1917-1918 *

A. Neutrals

Argentina
Chile
Colombia
Mexico
Paraguay
Salvador
Venezuela

B. Severed Relations with Germany

Bolivia	April 13, 1917
Dominican R.	June 11, 1917
Ecuador	December 7, 1917
Peru	October 6, 1917
Uruguay	October 7, 1917

C. Declared War

	Severed Relations	Declaration of War
Brazil	April 11, 1917	October 26, 1917
Cuba	April 7, 1917	April 7, 1917
Costa Rica	September 21, 1917	May 23, 1918
Guatemala	April 27, 1917	April 23, 1918
Haiti	June 17, 1917	July 12, 1918
Honduras	May 17, 1917	July 19, 1918
Nicaragua	May 18, 1917	May 7, 1918
Panama	April 7, 1917	April 7, 1917

* In some instances there were several stages in the process of severing relations and declaring war; the above dates generally represent decisive action. A variance in dates is also accounted for by the fact that the necessary steps were taken either by the legislative or by the executive authority or by both. (Dates obtained from *For. Rel.*; Martin, *Latin America and the War*; New York *Times*.)

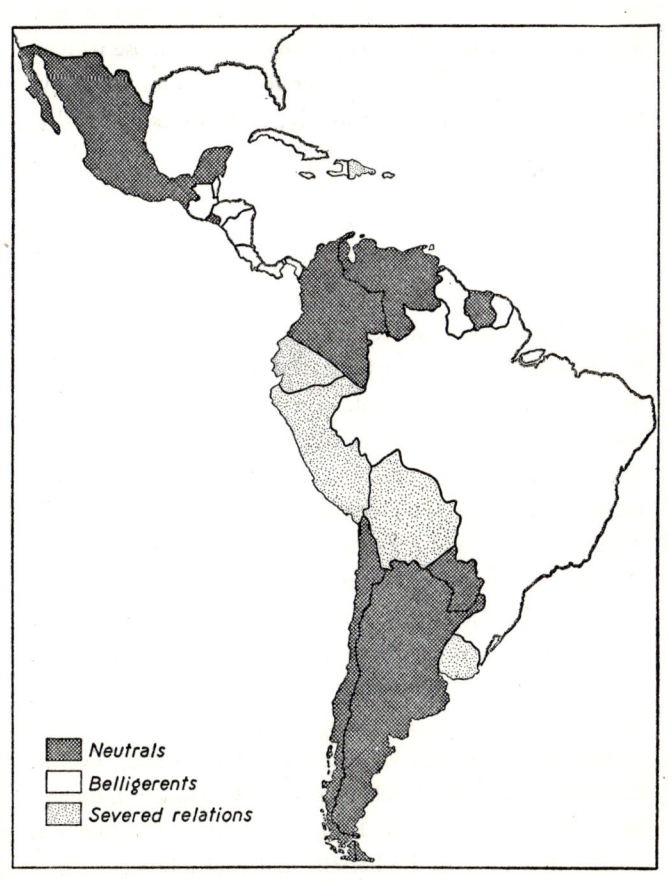

LATIN AMERICA, 1917-1918

which were not vitally touched by the war, which had no direct grievances to redress, and which felt that their best interests would be served by a neutral course. But by and large it seems clear that even among most of those nations that did not go so far as to sever relations with Germany, the majority opinion was pro-Ally; and this explains why, with one notable exception, Mexico, the neutral republics of Latin America were benevolently disposed toward the United States.

The absence of hemispheric solidarity on the issue of resisting the Central Powers was reflected in the division of the Latin American republics into three groups: those that became belligerents; those that severed relations; and those that remained neutral. The eight that declared war and became cobelligerents of the United States were Cuba, Haiti, Guatemala, Honduras, Nicaragua, Costa Rica, Panama, and Brazil. Only one of these, Brazil, was a South American state; and only one, also Brazil, ranked among the leading nations of Latin America in size, population, wealth, and influence. With the possible exception of Cuba, which supplied an enormous amount of sugar, none of the other countries in this group was of primary importance, except, in some cases, for strategic reasons.

The second group consisted of those states, five in number, that severed relations with Germany: Uruguay, Santo Domingo, Ecuador, Peru, and Bolivia. Uruguay was almost in a category by herself, and probably went closer to the brink of war than any of the other republics that merely broke with Berlin. This smallest of the South American nations was pro-Ally from the beginning, and after severing relations with Germany officially revoked its neutrality. More than that, on June 18, 1917, the government at Montevideo issued a famous decree:

First, that no American country, which in defense of its own rights should find itself in a state of war with nations of other continents, will be treated as a belligerent; *Second*, that existing decrees which may be in contravention to this resolution shall be null and of no effect.

In other words, the customary neutral restrictions upon Allied or United States vessels would not be invoked, nor would other hampering measures be taken against the Associated Powers.[2]

The other four republics that severed relations with Germany may be disposed of briefly. Santo Domingo was occupied by American marines and may thus be regarded as virtually a cobelligerent. Ecuador was strongly pro-Ally, at least among the cultured classes, and shortly after the severance of relations threw open her ports without restriction to the ships of the United States and the other Associated Powers.[3] Peru was pro-Ally from the outset of hostilities in 1914; declined to issue a proclamation of neutrality when the United States declared war on Germany; and subscribed to the declaration of Uruguay that no American nation (i. e., the United States) fighting in defense of its rights would be treated as a belligerent.[4]

[2] Martin, *op. cit.*, pp. 351, 362-63, 372. The translation is from *ibid.*, pp. 362-63. The full text in a different translation is in the *Official Bulletin*, June 20, 1917, p. 2. In July, 1918, Uruguay received an American squadron in her waters, and waived all regulations as to the length of its stay. Martin, *op. cit.*, pp. 366-67.

[3] *Ibid.*, p. 460, n.

[4] *Ibid.*, pp. 363, 383, 390. See statement of President Pardo, of Peru, before the Peruvian Congress, *Official Bulletin*, August 23, 1917, p. 1.

Bolivia, which next to Chile among the South American states was perhaps most deeply permeated with German influence, nevertheless showed strong pro-Ally sentiments and subscribed warmly to the declaration of Uruguay.[5]

All of the five that severed relations with Germany were neutral in that they did not enter upon a state of war, and in that they could resume relations with Berlin without the necessity of negotiating new treaties. Actually, however, they were neutral neither in spirit nor in deed. For our purposes, therefore, they will all be regarded as belligerents, except where they became involved in problems that require special attention.

ii

The seven Latin American states that remained neutral and did not break relations were Salvador, Paraguay, Colombia, Venezuela, Chile, Argentina, and Mexico. This group is significant in that it embraced, with the exception of Brazil, the three most important nations of Latin America, at least from the point of view of the United States in 1917-1918. All things considered, these seven neutrals were of more significance than their eight sister states which declared war, or the five which severed relations.

Salvador was not intimately involved in the submarine issue with Germany, and was repelled from entering the war on the side of the United States, partly because of the bitter controversy growing out of the Bryan-Chamorro Treaty, which the Wilson administration had signed in 1914 with Nicaragua. Nevertheless, Salvador pursued a policy that was

[5] Martin, *op. cit.*, pp. 363-64, 474.

benevolently neutral toward Washington, and so far departed from strict neutrality as to throw open her waters to ships of the Allies and the United States.[6] Paraguay likewise did not become involved in any serious difficulties with Germany, and although pro-Ally from the start, elected to remain out of the conflict.[7] Venezuela felt grateful to the United States for President Cleveland's intervention in her behalf during the boundary dispute with the British in 1895-96, and her intellectuals were pro-Ally from the beginning; but the government was Germanophile and as a consequence kept the nation neutral.[8] Although a majority of the Colombians were probably pro-French and pro-British, there was present a strong German influence; and Colombia could not bring herself to join the war on the side of a country which had despoiled her of Panama in 1903 and was failing to make prompt indemnification. In spite of a barrage of newspaper misrepresentation in the United States, the Bogotá government maintained a firm and dignified neutrality, with a benevolent disposition toward the Allies.[9]

Chile was of incalculable importance to the Allied war effort, primarily because of her nitrates. Although German influence was strong in her schools and army, German violations of Chilean territorial waters, together with the entrance of the United States into the war, gave a strong impetus to pro-Ally feeling, and by the end of the conflict

---

[6] *Ibid.*, pp. 511, 512, 513; *For. Rel., 1917, Supp. 1*, pp. 330-31; Naval War College, *International Law Documents, 1917*, p. 210.

[7] Martin, *op. cit.*, p. 480.   [8] *Ibid.*, pp. 461-62, 471.

[9] *Ibid.*, pp. 428, 435-36. George Creel found much bitter hostility in Colombia and Venezuela against the United States. Creel, *How We Advertised America*, p. 365.

sentiment was overwhelmingly in favor of the Associated Powers. There can be no question but that Chile interpreted her neutral obligations to the advantage of the United States.[10]

For various reasons, public opinion in Argentina was strongly pro-Ally, particularly after the Count Luxburg "spurlos versenkt" scandal involving Germany. As a matter of fact, Washington published these telegrams largely in the hope that both Argentina and Brazil, which were then wavering, would be brought into the Allied camp.[11] In September, 1917, both the Argentine Senate and Chamber of Deputies voted to break off diplomatic relations with Berlin, but President Irigoyen resolutely blocked the proposed action. He was apparently convinced that a neutral policy would best serve the interests of Argentina, and he did not want to follow in the wake of the United States. Although he was bitterly criticized at the time as pro-German, the evidence now available rather strongly supports the view that from beginning to end he was pro-Argentine rather than pro-German. Certainly, neutrality proved very profitable for Argentina, what with the enormous world demand for grain; and the support which Irigoyen received in the congressional elections of 1918 indicates that his policy commanded public support. In any event, Argentina was favorably disposed toward the United States.[12]

---

[10] Martin, *op. cit.,* pp. 265, 335, 345-48; *Neut. Press Supp.,* IV, 362. See also Beltran Mathieu, "The Neutrality of Chile during the European War," *Amer. Jour. of Int. Law,* XIV (1920), pp. 319-42.

[11] Lansing, *Memoirs,* p. 328.

[12] Martin, *op. cit.,* ch. III. In writing of both Chile and Argentina, Dana G. Munro concluded: "The chief motive of their policy has been their desire to compel recognition of their own

Mexico occupied a unique position among the Latin American neutrals. She was the only important one north of the Isthmus; she was a next-door neighbor of the United States and consequently in a position to cause more than an ordinary amount of trouble; and she was the only one of the neutrals that was not benevolently inclined toward the Colossus of the North. This antipathy went back to the middle of the previous century, to the time of the Texan Revolution and the Mexican War, and had been more recently intensified by such unfortunate developments as the Vera Cruz incident, the Pershing expedition, and the persistent friction between Wilson and President Carranza. Indeed, it seems probable that Mexican opinion was not so much pro-German as anti-Yankee. German influence and propaganda were strong in Mexico when the United States entered the conflict, but as time wore on and the American campaign of counterpropaganda began to prove effective, Mexican sentiment definitely changed.[13] In brief, if Mexico

---

importance as world Powers." Together they were the strongest of the non-European neutrals; it would be undignified to enter the war unless they could take a full part (something they were unprepared to do); hence it was better to pursue an independent course and enjoy the unaccustomed deference of the great powers of the world. There was also some feeling in both Chile and Argentina that it was undesirable to follow servilely the lead of the United States. Dana G. Munro, " Pan-Americanism and the War," *North American Review,* CCVIII, 717-18 (November, 1918).

[13] The Committee on Public Information later reported: " With the possible exception of Spain, in no other country outside of Mexico did the German propaganda attain such vigor and proportion and nowhere was it waged with more determination and vicious mendacity." *Report of Committee on Public Information,* p. 150. In June, 1918, the Committee brought a group of Mexican editors to the United States in pursuance of its propaganda campaign. President Wilson's remarks to them in Washington were well received. Baker, *Wilson,* VIII, 195, 204, 228.

was neutral in the letter of her decrees, she was not neutral in the manner of their enforcement. It is probable, however, that the official acts of Mexico City were more nearly neutral than those of most of the other Latin American governments. But the United States wanted sympathy rather than neutrality; and, by contrast with her neighbors, Mexico appeared to be markedly unfriendly.[14]

On the whole, we may conclude that from the point of view of this study the Latin American neutrals were much less important than those of Europe. They were separated by an ocean from beleaguered Germany, and they were effectively prevented from sending any appreciable amount of goods to the Central Powers by the British blockade and bunker restrictions. In fact, this was the basic reason why the export control regulations of the United States were applied much less stringently to Latin America than to the Northern Neutrals.

But we must not infer from these observations that the neutrals of Latin America were unimportant to the United States. Chile was vital for nitrates and copper; Argentina for grain; Mexico for oil and other necessities. Yet the

[14] In July, 1918, the Mexican ambassador in Washington, Ignatio Y. Bonillas, published a statement in which he pointed out that neutrality was a necessity with Mexico. She had been fighting at home throughout seven years for liberty and democracy, and she had to bend all of her energies toward reconstruction. The United States, which had been at peace for many years, could afford the luxury of a foreign war. *Forum*, LX, 45-46 (July, 1918). Secretary Lansing later wrote that there was "at least a reasonable doubt" as to Mexico's remaining neutral. Lansing, *Memoirs*, p. 308. This seems hardly probable. Mexico needed peace; she could not render direct aid to Germany; and if she joined the Central Powers she would be extremely vulnerable to attack from the United States.

owners of these products were no less anxious to sell to the Associated Powers than the Associated Powers were to buy. As a consequence, we may say that in general the relations of the United States with the Latin American neutrals consisted of the normal interchange of commodities that were needed by both sides. Only where problems arose involving an interpretation of neutral rights and international law, or the application of various kinds of pressure by the United States in pursuance of its war effort, shall we find material directly relevant to the general theme of this book.

iii

One of the most interesting of the early problems involving the United States and its southern neighbors concerned the calling of a conference of neutrals by the Argentine government in the spring of 1917. The invitation was finally extended to all of the Latin American republics, and its avowed object was " to obtain a uniformity of opinion on the war and to bring closer together the American republics and strengthen their position in the concert of nations." [15] Although Washington could hardly be expected to view with enthusiasm any grouping of the Latin American republics under the leadership of Argentina, President Irigoyen emphatically assured the American ambassador in Buenos Aires that the purpose of such an assembly was " far from hostile to the United States. . . ." [16]

[15] Quoted in Martin, *Latin America and the War*, p. 255.
[16] *For. Rel., 1917, Supp. 1*, p. 382. For earlier and fruitless moves by Paraguay, Ecuador, and Argentina in the direction of a neutral conference or mediation between Germany and the United States, see *ibid.*, pp. 232 ff. This, however, was before the United States became a belligerent, and hence is not altogether germane to the present subject.

All but two of the Latin American nations (Venezuela and Colombia) finally accepted the invitation, although Chile pointed to the unwisdom of excluding the United States, and Brazil accepted with reservations relating to the attitude of Washington. But by the middle of the summer all plans for the conference were temporarily abandoned. Among the factors contributing to the fiasco were the changed status of Brazil growing out of her break with Germany; the divergence of views among those republics that had accepted; and especially the unfavorable attitude of the United States.[17] To Honduras Secretary Lansing sent a thinly veiled warning against co-operation; to Panama he cabled that the Department wished the Isthmian republic to "have no participation in this conference"; to the Paraguayan government the United States minister made representations designed to discourage support of the movement; and to the American diplomatic representatives in Central and South America (except Argentina, Mexico, Panama, Cuba, Brazil, and the Dominican Republic) the Department of State cabled that it "does not consider that such a conference would serve any useful purpose at this time." This information was to be put to "discreet use" should the occasion arise.[18]

In October, 1917, the Argentine government made an attempt to revive the scheme when it invited all the Spanish American states to send delegates to a Latin American congress. This was not, however, to be a conference of neutrals, inasmuch as a majority of the nations of Central

[17] Martin, *op. cit.*, pp. 255-57; *Neut. Press Supp.*, II, 165.

[18] *For. Rel., 1917, Supp. 1*, pp. 280, 281, 289, 372. Honduras heeded the warning of the United States. Price to Lansing, October 31, 1917, State Dept., 763.72111/6732.

and South America had either declared war or had broken relations. Mexico alone responded with alacrity, and in January, 1918, a large Mexican delegation arrived at Buenos Aires only to find the congress postponed.[19] No other serious effort appears to have been made to call a conference of the neutrals.

This episode is not in itself of primary importance, and it is quite probable that the conference would have failed even if the State Department had not raised a hand. But the whole affair indicates that President Irigoyen was eager to assume leadership of the Latin American neutrals; that Mexico was conspicuously unfriendly to her northern neighbor; and that the United States did not hesitate to make representations against a movement that might be inimical to its war effort. There can be little doubt that the neutrals of Latin America were well aware of Washington's opposition, though the record does not reveal that the United States went beyond the conventional expressions of dissatisfaction, except perhaps in the case of Honduras, which had already severed relations.

iv

We have already noted that Mexico occupied a unique position among the republics of Latin America in that she was the only one conspicuously unfriendly to the United States. In addition, she was the neutral republic in which German activity was perhaps most pronounced; and little effort seems to have been made by Mexico City to restrain it. Not only was the usual type of German propagandist at work, but Germans from interned ships in Mexican

[19] Martin, *op. cit.*, p. 257; *For. Rel., 1918, Supp. 1*, I, p. 665.

harbors were reported to be busy with various kinds of enterprises harmful to the cause of the Associated Powers. In particular, the Navy Department in Washington was concerned over reports that the Germans, with Mexican acquiescence, if not active assistance, were attempting to fit out commerce raiders in the ports of Mexico.[20] During the period of American belligerency there was some little friction along the Mexican border; but this had been going on for decades. Much more important were problems involved in a possible shutting off oil supplies from Mexico;[21] in attempting to counteract German propaganda; in lifting the embargo on arms shipments to Mexico;[22] and in putting into effect the various export and import restrictions, particularly the embargo on food, which was finally lifted in July, 1918.[23] But all of these difficulties did not, to a noteworthy degree, involve those more fundamental neutral rights with which we are here concerned. It was in mari-

[20] Admiral W. F. Fullam to Daniels, April 4, 1918, State Dept., 763.72111M57/51. The State Department had evidence to show that Berlin was seeking submarine bases in Mexico. Lansing, *Memoirs,* pp. 310-11.

[21] *Ibid.,* pp. 314-16.

[22] In July, 1917, the Department of State announced the release of a considerable amount of ammunition purchased by the Mexican government eighteen months earlier. New York *Times,* July 21, 1917. President Wilson wrote Lansing a short time later in regard to the arms export problem: " It is my wish, for example, that we should deal with Mexico in this matter very generously from now on." Wilson to Lansing, August 15, 1917, War Trade Board Executive Files, State Dept.

[23] In July, 1918, it was announced that the export ban on food to Mexico had been lifted, on condition that the Mexican government would provide commodities needed by the United States. Mexico City was also to give guarantees against the re-export of imported goods. New York *Times,* July 11, 1918.

time activity that disputes of this nature with Mexico most conspicuously arose, and to them we shall turn.

V

Except for Salvador, which was not important, Mexico was the only neutral situated between the United States and Colombia. A great deal of traffic, both merchantmen and warships, passed between the Panama Canal and the west coast of the United States. In the case of small vessels with relatively little fuel capacity, such as subchasers and tugs, it was essential that stops be made en route at the various Mexican ports. These visits by American ships caused a number of incidents which resulted in a stir out of all proportion to their intrinsic importance.[24]

Altogether, there were some nine cases—at least nine protested cases—of United States warships remaining in Mexican ports longer than the customary twenty-four hours for provisioning or repair. In every case, or practically every case, the American officers in command reported extenuating circumstances, such as the stress of weather or the necessity of making extensive repairs. In no case do there appear to have been requests at the time from the local or central Mexican officials to leave within the twenty-four hours, for if such requests had been made they doubtless would have been complied with. In several instances the commanders of the United States ships received permission from the local authorities to stay beyond the customary time, or were told that the twenty-four hour rule did not mean anything.[25]

[24] The correspondence regarding these incidents may be found in the State Dept., 763. 72111M57.
[25] Admiral W. F. Fullam to Daniels, April 4, 1918, *ibid.*, 763. 72111M57/51.

In these cases, presumably, the port officials failed to notify Mexico City of their action.

The Mexican government lodged repeated protests in specific cases against permitting the vessels of the United States to remain in the ports of Mexico beyond the twenty-four hour limit, and based its contention on Articles 12 and 15 of the 13th Hague Convention of 1907. The Department of State took the position that this Convention was not binding, because three of the belligerents had not subscribed to it, and Article XXVIII specifically stated that the entire pact was not to be effective unless all the belligerents were signatories. Yet the instructions which were issued by the Navy Department to all commanders categorically stated that the twenty-four hour rule was to be observed, and Washington took the position that, although not legally bound to do so, it could be expected to abide by its own rules.[26] A determined effort was therefore made—and it was apparently successful—to avoid giving further offense to Mexico.[27]

---

[26] *Instructions for the Navy of the United States Governing Maritime Warfare, June, 1917* (Washington, 1924), p. 12. (Hereafter cited as *Naval Instructions, 1917.*) The argument can also be advanced that although the 13th Hague Convention was not adopted by all the belligerents, it was nevertheless generally regarded as declaratory of international law. See *Amer. Jour. of Int. Law*, XXXIV (1940), 581. It is also to be noted that, as Professor Quincy Wright points out, "A belligerent does not have a right to a twenty-four hour or any other length of sojourn for its ships in neutral waters. Such sojourn is a privilege which the neutral may grant, withhold or regulate." *Ibid.*, p. 239.

[27] Lansing informed the Mexican ambassador: "I have the honor to state that appropriate steps have been taken with a view to impressing upon the commanders of American ships of war that they should observe strictly the neutrality of Mexican territorial

What shall we say in general of the attitude of the United States in this matter? There can be no doubt that American warships violated the twenty-four hour rule, although, as we have observed, there were extenuating circumstances in all or almost all of the cases.[28] Technically speaking, these incidents were not a violation of the Hague Convention; nor were they violations of international law. The Department of State took the position, which seems to have been sound, that the twenty-four hour rule was a municipal regulation, rather than international law; and that the neutral which chose to invoke it should not only give satisfactory publicity to it but should apply it equally to all belligerents.[29] Interestingly enough, upon inquiry at London

---

waters, where it is unnecessary to protect jeopardized American interests, and it is confidently expected that no further instances will arise as to which the Mexican Government will feel warranted in making protest to this Government." Lansing to Bonillas, July 26, 1918, State Dept., 763. 72111M57/18.

[28] The instructions issued to naval officers allowed a prolongation of stay on account of damage or stress of weather. *Naval Instructions, 1917,* p. 12.

[29] Lansing to Bonillas, July 26, 1918, State Dept., 763. 72111M57/18. The German government did not regard the twenty-four hour rule as international law. Garner, *International Law and the World War,* II, 421, n. Following the disturbances early in Wilson's administration, the United States, with the consent of the Mexican government, stationed warships at Tampico for the purpose of protecting American lives and property. Two were still there when, in 1918, Mexico City protested against their presence on the grounds that their wireless communications to the United States interfered with those of Mexico, and on the further grounds that such a prolonged violation of the twenty-four hour rule would give other belligerents the basis for claiming the same right for themselves. The war came to an end before the matter was finally threshed out. In any event, it seems clear that this problem antedated the period we are considering, and that the

and Paris the State Department learned that the Mexican government had not made an announcement regarding the twenty-four hour rule; nor had it lodged any protests against British or French infractions.[30]

A not dissimilar situation arose from some eight cases involving an alleged violation of the three-ship rule by American men-of-war; that is, the presence of more than three vessels in a port of a neutral at the same time. The Mexican government again lodged repeated protests and cited Article 15 of the 13th Hague Convention of 1907. The Department of State took the position, as earlier, that the Hague Convention was not binding, and further pointed out that, strictly speaking, some of the American vessels involved were not warships at all because they were not carrying guns.[31] But, as before, the instructions issued to American naval commanders explicitly enjoined observation of the three-ship rule; [32] and since the United States could hardly complain when its own rules were invoked, it made strong efforts to comply with Mexico's wishes.[33]

---

continued acquiescence of the Mexican government in the presence of the American ships gave to the United States a kind of prescriptive right. See particularly Bonillas to Lansing, November 11, 1918, State Dept., 763.72111M57/78. Ambassador Page, in London, learned from British sources that the Mexican government considered the presence of American warships at Tampico as a pretext for a dispute if such should be desired with the United States government. Page to Lansing, February 16, 1918, *ibid.*, M57/55.

[30] *Ibid.*; Sharp to Lansing, February 15, 1918, *ibid.*, M57/1.

[31] These cases are all in *ibid.*, M57/18.

[32] *Naval Instructions, 1917,* p. 12.

[33] Admiral Fullam assured Secretary Daniels that " the Division Commander will continue the policy heretofore followed by him, taking every possible precaution to avoid precipitating a crisis in

vi

Several other cases involving Mexican rights rest on a somewhat different footing. Mexico City complained that certain American warships were hovering off the three-mile limit for the purpose of visit and search. One well-substantiated case involved the port of Mazatlán, where German sympathizers were notoriously active, and where it was feared that raiders might be fitted out or aid might be given to those at large. The Mexican government claimed that American hovering was an unfriendly act, inasmuch as the ports involved were far removed from the scene of hostilities, and inasmuch as Mexican ships were being searched even when there was no well-founded suspicion of contraband. The Department of State replied that the allegations of Mexico City had no bearing whatever on the time-honored right of a belligerent to visit and search outside the three-mile limit. But in view of the fact that Washington had earlier protested against British hovering as an unfriendly act, and in view of the further fact that Mexico found this practice objectionable, Acting Secretary of State Polk informed the Mexican ambassador that " out of regard to the wishes of Your Excellency's Government steps will be taken to conform so far as possible in the circumstances to the desire of the Mexican government in respect to the hovering of American war ships about Mexican ports." [34]

Mexico, searching vessels only when there is necessity for doing so and observing the neutrality of Mexican ports in accordance with previous instructions from the Department." Fullam to Daniels, April 4, 1918, State Dept., 763. 72111M57/51.

[34] Polk to Bonillas, August 6, 1918, *ibid.*, M57/25.

There were also several instances of American ships being detained or otherwise interfered with by United States warships in Mexican territorial waters. One clear-cut case occurred at Ensenada, in December, 1917, and involved the arresting of an American merchantman by the U. S. S. *Iroquois* while enforcing a statute of the United States. This was unquestionably a flagrant violation of Mexico's rights. The American consul who was responsible for the incident was reprimanded and the naval officer was removed from his command. The Judge Advocate General advised making an apology to Mexico City, and this was ultimately done in the form of an explanation to the Mexican ambassador. It would appear that this was the only one of these maritime cases where a United States naval officer was clearly and completely in the wrong; but punitive action was promptly taken and the appropriate apologies were tendered.[35] More than this could hardly be expected.

Several other cases were not so clear-cut. Mexico City protested against the searching of two Mexican ships in Mexico's territorial waters. If this had occurred, there would have been legitimate grounds for complaint; but the evidence supplied by the Navy Department indicated that these two vessels were about seven miles off the coast, in which case the searching was proper.[36] Mexico City also protested against firing solid shot across the bows of Mexican merchantmen on the high seas. The Navy Department

---

[35] Wilbur J. Carr to Smith (U. S. consul at Ensenada), May 28, 1918, *ibid.*, M57/63a.

[36] Secretary Lansing wrote to the Mexican ambassador: "In conclusion I may add that the Commanding Officers of American naval vessels have instructions to respect the neutrality of Mexican waters." Lansing to Bonillas, April 18, 1918, *ibid.*, M57/7.

explained that it had no blanks, and it complained that Mexican ships notoriously refused to heed American commands to heave to. In the case under consideration the vessel had attempted to escape, and the Navy Department contended that under these circumstances the ship could have been legitimately seized as a prize of war.[37]

Several general conclusions may be reasonably drawn from these cases. First of all, given the long haul between the Panama Canal and the west coast of the United States, it would have been strange indeed if a number of instances of this kind had not occurred. But as one examines the thick file of protests growing out of these rather trivial affairs, one finds it difficult to avoid the conclusion that the Mexican government was using this means of venting its unfriendliness against the United States. Possibly, as the Department of State suspected, these representations were being used as an offset to American protests on other matters. Whatever the truth, Secretary Lansing privately referred to the "irritated nature" of the complaints; and the Navy Department was of the opinion that they would not have been made if German agents had not persuaded

[37] Admiral Fullam added: ". . . It is most respectfully urged that the friendly and considerate attitude of Naval vessels on the Mexican coast toward Mexican vessels and the Mexican people, was probably without parallel in time of war, and that the searching and visitation of Mexican and other vessels was not begun until evidence of enemy activity and unneutral acts by Mexican officials and Mexican people against the United States made the occasional visitation and search of Mexican vessels a positive necessity." Fullam to Daniels, June 6, 1918, *ibid.*, M57/25. Daniels testified that Fullam had "repeatedly cautioned his force against giving any just grounds for complaint, and it is believed that the patrol is being carefully maintained in this spirit." Daniels to Lansing, May 15, 1918, *ibid.*, M57/18.

Mexico City to take action.[38] In any event, it is clear that some, if not most, of these protests were poorly founded, and were often drawn up without an adequate investigation of the facts.[39] It does not appear, either, that Mexican municipal regulations were properly announced, and it seems clear that the United States was singled out for discrimination, to the exclusion of Britain and France. At the worst, these incidents were all minor; most of them involved arguable infractions of international law. There was only one clear case of a violation of Mexican rights, and for this Washington took proper action. There can be no doubt that the United States Navy went to considerable pains and some inconvenience to avoid offending Mexico; that the Department of State was deferential and conciliatory; and that a genuine effort was made in Washington to avoid a further exacerbation of feelings that were already embittered.[40]

vii

An interesting situation involving Yucatán, nominally a political subdivision of Mexico, is of significance to us as revealing not what the United States did but what it refrained from doing.

[38] Lansing to Daniels, June 22, 1918; Fullam to Daniels, April 4, 1918, *ibid.*, M57/18, 51.

[39] On February 21, 1918, the Mexican government protested against some armed men from a merchantman taking photographs on the Mexican west coast. The Secretary of the Navy reported that this was an unarmed bathing party, one member of which took a small Kodak ashore; and that only one picture was taken, that being of a Mexican family group. Lansing to Bonillas, March 19, 1918, *ibid.*, M57/4.

[40] Lansing feared that the Mexican government might be seeking an excuse to intern United States ships. Lansing to Daniels, June 22, 1918, *ibid.*, M57/18.

The *Comisión Reguladora* of Yucatán, an organization closely affiliated with the local government, enjoyed an absolute monopoly of the only important supply of sisal in the world.[41] This product was used in the manufacture of binder twine, which was indispensable in the harvesting of American grain crops. The only possible substitute for sisal was hemp from the Philippines, but because of the shortage in tonnage and the extent of the demand, it was not possible to count on this source of supply.[42]

The *Comisión Reguladora*, which was virtually the government of Yucatán, was able, by monopolistic methods, to force the price of sisal up from four and one-half cents a pound in 1911 to nineteen and one-half cents in 1917. This amounted to a tax of some $50,000,000 annually on the American farmer, when compared with what he had paid before the war. The *Comisión* was threatening to push the price even higher if the Food Administration did not agree to the terms of an "outrageous" contract. The monopoly was fully aware of its power and of the necessities

[41] The official name was *Comisión Reguladora del Mercado de Henequén*.

[42] The affair is ably summarized in William C. Mullendore, *History of the United States Food Administration, 1917-1919* (Stanford University, 1941), pp. 311-16. This is the contemporary official report. Mark Requa, of the Food Administration, wrote: "Under no circumstances, be they whatever they may, can the United States harvest its wheat crop next year without this material." Requa to Polk, November 24, 1917, National Archives, F. A. A., 39H A3. Alexander Legge, of the War Industries Board, was disposed to take a less alarmist view. He pointed out that the crop could be harvested loosely without binding, but this would employ more labor and involve the rain hazard. He also noted that the market of the United States was as important to Yucatán as Yucatán was to the United States. Legge to Requa, November 6, 1917, *ibid*.

of the United States, for its attorney said to a representative of the Food Administration: "If we wanted to be brutal we might say that we have the material, that you must have it, and what are you going to do about it?"[43] By the latter part of 1917 the binder-twine factories in the United States were beginning to close down because of the exhaustion of supplies on hand; and Mark Requa, of the Food Administration, was forced to confess that the United States, if necessary, would have to pay fifty cents a pound or more in order to get the product.[44] He was of the opinion that this was the most important single problem then before the Food Administration.[45]

On November 10, 1917, Requa submitted a remarkable report to his superior, Herbert Hoover. Referring to these "pirates" who were making America the "vassal" of Yucatán by exacting "tribute," Requa concluded:

> I recommend that the matter be submitted to the State Department and that preparations be made for landing a force in Yucatan; that I be instructed to continue negotiations toward a final ultimatum, and that failing in this troops be landed and the country policed pending determination of what is the just price for sisal.[46]

Three days later, Hoover forwarded Requa's report to the Department of State, and in his covering letter made it clear that, while he did not necessarily favor force, he regarded

---

[43] Requa to Lansing, November 23, 1917, *ibid.*

[44] Requa to Lindley, January 11, 1918, *ibid.*

[45] Requa to Hoover, November 27, 1917, F. A. R., Hoover Library (Mark L. Requa).

[46] Requa to Hoover, November 10, 1917, National Archives, F. A. A., 39H A3.

the situation as critical. "We have got to have the sisal," he concluded.[47]

In reply to the representations of Requa and Hoover, the Department of State made it clear that the Administration preferred not to resort to violent measures, and that it would be desirable to make the best terms possible with the monopoly, even at nineteen and one-half cents a pound, rather than stir up trouble. Specifically, Polk pointed out that forcible methods were open to two objections. First, they would mean an armed conflict with Mexico. Second, war would completely interrupt the production of sisal, unless laborers were sent down with the troops; and even an attempt to secure the product under such conditions would encounter almost insuperable obstacles. Moreover, hostilities with Mexico would not only cut off the supply of sisal, but would interfere with the importation of Mexican oil, metals, and other necessities.[48]

The objections of the State Department proved decisive, and strong-arm measures were avoided.[49] The Food Ad-

[47] Hoover to Polk, November 13, 1917, F. A. R., Hoover Library (State Dept., Frank L. Polk). The next year Hoover recommended the landing of several hundred additional marines in Santo Domingo so as to forestall a large loss in sugar production. It is to be noted, however, that this republic had severed relations, and that it had been occupied by United States marines since May, 1916. Hoover to State Department, November 1, 1918, *ibid.* (State Dept., Lansing).

[48] Polk to Requa, November 24, 1917, National Archives, F. A. A., 39H A3.

[49] The excitable Requa wrote to Lansing: " The shade of Charles Jay [*sic*] Pinckney rises before us and his immortal declaration of ' Millions for defense but not a cent for tribute ' is a fit expression of the attitude of the Food Administration—which, however,

ministrator was able, however, to keep the price of sisal at nineteen cents by agreeing informally to arrange for the export of food and gold to Yucatán. This price was unsatisfactory but necessary.[50]

The entire incident is important as showing that Washington resisted the temptation to use violent methods in Yucatán.[51] It preferred to pay an exorbitant price and tax the American farmer many millions rather than disturb the already ticklish relations with Mexico. Although the Department of State pointed out that on the practical side armed intervention would probably not produce the sisal, it does not appear that this was the decisive consideration. The United States already had its hands full with one war; the neutrals throughout the world were not happy over the tactics that Washington was being forced to use; and apparently it was desirable to pay a monopolistic price, provided the sisal was obtained, rather than further blacken the good name of the United States.

---

recognizes the paramount authority of the Department of State and upon instructions from you must necessarily conform thereto." Requa to Lansing, November 23, 1917, *ibid.*

[50] As early as September 18, 1917, Hoover had suggested employing the financial club on the Mexican government. Hoover to Lansing, September 18, 1917, F. A. R., Hoover Library (State Dept., Robert Lansing). On November 26 Hoover urged use of the food embargo. Hoover to Polk, November 26, 1917, *ibid.* (State Dept., Frank L. Polk).

[51] One of my informants who prefers not to be named in this connection writes: "I had a feeling at the time that the Food Administration were making a record in order to put responsibility on the State Department." He adds that when Requa brought in his final recommendation he was told that it amounted to a declaration of war and that he had better take it across to the White House rather than leave it with the Department.

viii

In addition to Mexico, Argentina must be singled out for special consideration. This sprawling South American republic was of vital importance to the Allies because of its large surpluses of grain. Argentina, in turn, was heavily dependent upon the Associated Powers for coal, agricultural machinery, and other necessities. Coal was of particular importance, because without it the public utilities of the larger Argentine cities could not be kept running; and considerable difficulty was caused when the United States, operating under its blacklist, refused to permit the export of coal to concerns that were German-tainted.[52]

An interesting case of self-denial on the part of Washington arose in November, 1917. The British minister in Buenos Aires invited the United States ambassador, Frederic J. Stimson, to a conference with the Allied representatives on the means of bringing about internment of any German submarines that might arrive. Lansing promptly sent instructions that it was "inadvisable" to attend such a gathering, and Stimson was further warned "to make no expressions of opinion either personally or officially in connection with this matter."[53] President Wilson approved this stand, and on his own typewriter drew up the following statement:

Surely the Ministers of the Allies are going too far in trying this sort of thing on the impossible gentleman who is President of Argentina. The position they are purposing to take is the one the Allies tried to force on us when we were

---

[52] Stimson to Lansing, June 7, 1917, State Dept., 600.119/106; New York *Times*, December 5, 1917.

[53] *For. Rel., 1917, Supp. 2*, II, p. 1297.

neutral, and they must realize that they are putting us in a very awkward position. If Stimson does not join with them, he will seem, on our behalf, to put our sanction on the admission of the boats to Argentine harbours, which we desire as little as they do; and yet he cannot take part with them in any such representations. I suppose it is too late to head the whole thing off?[54]

The record does not reveal that the United States became involved in the proposed joint representations.

Argentina also entered into the calculations of the United States as an alternate source of grain for the hard-pressed neutrals of Europe, but the shortage of shipping and the fact that the haul from the Argentine was twice that from New York militated strongly against a satisfactory solution of the problem in this quarter. The Argentinians were particularly disturbed over the loss of their grain market in the European neutral countries as a result of American bunker coal and other shipping restrictions. Food Administrator Hoover proposed a scheme under which Argentina would be compensated for losing this market, but the difficulties encountered were of such a serious nature that nothing came of it.[55]

After prolonged negotiations, a convention was signed on January 14, 1918, between Buenos Aires on the one hand and the French and British governments on the other, under the terms of which Argentina was to sell 2,500,000 tons of grain and receive in return her needed coal. The

---

[54] Baker, *Wilson,* VII, 343.

[55] Hoover proposed that the United States take the three-year prewar average of Argentine exports to the embargoed neutrals, buy up this surplus, and then dispose of it as seemed best. Hoover to Polk, October 5, 1917, National Archives, F. A. A., 10H A7. See also F. M. Surface, *The Grain Trade during the World War* (New York, 1928), p. 295.

responsibilities of the United States under the agreement were to issue export licenses for coal and to assist in the providing of shipping.[56] The convention was promptly approved by the Argentine Congress and put into effect by executive decree on January 19, 1918.[57]

Some little difficulty arose between Washington and Buenos Aires over the proposed purchase by Argentina of the *Bahia Blanca*, a 15,000-ton interned German steamer. In March, 1918, the Argentinian government sought the approval of the United States, and Secretary Lansing provisionally replied that the State Department would be inclined to favor the transaction, provided proper guarantees were given against the ship's being employed for the benefit of the enemy. These assurances were forthcoming; but when the British began both to raise objections to the transfer and to lay down conditions for the use of the vessel, the United States swung around to the support of its Associate. The inference is that London exerted some pressure on Washington, and that Britain was concerned lest the purchase price, reportedly 2,500,000 gold pesos, reach the Germans and be used against the common cause. The British still registered opposition even when Argentina proposed to send the ship to Cette, France, with grain for Switzerland.

---

[56] Stimson to Lansing, January 2, 1918, F. A. R., Hoover Library (Argentina: Purchase of Wheat Crop by French and British). See also Stimson, *My United States*, pp. 415-18.

[57] Martin, *Latin America and the War*, p. 259; Adee to Hoover, January 23, 1918, F. A. R., Hoover Library (Argentina: Purchase of Wheat Crop by French and British). Britain did not formally accept the agreement, and there was some friction between her and the United States over coal distribution in the Argentine. Lansing to London Embassy, November 29, 1918, State Dept., 600. 119/1839b.

The Buenos Aires officials were evidently much displeased with Washington's about-face regarding the sale. They cited the Declaration of London, as well as American precedents, and in particular asserted that the State Department had not only approved of the transaction but had told the Argentine ambassador that the United States would be willing to advance the purchase price. The war came to an end with the *Bahia Blanca* dispute still unsettled, and with relations between Britain and Argentina definitely strained. The State Department in this matter apparently had no strong convictions, but merely followed the lead of the British.[58]

ix

The case of interned German ships in Chile, some eighty in number (including both steamers and sailers), presented fewer difficulties. In the spring of 1918 the Chilean government sought the permission of the United States for the leasing of three of these vessels. Both Washington and London gave their approval, subject to certain safeguards designed to keep the ships from operating for the benefit of the enemy. While the negotiations with Berlin for the leasing of the three ships were still going on, the German officers, evidently acting under orders, sabotaged or attempted to sabotage the vessels under their command. The Chilean government then put armed guards on the ships, and on November 5, 1918, when Germany was collapsing, seized the entire lot, presumably to prevent the crews from sinking them.[59] It is interesting to note that Washington

[58] The entire episode is treated in *For. Rel., 1918, Supp. 1*, II, pp. 1746-64. See also Stimson, *My United States,* pp. 414-15.

[59] *For. Rel., 1918, Supp. 1,* II, pp. 1748-51; New York *Times,* April 21, 24, September 28, November 5, 6, 1918.

was much interested in these negotiations, and that it withdrew a ship from the Chilean run with the obvious intention of bringing pressure to bear on Santiago.[60] Whether or not Chile would have acted without such prompting it is difficult to say; at all events, the United States apparently was to some extent responsible for inducing a neutral to adopt a type of seizure not dissimilar to that which had been employed in the wholesale requisitioning of the Dutch ships, although in the case of Chile the seizure was for the prevention of further sabotage rather than for the immediate employment of the interned vessels.

Two other South American republics, Uruguay and Peru, figured prominently in negotiations with the United States over the seizure of interned German tonnage. Uruguay, which, as we have noted, was perhaps the most conspicuously unneutral of those republics that severed relations, ran true to form when she took steps to seize eight German steamers as her contribution to the world shipping crisis. The necessary legislation was passed in November, 1917, and after the vessels had been reconditioned they were

[60] *For. Rel., 1918, Supp. 1*, I, pp. 716, 717, 719, 726-27. Chandler P. Anderson suggested to Frank L. Polk that Chile might employ a "converse application" of the right of angary. "In other words," he said, "if we are entitled to seize Dutch ships on account of the lawlessness of the German submarine activities, Chile should be entitled without loss of neutrality to seize German ships in Chilean waters to make good the interference with neutral trade resulting from German submarine warfare." Anderson recorded that Polk, who was "very much pleased with this suggestion," expressed the hope that "I could work it up to make it useful in our negotiations with Chile for getting the German ships out." "Diary of Chandler P. Anderson," March 18, 1918. Similar views were set forth by a Chilean jurist. Alejandro Alvarez, *La grande guerre européenne et la neutralité du Chili* (Paris, 1915), pp. 261-65.

leased to the Emergency Fleet Corporation of the United States, in May, 1918.[61] Peru took similar action with reference to ten German ships in her waters, and in September, 1918, entered upon a contract with the Emergency Fleet Corporation for the leasing of the vessels.[62] Thus it was that the United States quite properly became the beneficiary of action taken by two South American states which, though having severed relations with Germany, were still technically neutral.

x

Early in the war Washington became concerned over the possibility that American armed merchantmen engaged in the South American trade might be interned. It was finally decided to address inquiries to Chile, Peru, Colombia, Argentina, Paraguay, Venezuela, Ecuador, Honduras, and Guatemala, asking what the attitude of the governments of these respective countries would be regarding defensively armed merchantmen. In every case the reply was that these ships might freely engage in trade, although Argentina and Chile laid down inconsequential safeguarding conditions. A similar inquiry addressed to the Netherlands government as to its colonial ports elicited the response that such vessels, in accordance with Holland's previously announced policy, would not be received. The United States, while a neutral, had permitted defensively armed ships to enter its ports; hence it was asking of the Latin American states only what it had practiced. It is noteworthy, however, that all these republics which appear to have been consulted, whether

[61] Martin, *Latin America and the War*, p. 374.

[62] *Ibid.*, p. 407. These shipping seizures are discussed at length in file 862.85, State Dept. See also New York *Times*, July 14, September 8, 1918.

neutral or not, fell in with the wishes of the United States, though not pressed to do so.[63]

A somewhat similar problem arose in connection with the requisitioned Dutch vessels. The Washington government planned to put some of this tonnage in the South American trade, but it feared that the Dutch owners, through the courts of these countries, might bring legal action which would result in intolerable delays. Accordingly, the Department of State addressed inquiries to Uruguay, Peru, Argentina, and Chile; and in every case assurances were forthcoming that proper protection would be extended to these requisitioned vessels. The consent of Chile was particularly prompt and cordial, while the reply of Argentina contained the sole condition that munitions would have to be removed before the ships could enter her ports.[64]

It would appear, then, that in the case of both the armed merchantmen and the Dutch requisitioned steamers the republics of Latin America, whether technically neutral or not, revealed a definite willingness to co-operate with the United States.

xi

On the whole, the United States had less difficulty with the Latin American than with the European neutrals. The sister republics of the Western Hemisphere were all, with the notable exception of Mexico, benevolently disposed; they were not subject to invasion or serious German reprisal if they strayed from the path of neutrality in favor of the Associated Powers; and even if they had strongly favored

[63] *For. Rel.; 1917, Supp. 2*, II, pp. 1283-89; *ibid., 1918, Supp. 1*, II, pp. 1790-92.
[64] *Ibid.*, pp. 1792-97.

rendering active assistance to Germany, they were estopped by the British blockade and by Allied and American bunker control. In addition, as we have noted, they were in a position to dispose of valuable surpluses of their native products to the United States.

It is true that Washington permitted several of the Latin American republics to compromise their neutrality when it accepted unneutral use of their ports and other facilities; but inasmuch as these privileges were voluntarily offered, it would seem as though the Wilson administration was not guilty of any real offense.[65] It is also true that the United States became involved with Mexico in a series of disputes involving alleged violations of territorial waters; but only once does Washington appear to have been clearly in the wrong, and in this case it made ample amends. On the other hand, the United States discontinued its indubitable right to hover off the Mexican coast, declined to use drastic measures in Yucatán, and refused to join with its Associates in an attempt to bring about the internment of German submarines in Argentina. All in all, the record reflects creditably on the Washington government.

[65] For the cases of Guatemala and Nicaragua during the pre-belligerency period, see *ante*, pp. 28-29. It is a well-established principle of international law that a neutral may engage in unneutral acts, but if it does so it must abide the consequences. As Professor Charles Cheney Hyde says in his discussion of Latin American unneutrality: ". . . the law of nations does not contemplate that a State not at war shall fix or alter its obligations as a neutral according to its interest in the success of one belligerent rather than another. When a non-participant undertakes to do so, it must be normally deemed to accept responsibility for the harm which its action inflicts upon the State subjected to discrimination. The United States has vigorously advocated respect for this principle." *International Law Chiefly as Interpreted and Applied by the United States*, II, 766.

Chapter XI

BUNKERS AND BLACKLISTS

i

Long before America entered the war the British adopted and perfected an extraordinarily effective device for the control of neutral tonnage: the bunker-supply club. This involved the withholding of bunker coal and oil, as well as ships' stores and supplies (all of which were generally referred to as bunkers), until the neutral shipper agreed to fulfill certain conditions. As finally developed by the British, bunker control was used to accomplish four main objects:

1. To aid in the enforcement of the Allied blockade. (This was done by requiring the neutral vessel, when proceeding to Europe, to stop at a British port for examination.)

2. To prevent coal, oil, and other supplies from reaching enemy submarines and other commerce raiders. (This was accomplished by restricting the shipment of such supplies to approved consignees.)

3. To prevent the transportation of enemy reservists.

4. To conserve tonnage. (This was done by forbidding long trips in ballast, and by requiring neutral ships to perform a certain amount of service beneficial to the Allies.) [1]

As the war dragged on, and the German submarines began to take an increasingly heavy toll, conservation of tonnage became the most important of these four objects.

---

[1] This list is rather closely paraphrased from the *Report of War Trade Board*, p. 120.

It must be clearly understood at the outset that the general principle of bunker control was not at variance with international law but merely involved the exercise of a sovereign right. The coal and other supplies belonged to the British, who were at perfect liberty to prescribe conditions for their use. The neutral shipper could either accept these conditions or refuse them. If he refused them, his alternatives were to lay up his ship at a mounting loss, or to turn, if possible, to some other trade. Although theoretically his acceptance of bunker control was purely voluntary, actually his decision was the result of a form of duress.

America, while a neutral, had naturally found British bunker control annoying; but such protests as she made against it were generally coupled with the blacklist, to which it was closely related. This failure to make a strong issue of bunker restrictions as such was probably due primarily to the fact that the United States was not so heavily dependent as the European neutrals upon British bunkering facilities, particularly in American and Pacific waters. Nevertheless, at one time or another the Department of State did make representations in behalf of several United States ships which were being denied bunkers, and in each case Britain promptly acceded to the wishes of Washington.[2]

[2] On British-American relations regarding bunker control, see *For. Rel., 1916, Supp.*, pp. 423, 430, 436, 440-41, 443-45, 455, 457-59, 460, 465, 480, 489; *ibid., 1917, Supp. 1*, pp. 506-07, 507-09. On December 28, 1916, Lansing informed Page that several cases had arisen "recently where American steamship lines have been told that they could not charter or use ships of other neutral countries, which ships had signed bunker agreement [with the British], unless American company agreed to bind not only chartered ships but also all the ships owned by the American company." Lansing concluded that the British attempt to control chartered ships which were bound by agreements was understandable, but "the attempt

The chief obstacle to completely effective bunker control by the British was the United States, from which neutral ships were able to obtain large quantities of fuel. But after America's entry into the war it was evident that Anglo-American co-operation would result in practically airtight bunker restrictions.[3] The British officials, particularly those on the Balfour Commission, consequently revealed the details of their practices, and cautiously recommended the adoption of a common policy. They were certain that " since the Allies will be in control of practically the whole coal supplies of the world," " any conditions, short of compelling the neutral shipowner to run his ships at a loss, can be imposed as a *quid pro quo* for the supply of coal." [4]

In his highly revealing memorandum of May 17, 1917, the Law Adviser (then Solicitor Nominate) of the State Department, Lester H. Woolsey, indicated that Washington had considerable misgivings about following the British in their bunker control practices. The United States, of course, was fully prepared to distribute its own fuel in such a way as to prevent supplies or reservists from reaching the enemy. But the Administration would not be bound by the lists of undesirable ships drawn up by the British; rather, it would insist upon an equal voice in the determination of such lists.

---

to control American ships not requiring British facilities is entirely unreasonable and can not possibly be permitted by this Government." Page was instructed to investigate this situation; but nothing more seems to have come of it. *Ibid.,* p. 505.

[3] For figures on the large supplies of oil and coal provided by the United States to vessels in foreign trade, see *Report of War Trade Board,* p. 119. The War Trade Board declared: " Outside of the British Empire and the United States the sources of bunker fuel open to the shipping world were practically non-existent." *Ibid.*

[4] *For. Rel., 1917, Supp. 2,* II, p. 839. The various British documents appear in *ibid.,* pp. 811-12, 839-46, 849-51, 857-62.

(This principle was adhered to throughout the war.) Woolsey further pointed out that the United States was unwilling to force neutral ships to call at British ports for examination, but that the proposed system of American license control would render such a practice unnecessary. Nor would Washington proscribe all persons of enemy nationality or association; there would have to be reasonable grounds for supposing that they were actually helping the enemy. (This principle was persistently maintained.) The United States was willing, Woolsey added, to induce neutral ships to carry supplies to and from neutral countries, but it would not force them into the danger zone, either in American or Allied service.[5] (This principle was followed much less rigidly.) The inference that one draws from this interesting document is that the Administration would determine its own policy in its own good time, and would not resort to extreme restrictions on the neutrals.

ii

The United States adhered to its evident determination not to be hurried into some extreme form of bunker control. The earliest definite beginnings were somewhat belatedly announced in Wilson's first export control proclamation (July 9, 1917), which listed bunker fuel among those commodities that could not be exported without a license. During the ensuing weeks Washington gradually enlarged its concept of bunker control; and although it did not adopt certain British blockade practices, preferring rather to cooperate with the Admiralty in these, it did extend bunker restrictions to a point that must have been gratifying to

[5] *Ibid.*, pp. 867-69.

Downing Street. Among other things, the United States established a secondary bunker control at the Dutch West Indian island of Curaçao, at the Colombian port of Maracaibo, and at the Venezuelan ports of Puerto Cabello and La Guaira. All of these places were neutral; and since the coal supplies that were sold there as bunkers came from the United States, the War Trade Board properly and successfully enforced the condition that this fuel should not be sold without its consent.[6]

As far as the neutrals were concerned, American bunker control had three major objectives.[7] The first of these was to prevent aid from reaching the enemy, directly or indirectly; and to this end a number of specific regulations were laid down. No voyage could be made and no cargo could be carried without the consent of the American bunkering authorities.[8] No vessels were permitted to run, directly or

[6] *Report of War Trade Board*, p. 333. Bunker control was also exercised in some of the cobelligerents, notably Cuba. There the War Trade Board representative had absolute control over the bunker supply, which was shipped from the United States; and pressure exercised on the Cuban government seems to have been partially effective in stopping Spanish ships from going from Cuba to Mexico, where they were suspected of maintaining connections with Germany. For this episode see *For. Rel., 1918, Supp. 1*, II, pp. 1730-31, 1733-37, 1738-39, 1741, 1742-44, 1745-46.

[7] The most comprehensive statement of regulations seems to have been that issued by the War Trade Board, on January 19, 1918, and modified in minor particulars from time to time. Text in *ibid.*, pp. 946-49. An earlier statement of importance, dated October 5, 1917, appears in *ibid., 1917, Supp. 2*, II, p. 958. Most of the material in this section has been drawn from the *Report of War Trade Board*, pp. 59-61, 119-122, 329-45.

[8] See the strict regulations that two Spanish lines were forced to accept, including free accommodations for American representatives while on voyages. *For. Rel., 1918, Supp. 1*, II, p. 1730.

indirectly, in the interests of the enemy.[9] No ship accepting bunkers could be bought or sold without the previous consent of the United States authorities. No wireless communication could be made that would be of assistance to the enemy. Every shipper receiving bunkers bound himself, upon the request of the War Trade Board, to dispense with the services of the master, the officers, or any members of the crew that might be deemed inimical to American interests.[10] No vessels were permitted to carry cargoes to blacklisted firms. No enemy subject, unless due authorization was first obtained, could be transported by ships receiving American fuel. No surplus bunkers could be used for purposes other than those for which they were issued. No sailing vessels were allowed ships' stores for a voyage into the danger zone, lest these slow craft be overhauled by

[9] Through bunker control at the Canal Zone, the United States forced the execution of an agreement giving the American authorities complete control over certain Chilean and Peruvian lines that had been operating in the service of a German-owned sugar plantation in Peru. *Report of War Trade Board*, p. 59. In order to cut off German contacts with Latin America, the War Trade Board required certain Spanish lines to enter into an agreement which provided that in return for bunkers the ships would maintain fixed itineraries and make their first and last call on the American side of the Atlantic at New York or San Juan, Puerto Rico. After the Armistice, San Juan was changed to Key West. *Ibid.*, pp. 333-34. The War Trade Board seriously considered a plan to require all Spanish ships crossing the Atlantic to stop at Puerto Rico for bunkers, but this was finally disapproved by the Department of State. See *For. Rel., 1918, Supp. 1*, II, pp. 1738, 1740, 1742-44, 1745; see also *post*, pp. 401-03.

[10] This practice appears not to have been generally exercised. The master of a Norwegian ship was removed, but it so happened that this ship had come under the jurisdiction of the United States as a result of the Norwegian agreement. *Report of War Trade Board*, pp. 60-61.

submarines and essential supplies be taken off.[11] Bunkers were likewise denied to unarmed and unconvoyed steamers planning to enter dangerous waters with a deck cargo useful to raiders. As a means of enforcing all these regulations, the War Trade Board required the shipper who applied for bunkers to enter into an agreement to abide by the rules, and to list all the vessels under his control, so that if one was guilty of an infraction, all might be denied bunkering privileges.

The second major purpose of bunker control, and perhaps the most important one, was the conservation of tonnage. This was accomplished in several ways. No sailing vessels, with minor exceptions, were granted ships' stores for a trip into the submarine zone, primarily because the loss among these slow craft was greater than among steamers.[12] This regulation forced sailers into the coastal trade, and consequently drove steamers into transoceanic routes, where they were urgently needed. The War Trade Board also required vessels to be loaded to capacity, and pursued a policy of

[11] This was one of the earliest restrictions. See resolution of the Exports Administrative Board, September 19, 1917. *For. Rel., 1917, Supp. 2,* II, p. 957. Exceptions were made, notably in the case of Swiss " safe-conduct ships " going to Cette (France), and certain regulations were laid down for storing in inaccessible parts of the vessel supplies that would be useful to submarines. *Ibid., 1918, Supp. 1,* II, pp. 997-98, 1005-06. The restrictions on sailing ships were among the first to be lifted after the Armistice. "Minutes of the War Trade Board," IV, 478 (November 21, 1918).

[12] When this policy was first inaugurated exceptions were made in favor of ships that had been granted prior charters. *For. Rel., 1917, Supp. 2,* II, 1006. The restrictions on sailing craft were also motivated by the fear that their owners might sell out when they reached a European port. *Second Annual Report of U. S. Shipping Board,* p. 44.

discouraging unnecessarily long hauls. In December, 1917, for example, United States bunker control forced several ships to forsake the South African trade and ply in South American and West Indian waters.[13] In addition, no vessel could be laid up, except for repairs, without the consent of the proper American authorities.[14] Finally, the most effective way of securing and retaining the services of neutral tonnage was to require that the ships receiving bunkers for the outward voyage agree to return to the United States, in some cases by such routes and with such cargo as the bunkering officials stipulated.[15] This type of control not only forced much neutral tonnage to ply in American interests but also served to keep certain commodities out of the hands of the enemy. As early as September, 1917, for example, the owners of a Danish steamer sought bunkers for a trip from the United States to Brazil, where they planned to take on a large supply of coffee for one of the Northern Neutrals. Fearing that the cargo ultimately would fall into German hands, the American bunkering authorities exacted an agreement that this ship would return to the United States.[16]

The third primary purpose of bunker control was to

---

[13] *Report of War Trade Board*, p. 121.

[14] Very little concerning these regulations appeared in the press. In February, 1918, however, it was reported that coal had been refused Norwegian vessels unless their owners signed guarantees that the ships would not be withdrawn from service. New York *Times*, February 20, 1918.

[15] This regulation was applied effectively to Dutch shipping in the Pacific. *For. Rel., 1917, Supp. 2*, II, p. 1135.

[16] *Report of War Trade Board*, p. 331. The Spanish consul at "a gulf port" objected strongly to the demands of Washington that three Spanish ships be required to return to the United States. New York *Times*, March 8, 1918.

secure essential commodities. This was done by requiring, as a condition for receiving the bunkers, that the vessel, on its return trip, bring back certain products needed by the United States. Such regulations were particularly binding in the case of a considerable number of sailing vessels plying in American and Pacific waters. Some of them were actually required to go to specific places and bring back specified cargoes.[17] An interesting corollary to the securing of essential commodities was the insistence of the War Trade Board that the shipper keep his freight rates within reasonable bounds or go without bunkers. This device proved effective in the case of certain Spanish steamers and in the case of other vessels engaged in the coffee trade with Brazil.[18]

iii

What conclusions shall we draw regarding American bunker control? There can be no doubt that from the standpoint of the neutrals it was extraordinarily binding, that it worked considerable hardship,[19] and that it was achieved by a type of coercion. We must note, however, that it was applied to all shipping leaving American waters, whether that of neutrals, of cobelligerents, or even of the United States. Indeed, some of the most interesting cases of severity involved the Allies. We may further observe that the neutral governments, so far as this investigation revealed, made no serious protest against bunker control, and the few

[17] *Report of War Trade Board,* pp. 334-35.
[18] *Ibid.,* p. 340. The War Trade Board here instances one case of a Japanese line which was forced to lower its proposed rate on carrying United States mail to South Africa.
[19] Exports markets, notably in the case of Argentine grain, were disrupted by bunker restrictions. See *ante,* p. 332.

minor complaints that were registered concerned matters of detail rather than of principle.[20] It must be conceded, however, that the neutrals may have been discouraged from making representations by the evident determination of the United States to use its dominant control of fuel for the prosecution of the war. Although there doubtless were instances of individual grievances that never became the subject of formal protest or court action, it seems clear that as a matter of general policy the War Trade Board exercised bunker control without discrimination among the neutrals, and that Washington did not go so far as it might have gone, notably when it refused to force neutral shipping into the danger zones.[21]

So much for the actual working of bunker control. What about the legal principles involved? It would be difficult to maintain, as we have noted, that the general policy of bunker control was a violation of international law. America was involved in a desperate war; her supplies of fuel, food, and other ships' provisions were limited; the labor for

[20] Upon complaint of the Danish government, certain exemptions as regards bunker control were granted to ships bound by the existing agreement. *For. Rel., 1918, Supp. 1*, II, pp. 1312, 1317. The neutral press, however, was quite vocal in its condemnation of bunker restrictions. For minor Swedish objections, see *ibid.*, pp. 1210-11, 1212. The Spanish government protested against the restrictions on sailing ships, but this difficulty appears to have been amicably settled by exempting those vessels bound by prior arrangements. *Ibid., 1917, Supp. 2*, II, pp. 1006, 1211.

[21] Compare with the Woolsey memorandum of May 17, 1917, *ibid.*, pp. 867-69. The State Department vetoed a suggestion of its representative in Madrid that it use the bunker club to force Spain into a hostile attitude toward Germany at the time of the crisis over the contemplated seizure of German ships. *Ibid., 1918, Supp. 2*, II, pp. 1721-22, 1724-25. See *ante*, pp. 301-02.

producing and making those commodities available was scarce; the tonnage for hauling the coal to outlying stations was hard to obtain. There can be little doubt that the United States was justified in insisting that its own supplies should not be used against it for the benefit of the enemy. As for forcing neutral shipping into services beneficial to the Associated Powers, the case rested on somewhat different foundations. The neutral country needed supplies; the United States was short of those supplies. If the neutral shipper was to secure them, he was forced to agree to a *quid pro quo*; namely, such conditions as Washington should lay down. Theoretically, the neutral had a free choice: he could accept these conditions or refuse them; but since the alternative was ruinous, he exercised that free choice to accept American terms.

iv

A discussion of bunker restrictions leads naturally and logically to the blacklist. In the first place, bunker control was a specialized form of the blacklist, confined solely to shipping. In the second place, bunker control was one of the most effective instruments—perhaps the most effective instrument—in the enforcement of the blacklist. In turn, the blacklist, with the exception of the blockade and export control, was probably the most potent single weapon that the Allies employed against the neutrals.

The blacklist was a list of persons or firms in a neutral country which were in one way or another helping the enemy, or were reasonably thought to be helping the enemy. To weaken these organizations, the belligerent in question forbade its nationals to have any traffic with them, except under a carefully supervised system of licensing. In short, the blacklisted firm could be affected only by boycott methods; the person trading with it would be subject to the penalties prescribed by the law of his own country. The effectiveness of this instrument is eloquently attested by the fact that it was adopted during the war by most of the principal belligerents.[22]

Before the United States entered the conflict, the British had brought their blacklist to a high state of perfection. Its most obvious feature was the published or statutory list, which was issued under statutory authority and which forbade, under penalty of the law, any British subject or firm to trade with the proscribed organizations. A second and earlier grouping was the confidential list, which for various reasons was not published but which was used by the licensing authorities in approving consignees, and by the customs authorities in examining imported goods.[23]

The British tests for eligibility to the blacklist are of particular interest to us, because to a degree they were later followed by the United States. In addition to those persons whose normal business was in some way connected with the enemy, the British lists included persons or firms (1) who were backed by enemy capital or controlled from an enemy country; (2) who sent money to the enemy or subscribed to enemy war loans; (3) who engaged in propaganda activities, espionage, sabotage, or the fomentation of rebellion; (4) who abused cable privileges by sending secret messages; (5) who gave aid to enemy cruisers or submarines; and (6) who bought up stocks of commodities to keep them from

[22] See Bailey, "United States and the Blacklist during the Great War," *Jour. of Mod. Hist.*, VI (1934), 14 ff.

[23] *Report of War Trade Board*, p. 46. The confidential list had at least two gradations. *For. Rel., 1917, Supp. 2*, II, p. 851.

the Allies. Under British and French law a person of enemy nationality resident in a neutral country was subject to blacklisting, even though he was not actively engaged in helping the enemy. In general, the policy of the Allies was to weaken all firms connected with the Central Powers, for even though such organizations did not actively succor the enemy, they helped his morale by building up credits and stores of raw materials in anticipation of peace. The British believed, not without reason, that the gradual undermining of German branch firms in neutral countries would cause the parent organization to bring pressure on Berlin to end the war.[24]

When a company was once blacklisted by London, all British subjects were forbidden to trade with it; cable and mail facilities were denied it; marine insurance, banking, and credit arrangements were withdrawn from it; ships' stores and bunker fuel were not made available to it. In addition, the threat of blacklisting, or a desire to get off the list, or fear of a postwar boycott, often induced the neutral firm in question to discharge its German employees, and in some cases, apparently, to reveal German trade secrets. There was a natural disposition on the part of the British to accord preferential treatment to those concerns in neutral countries which were on the German blacklist—hence presumably pro-Ally—and in general to boycott companies of questionable sympathies in favor of those that clearly favored the Allied cause.[25]

---

[24] *Report of War Trade Board*, pp. 46, 170; *For. Rel., 1917, Supp. 2*, II, pp. 853, 871. A useful account of the British blacklist appears in Chapter VII of Otto Jöhlinger, *Der britische Wirtschaftskrieg und seine Methoden* (Berlin, 1918).

[25] Turlington, *Neutrality*, p. 81; *For. Rel., 1917, Supp. 2*, II, pp. 870-71.

The British stoutly maintained that the blacklist was purely domestic legislation, and that it was their business if they declined to have dealings with any particular foreign concern. They asserted, moreover, that the blacklist prescribed penalties for only British subjects, and that as a consequence the blacklisted neutral firms had no legal cause for complaint. But whatever the legalities of the question, in actual practice not only was the blacklistee affected, but a great many other persons as well. A large number of concerns which had formerly done business with the proscribed organization discontinued doing so for fear that this association might result in their being added to the blacklist. Some organizations were bold enough to continue their traffic with a blacklisted house, but they frequently found that more timid concerns stopped doing business with them for fear of being proscribed. This whole atmosphere of uncertainty and fear was heightened by the knowledge that there were confidential lists; that many blacklisted companies did not know why they were singled out; and that as the British authorities were inclined to err on the side of severity, many innocent firms were mistakenly banned. In some instances this was brought about by one organization deliberately spreading lies to the effect that its competitor was pro-German.[26] Such developments as these caused the blacklist to have many of the widespread and paralyzing features of a secondary boycott. Indeed, it would be difficult to point to any other weapon devised by the belligerents during this war that was more vicious in its operation within neutral countries, or more widespread in its ramifications.

[26] Geering, *Handel und Industrie der Schweiz*, p. 34.

V

Following the passage of the British Trading with the Enemy Act of December 23, 1915, which authorized the statutory blacklist, Secretary Lansing served notice on the British government that "this act is pregnant with possibilities of undue interference with American trade," and that the Department of State reserved the right to protest against its application to the United States.[27] Whether deterred by these stern words or not, the British delayed announcing a blacklist for the United States until July 18, 1916, long after they had applied one to other countries; and the list of eighty-five American persons or concerns was disproportionately small, particularly when compared with the long blacklists for other neutral nations and with the large number of enemy subjects resident in the United States.[28]

Despite these evidences of mildness, public opinion in America, already smarting under other British trade restrictions, was mightily aroused; and Congress clothed the President with retaliatory power which, as it turned out, he never used.[29] The country was in the midst of a bitter presidential campaign, in which the pro-German vote was being assiduously courted, and it was good politics if not

---

[27] *For. Rel., 1916, Supp.*, p. 339. For the attitude of the Wilson administration toward the blacklist, see Charles C. Tansill, *America Goes to War* (Boston, 1938), pp. 535-47. The Department of State had already made representations to the British Foreign Office regarding the harmful effect of the confidential blacklist on American interests in China. Lansing to Page, December 18, 1915, *For. Rel., 1915, Supp.*, pp. 641-42; Lansing to Page, January 10, 1916, *ibid., 1916, Supp.*, p. 330.

[28] Bailey, *loc. cit.*, pp. 20-21.   [29] *Ibid.*, pp. 23-24.

good law to lodge a resounding protest against what was regarded as the latest evidence of British arrogance. The resulting note of Acting Secretary Polk, dated July 26, 1916, is worthy of careful analysis.[30]

Both preceding and following his discussion of the widespread ill effects that the blacklist would have on American commerce Polk referred to a "sweeping" policy of "arbitrary interference with neutral trade"; to the "harsh and even disastrous effects of this policy upon . . . neutral rights"; to measures that "are inevitably and essentially inconsistent with the rights of the citizens of all the nations not involved in war"; and to the "many serious consequences to neutral right and neutral relations which such an act must necessarily involve." In particular, Polk insisted upon the right to freedom of trade, and he also protested against proscription without a hearing.

Conspicuous among the principles which the civilized nations of the world have accepted for the safeguarding of the rights of neutrals is the just and honorable principle that neutrals may not be condemned nor their goods confiscated except upon fair adjudication and after an opportunity to be heard, in prize courts or elsewhere. Such safeguards the blacklist brushes aside. It condemns without hearing, without notice, and in advance. It is manifestly out of the question that the Government of the United

---

[30] Mr. Paul Fuller, Jr., whose law firm at this time was counsel for the British Embassy, remembers that the so-called Polk note "was written personally by the President, and his [Wilson's] opposition to a blacklist was well-known, both to the British representatives in Washington and to the President's friends and colleagues." Fuller to writer, December 24, 1941. Mr. Polk has no clear recollection of the authorship of the note. But the evidence, both direct and circumstantial, strongly supports the view that the President had a large hand in its composition. See particularly Tansill, *America Goes to War*, p. 539.

States should acquiesce in such methods or applications of punishment to its citizens.

In his concluding paragraph, Polk stated that the government of the United States was "constrained to regard" the blacklist "as inconsistent with that true justice, sincere amity, and impartial fairness which should characterize the dealings of friendly governments with one another." [31]

Strong though this protest was in tone, it is evident that Polk brushed aside considerations of international law and based his plea on the "higher law" of international morality and fair dealing. The reply of Sir Edward Grey, dated October 10, 1916, came down to earth. The British Foreign Secretary reiterated the view that the blacklist was the result of "purely municipal legislation."

That is all. His Majesty's Government neither purport nor claim to impose any disabilities or penalties upon neutral individuals or upon neutral commerce. The measure is simply one which enjoins those who owe allegiance to Great Britain to cease having trade relations with persons who are found to be assisting or rendering service to the enemy.
I can scarcely believe that the United States Government intend to challenge the right of Great Britain as a sovereign state to pass legislation prohibiting all those who owe her allegiance from trading with any specified persons when

---

[31] *For. Rel., 1916, Supp.*, pp. 421-22. On September 22, 1916, Lansing prepared an instruction for the United States chargé in London (it apparently was not sent because of Wilson's objections) in which he said: "It [the blacklist] is clearly an invasion of the independence and sovereignty of the United States by an endeavor to enforce indirectly, if not directly, British laws upon American soil and to impose restraints upon trade in the United States. Not only do the British Government control the actions of British subjects here but seek to control the actions of the American traders." Savage, *Maritime Commerce*, II, 524.

such prohibition is found necessary in the public interest. The right to do so is so obvious that I feel sure that the protest which your excellency handed to me has been founded on a misconception of the scope and intent of the measures which have been taken.

Grey emphatically denied that the blacklist was designed to drive out American competition to the advantage of the British, or that it adversely affected the rights of the blacklistees.

> . . . No rights or property of these specified individuals are interfered with; neither they nor their property are condemned or confiscated; they are as free as they were before to carry on their business. The only disability they suffer is that British subjects are prohibited from giving to them the support and assistance of British credit and British property.[32]

In retrospect, it seems clear that neither the British nor the American note came squarely to grips with the problem. Polk was careful to base his case on international morals rather than on international law. Grey oversimplified his case and completely ignored the demoralizing effects of the secondary boycott. A man of his intelligence must have known—assuming that he read the note carefully before signing it—that blacklisted firms were not " as free as they were before to carry on their business." But from a purely legalistic standpoint he seems to have been on sound ground. Technically, the blacklist was the result of municipal legislation over which no other nation had control—a device so new that it was neither recognized nor proscribed by international law. It seems fair to conclude, therefore, that Polk was correct when he stated that the blacklist would have " harsh " effects upon " neutral rights "; and

[32] *For. Rel., 1916, Supp.*, pp. 462-65.

that Grey was correct when he declared that the blacklist was legally unassailable.[33]

vi

After America entered the war, Great Britain and France removed the proscribed firms in the United States from their blacklists.[34] The British were naturally anxious to have Washington join with them in the application of this weapon to the remaining neutrals; but in view of the strong position taken by the Department of State in its protests, London at first seemed to have hoped for nothing better than "an attitude of benevolent neutrality."[35] During the discussions in Washington, in April and May, 1917, the members of the Balfour Commission and of the British Embassy urged upon the United States the desirability of adopting the blacklist, emphasizing particularly that the absence of a common policy would create friction and rivalry in Allied trade relationships. If, for example, London blacklisted an organization in Mexico, while American firms not only continued to ship goods to it but supplied the deficiency caused by the withdrawal of British trade, the net result would be much unpleasantness. In addition, the British officials pointed to the proved effectiveness of the blacklist in weakening the enemy, and they made it clear that the United States would be assuming a grave responsibility for prolonging the conflict if it deliberately refrained from "the use of a powerful and humane weapon which lies ready to their hand. . . ."[36]

---

[33] For the legal aspects of the question see Garner, *International Law and the World War*, I, 233.

[34] *For. Rel., 1917, Supp. 2*, II, pp. 801, 807, 816-17.

[35] *Ibid.*, p. 804; also pp. 851-53.

[36] *Ibid.*, p. 871; also pp. 852-53, 878.

Law Adviser Woolsey pointed out, in his comprehensive memorandum of May 17, 1917, that the United States was "not prepared to accept the British and French blacklists in their entirety." But irrespective of such lists, Woolsey continued, Washington was willing to prohibit the export of goods to persons in neutral countries who were using such goods in any way for the benefit of the enemy, and to persons who, "for special reasons," were objectionable, such as revolutionists in Central America. As for import transactions, the United States would not refuse to buy goods from blacklisted firms in neutral countries unless there was satisfactory evidence that this business was in some way benefiting the Central Powers. In short, the United States, unlike the British and French, would not blacklist a person just because he was an enemy national; there had to be reasonable grounds for believing that he was in some way actually trading with or for the benefit of the enemy. Touching upon a materialistic note, Woolsey explained:

The United States is in a different position from European countries as to such trade with South America, in that it can not afford to rouse the ill-feeling of Latin American countries nor to lose the profits which accrue from trading with Germans in those countries—profits which go toward defraying the expenses of the war.[37]

As Vance C. McCormick later testified, and as was well known in Washington at the time, President Wilson thoroughly detested the blacklist, and held out against it as long as he could.[38] Even after the signing of the Trading with the Enemy Act (October 6, 1917), which authorized

[37] *Ibid.*, p. 869.
[38] Interview with writer on March 23, 1941; also Paul Fuller, Jr., to writer, December 24, 1941.

the issuance of blacklists, he was reluctant to go ahead. As earlier foreshadowed by Woolsey and others, this law did not accept the Allied definition of an enemy, which *ipso facto* embraced everyone in a neutral country of enemy nationality; rather, the test was enemy activity.[39] For example, a German merchant in Chile who was in no way helping the Fatherland would not necessarily be put on the American blacklist; but a German or Norwegian found to be engaged in pro-enemy activity in Chile would ordinarily be blacklisted.[40] Exceptions were also made in favor of certain border neutrals (notably in the Norwegian-American agreement) who were merely engaged in normal trade with Germans.

[39] German subjects anywhere could be blacklisted if the President, finding that "the safety of the United States or the successful prosecution of the war shall so require," issued a proclamation declaring such persons enemies. This power seems never to have been exercised against enemy subjects in neutral countries. Section II of Trading with Enemy Act, *U. S. Statutes at Large*, XL, pt. 1, p. 411.

[40] Comment of Paul Fuller, Jr. (December 24, 1941): "There may, of course, have been exceptions, but I believe there were very few cases where German nationals doing business in neutral countries were not put on the list. You will recall that there was a Bureau of Enemy Trade which was created especially to take care of cases where it was to our advantage to trade with a merchant in a neutral country, even though he were of enemy nationality. If sound reasons were given to the Board to show why trading with a firm on the list was to our interest, a license was issued by the Bureau of Enemy Trade. I remember one instance in which one of the nitrate exporters in Chile was on the blacklist. The War Industries Board considered it almost essential for American explosive manufacturers to get large quantities of nitrate, which were apparently only available through this so-called 'enemy' source. The enemy firm was not removed from the blacklist, but licenses were issued which allowed importation of the nitrates in question."

As finally perfected, the American enemy trading lists were divided into four categories.[41] First, and most conspicuous, the published Enemy Trading List. Second, the Confidential Enemy Trading List (also known as the Confidential Suspect List), which was about forty per cent shorter than the largest published list and which included the names of those whose official connection was such that it was inexpedient to ban them publicly; or firms that could be handled as effectively or more effectively in private; or concerns of such small consequence that it was deemed unwise to swell the published list by the addition of their names.[42] In short, if more was to be lost than gained by a public listing, the organization was not proscribed; and in this connection care had to be exercised not to drive out of business firms that were supplying essential war materials to the United States, such as nitrates. The third category was the Confidential Cloaks List, which was also about forty per cent shorter than the largest published list and

---

[41] On the American blacklisting policy in general, see *For. Rel., 1918, Supp. 1,* II, pp. 1031, 1042-46; *Report of War Trade Board,* pp. 49-50, 55-56.

[42] *Confidential List (Revised to December 18, 1918) Superseding all Previous Confidential Lists, Cloaks Lists, Supplements, and Announcements,* no. 3, December 18, 1918 (Washington, 1918). This was published by the War Trade Board and bore the injunction, "For the Use of Officials of the United States and Associated Governments only." State Dept., War Trade Board, 774. 5. Comment of Paul Fuller, Jr. (December 24, 1941): "You refer in Chapter XI to certain unofficial lists. These, according to my recollection, were entirely confidential, and were only used for interdepartmental information and convenience, and in order to save time." In short, the published list was designed as a warning to American houses not to trade with the firm designated; the unpublished lists were for the guidance of the War Trade Board in such matters as the issuance of export licenses.

which consisted of fictitious concerns that were used to mask enemy operations.[43] The fourth type of enemy trading list was the white list, a less formal and complete grouping of those firms whose nonenemy connection was beyond question. Other concerns in the same country might not be objectionable, but those on the white list were of well-established purity.[44]

American representatives abroad, particularly consular and War Trade Board officials, were instructed to collaborate with their Allied colleagues in collecting evidence regarding names that should be blacklisted.[45] In connection with such activity, the Department of State, on August 30, 1918, sent an important circular instruction to its diplomatic and consular representatives in Latin America. It was emphasized that the blacklist was not an outlet for vindictiveness or a device for punishment but a means of striking at the enemy. Hence there was little profit, and possible

---

[43] The Cloaks List covered only Latin America, Spain, and the Netherlands Indies, and was shared by the United States with its Associates. See *Cloaks List for Spain and the Countries of Latin America*, no. 1, September 5, 1918 (Washington, 1918). This was issued by the War Trade Board and bore the injunction, "For the Use of Officials of the Associated Governments only." State Dept., War Trade Board, 774. 3.

[44] At first the United States refused to establish a white list; and at best adopted the principle only half-heartedly. See *For. Rel., 1918, Supp. 1*, II, pp. 1023, 1028. There was also a Confidential Consignors' List, consisting of firms in the United States to which licenses would be denied. But this did not directly affect the neutrals. See State Dept., War Trade Board, 774. 4.

[45] *For. Rel., 1917, Supp. 2*, II, pp. 997-1002; *ibid., 1918, Supp. 1*, II, 1016-17, 1019-20, 1026, 1031. Circular telegram of Department of State to missions in Scandinavia, the Netherlands, Switzerland, and Greece, February 23, 1918, State Dept., 763. 72112/8109b.

harm, in the indiscriminate proscription of quiet, inoffensive Germans, even though they had expressed a belief in the justice of the Fatherland's cause. The Department of State further declared that German nationality alone was not a cause for blacklisting, though this would be an important factor if other evidence as to connection with the Central Powers was uncovered. If the suspect was a neutral, and he could be induced to swear before a proper official that he had severed his enemy relationship, this procedure might be preferable to immediate listing. The Department of State cautioned its representatives to exercise particular care in recommending newspapers and other organs of opinion for inclusion on the blacklist, because the United States did not want to become involved in a controversy over the freedom of the press. If newspapers merely favored the enemy cause they were not to be proscribed; but if they were backed by Berlin or by German propagandists, they were to be nominated for listing.[46]

vii

Altogether, the War Trade Board published three comprehensive enemy trading lists (blacklists). The first, brought up to October 6, 1917, was not made public until early in December.[47] It embraced a total of 1,524 names,

---

[46] *For. Rel., 1918, Supp. 1*, II, pp. 1042-46.

[47] It was published in the New York *Times* on December 5, 1917. In connection with this first list, Mr. Paul Fuller, Jr., remembers that late in November, 1917, he had an interview with Wilson, in company with Thomas D. Jones, of the War Trade Board, who was very nervous because of Wilson's well-known antipathy to the blacklist. "I explained to the President that I had come to urge the necessity of a blacklist, and very briefly

BUNKERS AND BLACKLISTS

and applied only to the twenty republics of Latin America. They were all included, whether they had declared war, severed relations, or remained neutral. The republic of Brazil, a cobelligerent, had the largest representation, 340 names—an eloquent testimonial to its large and commercially important German population. Mexico was a close second, with 326 names, while Argentina, Chile, Bolivia, and Venezuela followed in that order. None of these four was a belligerent, and only Bolivia had severed diplomatic relations.[48]

---

outlined our arguments in favor of this action. He said that he would like to ask me two questions:

"*First:* what would be, in my opinion, the effect upon public opinion in this country; and

"*Second:* what would be the effect on public opinion in Latin America?

"I told him that I was certain that all American exporters would welcome the publication of the list with enthusiasm; that the great majority were patriotic American citizens who were anxious to do their part in the war, and who did not wish under any circumstances to do any trading with the enemy; that, where an uncertainty existed as to what constituted enemy firms, they should consider the list of great assistance in dealing with importers. I told him that in South America exporters and importers were so accustomed to the blacklist, since it had been in use by the British there for several years, that I did not think that our publishing of the list would have any effect there whatsoever.

"He seemed entirely satisfied with these two answers, and I then told him (with some slight trepidation) that I had prepared a printed list, and had it in my pocket. He asked to see it; read the head note rapidly and made two or three changes of form; then signed the famous 'W. W.,' and thus the publication of an American blacklist was authorized." Fuller to writer, December 24, 1941.

[48] War Trade Board, *Trading with the Enemy: Enemy Trading List,* No. 1, October 6, 1917 (Washington, 1917).

ENEMY TRADING LISTS OF THE UNITED STATES

Country	List 1	List 2	List 3	Confidential List	Cloaks List
Argentina	131	274	346	287	291
Bolivia	106	130	154	229	263
Brazil	340	460	496	95	245
Chile	108	230	284	230	226
Colombia	61	79	94	21	45
Costa Rica	45	34	68	18	23
Cuba	27	23	51	36	25
Denmark	—	126	144	117	—
Dominican R...	7	14	15	—	—
Ecuador	36	83	120	52	60
Greece	—	112	106	—	—
Guatemala	18	23	72	14	7
Haiti	23	28	35	7	10
Honduras	27	27	35	40	42
Iceland; Faroes.	—	10	10	1	—
Mexico	326	324	823	309	550
Morocco	—	109	148	—	—
Netherlands	—	411	517	170	—
Neth. E. Indies.	—	—	538	—	34
Neth. W. Indies	—	—	1	—	2
Nicaragua	10	14	18	3	3
Norway	—	276	303	40	—
Panama	10	13	21	2	2
Paraguay	10	26	30	17	14
Peru	70	109	140	143	125
Salvador	12	14	34	25	45
Spain	—	702	980	168	75
Sweden	—	245	278	102	—
Uruguay	71	91	95	49	67
Venezuela	86	83	120	181	193
	1524	4070	6076	2356	2347

In a prefatory statement, the War Trade Board explained that this first blacklist was published for the guidance of

American merchants, shippers, and bankers, all of whom were forbidden by law to trade with persons or firms of enemy connection, unless they first applied for and obtained licenses.[49] The Board further warned that this list was by no means complete. American concerns should exercise great caution in their foreign trade, for continued traffic with firms of enemy association, even though they had not yet been formally blacklisted, would not relieve the offender of the heavy penalties prescribed by the Trading with the Enemy Act.[50] The War Trade Board realized that the abrupt severance of commercial relationships with a given organization in a neutral country might seriously dislocate the business of certain American importers or exporters, and it therefore announced that it would co-operate fully in securing the names of pro-Ally or genuinely neutral concerns that might be used as substitutes.

The War Trade Board perfected elaborate machinery, in conjunction with the Allies, by which American representatives abroad forwarded evidence to Washington regarding the character of firms under suspicion.[51] Names were dropped from the original list upon satisfactory proof of their unobjectionable activity; names were added to the list upon evidence of their pro-enemy taint. These excisions or additions were published by the War Trade Board every

---

[49] Comment of Paul Fuller, Jr. (December 24, 1941): "It was obvious to me from the start of my work in Washington that the blacklist was not only necessary if we were to contribute to an Allied victory by carrying on an economic warfare, but that with the passing of the Trading with the Enemy Act it was only fair and just to honest and patriotic American firms and merchants to inform them who constituted enemy firms in neutral countries."

[50] This was not put so strongly in the preface to the second list.

[51] See *For. Rel., 1917, Supp. 2,* II, p. 1003.

two weeks, and were given considerable publicity in the American press.[52]

The first general blacklist, as we have noted, applied to Latin America alone and left the European neutrals completely untouched. In licensing shipments to them, the War Trade Board was forced to rely on the British and French blacklists, a procedure which made for considerable clumsiness and some friction. The second list of the United States corrected this difficulty. Revised to March 15, 1918, and superseding all preceding lists and supplements, it was published by the War Trade Board on April 20, 1918.[53] Not only did it add some 2,500 names for all of the European neutrals (except Switzerland),[54] but it increased the number for Latin America as well. In addition, firms in Greece and in Morocco were proscribed.[55] Altogether, the second general blacklist embraced 4,070 names, as compared

[52] By August 30, 1918, the Board was releasing these supplementary lists every other Friday. File 763.72112a of the Department of State contains the records of a tremendous amount of routine in connection with this activity.

[53] War Trade Board, *Trading with the Enemy: Enemy Trading List Revised to March 15, 1918* (Washington, 1918).

[54] The publication of a blacklist for Switzerland seems to have been delayed largely because both the *Société Suisse de Surveillance Économique* and the British and French confidential lists were controlling enemy trade with reasonable satisfaction. By July 3, 1918, the War Trade Board approved in principle the creation of a blacklist for Switzerland, but in part because of certain difficulties with the French no such list was published by the time hostilities ceased. See *For. Rel., 1918, Supp. 1*, II, pp. 1031, 1037, 1039-41, 1054, 1057-58, 1058-62, 1072; McFadden to War Trade Board, November 6, 1918, F. A. R., Hoover Library (Switzerland: Exports and Imports).

[55] The War Trade Board co-operated with the Allies in blacklisting firms in Persia, a neutral, although the United States published no blacklist for that country. *For. Rel., 1918, Supp. 1*, II, p. 1015.

with 1,524 for the first. The preface to the new list contained the same suggestions and warnings as the earlier one, and in particular pointed out that the proscription of one member of a partnership applied also to his business associates.

It is interesting to note that of all the neutrals Spain was most generously represented in the second list, with 702 names. Of the other European neutrals, the Netherlands, Norway, Sweden, and Denmark may be listed in that order.[56] In Latin America, Brazil, though a cobelligerent, held the lead, with 460 names. Mexico was still in second place with 324, while Argentina, Chile, and Bolivia retained third, fourth, and fifth positions. Roughly, these figures give an index to the comparative extent of pro-German activity in each of these countries.

The third and final comprehensive list was published by the War Trade Board early in 1919, and was revised to December 13, 1918, significantly more than a month after the Armistice. It contained 6,076 names, or 2,006 more than the second blacklist, and included all of the countries or places on the second list, with the addition of the Dutch East Indies and the Dutch West Indies. The relative positions of the various neutrals had not materially changed, though Mexico had ousted Brazil from first place in Latin America; and Switzerland was still unrepresented.[57]

[56] A great many firms in the border neutrals continued their normal business dealings with Germany; and the British and Americans established a policy of leniency in treating this type of organization, in part because they would unnecessarily hurt their own trade if they did not. The French, who had no comparable commercial stake, opposed such a policy. See *ibid.*, pp. 1065-66.

[57] War Trade Board, *Trading with the Enemy: Enemy Trading List Revised to December 13, 1918* (Washington, 1919).

One of the most interesting features of the blacklist is that perhaps alone of the major economic weapons which the Associated Powers used against the neutrals, it was not relaxed shortly after the Armistice.[58] Instead, as we have observed in analyzing the third list, it was sweepingly extended, primarily for the purpose of keeping Germany prostrate pending the conclusion of a dictated peace. It was also designed to prevent the concealment of reparations assets and to squeeze out future German competition in favor of Allied and American trade. As the exhaustion of Germany became increasingly evident, and as complaints from American merchants mounted stridently, a policy of relaxation was plainly necessary. On April 4, 1919, the 3,051 names on the Latin American list were reduced to some 170. And on April 27, the Supreme Economic Council voted to suspend all enemy trading lists, effective April 29. Following this action, the War Trade Board, on April 27, 1919, announced a withdrawal of all blacklists as of April 29.[59]

viii

We should be greatly in error were we to suppose that the final perfection of the blacklist was accomplished without some little friction among the Associated Powers.[60]

[58] See particularly Polk to London Embassy, December 31, 1918, State Dept., 600. 119/1895.

[59] *Report of War Trade Board,* pp. 170-73; New York *Times,* April 28, 1919. The British withdrew their blacklists as of the same day, April 29.

[60] Comment of Paul Fuller, Jr. (December 24, 1941): "On the whole (I speak from recollections only), there were no serious differences. An informal and unwritten plan was worked out, by which the United States accepted the British list for Scandinavian countries prima facie, and the French list for Spain; and the

Initially, the lists announced by the War Trade Board were not the same as those of the Allies; and much confusion and ill feeling resulted when British facilities were denied to Americans who were dealing with firms which were on the Allied blacklists but which were not proscribed by the War Trade Board. Conversely, the British merchants were greatly annoyed when American houses took advantage of the British enemy trading lists to exploit markets abandoned by their competitors. Indeed, trade rivalry between the British and the Americans was an important and constantly recurring obstacle to co-ordination of the war effort. In July, 1918, however, after protracted negotiations, elaborate machinery for integrating the American and Allied lists was provided for, and "substantial identity" of the published blacklists of Britain, France, and the United States was secured. Italy approved the new policy in principle; and Japan was belatedly brought into the co-ordination conferences. But as this problem concerned the Associated Powers rather than the neutrals, a detailed discussion of it is not relevant to the present study.[61]

Not only was there friction among the principal Asso-

Allies all accepted our recommendations for Latin America. We organized an informal blacklisting committee consisting of representatives of the British, French, Italians and ourselves. The presence of the French and Italian representatives was largely complimentary. Most of the work was done by the American and British representatives on this informal committee. This tended to avoid friction, and, on the whole, a very real system of co-operation existed between the British, French, and ourselves. The Italian representative was entirely in accord with the policy of the blacklist, but was not at all active upon the committee."

[61] On co-ordination see *Report of War Trade Board*, pp. 52-56; also *For. Rel., 1918, Supp. 1*, II, pp. 1017 ff. For evidence of British-American friction over trade, see *ibid.*, pp. 1051, 1073-74.

ciated Powers, but the policy of proscribing firms in cobelligerent countries created much dissatisfaction. The War Trade Board did not publish a blacklist for Great Britain, France, Italy, Japan, and certain other Associated Powers, but it did for Greece and all of the Latin American countries, whether belligerents or not. The republics of Latin America naturally felt that those who had entered the war or had severed relations were entitled to greater consideration in the matter of blacklisting than those who had not; and on February 25, 1918, the Department of State recommended to the War Trade Board that close co-operation be established with the Latin American cobelligerents in adding names to the list or dropping them from it.[62]

Yet in spite of all this jarring and working at crosspurposes, the blacklist was a potent weapon in dealing with neutrals. Even those firms that were not actually proscribed were subjected to the Damoclean fear that they might be in the near future, or that their names were already on a confidential list. And it must be remembered that those on either the published or unpublished lists were denied bunkering and other facilities. In some instances enemy-tainted firms were forced completely to the wall by the application of the blacklist; in others their business dropped to seven per cent of the normal total. In such cases the lost trade was frequently thrown into the hands of pro-Ally firms approved by the War Trade Board; and quite often American or British houses got the business.[63] In

[62] For this most interesting statement see *ibid.*, p. 1020. Of course, the absence of the name of a neutral or a cobelligerent from the published lists did not necessarily mean that it was not affected by the confidential lists.

[63] Specific instances are given in *Report of War Trade Board*, p. 57.

other instances, neutral concerns severed their German connections or discharged their German employees in the hope of keeping off the blacklist or of being removed from it.[64] In addition, Washington informed American firms in Latin America that they were under a patriotic obligation to dismiss their enemy employees.[65]

Onerous though the American blacklist undoubtedly was, the present investigation disclosed no single instance of a formal protest by one of the neutral countries against its basic principles.[66] It is possible, however, that there were many unrecorded informal remonstrances; and objections were certainly voiced against the inclusion of specific names. For example, Salvador, the only Central American republic to remain neutral, protested against the inclusion of the Banco Salvadoreño on the United States blacklist. The Washington government, upon the receipt of proper guarantees, acceded to Salvador's wishes and removed this institution.[67] It is also worthy of note that when, in Sep-

[64] For evidence that blacklisted Dutch East Indian firms were discharging their German employees, see New York *Times,* August 2, 1918.

[65] Department of State to embassies and legations in South America and Mexico, March 7, 1918; State Department to Buenos Aires Embassy, May 15, 1918, State Dept., 763. 72112/7413a, 7659. The penalties prescribed by the Trading with the Enemy Act were applicable only to American citizens living in the United States. Nevertheless, the Department of State instructed some of its diplomatic representatives to discourage Americans in foreign lands from engaging in transactions with aliens which would have been violations of the law had they been carried on in the United States. *For. Rel., 1918, Supp. 2,* pp. 427, 429, 432, 434, 442-43.

[66] During the negotiations with Switzerland over a blacklist, which was never established, the Berne government objected to the employment of such an instrument. *Ibid., Supp. 1,* II, pp. 1057-58.

[67] *Ibid., 1917, Supp. 2,* II, pp. 1004-05, 1007.

tember, 1918, Spain protested against the French and British blacklists, she did not address a similar complaint to the United States, whose list was substantially identical with those of the other two powers.[68]

The absence of official protests against the blacklist may be attributed to several factors. In the first place, it was already some two years old when the United States publicly adopted it. By that time the neutrals not only had become accustomed to this new form of economic warfare but they had discovered that their representations were so many wasted words.[69] In the second place, the technical legality of the blacklist, and the evident determination of the United States to co-operate with its Associates in using it, probably acted as a strong deterrent against further fruitless protests.

ix

Intimately associated with the blacklist was the British proposal, made on April 10, 1917, that the United States join with the Allies in a financial blockade of the enemy. This was to be accomplished by using the combined facilities of the Associated Powers for the purpose of compelling banking firms in neutral countries to refrain from engaging in transactions that would benefit the enemy. Prior to April, 1917, the Allies had been able to bring considerable pres-

[68] *Ibid.*, *1918*, *Supp. 1*, II, pp. 1064-65, 1069. In Spain the blacklistees formed a kind of league for mutual protection. *Neut. Press Supp.*, III, 728.

[69] Much dissatisfaction was caused in Latin America by the United States blacklist, and feeling probably would have mounted higher had these people not already vented their wrath against the earlier British blacklist. See Martin, *Latin America and the War*, pp. 41-45, 190, 356.

sure to bear upon these houses, but the latters' free access to the money centers of the United States constituted a serious gap in the financial blockade. The London government naturally expressed the hope that its new Associate would be willing to plug the leak.[70]

Whether in response to the British overture or not, the Department of State suggested to the Governor of the Federal Reserve Board, W. P. G. Harding, the desirability of guarding against the transfer of banking credits to neutral countries for the account of enemy nationals, and against the use of domestic credits for similar purposes. On May 10, 1917, Harding informed the Department that the members of the Federal Reserve System had been advised both to co-operate in such a program and to urge nonmember banks and agencies within their districts to follow suit. But this, though a step in the right direction, was not what the British had suggested, and late in June they renewed their representations in Washington. Not until August 7, 1917, did Secretary Lansing belatedly reply that until the Trading with the Enemy Act was passed nothing could be done. Meanwhile, as he pointed out, certain steps had been taken by the Federal Reserve and other agencies to prevent neutral houses from helping the enemy.[71]

Late in August, 1917, the British government drafted a warning to neutral financial houses, and proposed that the

---

[70] *For. Rel., 1917, Supp. 2,* II, p. 809.

[71] *Ibid.,* pp. 814-16, 898-902, 918-19. Lansing further pointed out that since as early as April 2, 1917, banks in New York had voluntarily reported all foreign exchange transactions and often had, on their own initiative, refused to take questionable business. Furthermore, the cable censor was refusing to pass suspicious financial cables.

United States and the other Associated Powers give formal adherence to its publication.[72] Lansing thereupon solicited the opinions of three of the executive departments. Secretary of Commerce Redfield, while not prepared to discuss the legal aspects of the problem, regarded the means proposed as legitimate and the course as practicable. Attorney General Gregory did not think it "wise or just" for the United States to assent to the British proposition, inasmuch as it would result in "the most extreme form of blacklist of citizens of neutral nations. . . ." (This, it will be remembered, was before the United States published its first blacklist, and while there was some hesitancy about reversing the position taken as a neutral.) Acting Secretary of the Treasury Crosby was of the opinion that the objects of the British plan could in considerable measure be achieved by control over both foreign exchange and the transmittal of various forms of commercial paper. To go beyond this, he felt, would raise "grave questions of international relationship. . . ." Nevertheless, if the State Department still wished to join in the proposal, and found that "no question of neutral rights would be involved," the Treasury Department would acquiesce.[73] With these three opinions before him, Lansing informed the British Ambassador, on September 17, 1917, that "it is deemed inexpedient at present for this Government to join in issuing the proposed notice, but that this Government will give the matter further consideration."[74]

Following this decision by the Department of State, the

---

[72] *Ibid.*, pp. 924-26.
[73] *Ibid.*, pp. 938, 940, 940-41, 942-43.
[74] *Ibid.*, p. 946.

British suggested certain modifications of their financial blockade. Acting Secretary of State Polk, while finding certain aspects of the plan unobjectionable, left the final decision with the Secretary of the Treasury, on the grounds that this was chiefly a monetary problem. In two subsequent communications the Treasury Department declared that it was opposed, at that time at least, to the British scheme, and it pointed to the President's executive order of January 26, 1918, which provided for a close supervision of foreign banking transactions, and which could be tightened into any kind of financial blockade desired.[75] From the documents that were examined for this study it does not appear that the United States, either formally or informally, ever joined with its Associates in the type of financial blockade proposed by the British.

The question naturally arises: Why did the United States assume such an un-co-operative attitude toward this weapon, while resorting to other measures of a no less objectionable character? It will be remembered, first of all, that when the British proposal was made the Wilson administration was not at all sure whether it would adopt the blacklist, and that the question of the financial blockade seems to have been disposed of, as far as Washington was concerned, before the blacklist was fully adopted. The questions of neutral rights involved in a financial blockade, as well as the outcry that would arise from the neutrals should the United States join in a public proclamation of the British scheme, were undoubtedly factors making for hesitation. But the decisive argument seems to have been that Washington,

[75] *Ibid.*, pp. 959-60, 985, 1005; *ibid., 1918, Supp. 1,* II, 951, 953-55, 965-68, 977.

without becoming unpleasantly involved with its Associates or further provoking the neutrals, could accomplish all of the objects in view through cable censorship, mail censorship, domestic banking control, and the blacklist itself. The fact should not be overlooked that a good many financial houses appeared on the various types of blacklists. So we may conclude that the United States, while going essentially as far as the British wished, did so more discreetly.

X

A final question remains to be answered. Did the United States violate the rights of the neutrals in its use of the blacklist? In this connection, it seems desirable to make a distinction between violations of international law and what Polk described as " harsh " effects upon neutral rights. The first of these distinctions may be quickly dismissed by repeating what we have already observed; namely, that a weapon so new as the blacklist was unknown to international law, and consequently was not specifically interdicted by it.

As for " harsh " effects upon neutral rights in general, we approach a larger and more elusive problem. The War Trade Board proceeded on the assumption that the blacklists were designed solely for the guidance of American firms, and were to be used by them in avoiding the penalties prescribed by the Trading with the Enemy Act. But the lists, when published, quickly found their way into the neutral countries concerned, and the whole demoralizing influence of the secondary boycott soon made itself felt. Furthermore, the War Trade Board virtually advised American traders to make their own blacklists, for it warned them that they would suffer severe penalties if they trafficked with firms of enemy taint that had not yet been formally banned. How much business was driven away from the neutrals by such unofficial lists we shall probably never know.

Certain commentators have stressed the fact that the first United States blacklist contained 1,524 names and applied to twenty different countries, as compared with the first British published list (February 29, 1916) of only 363 names in seven different countries.[76] But when we consider that the blacklist was in an experimental stage when Great Britain adopted it, and that it was nearly two years old when the United States announced one, the two cases do not stand on all fours. A much fairer comparison would be to contrast the first American list with the consolidated British list of July, 1916, which contained 1,530 names.[77] It should be repeated, however, that in two important respects the United States did not go so far as its Associates. First, it did permit trade with a blacklisted firm if the American exporter secured a proper license; whereas the British practice was to forbid all business whatsoever with the blacklisted firm.[78] Second, unlike the British and the French, the United States declined to consider all enemy subjects in neutral countries as *ipso facto* subject to blacklisting; there first had to be evidence of pro-enemy activity. And despite strong pressure from its Associates to act against all enemy aliens, the United States

---

[76] See Turlington, *Neutrality*, p. 80.

[77] Bailey, *loc. cit.*, p. 21.

[78] *For. Rel., 1917, Supp. 2*, II, p. 851. It has also been pointed out that in certain of the trade agreements, notably those with Norway and Denmark, the blacklist was not to be applied to persons engaging in normal trade with the enemy. See *ibid., 1918, Supp. 1*, II, pp. 1342-43 for Denmark; p. 1177 for Norway.

steadfastly clung to this rule.[79] In brief, the blacklists of the War Trade Board were as wide as, if not wider than, those of the Allies, but they did not penetrate so deeply.

Yet when all is said that can be said in extenuation of the American version of the blacklist, it is clear that as far as the neutrals themselves were concerned it was a vicious weapon. All firms that were placed on the published or confidential lists were condemned without a hearing, frequently on the basis of poor evidence, sometimes primarily on suspicion. So great was the premium on haste, and so profitable was it to err on the side of severity, that guiltless organizations were inevitably posted.[80] Unoffending employees were discharged; innocent businesses were ruined by the mere threat of the blacklist; unprincipled concerns spread lies about their competitors. Suspected organizations were forced to line up with Allied interests by the potent threat that their business would be discriminated against after the war ended.[81] As firms went bankrupt and business declined, governmental revenues derived from customs duties and other taxes fell off. The whole witches' cauldron of greed, rivalry, mendacity, suspicion, and fear produced a brew that unquestionably did widespread harm in neutral lands.

If we define neutral rights even as narrowly as the right of an innocent neutral firm to engage in domestic commerce within its own country without interference from the belligerents, it is clear that the blacklist had a "harsh" effect upon "neutral rights," even though it may not have run

[79] *Ibid.*, pp. 1022, 1025, 1036.
[80] Morris, *American Legation*, pp. 80-81.
[81] *Ibid.*, p. 81.

counter to any well-established precepts of international law. "But," as Ira Nelson Morris, United States minister in Sweden put it, "the exigencies of warfare, unfortunately, cannot take much account of the rights of the weak. The only excuse to be offered is that these blacklists helped win the war. And that was all we were thinking of at that time." [82]

[82] *Ibid.*

Chapter XII

PROBLEMS INVOLVING FREEDOM OF THE SEAS

i

In the year 1909 a conference of the powers met in London and drew up a comprehensive and relatively humane code for the conduct of maritime warfare. As the signatures of the plenipotentiaries attested, and as one of the provisions definitely stated, the Declaration of London corresponded "in substance with the generally recognized principles of international law."[1] Although this document was not finally accepted by the powers, owing largely to the opposition of big-navy Britain, it was nevertheless an important statement of what enlightened jurists conceived international law to be on the eve of the World War.

The Declaration of London divided contraband into the three traditional categories: (1) absolute contraband; (2) conditional or relative contraband; and (3) noncontraband or the free list. Absolute contraband embraced articles, such as arms and explosives, that were employed in the actual prosecution of war. Conditional contraband consisted of those things, such as foodstuffs, that could be used for both peace and war, and the status of these articles as contraband depended on whether or not they were destined for the armed forces of the enemy. Noncontraband included those

[1] James Brown Scott, ed., *The Declaration of London, February 26, 1909* (New York, 1919), p. 114. The entire text of the Declaration, together with other relevant documents, is printed in this useful volume.

items that were not susceptible of use in war—at least the kind of war envisaged in 1909—and embraced such materials as raw cotton, wool, silk, rubber, raw hides, and metallic ores. Although provision was made for declaring conditional contraband absolute contraband, the articles listed as noncontraband were not subject to such a designation. The Declaration also contained certain stipulations regarding the character of a legal blockade and the doctrine of ultimate destination or continuous voyage.[2] As limited by the Declaration of London, the doctrine of ultimate destination could be applied only to absolute contraband destined by a circuitous route to the enemy. In general, conditional contraband or noncontraband could not be seized under this doctrine.[3]

At the outset of the war, the Allies were well aware that large quantities of noncontraband and conditional contraband were flowing into Germany through the Netherlands and the Scandinavian states. If the British had shackled their hands by ratifying the Declaration of London, they would have been unable to stop this traffic, because, as we have seen, that instrument exempted all but absolute contraband from the doctrine of continuous voyage. Taking advantage of its freedom of action, London, on August 20,

[2] A voyage which, in view of its purposes, is regarded by the blockading power as a single voyage, even though circuitous or interrupted.

[3] *Ibid.*, pp. 120, 200. Certain exceptions were made in the case of a belligerent that had no seacoast. The United States and what were to be the Allied Powers favored the extension of continuous voyage to conditional contraband also, but they were forced to yield. See James W. Garner, "Violations of Maritime Law by the Allied Powers during the World War," *Amer. Jour. of Int. Law,* XXV (1931), 26-27.

1914, issued an Order in Council which authorized the seizure of conditional contraband of presumed enemy destination. The United States feared the effects of such a practice on American commerce, and consequently made several attempts to induce the British to subscribe to the Declaration of London. For various reasons, into which we need not go, these all ended in failure; and on October 22, 1914, the United States withdrew its suggestion and fell back upon the shifting sands of international law.[4]

During the ensuing months, the British extended their contraband lists, and further strengthened their interpretation of continuous voyage by applying it to their blockade.[5] The United States entered no general protests against these steps, in part because it had used the doctrine of ultimate destination in a less extreme form to strangle the Confederacy from 1861 to 1865, and in part because the Wilson administration was sympathetically disposed toward the Allies.[6]

[4] This story is fully told in Tansill, *America Goes to War*, ch. VI.

[5] This practice, which was forbidden by the Declaration of London and presumed to be illegal when directed against neutral ports, was put into effect by the British Order in Council of July 7, 1916. Against it most of the neutral complaints were directed. See Malbone W. Graham, Jr., "Neutrality and the World War," *Amer. Jour. of Int. Law*, XVII (1923), 710.

[6] In his note to the British, on December 26, 1914, Secretary Bryan stated that commerce between nonbelligerents "should not be interfered with by those at war unless such interference is manifestly an imperative necessity to protect their national safety, and then only to the extent that it is a necessity." *For. Rel., 1914, Supp.*, p. 373. On January 20, 1915, Bryan declared in a letter to Senator Stone: "It is thus seen that some of the doctrines which appear to bear harshly upon neutrals at the present time are analogous to or outgrowths from policies adopted by the

ii

The struggle for neutral rights entered upon a new phase when, in February, 1915, the German government proclaimed a submarine blockade of the British Isles. As a retaliatory measure, the British announced that they were going to stop all goods exported from or imported to Germany, regardless of their nature as contraband and regardless of whether they were being transported to Germany directly, or indirectly through the neutrals.[7] This was the so-called British blockade—"so-called" because it was never officially proclaimed as such, and because it violated most of the basic features of the traditional blockade. In particular, it was not the conventional close-cordon type;[8] it was extended to neutral ports; it did not apply equally to the ships of all nations; and it was not effective, particularly in the Baltic. But whatever the question of legality, it is clear that the operation of this blockade, coupled with both the extension of continuous voyage and the rationing

---

United States when it was a belligerent. The Government therefore can not consistently protest against the application of rules which it has followed in the past, unless they have not been practiced as heretofore." *Ibid.*, p. ix.

[7] For texts of the British note of March 1, 1915, and of the Order in Council of March 11, 1915, see *ibid., 1915, Supp.*, pp. 127-28, 143-45. The British blockade was less severe than the traditional blockade in its penalties upon seized ships. Ordinarily, both the ship and its entire cargo were subject to confiscation if running the blockade. The British system was not to seize ships but only such part of the cargo as was contraband, and to restore or pay for noncontraband, as the prize court should decree. Garner, *International Law and the World War*, II, 324.

[8] On March 5, 1915, Secretary Bryan conceded that, within limits, the long-range blockade might be defended in the light of changed conditions of warfare. *For. Rel., 1915, Supp.*, p. 133.

of neutrals, virtually terminated American commerce with Germany.

The enforcement of the British Orders in Council resulted in the detention of scores of American ships and the confiscation of their contraband cargoes. Although noncontraband goods were normally released or paid for, and although the shippers in many cases made satisfactory profits, public opinion in the United States was greatly angered. Accordingly, the Department of State made insistent representations to London against the operations of a blockade which seemed to be clearly illegal, at least on the basis of international law as of 1914. The ablest and most comprehensive statement of American grievances was the note of Secretary Lansing, dated October 21, 1915.[9] If we may judge from the repeated references to it after America became a belligerent and was troubled by charges of inconsistency, this protest was regarded by Washington as the most significant document of its kind to emanate from the Department of State during the neutrality period.

For our purposes it is not necessary to discuss this note in detail. It will suffice to observe that Lansing protested strongly against the detention of American vessels and cargoes at British control stations (especially the practice of sending them there and later searching for evidence of contraband); against the British prize-court procedure; and particularly against the blockade. This, Lansing insisted, was "ineffective, illegal, and indefensible. . . ."[10]

---

[9] Comment of Lester H. Woolsey (January, 1942): "There were many fingers in this pie, but I drew the draft which was revised by R. L. [ansing] and W. W. [ilson]."

[10] *For. Rel., 1915, Supp.*, pp. 578-589.

iii

In view of Washington's unequivocal stand, it could hardly be expected that America would about-face, after entering the war, and accept the Allied blockade as legal.[11] The documents regarding the work of the Balfour Commission are singularly lacking in references to the blockade, and it may be assumed that the British, knowing the views of the United States, had no intention of pressing the Department of State for a reversal of its position.[12] And, on the practical side, it was clear that the British were fully capable of enforcing the blockade themselves without the active co-operation of the United States Navy.

In British eyes the important objective was to induce the Wilson administration to establish an export embargo, about which there would be no question of legality, but which would most effectively supplement the blockade. This, as we have noted, the United States reluctantly consented to do. The licensing of exports by the War Trade Board was finally made so effective that it was possible to consider the elimination of British letters of assurance (navicerts). In February and March of 1918 a system was worked out by London and Washington under which these documents were discontinued in favor of a scheme involving close co-operation between the American exports licensing authorities and the British blockade and rationing officials.[13]

---

[11] The Woolsey memorandum of May 17, 1917, declared: "Great Britain has heretofore attained the objects set forth above through her exercise of belligerent maritime measures, depending upon the prize court to condemn property violating those measures. The United States regards certain of the measures in question as illegal. . . ." *Ibid., 1917, Supp. 2,* II, p. 867.

[12] Comment of Frank L. Polk (January, 1942): "This is true."

[13] This was in line with the Woolsey memorandum of May 17,

Although the Department of State was willing to cooperate with the British in substituting export licenses for letters of assurance, it took an entirely different position with respect to prizes of war. Early in the conflict the Allies asked the United States to enter into an agreement involving the reciprocal transfer of such vessels. Thus, neutral or belligerent ships captured by the British in American waters would be turned over to an American prize court, and ships seized by United States cruisers in European waters would be turned over to a British prize court. But, Solicitor Woolsey recorded, " the United States refused to enter into such an agreement, as it appeared probable that its naval forces would not seize vessels and return them to the United States for adjudication but would allow the cobelligerents to take the onus of seizure and bringing in the prizes of war." [14] It will again be noted that Washington was quite willing to have the already much-condemned British bear the opprobrium of this practice, while the United States continued with a policy for which it had stood as a neutral.

The Navy Department took a stand fully in harmony with

1917. *For. Rel.*, *1917, Supp. 2*, II, p. 867. The British Embassy had begun formally to issue letters of assurance in March, 1916, even while America was still a neutral. This anomalous situation whereby an American shipper applied to the British Embassy in his own country for permission to export his goods was tolerated because it removed serious delays caused by the blockade. *Ibid., 1916, Supp.*, pp. 496-97. On the elimination of navicerts after America became a belligerent, see *ibid., 1917, Supp. 2*, II, pp. 806, 849, 882, 948, 955-56, 985-86, 995; *ibid., 1918, Supp. 1*, II, pp. 963-65, 968; also " Minutes of the Exports Administrative Board," p. 123 (August 23, 1917).

[14] Memorandum of Woolsey to Auchincloss, July 18, 1918, on the subject of German safe-conducts under international law. State Dept., 763. 72112 Sa/119.

that of the Department of State. The printed instructions which were placed in the hands of naval officers, and which guided the conduct of operations throughout the war, contained important rules regarding the blockade—rules that had been worked out in close collaboration with the State Department.[15] These were taken almost verbatim from the Declaration of London and stipulated that (1) a blockade must not bar access to neutral ports or coasts; (2) a blockade, to be binding, must be effective; and (3) a blockade must be applied equally to the ships of all nations. Inasmuch as Secretary Lansing had found British practice wanting on all of these counts, it would follow that such instructions estopped the United States from playing an active part with the Allies in the enforcement of their blockade. This, of course, worked no hardship on the Allied war effort, because the American Navy was concerned primarily with antisubmarine operations, with the convoying of troop and supply ships, and with containing the German High Seas Fleet.

iv

During and after the war several communications were directed to the Department of State from international lawyers and others who were interested in knowing to what extent, if any, America had participated in British blockade measures. On January 30, 1919, the Assistant Secretary of State addressed a communication to the Secretary of the Navy in which he requested specific information as to

[15] *Naval Instructions, 1917,* pp. 16-17. Comment of Lester H. Woolsey (January, 1942): "Naval Instructions 1917 were drafted in conjunction with State Department (my office)."

whether naval vessels of the United States had co-operated with the British in the execution of the type of search and seizure protested against in Lansing's memorable note of October 21, 1915. Secretary Daniels, in his reply, stated that since the naval records had not been completely assembled, it was impossible to give a categorical answer.[16] Ten years later, in 1929, the Department of State reopened the question, and Secretary of the Navy Adams replied, on March 30, 1929, in a letter that is of the first importance. Adams noted at the outset that the official instructions issued to the Navy stated: "Commanders of all Naval vessels shall whenever possible take the necessary steps to assure themselves of the character of all vessels sighted on the high seas in accordance with international law and usage." Replying to the State Department's first question, Adams declared: " The right of visit and search of neutral ships was exercised by the United States Navy constantly during the war. . . ." The Secretary of the Navy continued:

The answer to the second question is that there is no record in the Navy Department of any neutral ships or cargoes being brought into port by vessels of the United States Navy during the World War for adjudication as prizes.

[16] *For. Rel., 1918, Supp. 1,* II, pp. 932-36. In an earlier letter to the Secretary of State, dated January 6, 1919, Secretary Daniels had noted that the introduction to the published instructions of the United States Navy stated that the volume was " prepared in accordance with international law, treaties, and conventions to which the United States is a party, the statutes of the United States, and, where no international agreement or treaty provision exists covering any special point, in accordance with the practice and attitude of the United States as hitherto determined by court decisions and Executive pronouncements." Daniels added: " The Navy Department has no knowledge of any violations of these instructions by United States naval vessels." *Ibid.,* pp. 931-32.

FREEDOM OF THE SEAS

The answer to the third question is that there is no record in the Navy Department of any case of search and seizure by vessels of the United States Navy of the kind contested in the American note of October 21, 1915. . . .[17]

On the basis of this evidence it would seem as though the United States is not open to the charge of having reversed itself by actively co-operating with the British in their blockade.[18]

[17] *Ibid.*, p. 934, n. On November 10, 1917, Secretary Lansing sought the advice of Secretary of the Navy Daniels as to whether the United States should subscribe to a convention entered into by Great Britain and France, and acceded to by Italy, concerning prizes captured during the war. In his reply Daniels listed certain objections, the most important of which in his judgment was " a seeming approval of certain practices and principles against which the United States has already protested, as in the note from the Secretary of State to Ambassador W. H. Page, dated October 21, 1915." Accepting Daniels' views, Lansing concluded that the United States would take no action unless the character of the war should so change as to give the subject more pressing importance. *Ibid.*, pp. 922-24. Replying to an inquiry from the Dutch chargé in Washington, on November 29, 1918, Assistant Secretary of State Phillips replied for the Secretary of State: " There appear to have been no cases brought before the United States courts concerning prizes during the existence of the present war." *Ibid.*, p. 931.

[18] In consenting to the rationing agreement between Holland and the Associated Powers, the War Trade Board made it clear that it would not be a party to any examining of ships done under the British blockade, but that all searching of Dutch vessels as envisaged by America's responsibility under the agreement would be done in United States ports. *Ibid.*, pp. 1591-92; also *ante*, p. 235. The present writer has heard rumors to the effect that American naval vessels clandestinely passed on to British ships information as to the movement of neutral merchantmen, thus helping in the enforcement of the blockade. In response to an inquiry on this point, Captain Dudley W. Knox, Officer-in-charge of the Office of Naval Records and Library, Navy Department, Washing-

V

A possible exception to the conclusion just drawn has sometimes been cited.[19] The United States, it is true, collaborated with its Associates in setting up and directing machinery for the co-ordination of embargo and blockade practices. The most important of these agencies, the Allied Blockade Committee (A. B. C.), held its first meeting in London on March 15, 1918, and its membership consisted of representatives of the United States, Great Britain, France, Italy, and (later) Belgium. This organization, together with the other committees associated with it, was not a policy-making but a policy-executing body, and consequently occupies but a small place in our discussion. Its functions were purely supervisory and advisory. It did not even have final authority to accept or reject export licenses. This function was reserved for the export control organization of the constituent governments (the War Trade Board in the case of the United States), which merely considered the recommendations of the A. B. C. On all matters of

---

ton, D. C., wrote on November 4, 1941: "I would doubt very much that in actual practice the active operating vessels of the Navy failed to follow carefully the official policies of the Government in these or in any other respects. Of course, it is possible that there might have been an occasional exception. I doubt any exceptions, but if there were any they would be very few, and I think it likely that the suspicions and rumors that you mention are out of all proportion to the facts.

"I am sorry not to be more specific in the matter, but we have very little data here. At any rate, had the facts been contrary to my opinion stated above, I feel certain that I would have heard of it either in London where I was on duty from December 1917 to the end of the war, or here."

[19] See Garner, "Violations of Maritime Law by the Allied Powers during the World War," *Amer. Jour. of Int. Law*, XXV (1931), 46-47.

importance the A. B. C. was not supposed to act without specific directions from the governments represented.[20]

It has also been alleged that the American embargo was to all practical intents and purposes a part of the British blockade system, and that by co-operating to this extent the United States was more or less in the same compromising position as the Allies.[21] We have already observed that the embargo supplemented and strengthened the blockade; and from the point of view of the neutrals it made little difference whether American goods were cut off in America by governmental action or stopped en route by the British fleet.[22] But we have also observed that the embargo was

[20] *For. Rel., 1918, Supp. 1,* II, pp. 974, 978-79; *Report of War Trade Board,* pp. 18-19. See *ibid.* for the work of the Contraband Committee, the War Trade Intelligence Department, the War Trade Statistical Department, the Interallied Trade Committees, and the *Commission Internationale de Contingents.* See also Louis Guichard, *The Naval Blockade* (New York, 1930), pp. 108-09.

[21] Comment of Charles Warren (December 18, 1941), who as Assistant Attorney General drafted the Export Title of the Espionage Act: " I think you should make clearer the difference between the British control of trade with neutrals and their interference as a belligerent, and the American control and interference. The first was exercise of unwarranted powers on the sea. The second was exercise under a domestic statute (the Export Title of the so-called Espionage Act) enacted under the plenary powers of control and embargo of the American Congress to regulate a foreign commerce vested in it by the Constitution."

[22] Garner (*loc. cit.,* pp. 47-48) uses quotations from British statesmen and publicists in an attempt to show that the United States, by employing the embargo, was tarred with the blockade brush. Fayle points out (*Seaborne Trade,* III, 234) that following the American embargo the number of neutral ships plying between the Northern Neutrals and the United States fell off so sharply that British armed cruisers on the Northern Patrol were largely withdrawn for antisubmarine work. Thus the American embargo made easier the enforcement of the blockade.

undeniably legal; and since we are at present concerned with legalities, it is not pertinent to develop this theme at length.

It could be argued, as some have, that by acquiescing in British practices and by indirectly co-operating with them, the United States was guilty of being a *particeps criminis*;[23] and although it did not actually engage in these objectionable blockade measures, it must to some extent share the odium of having violated neutral rights. This argument, however, is not without certain elements of weakness. The Washington government, while neutral, had been unable or unwilling to force an abandonment of Britain's practices, even though it possessed the strong weapons of naval power and a potential embargo. One could hardly expect the United States, as a belligerent, to turn against its associates in arms, and hamper the common effort by attempting to interfere with measures that it had tolerated while a neutral.

vi

During the period of neutrality the United States did not take nearly so strong a position on the issue of contraband as on the blockade and other matters. Indeed, on this question Washington showed a greater degree of willingness to sympathize with the point of view of the belligerents

---

[23] Sir Edward Grey later reminisced: "That was a blockade such as the world had never known, but it was possible only because the United States was not criticizing but co-operating.... The reason was, that the point of view of the United States had changed from that of a neutral to that of a belligerent with superior sea-power. In matters of blockade and contraband the point of view makes the whole difference." Edward Grey, *Twenty-five Years, 1892-1916* (New York, 1925), II, 117-18.

than on others. In a public circular, issued on August 15, 1914, by the Department of State, reference was made to the traditional categories of contraband (absolute and conditional); and it was stated that the position of the United States on disputed points was "to be determined by international law and usage, influenced in some degree by the positions assumed by the belligerents."[24]

At first the United States seemed disposed to insist that food not destined for military purposes was not contraband; but a German decree establishing governmental control of foodstuffs appears to have made such a distinction untenable, or at least of arguable validity. The Department of State also concluded that it could not reasonably protest against the inclusion of petroleum in contraband lists, so vital had this commodity become in mechanized warfare. The question of cotton was of considerably greater importance. The British were anxious not to arouse the South against the blockade, and as a consequence they early informed Washington that as far as they were concerned cotton was not contraband. Nine months later, after the blockade had became more firmly established, Downing Street announced that it would add cotton to the contraband list. The Secretary of State told the British ambassador that much resentment would be created in the United States by a feeling that

[24] *For. Rel., 1914, Supp.*, p. 276. As further illustration of the flexibility of the American position, we may note that the Italian government, in May, 1915, requested the consent of the United States to the inclusion of articles in a proposed contraband list which were not listed in the treaty of 1871 between the United States and Italy. The State Department, noting that other belligerents had lengthened their contraband lists, replied that it would not object to such additions on the grounds of nonconformity with the treaty of 1871. *Ibid., 1915, Supp.*, pp. 164-65.

London had broken a solemn promise; yet so clearly did cotton enter into the manufacture of explosives, and so willing were the British to buy large quantities of the fiber themselves, that Washington did not protest when, on August 20, 1916, Great Britain officially added cotton to its absolute contraband list.[25]

Throughout these discussions, the Department of State was aware that in the past it had stood for a restricted contraband list while a neutral, and for a liberal list while a belligerent.[26] And as the conflict progressed it became increasingly evident that in a struggle of this nature there were few, if any, articles of any importance that could not in some way be associated with the war effort. Doubtless with such considerations in mind, Washington generally pursued a noncommittal attitude. In his comprehensive note

---

[25] Similarly, the Washington government was disturbed when the British, revoking previous assurances to the contrary, added turpentine and rosin to their list of absolute contraband. The Department of State viewed this addition "with profound regret" and unsuccessfully sought, without actually lodging a formal protest, to induce the British to rescind their action. In this, as in the cotton issue, the necessity of quieting domestic producers was probably more important than questions of pure legalism. For the diplomatic interchange see Savage, *Maritime Commerce*, II, 15-16, 35-37, and supporting documents.

[26] In a letter to Senator Stone, Secretary Bryan wrote on January 20, 1915: "But the rights and interests of belligerents and neutrals are opposed in respect to contraband articles and trade and there is no tribunal to which questions of difference may be readily submitted.

"The record of the United States in the past is not free from criticism. When neutral, this Government has stood for a restricted list of absolute and conditional contraband. As a belligerent, we have contended for a liberal list, according to our conception of the necessities of the case." *For. Rel., 1914, Supp.*, p. ix.

of October 21, 1915, Lansing said that the United States had no disposition to waive any objections that it might entertain regarding the British contraband list; and, while not actually protesting, he reserved the right to make a later communication on this subject.[27]

On April 13, 1916, the British announced that they would consider all contraband articles, whether conditional or absolute, as absolute contraband. As early as January 9, 1915, the then Secretary of State, William Jennings Bryan, had privately come to the conclusion that the distinction between conditional and absolute contraband had proved "valueless." [28] Probably a not dissimilar conviction was responsible for the fact that Secretary Lansing waited for seven months before officially commenting on the British innovation; and he then notified London " of the reservation of all rights of the United States or its citizens in respect of any American interests which may be adversely affected by the abolition of the distinction between these two classes of contraband, or by the illegal extension of the contraband lists during the present war by Great Britain or her allies." [29] This, it will be observed, was not a protest, but a reservation of rights, should they become adversely affected.

vii

In view of all these developments, it is not surprising that when the United States became a belligerent it kept

[27] *Ibid., 1915, Supp.*, pp. 588-89. The German government, like the British, made extensions in its contraband lists.

[28] See the entire memorandum. Savage, *Maritime Commerce*, II, 533, n.

[29] Lansing to Page, November 11, 1916, *For. Rel., 1916, Supp.*, p. 483.

pace with current developments and issued a most inclusive contraband list. This embraced virtually every item that could be of use to the enemy in the prosecution of a modern war.[30] The United States also followed the British in abolishing all expressed distinction between absolute and conditional contraband, although by making destination the deciding factor Washington actually retained in some degree the old classification.[31] But a discussion of this question in connection with American belligerency is primarily academic. Inasmuch as the United States did not actively cooperate with the British in their blockade, and inasmuch as it took no neutral prizes, it was not involved in any important issue with the neutrals as regards contraband. In any event, its paper position was not seriously at variance with its pronouncements while a neutral, and with the exigencies of a modern war involving an enemy located in the position of the Central Powers.

Precisely the same thing can be said about the doctrine of continuous voyage. The United States adopted Allied presumptions as to the destination of absolute contraband, and departed from the Declaration of London by returning to a former position and applying continuous voyage to conditional as well as to absolute contraband.[32] But it must be remembered that the American delegates had surrendered

---

[30] For list see *Naval Instructions, 1917*, p. 15. When, in April and May, 1918, the British Embassy in Washington requested the United States to add certain articles, including sodium fluoride and citric acid, to the list of absolute contraband, it was informed that these items were already regarded as covered by the American list. *For. Rel., 1918, Supp. 1*, II, pp. 917-19.

[31] This was the interpretation of the Acting Judge Advocate General of the Navy. *Ibid.*, p. 919.

[32] See *Naval Instructions, 1917*, p. 15.

this claim at the London Conference, and that the Declaration of London was never ratified.[33] In any event, since the United States did not participate in the Allied blockade and did not take any neutral prizes, the doctrine of continuous voyage did not become an issue involving the neutrals, and as a consequence Washington cannot be charged with inconsistent practice. But the theoretical position of the United States was in part a return to its historical stand, and in part a recognition of the changed conditions of modern warfare.

viii

We have already observed that the United States " constantly " exercised the unquestioned right of a belligerent to visit and search on the high seas.[34] This, of course, was unobjectionable, if done in accordance with international law. But the removal of enemy nationals from neutral ships raised other and more serious questions. As a neutral, the Washington government had strongly protested against the Allied practice of stopping American merchantmen on the high seas and seizing German reservists on board.[35] As a belligerent, the United States firmly resisted all invitations to reverse itself in this matter. One example will suffice.

On March 6, 1918, the U. S. S. *Bainbridge* was dispatched from Gibraltar by the British Senior Naval Officer, with

---

[33] Scott, *Declaration of London*, p. 200.

[34] American boarding parties deviated from their published instructions in not making entries in ships' logs when " such entries would give information facilitating unlawful attack by enemy submarines." *For. Rel., 1918, Supp. 1*, II, p. 925.

[35] Thomas A. Bailey, " World War Analogues of the *Trent* Affair," *Amer. Hist. Rev.*, XXXVIII (1933), 286-90.

instructions to intercept a Spanish (neutral) merchantman and remove from it a certain passenger with a Germanic name. When the American commander in this area learned of these orders, he promptly protested against them and secured their revocation. Shortly thereafter the British Senior Naval Officer was instructed by the Admiralty in London that United States warships should not be employed to remove enemy or other persons from neutral merchantmen.[36] In short, if the British wanted this sort of thing done, they would have to do it themselves.

The United States Navy also declined to share in the mandatory routing of neutral vessels for purposes of detention and search, inasmuch as this was precisely the practice against which Lansing had emphatically protested in his note of October 21, 1915. It is true that the Navy did require neutral ships in American convoys to follow certain routes, and in some cases to put into a port of call prior to arriving at the harbor of ultimate destination. But all such restrictions were designed to insure the greatest possible safety and to bring about as speedy a voyage as was consonant with this general objective.[37]

It is clear, then, that the United States Navy did not follow the example of the British in using force, or a show of force, to bring neutral ships into control stations where they could be searched for contraband. But it will be recalled that the movements of such vessels were controlled by the War Trade Board through the bunker club and the tonnage agreements.[38] This, however, was done primarily

[36] *For. Rel., 1918, Supp. 1,* II, p. 934, n.
[37] *Ibid.,* pp. 935-36.
[38] The bunker regulations of January 19, 1918, provided: " Every vessel which proceeds from or to the United States, to or

for the purpose of conserving shipping, of preventing neutral craft from operating to the advantage of the enemy, and of forcing vessels to move in the interests of the Associated Powers. The bunker club and the tonnage agreements were also used to enforce the American embargo. But they did not involve a threat of naval coercion, and they were not used by the United States for the purpose of enforcing a blockade which the State Department had declared illegal.

ix

Before leaving the subject of mandatory routing, we should observe that the United States seriously considered—but did not finally adopt—a scheme for resorting to such a practice. This grew out of a desire to end the call which the Northern Neutrals were forced to make at Halifax, en route to the United States or en route to Europe, for purposes of examination by the British authorities. Washington considered this procedure both an uneconomical use of tonnage and, in most cases, unnecessary. It was uneconomical because the vessels ordinarily lost several days; it was unnecessary in the case of European-bound vessels which were subjected to a rigorous search before leaving New York.[39] After prolonged discussions between the American and British officials, it was decided, in March, 1918, to eliminate the Halifax calls for eastbound vessels taking on their cargo at New York and proceeding

---

from Norway, Sweden, Denmark (including Iceland and the Faroe Islands), Holland, Spain, or to or from any neutral port in the Mediterranean Sea, shall call for examination as may be directed by the War Trade Board." *Ibid.,* p. 948.

[39] *Ibid.,* p. 941; "Minutes of the War Trade Board," I, 239-40 (January 12, 1918); I, 277 (January 21, 1918).

to one of the Northern Neutrals.[40] The search of these ships at New York was to be undertaken in collaboration with the British, who sent over experts to tutor their American cousins in the fine points of such work.[41]

The new arrangements were not wholly satisfactory to the United States. American-bound traffic from the Northern Neutrals was not covered, though some Scandinavian ships were exempted from the call at Halifax, provided they were destined directly for New York.[42] Moreover, European-bound vessels touching at New York, but not loading all their cargo there, were still required to stop at Halifax, no matter how thorough the American search. This raised the strong suspicion that the British were anxious to examine as many ships' papers as possible in order to ferret out trade secrets. For the purpose of eliminating such difficulties, the British Foreign Office and the Admiralty in London, co-operating

---

[40] See records of the conference at the New Willard Hotel, Washington, February 6, 1918, State Dept., War Trade Board (Search of Vessels . . .); also *For. Rel., 1918, Supp. 1,* II, pp. 957, 969.

[41] By the early winter of 1918 the War Trade Board felt that American searchers had been thoroughly taught, and expressed resentment at the continued participation of the British. War Trade Board to Sheldon, November 30, 1918, marked "draft not sent," State Dept., War Trade Board (Search of Vessels . . .).

[42] Memorandum of L. L. Richards, of the War Trade Board, to Thomas L. Chadbourne, October 10, 1918, *ibid.* Richards said in this memorandum: ". . . The Navy Department has informed us very confidentially that they are of the opinion that the Halifax call was entirely for commercial purposes, and to obtain commercial information from the ship papers, etc. The Navy regarded the search at Halifax as both superficial and unnecessary, particularly in view of the thorough search in New York." See also Vance C. McCormick to R. S. Hudson (British Embassy), October 11, 1918, *ibid.*

with American naval representatives there, finally drew up an elaborate proposal for requiring east- and west-bound European traffic to stop at joint British-American examination stations, conveniently situated. Those for the United States, in addition to New York, were to be at Philadelphia, Norfolk, New Orleans, and Colón.

The scheme proposed in London for the elimination of the general call at Halifax was widened in scope and approved by the War Trade Board after consultation with the Navy Department.[43] The amended plan provided for the creation of two additional examination ports: St. Thomas in the Virgin Islands and San Juan in Puerto Rico. These were to be established primarily for the purpose of accommodating east- and west-bound Spanish ships, which would be forced into these ports for examination. It was also contemplated that in the case of Spanish vessels on certain routes it might be well to establish an American examination port at Rio de Janeiro, in cobelligerent Brazil (a subject that was then under diplomatic discussion), or at some other convenient point in South America.

The members of the War Trade Board and the Navy Department who favored this ambitious plan were evidently much less concerned about consistency and precedent than the Department of State. Solicitor Woolsey examined the

---

[43] "Minutes of the War Trade Board," IV, 370 (November 4, 1918). The amended plan was in the form of a memorandum entitled: "Memorandum for a Plan of Examination of Northern Neutral Vessels with a View of Eliminating the Call at Halifax and to Provide for the Examination of Spanish Vessels." It is not dated, but a copy was sent by Lawrence Bennett to Dr. Alonzo E. Taylor of the War Trade Board under date of November 1, 1918. F. A. R., Hoover Library (Neutrals).

scheme emanating from London, as amended by the War Trade Board, and prepared a highly significant memorandum. He pointed out (November 11, 1918), that under existing arrangements the United States was pursuing a policy "based upon our correspondence with Great Britain in respect to the diversion and examination of vessels in her ports while we were neutral." He further observed that the British "continued to do this, and we took no part in it, on account of our position in the diplomatic correspondence." Woolsey concluded:

> Under the new plan adopted with some modifications by the War Trade Board, the United States is integrated with the Allies in this matter. If it is adopted by the United States, our contentions while neutral, and the claims of American citizens admitted by us to be good at the time, are, it seems to me, cast aside. I doubt whether the Government as a matter of policy, or law, ought to or can invalidate such claims as may be good, by action of this kind. This was the view entertained by Mr. Anderson, when he considered the subject. Another objectionable feature is that the new plan proposed to have an examination port in the Panama Canal Zone—a procedure which I understood the Department had opposed consistently, inasmuch as it is clearly an exercise of belligerent rights in the Zone.[44]

The opposition of the State Department apparently proved decisive, for some two weeks later the War Trade Board informed its representative in London that the Department had vetoed the plan, and that the War Trade Board and the State Department were in consultation for the purpose of preparing a revised scheme.[45] The records

---

[44] *For. Rel., 1918, Supp. 1*, II, pp. 1010-11.

[45] War Trade Board to Sheldon, November 29, 1918, *ibid.*, pp. 1012-13. This is a brief telegram. A much longer one, dated November 30, 1918, and marked "draft not sent," may be found

consulted for this study do not reveal that any such proposal was adopted.[46] When the year 1918 ended, those neutral vessels which had not been properly examined at New York were still required by London to stop at British ports. And although many neutral shippers would doubtless have preferred being forced into a conveniently located American harbor, rather than going out of their way to touch at a British station, the United States made a virtue of consistency and kept its record clean.[47]

---

in State Dept., War Trade Board (Search of Vessels . . .). This repeated almost verbatim Woolsey's objections, and stated further that the War Trade Board wished to eliminate the Halifax call by searching in American ports all neutral ships that called there in due course, including those bound by agreement with the United States. This presumably would meet the charge of mandatory routing. Woolsey was reported in a War Trade Board memorandum (December 11, 1918) as having said:

"1. There should, of course, be no forcible deviation in a vessel's voyage in order to bring about a search in an American port.

"2. All vessels, either loading at our ports or unloading at our ports, may be searched for all purposes whatsoever.

"3. Vessels that touch at our ports purely voluntarily, that is to say, not as the result of a Trade Agreement or a Bunker Agreement, may be searched for the sole purpose of determining whether they have on board contraband consigned to the enemy.

"4. Vessels that touch at our ports voluntarily, but as the result of a Trade Agreement or a Bunker Agreement. Mr. Woolsey prefers to express no opinion in connection with such vessels until he has had an opportunity to study both our Trade Agreements and our Bunker Regulations.

"5. There should be no search, of course, in the Canal Zone."

Apparently Woolsey's opinions were followed by the War Trade Board. *Ibid.*

[46] *For. Rel., 1918, Supp. 1,* II, p. 1745, n.

[47] A memorandum by T. M. Phifer, dated December 11, 1918, stated: " Neutral representatives have repeatedly requested us to

X

Any consideration of America's attitude toward maritime rights during the period of her belligerency necessarily involves some mention of German safe-conducts. These were documents issued by Berlin to neutral shippers granting them protection against the U-boats. The nature and destination of the cargo were approved by the German authorities before issuance of the safe-conduct; and when this was done the neutral ship was instructed to carry markings easily recognizable by the submarine commanders. The scheme had certain advantages from the point of view of both parties. The neutrals were granted immunity from destruction, as well as freedom from the annoyance and delay caused by visit, search, and possible diversion. Indeed, the alternative to the safe-conduct was the risk of being sunk at sight.[48] To the Germans, on the other hand, this device was of value primarily because it forced the neutrals into services that were useful to the Central Powers and disadvantageous to the Allies. In fact, the safe-conduct was probably devised in part as a countermove against the tonnage agreements into which the neutrals were being driven by the American embargo.[49]

Throughout the controversy with the neutrals over safe-conducts, the British seem to have been much less disturbed

---

use our good offices with the British authorities to make a joint search at Norfolk in particular in order to avoid the call at Halifax." State Dept., War Trade Board (Search of Vessels . . .).

[48] According to Minister Morris in Stockholm, the Swedes found that the advantages of this system outweighed the disadvantages. *For. Rel., 1918, Supp. 1,* II, pp. 1086-87.

[49] The United States chargé in Denmark came to this conclusion. *Ibid.,* pp. 1087-88.

than either the Americans or the French. The Department of State gave a preliminary opinion to the Chairman of the War Trade Board that a neutral vessel proceeding under a safe-conduct was subject under international law to treatment as an enemy ship.[50] After more mature consideration, Solicitor Woolsey drew up a memorandum on this question, dated July 18, 1918. Although Woolsey could find no exact precedents in American action, he concluded that the acceptance of safe-conducts by a neutral nation assimilated it closely to the belligerent which issued them, and that vessels carrying such documents " probably " would be condemned if seized and brought before an American prize court. He felt, however, that it might be wise to avoid becoming involved in such a practice. Noting that earlier in the war Washington had declined to enter into an agreement with its Associates for a mutual exchange of prizes, he suggested that unless there were compelling reasons to the contrary, it would be well for the United States " not [to] take the initiative in making captures in distant waters, but . . . leave the working out of the policy and procedure in such cases to its co-belligerents which have their own prize court machinery and methods established and in operation." In any event, Woolsey believed that no neutral ships carrying safe-conducts should be seized until due notice had been given and the vessels had had time to complete their voyages.[51]

Washington was anxious to take action before the neutrals

[50] " Minutes of the War Trade Board," III, 192 (July 15, 1918).

[51] Memorandum to Auchincloss from Woolsey, July 18, 1918. Subject: " Status of licenses or German safe-conducts under international law." State Dept., 763. 72112 Sa/119.

became accustomed to the German safe-conduct scheme and gave it general recognition. Accordingly, on July 25, 1918, the War Trade Board, with the approval of the State Department, proposed that the Associated Governments present an identic communication to the European neutrals stating that the acceptance of a safe-conduct might " operate to deprive vessels accepting the same of their neutral character," and that the Associated Powers " reserve the right to deal with any vessel which has subjected itself to enemy control as the circumstances in each case may warrant." Two days later, the representative of the War Trade Board in London reported that the British government " generally approved " the American proposal, subject to certain relatively minor changes.[52] Encouraged by this favorable response, the Department of State, early in August, 1918, sent a substantially identical declaration to its representatives in Spain, Sweden, Norway, the Netherlands, and Denmark, which they were to present to the respective foreign offices upon learning that their British, French, and Italian colleagues had received similar instructions.[53]

Although the Italian government was prepared to acquiesce, the French raised some objections to the proposed joint warning; and the British, despite their tentative acceptance, now regarded the scheme as unwise, primarily because they felt that on the whole safe-conducts facilitated the movement of neutral shipping.[54] The War Trade Board was much annoyed by this British reversal, and persisted in pushing its proposal.[55] But the plan for identic action

---

[52] *For. Rel., 1918, Supp. 1*, II, pp. 1090-93. [53] *Ibid.*, p. 1093.
[54] *Ibid.*, p. 1095; Sharp to Lansing, August 6, 1918, State Dept., 763.72112 Sa/29.
[55] *For. Rel., 1918, Supp. 1*, II, pp. 1096-98.

was finally abandoned, lest such a concerted move unduly alarm public opinion in the neutral countries; and early in September, 1918, the Associated Powers undertook to make their representations individually, either formally or informally, oral or written, as the delicacy of the situation in the country concerned seemed to require. Thus, in substance, the American plan for presenting a warning to each of the European neutrals against the acceptance of safe-conducts was ultimately adopted.[56]

The subject of safe-conducts is not of primary importance to us, for it does not appear that the American position ever got beyond the warning stage. Certainly no neutral vessels were halted by the United States Navy and taken into port for sailing with these documents. Washington did not actually threaten to seize such ships, and its practice throughout the war was against such a course. The safe-conducts closely resembled letters of assurance, which the United States had tolerated while a neutral; and to have confiscated vessels for carrying them would have led to much ill feeling. The whole episode shows that in this matter Washington took a much more active and aggressive attitude toward the neutrals than any of the Allies. The policy of the United States was legalism tempered by expediency, for on a strict basis of international law the Associated Powers could have made out a good case for seizing neutral ships carrying safe-conducts. The final American representations were in part a recognition of the fact that the neutrals were in a difficult position, situated as

[56] *Ibid.*, pp. 1102-03. The United States protested to Sweden on the additional grounds that the acceptance of safe-conducts violated the Swedish-American agreement of May 29, 1918. *Ibid.*, pp. 1103-04. The protest to Spain seems to have been handled with the greatest delicacy. *Ibid.*, p. 1104.

they were between the nether millstone of the German submarine and the upper millstone of the British naval blockade.

xi

For some reason that has never been satisfactorily explained, the United States, while a neutral, did not take so positive a stand against belligerent mining of large areas of the open sea as on certain other innovations produced by the war. On November 3, 1914, the British government, alleging that the Germans had scattered mines indiscriminately in the North Sea, announced its determination to mine that body of water and denominate it a "military area." [57] Although this was a sufficiently drastic departure from the ordinary procedure of warfare to justify representations on the part of the United States, Secretary Bryan declined an invitation from Norway to join with the three Scandinavian countries in a protest, remarking that Washington did "not see its way at the present time" to take such action.[58] Here the matter rested, while the

[57] *Ibid., 1914, Supp.*, p. 464. On August 11, 1914, the British Embassy informed the Department of State that the Germans were "scattering contact mines indiscriminately about the North Sea," and warned the United States that the British government held themselves "at liberty to adopt similar measures of self-defense. . . ." Interpreting this, apparently erroneously, as a statement of the right to use floating mines, Secretary Bryan lodged a protest against the use of such a weapon. *Ibid.*, pp. 455-56. It does not appear, however, that the British, if for no other reason than the danger to their own merchant fleet, made a practice of scattering floating mines in the open sea.

[58] *Ibid.*, p. 466; also Savage, *Maritime Commerce*, II, 51. See the somewhat evasive answer of Secretary Bryan (January 22, 1915) to an invitation from the Swedish government to state the position of the United States on the question of mining. *For. Rel., 1914, Supp.*, pp. 473-74.

Department of State laid itself open to charges of inconsistency by protesting vigorously against the German proclamation (February, 1915) of a submarine area around the British Isles. To some observers there was no essential difference between a mined war area and a submarine war area.

Not until February 19, 1917, on the eve of America's entry into the war, did the Department of State make anything suggesting a protest to London against mining areas in the open sea, and on this occasion the representations were apparently not inspired by the original announcement but by a later refinement of it. Secretary Lansing declared:

As the question of appropriating certain portions of the high seas for military operations, to the exclusion of the use of the hostile area as a common highway of commerce, has not become a settled principle of international law assented to by the family of nations, it will be recognized that the Government of the United States must, and hereby does, for the protection of American interests, reserve generally all of its rights in the premises, including the right not only to question the validity of these measures, but to present demands and claims in relation to any American interests which may be unlawfully affected, directly or indirectly, by virtue of the enforcement of these measures.

This, it will be recognized, was not a protest to Britain against mining the open sea, but merely a reservation of the right to protest, should such a course be deemed necessary. In any event, it is clear that the Washington officials regarded this practice as challengeable, inasmuch as it was not specifically recognized by international law.[59]

---

[59] *Ibid., 1917, Supp. 1,* pp. 519-20. On February 20, 1915, Secretary Bryan proposed to the British and German governments, without success, that " they should not sow floating mines on the high seas or in territorial waters, and should not plant anchored mines on the high seas ' except within cannon range of harbors for defensive purposes only. . . .' " Savage, *op. cit.,* II, 16.

Upon entering the war the United States was faced with the problem of combating the German submarines, which were a grave menace to American troop and supply ships. The Navy Department took the initiative in urging a proposal for planting an immense mine barrier across the North Sea, from northern Scotland to the coast of Norway, which would close that important exit to German U-boats.[60] The British at first opposed the scheme, apparently because of the impracticability of such a huge undertaking rather than because of any scruples involving international law. But once decided upon, the project was carried through with great energy. Beginning in June, 1918, an area 230 miles long and 15 to 35 miles wide was mined by over 70,000 contact mines, some 56,000 of which were laid by the Americans.[61]

What may be said in extenuation—if extenuation seems necessary—of America's having taken the initiative and played the largest role in roping off one of the world's important channels of commerce? Was she guilty of inconsistency in so doing? In this connection it will be remembered that Lansing, in his representations to the British of

[60] See Baker, *Wilson*, VII, 21. The scheme was strongly supported by Assistant Secretary of the Navy Franklin D. Roosevelt. *Ibid.*, p. 334. Wilson was much interested in shutting up "the hornets in their nests," and was impatient of delays. Josephus Daniels, *Our Navy at War* (New York, 1922), pp. 134, 144.

[61] See Navy Department, Office of Naval Records and Library, Historical Section, *The Northern Mine Barrage and Other Mining Activities* (Washington, 1920). The component parts of the mines were manufactured in America and assembled in Scotland. See also William S. Sims, *The Victory at Sea* (Garden City, N. Y., 1921), ch. IX; and Captain Reginald R. Belknap, "The North Sea Mine Barrage," *National Geographic Magazine*, XXXV, 85-110 (February, 1919). Captain Belknap was in direct command of the United States mine-laying squadron.

February 19, 1917, had not declared that laying stationary mines in the open sea was a violation of international law; rather he had expressed doubts as to the legality of such a practice and had reserved the right to protest. So, unlike the blacklist, it cannot be said that the United States took precisely the same kind of action against which it had specifically and emphatically protested while a neutral.[62]

It should also be pointed out that the mine barrage worked no serious hardship on the already badly battered neutrals, for the British provided innocent shipping with safe sailing directions.[63] Had the situation been otherwise, the neutrals would almost certainly have protested to Washington; and the files of the State Department that were examined on this subject revealed no such action. This does not necessarily mean that the neutrals accepted this sweeping use of the mine field as entirely consonant with the

[62] Comment of Charles Warren (December 18, 1941): "I do not think that there can be any doubt but that both the British and German policies as to mining of the seas were utterly without foundation in international law. I could never understand the weak attitude of the United States on this subject from the beginning. . . . I have no doubt that our North Sea mine barrage was equally lawless." See also Mr. Warren's statement in his "Lawless Maritime Warfare," *Foreign Affairs,* XVIII (1940), 429, in which he points out that as far as international law in general is concerned the question of mining the high seas is still "unsettled."

[63] The United States took prompt and energetic measures to remove the mines, a task that was completed only after extraordinary hardship and labor. The removal of the mines, no less than their laying, remains one of the great sagas of the seas. See Navy Department, Office of Naval Records and Library, Historical Section, *The Northern Barrage: Taking up the Mines* (Washington, 1920).

precepts of international law.⁶⁴ Having already exhausted their quiver of arguments against Great Britain, without any appreciable effect, these small countries probably were impressed with the futility of fashioning new arrows for use against the United States.

xii

The North Sea mine barrage neared the three-mile limit of Norwegian territorial waters about August 5, 1918. Even before this time it had become apparent to the British and American naval experts that unless Norway could be persuaded to close this gap with her own mines, or unless the Allies forcibly mined the area themselves, considerable numbers of German submarines would continue to slip past the barrier, and the enormous expenditure of money and effort would have gone largely for naught. To lay mines in open sea was one thing; to lay them within the territorial waters of a neutral without the consent of that neutral was another. The role played by the United States in the negotiations on this point is of the first importance in our present study.

⁶⁴ Professor Charles Cheney Hyde generalizes as follows: "The absence of any belligerent right to assert control over definite and substantial areas of the high seas, and to divert neutral ships therefrom, serves to render generally unlawful the anchoring of mines in such places." But with reference to the North Sea mine barrage he is disposed to make an exception. "The nature of the service in which those vessels [submarines] were then engaged, and the effect of their operations (if not so thwarted) upon the duration if not the outcome of the conflict, together with the insufficiency of other means of combating them, will doubtless be acknowledged to have justified recourse to this extraordinary and efficacious measure, despite the restrictions which it necessarily imposed upon neutral shipping." *International Law Chiefly as Interpreted and Applied by the United States,* II, 415, 422.

Downing Street at first decided to work independently of the United States, and on August 8, 1918, the British minister in Christiania informed his American colleague that he had been "urgently and peremptorily instructed to demand" that Norway close the gap within four days. Having carried out his instructions, the British envoy suggested to his government that the United States be invited to join in these representations.[65] President Wilson promptly and vigorously vetoed this suggestion. We have already seen that he had taken an unusual interest in the earlier rationing negotiations with Norway, and that he had then insisted upon a lenient course. In connection with the mining problem, he sent three memoranda to the State Department, a summarized form of one of which emphatically stated that he was "opposed to joining any other Government in peremptory representations of any kind."[66]

The policy laid down by President Wilson was followed consistently by the Department of State. The American representations to Christiania were never "peremptory" and they were always made independently of the British. In conformity with this policy, the instructions sent by Lansing to Chargé H. F. A. Schoenfeld, on August 13, 1918, requested the Norwegian government to "proceed with such new and effective measures as will prevent effectually the passage of German submarines through Norwegian territorial waters. . . ." It is significant that the United States did not ask Norway specifically to lay mines;

[65] *For. Rel., 1918, Supp. 1,* II, pp. 1769-70.
[66] None of the originals of these three memoranda could be located in the relevant file in the State Department, or in the private collections of Wilson or Lansing. A summarized form of the one quoted is in State Dept., 763. 72111N83/91.

but although this delicate subject was not then mentioned, the meaning was clear. The State Department based its request upon the assumption that Christiania, by permitting the passage of German submarines through its waters, was not enforcing its own decree of January 30, 1917, which categorically forbade such privileges to belligerents. The United States, Lansing declared, had respected this proclamation; Germany had not.[67]

Meanwhile, the Christiania Foreign Office had presented an argumentative and evasive answer to the British demand for mining the gap, and had rested its case on the premise that Norway could not be dictated to by one of the belligerents.[68] London thereupon instructed its envoy to inform the Foreign Minister that " unless the Norwegian Government are prepared to mine efficiently the waters involved, or to allow Great Britain to do it for them, the British Government are fully resolved to carry out the work themselves." A time limit was not attached to this ultimatum, although the British then had in mind a delay of about a fortnight. The London government, as well as the Allied representatives in Norway, apparently did not think that unilateral mining by the Associated Powers would cause Germany to invade Norway, in part, presumably, because of current German reverses on the Western Front.[69]

The Norwegian government took a week to prepare its

[67] *For. Rel., 1918, Supp. 1*, II, pp. 1772-73. Schoenfeld was here specifically instructed not to take joint action with the British minister. In his reply Schoenfeld reported that he did not mention mines in his representations, and that he made it clear that he was acting independently of the Allies. *Ibid.*, pp. 1773-74.

[68] *Ibid.*, p. 1771; Schoenfeld to Lansing, August 14, 1918, State Dept., 763. 72111N83/17.

[69] *For. Rel., 1918, Supp. 1*, II, pp. 1775-76, 1780-81.

reply to the American note, and, on August 20, 1918, submitted a document that was no more satisfactory than that to London. The Foreign Office denied that Norway had not upheld her neutrality, and asked for concrete evidence that her waters had been violated by German submarines. Throughout the war the neutrals had generally pursued a policy of evasion and procrastination when confronted with demands from one set of belligerents that were offensive to the other; and in this instance Norway proved to be no exception to the rule. Although Chargé Schoenfeld dropped all circumlocution and suggested mining, and although he pointed out that German U-boats which passed through the gap were sinking Norwegian shipping, the government of Norway seemed determined to prolong the discussion and avoid action as long as possible.[70]

By this time more than two weeks had elapsed since the mine barrage had been brought to the Norwegian three-mile limit; and the United States Navy Department was naturally much disturbed that its Herculean efforts should be substantially negatived by the failure of Washington to co-operate with the British in employing strong measures.[71]

---

[70] *Ibid.*, pp. 1778-80; Schoenfeld to Lansing, August 21, 1918, State Dept., 763.72111N83/62. Part of the delay was due to the fact that Norway discussed the problem with Sweden and Denmark. Schoenfeld to Lansing, September 17, 1918, *ibid.*, 763.72111N83/35.

[71] It should be noted, however, that the mine barrage was never completely effective, and to the very end a few submarines apparently got through it. U-boat losses in the barrage itself have been estimated at between ten and twenty craft. But the existence of the barrier was shattering to the morale of U-boat crews, and is thought to have been an important factor in the great naval mutiny near the end of the war. Daniels, *Our Navy at War*, pp. 126-29.

The Chief of Naval Operations, Admiral William S. Benson, sent a memorandum to the State Department in which he pointed out that "the only recourse for the Allies" was to demand that Norway mine her own waters, and "if Norway will not do it, the Allies must do it for her." Lansing passed this extraordinary document on to Wilson, who promptly vetoed it with these words: "It is plain to both of us that we are taking the right course in Norway and cannot accept the suggestions of method made by the Navy Department in their very natural eagerness to see the northern barrage effective." [72]

In conformity with President Wilson's views, Lansing hastened to inform Schoenfeld that Washington was "not in sympathy with the course the British Government is taking," and that it was "important that they [the British] should understand that this Government does not wish to act in a way which can be construed as an infringement of the territorial sovereignty of Norway." [73] The position of Wilson seems to have had a restraining influence on the London officials, for when they learned that neither the United States nor France was in favor of drastic methods, they decided not to attach a definite time limit to the ultimatum they had previously presented.[74]

[72] Benson to State Department, August 9, 1918; Wilson to Lansing, August 22, 1918, State Dept., 763.72111N83/12, 65. One American journal took the view that the Norwegians had forfeited their neutral rights by permitting German U-boats to pass through their territorial waters; hence the Allies were justified in taking strong measures. *Scientific American,* CXVII, 110 (August 18, 1918). According to Articles IX and X of the 13th Hague Convention of 1907, a neutral could allow belligerent warships to pass through its waters, provided it showed no partiality. Malloy, *Treaties,* II, 2359-60.

[73] *For. Rel., 1918, Supp. 1,* II, pp. 1781-82.   [74] *Ibid.,* p. 1782.

Meanwhile Schoenfeld had continued to press his arguments with such tact and skill as later to merit the special approbation of the State Department. He particularly stressed the friendly sentiments of the United States toward the Norwegians, and the desire on the part of Washington to assist them in protecting their neutrality. By August 30, 1918, he was able to report that Norway had taken certain steps regarding shipping lights that would make navigation more difficult for German submarines.[75] Although the British minister in Christiania was unsympathetic with these velvet-glove tactics, and although Allied press discussions of Norway's recalcitrance threatened to disrupt the negotiations, the Norwegian government slowly came around, and on September 30, 1918, the Foreign Minister informed Schoenfeld that the gap would be closed to ordinary traffic on October 7, 1918.[76]

xiii

It is noteworthy that the barrage was laid to the edge of Norway's territorial waters about August 5, 1918, and that the gap was not finally closed until October 7—a period of two months. During this time German submarines were presumably slipping through Norwegian coastal areas to attack American and Allied troop and supply ships.

---

[75] *Ibid.*, pp. 1782-84, 1784-85.

[76] *Ibid.*, pp. 1788-89. The British and French press created an unfortunate impression in Norway by their discussions of the desirability of using strong measures. Schoenfeld felt that this would also put the Germans on their guard, and as a result of his advice Washington took appropriate action, through warnings to the press and through cable censorship, to keep the matter quiet. Schoenfeld to Lansing, August 27, 1918, September 5, 1918; and memorandum attached to Barclay to Lansing, September 7, 1918, State Dept., 763. 72111N83/21, 79, 31.

From the standpoint of pushing the war to a speedy and successful conclusion, it was doubtless a mistake to permit this delay. Indeed, the struggle was virtually over before the barrier was finally closed. If the Associated Powers had promptly mined the gap themselves, the submarines would have been more effectively muzzled, lives probably would have been saved, and German morale would have been dealt another body blow. Certainly Norway was in no position to resist forcible measures by the Allies; nor did Germany appear to be free to indulge in effective retaliatory action.

In short, grim military necessity dictated prompt and energetic measures; and it seems clear that those stern measures would have been taken by Great Britain if the United States had not opposed them. It is possible that Washington would have fallen in with British desires, or at least tacitly acquiesced in them, as it did in the blockade, had it not been for the idealism of Wilson, whose active intervention effectively banished all hope of employing such methods. This was perhaps the most conspicuous case where the United States, even at an appreciable cost to its war effort, insisted upon the maintenance of principle.

Whether America gained enough in neutral good will to compensate for her self-denial can never be determined. The naval officers in Washington, if asked, probably would have replied in the negative. The conciliatory methods pursued by the United States did, it is true, bring success—when the war was virtually over. Yet it is probable that the impending collapse of the Central Powers had a good deal more to do with Norway's concession than the tactics employed by Washington.[77] Significantly, Christiania an-

[77] Schoenfeld drew attention to the fact that Norway's action

nounced its decision as inconspicuously as possible, presumably in the hope of not giving undue offense to semi-prostrate Germany.[78] Nor can the United States be charged with having induced Norway to violate her neutrality by laying mines within her own territorial waters. Such action was an undeniable sovereign right, and it had already been exercised with perfect propriety by Sweden and Denmark. All things considered, it is clear that Washington, under the leadership of Wilson, resisted a strong temptation to use forcible measures—measures which would have been a serious attack on the rights of neutrals and which would have indelibly blackened the good name of the United States.

xiv

By way of analysis and summary it will be convenient to divide the subject matter of this chapter into two categories: first, arguable violations of neutral rights or international law, and second, action that was distinctly to the credit of the United States.

Turning to the first category, we find that although the United States did take a stand on contraband and continuous voyage similar to that of the British and hence objectionable to the neutrals, on the whole the position of Washington was not seriously at variance with its prebelligerent stand. In protesting against the use of safe-conducts, the United States took a somewhat illiberal view, but used nothing more effective than words. The planting of

---

came at the time of Allied victories and the news of Bulgaria's capitulation. Schoenfeld to Lansing, September 30, 1918, *ibid.*, 763. 72111N83/38.

[78] Schoenfeld to Lansing, September 29, 30, 1918, *ibid.*, 763. 72111N83/37, 38.

mines in the open sea, particularly the construction of the North Sea mine barrage, seems to have been a most serious offense against neutral rights. But even here there were extenuating circumstances; and it must be remarked that the United States had not protested against such a practice while neutral. It had merely entered a reservation of its rights.

On the other side of the ledger, there is much to commend. Washington declined to engage in British blockade practices and refused to consent to a reciprocal exchange of prizes. One may argue, however, that the position of the United States was weakened by its co-operation with, although not actual participation in, the British blockade. Washington also refused to depart from its traditional policy and remove enemy subjects from neutral ships on the high seas; it took a leading part in the partial elimination of the inconvenient call at Halifax; and it rejected all proposals for a mandatory routing of shipping by forcible methods, though milder types of coercion were employed. Most noteworthy of all, Wilson refused to close the North Sea mine barrage by a violation of Norway's territorial waters.

In general, this record reveals that Washington was reluctant to depart from the position it had taken during the neutrality period, and that the rights of weak neutrals were a major concern of President Wilson.

Chapter XIII

PROBLEMS OF INTERNATIONAL LAW AND NEUTRAL TREATY RIGHTS

i

Long before America declared war the British adopted the practice of removing mail from neutral ships on the high seas, or of forcing these vessels into port, where both first-class mail and parcel post could be subjected to a leisurely and thorough search. From the point of view of the Allies, there were at least two compelling reasons for such a policy. First, the submarine hazard was so great that it was foolhardy to attempt a satisfactory search of mail pouches on the high seas. Second, there could be no denying the fact that a very considerable amount of contraband, concealed in parcel post, was leaking into Germany through neutral hands.

Public opinion in the United States reacted violently against the British censorship and seizure of American mails. In the first place, the delays resulting from this practice were not only annoying but, in the case of certain business transactions, exceedingly costly. In the second place, the mail that was forcibly diverted from the high seas, where it was under the jurisdiction of international law, became subject to the much more stringent municipal statutes of Great Britain. And finally, the rigorous searching of American pouches appears to have resulted in the disclosure of trade secrets that would be welcome to British competitors. Public opinion in the United States concluded, on the basis of inference rather than positive proof, that these secrets were deliberately passed on to British firms by the postal censors, and this probably more than anything else was responsible for the anger of American businessmen.[1]

Early in 1916 Secretary Lansing filed a vigorous protest against mail censorship with the British Foreign Office, and followed it up with one to the French. His general position was first, that all first-class mail ("genuine correspondence"), whether neutral or belligerent, was inviolate on the high seas;[2] second, that the Allies had no right forcibly to divert neutral ships into port in order to search their pouches; and third, that all parcel post (as well as securities and negotiable instruments under seal) could be searched and seized for contraband, but such search and seizure could be legally done only on the high seas. (This, of course, was a damaging admission, for how could the British satisfy themselves that letters were not carrying money unless all "genuine correspondence" could be opened?) Lansing went even further—and this is of considerable importance from the point of view of the present study—in his position regarding mail on vessels that stopped in transit at a belligerent harbor:

In cases where neutral mail ships merely touch at British ports, the Department believes that British authorities have

---

[1] *For. Rel., 1914, Supp.*, pp. 531-43; *ibid., 1915*, pp. 731-43; *ibid., 1916*, pp. 591-630; *ibid., 1917, Supp. 1*, pp. 520-26. On the general subject of postal and cable censorship see Tansill, *America Goes to War*, pp. 548-58; Turlington, *Neutrality*, pp. 89-95; Savage, *Maritime Commerce*, II, especially pp. 529-32; Garner, *International Law and the World War*, II, 350-62; Lansing, *Memoirs*, pp. 125-27.

[2] This was in accordance with the Chapter I, Article I, of the Eleventh Hague Convention of 1907. Malloy, *Treaties,* II, 2347-48.

INTERNATIONAL LAW AND TREATIES 423

no international right to remove the sealed mails or to censor them on board ship. Mails on such ships never rightfully come into the custody of the British mail service, and that service is entirely without responsibility for their transit or safety.[3]

The same rule held, Lansing believed, whether the ship was brought into an Allied port through physical force or some other kind of pressure.

They [the Allies] compel neutral ships without just cause to enter their own ports or they induce shipping lines, through some form of duress, to send their mail ships via British ports, or they detain all vessels merely calling at British ports, thus acquiring by force or unjustifiable means an illegal jurisdiction. . . . For there is, in the opinion of the Government of the United States, no legal distinction between the seizure of mails at sea, which is announced as abandoned, and their seizure from vessels voluntarily or involuntarily in port.[4]

The British were never willing to accept the American point of view, and it must be confessed that they had strong arguments on their side.[5] Chapter I of the Eleventh Hague Convention of 1907, which related to the searching of mails, was technically inoperative, because several of the belligerents had not subscribed to it. And even if it had been binding no one could deny that conditions had been materially changed by the existing war. Parcel post had

[3] *For. Rel., 1916, Supp.*, p. 592.   [4] *Ibid.*, p. 605.
[5] The pro-British Lansing later wrote: "While the United States was bound to protest against this violation by Great Britain of the established international rule in regard to the opening and examining of sealed mail, I confess that it was done half-heartedly as a matter of form and with no intention to force the issue, because the British had strong reasons for their course of action." Lansing, *Memoirs*, p. 125.

experienced a tremendous and unforeseen expansion; the work of spies and saboteurs could be directed through "genuine correspondence"; and the introduction of the submarine had made extremely hazardous the traditional methods of examination. If, as Lansing admitted, it was permissible to search for contraband on the high seas, the British were certainly conforming to the spirit of that search when they carried it on in port, where conditions were safe and where the proper facilities existed.

ii

When America entered the war, Downing Street was naturally anxious that Washington should tighten the noose about Germany by adopting a strict mail censorship. Britain and France urged, in particular, that the United States establish postal control over the important and virtually virgin fields of Latin America and the Far East. The Allies were not primarily concerned about the Northern Neutrals, for British censorship took care of them, nor about Switzerland, for the French exercised satisfactory control in that quarter.[6] London even went so far as to offer the services of experienced men who would properly instruct American officials in the intricacies of mail censorship.[7]

As was true with most of the practices which the United States had earlier found objectionable, the Wilson administration was reluctant to take active steps in the direction of postal censorship. On May 3, 1917, Postmaster General Burleson wrote Wilson that in his judgment such censorship

[6] *For. Rel., 1917, Supp. 2*, II, p. 1231.
[7] *Ibid.*, I, 9; II, 1232; Page to Lansing, February 5, 1917, State Dept., 811. 711/23.

was not necessary. The Allies had complete control over all routes to Europe, except perhaps to Spain, as well as over the land and water communications (but not the wireless channels) from Spain to Germany. The only mail from the United States that was not subject to censorship by the Allies was that for Mexico and the other neutrals of Latin America. Burleson concluded that in general the institution of censorship would be "unnecessary" and "futile," primarily because it would merely be a duplication of work that was already being better performed. This, however, was not strictly true. As the Postmaster General himself admitted, there was no satisfactory censorship over mails from the United States to the Latin American neutrals.[8] Secretary Lansing disagreed with Burleson's general position and pointed out to President Wilson that much damage could be caused by leaving this channel to South America open. Adequate censorship would nip in the bud much German propaganda, intrigue, and espionage. It would also prevent the transference of money and military information, and hamper arrangements for the fitting out and succoring of raiders.[9] Wilson, however, was disposed to agree with Burleson's conclusions, "at any rate for the present." But he was careful to point out that "Circumstances which we do not know may come to light and existing circumstances may change."[10]

[8] Burleson to Wilson, May 3, 1917, Wilson Papers, Library of Congress.

[9] *Lansing Papers,* II, 11-12, 13-14.

[10] Baker, *Wilson,* VII, 47. Comment of Vance C. McCormick (November 4, 1941): "Referring to your chapter on mail and cable censorship, I have a very clear recollection of how distasteful to President Wilson was this whole matter of censorship and of how it was approved by him only because it was absolutely necessary to successfully carry on the war."

"Existing circumstances" did change; and on October 12, 1917, under authority conferred by the Trading with the Enemy Act, Wilson set up the Censorship Board as an administrative agency. Before the end of the war a total of nineteen censorship stations and substations were established at strategic points ranging from New York to Manila.[11] When the Armistice was signed, American businessmen and others brought strong pressure to bear on Washington to end this censorship, but primarily because of the value of such a weapon in maintaining the blockade, it was not until June 21, 1919, that the practice was discontinued.[12]

The United States was not unaware of its earlier representations to the Allies, and it carefully refrained from exercising postal censorship on the high seas. The official instructions issued to United States naval officers repeated practically verbatim most of the essential portions of the Eleventh

[11] The list is given in James R. Mock, *Censorship 1917* (Princeton, 1941), p. 62. See also *Annual Report of the Postmaster General, 1918* (Washington, 1919), p. 12. The Censorship Board consisted of representatives of the Postmaster General (who was chairman), of the Secretary of War, of the Secretary of the Navy, of the War Trade Board, and of the Chairman of the Committee on Public Information. For details of organization see Mock, *op. cit.*, pp. 55 ff.

[12] This was done by resolution of the Censorship Board on June 18, 1919. Polk (Acting) to American diplomatic and consular officers in many European countries, June 25, 1919, State Dept., 841.711/2684a. The reasons for continuing mail censorship are fully set forth in Fuller to McCormick, December 11, 1918, State Dept., War Trade Board (Censorship-General). President Wilson, then in Paris, agreed fully with McCormick that the censorship should be maintained. Auchincloss to Polk, December 19, 1918 (received), *ibid.* There was some little friction in the post-Armistice period over alleged British censorship of American mail in the interests of British business.

Hague Convention of 1907, and Section 87 of the same instructions clearly supported the prebelligerent position of the Washington government: "The genuine postal correspondence of neutrals or belligerents, found on board a neutral or enemy ship at sea, is inviolable. If the ship is detained, such postal correspondence is to be forwarded by the captor with the least possible delay." [13]

In addition to refraining from exercising postal censorship on the high seas, the United States did not extend such censorship to vessels passing through its ports destined for one or more of the Northern Neutrals. This was already being effectively done by the British, and American participation would only have complicated matters. Washington also declined to fall in with the suggestion of London that it resort to the extraordinary practice of searching diplomatic mail for enemy communications that were being sent by this medium.[14] The United States likewise refused to censor private mail addressed to chiefs of mission in the United States. Unfortunately, this concession brought a great deal of complaint, for through the ignorance or carelessness of subordinates many such letters were inadvertently opened.[15]

iii

On the other side of the ledger, the record on postal censorship is not so praiseworthy. The Washington govern-

[13] *Naval Instructions, 1917*, p. 33.

[14] *For. Rel., 1918, Supp. 1*, II, p. 1760.

[15] Numerous complaints of the diplomats in Washington accompanied by improperly opened envelopes may be found in State Dept., file 811. 711. In extending this courtesy the Department requested that the chiefs of mission turn over to it all irregular communications coming to them. Polk to Maddox, December 18, 1917, State Dept., 811. 711/154; *For. Rel., 1918, Supp. 1*, II, pp. 1755, 1757.

ment, despite its earlier protests against searching the pouches of neutral ships that casually touched at British ports, finally adopted the policy of examining all mail, whether " genuine correspondence " or parcel post, which, even in transit, reached its territorial waters on neutral ships. In general, this censorship was not applied to vessels destined for European routes that were controlled by the British and French; it was most rigorously applied to pouches passing to and from the United States and Latin American ports, and, wherever possible, between Latin American ports and Spain.[16] More than that, Washington used its control over bunker fuel to force neutral ships to change their routes so that they would put in at American harbors and consequently come within the jurisdiction of the Censorship Board.[17] This was done in spite of the earlier protest that ships forced into Allied ports under any " form of duress " could not properly be subjected to postal censorship. We should also note that the examination of

[16] *Ibid.,* pp. 1729, 1731. There was also a rigorous search of Asiatic mail.

[17] Maddox to Lansing, August 19, 1918, State Dept., 811.711/508; " Minutes of War Trade Board," III, 455 (August 22, 1918). The problem of how to censor mail being carried directly between Spain and the South American republics was a knotty one. On September 5, 1918, the Censorship Board passed a resolution to the effect that a censorship station be set up at the Azores; that United States, British, French, and Portuguese officials operate it jointly; and that the American bunkering authorities use their power so as to force neutral ships to stop at the Azores. The Censorship Board requested the Secretary of State to make the necessary diplomatic representations to London, Paris, and Lisbon. The present writer found no evidence that this was done. The War Trade Board, however, approved the scheme in principle. Maddox to McCormick, September 9, 1918; Maddox to Lansing, September 9, 1918; McCormick to Maddox, September 20, 1918, State Dept., War Trade Board (Postal Censorship).

INTERNATIONAL LAW AND TREATIES   429

mail on neutral vessels revealed much information that was of vital importance in administering the blacklist.[18]

The policy that the United States pursued toward two of its cobelligerents, Cuba and Panama, constitutes an interesting phase of this subject. Early in November, 1917, at the instance of American officials on the Isthmus, Panama readily agreed to institute a secret postal censorship under the supervision of the United States canal authorities. The government at Panama City appointed two Panamanians to co-operate in the work, although their salaries were to be paid by Washington.[19]

The United States was particularly anxious to have a postal censorship established in Cuba, inasmuch as an important Spanish line plied between Spain and Mexico by way of that island; and it was feared that these vessels brought information and money for propaganda, espionage, and other subversive activity among German agents in Mexico. The president of Cuba responded sympathetically to the overtures from Washington, and two American army officers were sent to Cuba to represent the Censorship Board.[20] On March 13, 1918, Acting Secretary Polk, not completely satisfied with the measures that had been undertaken, cabled the United States minister in Cuba:

> It is desired that when authority for censorship of Spanish mails under direct American control and supervision be granted it be so comprehensive as to permit at the same time a thorough search of the entire ship, passengers, officers, and crew in discretion of American official. This form of search has been carried out for nearly two years by British Government, all neutral vessels being so searched

---

[18] *Report of War Trade Board*, pp. 170, 172.
[19] Price to Lansing, November 7, 1917, State Dept., 811. 711/146.
[20] This story is told in *For. Rel., 1918, Supp.1*, II, pp. 1729 ff.

by them. *It is being done by the United States.* The great importance of having this work thoroughly and efficiently done under United States control and supervision can not be overestimated. Use your best efforts in arranging for immediate creation by Cuba of such a system.[21]

When the American minister presented this instruction in a somewhat more deferential form, he secured the ready acquiescence of the Cuban president. The Mexican government objected strongly to Cuban censorship of its mails; but this was a problem that directly concerned Mexico and Cuba, not Mexico and the United States.[22] The negotiations with Cuba are of value to us in showing that by March, 1918, Washington had not only adopted a rigorous form of postal censorship itself, but was using all of its influence to secure acceptance of similarly rigorous methods by its co-belligerents. It is also interesting to observe that in justifying the adoption of these practices the Department of State used arguments that were strikingly similar to those used by London when it was attempting to defend its position against the representations of Washington.[23]

It is clear, then, that the United States turned its back upon its early protests to Britain and France, particularly in the matter of examining the mail of ships that merely touched at American ports, and in using the bunker club to divert neutral merchantmen, primarily or secondarily for purposes of search. The British, on the other hand, used physical force to accomplish such diversion; and the bunker club, although more subtle, was hardly less effective.

---

[21] Italics inserted. *Ibid.*, p. 1732.

[22] The Cuban government sought the assistance of the United States in framing a reply to Mexico. *Ibid.*, pp. 1739-40.

[23] See *ibid.*, pp. 1739-40.

INTERNATIONAL LAW AND TREATIES 431

Nevertheless, as we have had occasion to observe earlier, a protest against a certain practice does not necessarily mean that this practice is a violation of international law; and it would be difficult to maintain that in its policy of postal censorship the Washington government was guilty of transgressing any well-established principle of the law of nations.[24] Perhaps we may most fairly conclude that the United States did not violate international law but that it did resort to practices that bore harshly upon neutral rights.

iv

Shortly after the outbreak of hostilities in 1914, London began to censor, detain, or suppress (in some cases without notifying the sender) a considerable number of messages to or from the United States going over British cable facilities. This disagreeable practice worked great hardship on a number of American business concerns, and again raised the presumption that censorship was being used to assist British competitors.[25] In response to pressure from various quarters, therefore, the Department of State, in 1914 and 1915, lodged repeated protests with Downing Street. The United States did not claim that British practices in the use of British cables were illegal; rather it pressed for an amelioration of the conditions attendant upon strict censorship and for a "more reasonable attitude." In short, the position of

---

[24] The present writer found no formal protest against the American practice of postal censorship, although the Spanish ambassador lodged a remonstrance with the Censorship Board against removing mail pouches from a Spanish steamer at New York which was en route to Vera Cruz. Phillips to Maddox, January 2, 1918, State Dept., 811.711/153.

[25] Lansing, *Memoirs,* p. 125.

the Department of State was based upon the inconvenience, delay, and loss that were caused innocent American concerns.[26] Any other position would have involved the United States in an embarrassing inconsistency, for on August 5, 1914, almost immediately after the outbreak of war, the Washington government established a strict censorship over its wireless facilities with the object of avoiding charges of unneutral conduct. A partial censorship was also applied to cable messages.[27]

In these circumstances, it is not surprising that the State Department based its case on international comity rather than on international law. There can be little doubt that the British officials were exercising an indisputable sovereign right in censoring messages passing over their territory and facilities, particularly those messages that contained information useful to the enemy.[28] In fact, Downing Street took the position that to permit the neutrals to use these cables at all was an act of " goodwill " or " grace." But the British recognized that their practice was offensive to America, whose favor they coveted; and when they had made certain concessions and had also become more skilled in exercising their censorship, very little legitimate American business suffered.[29]

---

[26] On this whole subject see *For. Rel., 1914, Supp.*, pp. 503-31; *ibid., 1915, Supp.*, pp. 697-731.

[27] Mock, *Censorship 1917*, pp. 73-74. The German government and affected firms protested vigorously against the American wireless censorship. From faraway Guam came strong objections to the restrictions that were placed on cablegrams.

[28] Garner, *International Law and the World War*, II, 413, n. For the British case see *For. Rel., 1915, Supp.*, pp. 707-08.

[29] In 1915 the British, in response to American representations that alternate lines could be used, abandoned censorship on their

INTERNATIONAL LAW AND TREATIES 433

This was the general situation when, on April 28, 1917, three weeks after America declared war, President Wilson issued an executive order authorizing censorship over cables, as well as over telegraph and telephone lines.[30] As finally established, cable censorship was exercised by the Navy Department through the office of Chief Cable Censor, and he in turn worked in close co-operation with the censorship agencies of Britain, France, Portugal, Brazil, and Cuba. Ultimately, representatives of the Chief Cable Censor were placed at every postal censorship station.[31] At first United States cable censorship was applied only to South and Central America, Mexico, and the Orient; while transatlantic cables were temporarily exempted in order that there might be time to work out satisfactory co-ordination with the British and French. But late in July, 1917, in addition to British censorship, the American authorities began to censor all messages passing over Atlantic cables to, from, or in transit through the United States. Although this involved some duplication of effort, the chief responsibility of Washington was in the Western Hemisphere, the Pacific, and the Far East, in all of which theatres Allied censorship had hitherto been relatively ineffective.[32]

On the whole, the United States reversed itself and did what it had protested to the British for doing. Special

---

cables passing between North and South America. After the United States became a belligerent this censorship was restored at the request of Washington. *Ibid., 1917, Supp. 2*, II, pp. 1233, 1234-35.

[30] *Ibid.*, pp. 1233-34.

[31] *Annual Report of the Secretary of the Navy, 1918* (Washington, 1918), pp. 23-24. See Mock, *Censorship 1917*, p. 80, for further details.

[32] *Official Bulletin*, July 18, 1917, p. 1; *For. Rel., 1917, Supp. 2*, II, p. 1241.

vigilance was exercised to see that cablegrams from neutral countries did not contain information that would be helpful to enemy spies, propagandists, and saboteurs; or that would strengthen firms which directly or indirectly were helping the enemy.[33] Naturally, such surveillance netted much data upon which to form the various blacklists. One interesting phase of this work is that the American authorities suppressed (apparently in some cases without notifying the sender) cablegrams to and from the neutrals, particularly those in South America.[34] In general, these involved the placing of orders which, if filled, would have run counter to the conservation program of the United States or to the statutes prohibiting trading with the enemy.[35]

---

[33] Conversely, American censors kept a careful eye on press dispatches going to neutral countries, lest information leak out that would bolster enemy morale or militate against a friendly spirit among the peoples of those countries. See Mock, *Censorship 1917*, pp. 82-83.

[34] Comment of Lester H. Woolsey (January, 1942): "Some of these messages were code messages in plain language of German saboteurs posing as travelling salesmen."

[35] Memorandum from F. Ayer, Jr., to Herbert Hoover, October 17, 1917, F. A. R., Hoover Library (War Trade Board Cable Censorship Memorandum). On August 18, 1917, Lansing suggested to Hoover that Somner Larsen (apparently a Swedish merchant) had laid himself open to suspicion as a result of a cablegram involving Argentine grain, and urged that "his cables be held up for the time being." "It has occurred to me," Lansing added, "that it might also be well to ask the Censor to interfere generally with messages such as these regarding speculation in food stuffs in this country as well as in South America." Hoover replied: "I am . . . strongly of the opinion that we should stop the transmission of cables regarding Argentine dealings as we do not want them cornering that market in advance against the other buyers. It all builds up the world's prices." Lansing to Hoover, August 18, 1917; Hoover to Lansing, August 18, 1917, *ibid.* (State Dept., Lansing.)

After the signing of the Armistice, agitation developed among businessmen, both in England and in America, for the lifting of cable censorship. But there was strong counterpressure to keep it in effect as a means of enforcing both the blockade arrangements and the Armistice terms; and it was not completely lifted until late in June, 1919, at about the same time that similar action was taken on postal censorship.

In brief, we may say that judicious cable censorship was not contrary to international law, and that America, though protesting against it as a neutral, based her position on comity rather than on legality. No fundamental violation of neutral rights was involved; yet it must be confessed that the operation of cable censorship was an unpleasant business which, while ferreting out much enemy activity, necessarily worked some hardship on unoffending neutrals.[36]

V

The practice of drafting aliens from neutral lands into the American army evoked many more protests from the neutrals than all of the other objectionable measures of the United States put together. This problem of alienage involved both treaty rights and international law, and the attempts that were made to solve it throw into clear relief the general policy pursued by the Wilson administration during these years.[37]

---

[36] The Swedish minister complained that official correspondence between the Swedish legation in Washington and that in Mexico City was being censored by the American authorities. Polk to Daniels, December 8, 1917, State Dept., 811.711/148.

[37] Materials for this subject were found in the *Lansing Papers*, II, 174-98; *Second Report of the Provost Marshal General to the*

The Selective Service Act of May 18, 1917, made provision for the drafting of all male persons in the United States between the ages of 21 and 30, except enemy aliens and all other aliens who had not declared their intention of becoming citizens. As regards the neutral countries, for example, if the individual in question was a declarant (i. e., one who had declared his intention of becoming a citizen and had taken out his first papers) he was eligible to be drafted; if he had not done so he was exempt. But the War Department took the position, which was the most practicable one, that the burden of proof was on the draftee to declare and establish that he was an alien. The result was that many persons from neutral countries who, under the law, were entitled to exemption, became conscripts in the American army. In some cases the alien selectee voluntarily and enthusiastically waived his rights so that he might join with his adopted countrymen in the great fight for democracy. Other alien nondeclarants volunteered when they were told that they would certainly be drafted. A few of these volunteers later changed their minds and caused considerable difficulty when they called upon their diplomatic representatives in Washington for assistance. But it is undeniable that in a great many other cases neutral aliens were inducted into the army against their will.[38] Some, because of language or other handicaps, were ignorant of their rights; others found it difficult to present documentary proof of their nationality; others were induced to enter the

---

Secretary of War on the Operations of the Selective Service System to December 20, 1918 (Washington, 1919), pp. 86-108; and file 811. 2222, State Dept., which consists of fourteen large manuscript volumes.

[38] See *Provost Marshal General's Report*, p. 96.

army through the persuasiveness of local draft boards (whose methods at times involved coercion); others encountered prejudiced boards who were determined to combat the current "slacker spirit";[39] and still others found that appeals to the district boards were too complicated, costly, and entangled with red tape. In any event, there were several hundred neutral aliens in the conscript army of the United States who did not want to be there and who, under the Selective Service Act, had every right to exemption.

But many of the neutrals thus caught in the draft net had other and better grounds for complaint. The United States had treaties with Argentina, Paraguay, Spain, and Switzerland specifically exempting the nationals of those countries from compulsory military service. Although the Selective Service Act included declarants, these treaties clearly exempted declarants, because the Supreme Court had held that a declarant was still a citizen or subject of his native land. Several other neutral countries had naturalization treaties with the United States which stipulated that declarants were not citizens, and thus, by inference though not by explicit exemption, immune from the draft. These nations were Peru, Salvador, Sweden, Norway, Uruguay, and, by one way of interpretation, Denmark.[40] Those

---

[39] Three Swedish declarants, who refused to sign enlistment cards and don uniforms on the grounds that they were aliens and conscientious objectors, were sentenced to imprisonment for twenty-five years. *Lansing Papers*, II, 187. In Illinois, seventy-six Swedes who refused en masse to register for the draft, were imprisoned for one year and steps were taken to deport them. But this was an organized attempt to violate the Selective Service Act and was on a different footing from the questions here considered. These cases and others appear in State Dept., 811. 2222.

[40] *Lansing Papers*, II, 185-86.

countries that had specific treaties protested against the forcible induction of their nationals on the grounds of treaty rights; the others based their position on international law and custom.[41] It is a striking fact that in the haste attendant upon passing war legislation it was not even pointed out in Congress that the portion of the Selective Service Act which claimed declarants ran directly counter to solemn treaty engagements with a number of the neutral countries.[42]

vi

Altogether, the neutral diplomats in Washington made protests to the Department of State against the drafting of 2,730 of their nationals.[43] So numerous were these cases and

---

[41] The Swedish minister in Washington pointed out that, according to Article 17 of the Fifth Hague Convention, a neutral could not avail himself of his neutrality if he committed hostile acts against a belligerent country. Hence, a belligerent country could not require a neutral person to take an active part in war, as that would entail loss of neutral character. Ekengren to Lansing, October 10, 1917, State Dept., 811. 2222/1019.

[42] *Cong. Record,* 65 Cong., 2 sess., pp. 4854-55.

[43] The list follows (including those that severed relations):

Argentina	5
Chile	2
Colombia	7
Denmark	241
Ecuador (severed)	4
Mexico	109
Netherlands	85
Norway	404
Persia	61
Peru (severed)	4
Santo Domingo (severed)	1
Spain	592

INTERNATIONAL LAW AND TREATIES   439

so difficult was it to dispose of them expeditiously that while representations were being made men were being inducted into the army, sent overseas, and even, in some instances, killed in action.[44] It is not to be wondered at that the neutral diplomats expressed great annoyance, resentment, and even bitterness.[45] The Spanish ambassador, Señor Juan Riaño, was particularly distressed over the policy of Washington, and went so far as to suggest reprisals if satisfactory

---

Sweden	216
Switzerland	995
Venezuela	4
	2730

Provost Marshal General's Report, p. 400.

[44] *Lansing Papers,* II, 196; Polk to Wilson, March 12, 1918, State Dept., 811.2222/5356; "Diary of Chandler P. Anderson," June 23, 1918. Men under protest were sent abroad, though this was not done in certain other cases where appeal was still being taken. This unfortunate situation was later rectified by the War Department. *Lansing Papers,* II, 195. Alien declarants who had been forced to register for the draft found their movements circumscribed.

[45] Lansing wrote to Wilson on August 27, 1917: "The lack of definite rule as to the drafting of aliens is causing me extreme embarrassment. I am daily besieged with the diplomatic representatives of countries with which we are at peace begging me to define our policy so that they can reply to the large number of letters of appeal which they are receiving. This has been going on for some time but as September 1st approaches the representatives are growing more and more insistent on a statement. In fact they begin to show considerable resentment at not being told what the authorities intend to do." *Ibid.,* II, 176. Comment of Lester H. Woolsey (January, 1942): "My recollection is: previous to this R. L. [ansing] had tried to get War Department to interpret the Act so as to exempt declarants. This as early as a few days after the passage of the Act, I believe. I doubt if the Department of State ever saw this provision until it was passed."

action was not taken.[46] This whole situation, of course, played into the hands of the German propagandists in the neutral European countries, who alleged that the United States was so short of man power that it was forced to resort to the inhuman practice of conscripting neutral aliens.[47]

The War Department found this whole business bothersome and entirely irrelevant to the main purpose of winning the war. The draft quotas for the various states had been based on the entire male population, alien and nonalien; and to exempt alien declarants after the quotas were established would work a great hardship on certain sections where there was a large foreign-born element. In some cases, for instance, the burden on the native population would be increased as much as fourfold.[48] The army needed all the able-bodied men it could get; it would be harmful to both discipline and organization to be discharging a steady stream of neutral aliens; and the task of investigating all these cases was, from the standpoint of the War Department, time consuming and otherwise annoying.[49] The army officials therefore resorted to the argument, which was legally unassailable from a domestic point of view, that a statute of Congress takes precedence over treaties, and that

[46] Polk to Wilson, March 12, 1918, State Dept., 811. 2222/5356.

[47] *Ibid.*; Lansing to Dent, February 14, 1918, *ibid.*, 811. 2222/6072b. Some little discontent was expressed in Sweden, Switzerland, and Norway over the alienage situation. *Neut. Press Supp.*, II, 414; III, 196, 248; IV, 200; *For. Rel., 1917, Supp. 2*, II, p. 1055; *Nachrichten der Auslandpresse*, August 29, 1918, p. 2; August 30, 1918, p. 4; September 7, 1918, p. 4.

[48] *Lansing Papers*, II, 175.

[49] Baker to Lansing, May 14, 1918, State Dept., 811. 2222/9902.

the draft should go on.[50] And after all, the War Department suggested, why should not the alien declarants from neutral countries serve with the colors. They came to America; enjoyed its liberties; made a livelihood there; thought enough of it to take out their first papers. Then, when the crisis came, they were clamoring for benefits without burdens.[51]

Secretary Lansing was prepared to admit that technically an act of Congress supersedes a treaty; but this did not relieve the United States of its responsibilities toward those neutral nations with which it had contractual obligations. And even in the case of the countries that did not have specific treaty safeguards, Lansing felt that they could " with some force " claim exemption on the basis of international custom. The position of the neutrals was strengthened, moreover, by the fact that America had never resorted to the conscription of aliens as she was then doing. Lansing therefore wrote the President that " the honor and good name of the United States " depended upon the discharge of these neutral draftees.[52]

Apparently the only way to afford reasonably prompt relief was for the President, by virtue of his authority as commander in chief of the army, to discharge exempted neutral declarants upon the presentation of satisfactory

[50] *Lansing Papers*, II, 179. The United States District Court, Southern District of California, specifically ruled, on October 6, 1917, that the draft law took precedence over treaty obligations. The case involved four Spanish declarants who were arrested off the coast of Mexico for attempting to evade the draft. 249 *Fed. Rep.* 981-82.

[51] *Provost Marshal General's Report*, p. 87.

[52] *Lansing Papers*, II, 191; also pp. 176, 182-83; Lansing to Dent, February 14, 1918, State Dept., 811. 2222/6072b.

evidence as to their status. On April 11, 1918, therefore, Wilson issued an order to the War Department, authorizing the prompt release of both declarants and nondeclarants from countries with which the United States had binding treaty obligations. Declarants of nontreaty countries were not to be affected by this order.[53]

vii

The makeshift device adopted by Wilson was still far from a satisfactory solution of the alienage problem. The mere fact of induction into the army, whether later accompanied by a discharge or not, constituted a violation of the treaties in question. In addition, the Selective Service Act was explicit on the subject of drafting all alien declarants, and for the President to discharge such persons amounted to a negation of one of the statutes which he had solemnly sworn to uphold. The War Department, moreover, was inundated with applications for release, largely as a result of the widespread newspaper publicity given to President Wilson's new order. But even when the men were discharged, as some were, they were subject to being drafted again; and a considerable number were so drafted.[54] While the Department of State was promising that neutral declarants exempted by treaty would be released, and while the men in question were actually being sent overseas to the fighting front, the neutral diplomats had the new grievances of broken promises and bad faith in addition to the old ones of violated treaty rights and international law.

The only practicable solution of this vexatious problem was to amend the Selective Service Act so as to exempt alien

[53] *Lansing Papers*, II, 188. [54] *Ibid.*, pp. 183, 186.

declarants. Secretary Lansing drafted an amendment for submission to the War Department; and, presumably to make it more palatable, he pointed out that it would affect only some 29,000 men, of whom from 30 to 50 per cent would be exempted from service. "In essence," he said, "the amendment gives up a claim to this amount of manpower in order to preserve our treaty obligations and to maintain a sound rule of international practice."[55] President Wilson, in a letter to the Chairman of the House Committee on Military Affairs, strongly supported the proposal in language that suggests his idealistic position at the time of the Panama Canal tolls repeal controversy:

> Whatever the general merits of the question, if we could consider ourselves absolutely free with regard to it, we are unfortunately not free but are bound by definite treaty obligations, which I should deem to take precedence of our temporary convenience, and I hope very much that it will seem best to the committee to report the amendment and the House to adopt it. It is a matter that touches our honor as a Nation, and I am sure will be dealt with as such.[56]

The House took favorable action on the amendment, on April 9, 1918, after it was pointed out that the United States must protect its good name;[57] but the Senate delayed until June 29. In its final form the amendment (which was written into the Army Appropriation Bill of July 9, 1918) provided that declarants of all neutral countries could be relieved of liability to military service by retracting their

[55] *Ibid.*, p. 184.

[56] *Cong. Record*, 65 Cong., 2 sess., p. 4854 (Wilson to Dent, March 8, 1918).

[57] *Ibid.*, p. 4859. Representative Kahn declared: "In this war it is exceedingly desirous that we clear our skirts, and that we do not put it into the mouths of the autocrats in Germany to say that we have violated our sacred treaty obligations." *Ibid.*, p. 4857.

declaration of intention, but everyone who did so "shall forever be debarred from becoming a citizen of the United States." This last proviso was proposed by Senator Lodge of Massachusetts, who felt that declarants ought to be willing to fight for the country they had made their home.[58]

By September 11, 1918, a total of 818 neutral declarants, or 3.16 per cent of the 25,918 who had been put into Class I, had taken advantage of this opportunity to escape compulsory military service.[59] A good many others declined to do so, and, availing themselves of the recently liberalized naturalization law, became citizens in wholesale ceremonies. There can be no doubt that a large number did this willingly and gladly; but there can also be no doubt that a considerable amount of pressure, both moral and physical, was exerted to restrain declarants from leaving the army.[60] Perhaps the most important instance of this kind to receive diplomatic attention was that of three Norwegians who

[58] *Ibid.*, p. 8485. The text of the amendment is in *U. S. Statutes at Large*, XL, pt. 1, p. 8851. Senator Jones of Washington went so far as to introduce a bill in the Senate providing for the expulsion of aliens who withdrew their declaration of intention in order to avoid military service. Acting Secretary of State Polk wrote to him urging the withdrawal of this measure in the interests of amicable relations with foreign countries. Polk to Jones, January 7, 1919, State Dept., 811. 2222/14579.

[59] The total of neutral declarants registering between June 5, 1917, and September 11, 1918, was 77,644. *Provost Marshal General's Report*, p. 102. In one camp alone 84 out of 200 declarants applied for release. *Ibid.*, p. 101.

[60] The Mexican ambassador protested against coercive measures. Bonillas to Lansing, June 11, 1918, State Dept., 811. 2222/11987½. On August 14, 1918, a general order was issued to the army forbidding the use of persuasive or coercive measures in such cases. Memorandum from War Department, *ibid.*, 811. 2222/14422. See also *Lansing Papers*, II, 192, 194.

were set upon and roughly handled by a mob in Ketchikan, Alaska, when they withdrew their declarations of intention. The case was finally dropped when the grand jury refused to indict, and when it was discovered that the three men were not so badly injured as had been feared.[61] There were other and less notorious incidents; in fact, considerable injustice was still being done to neutral declarants up to the signing of the Armistice.[62]

In leaving this subject of alienage we may note that the United States government, as Lansing himself privately conceded, violated its own treaty obligations and perhaps international law as well.[63] This situation, however, was the inadvertent result of hasty legislation, not of a deliberate purpose to flout solemn commitments. When the unfortunate cases growing out of drafting alien declarants were protested by the neutral diplomats in Washington, the Department of State moved as rapidly as possible to rectify the condition. The War Department, which was heavily involved in the task of creating a great army and which was

[61] State Dept., 811. 2222/14455, 14594. Other cases in this file relate to the rough handling of several Swedes and Norwegians. *Ibid.,* 811. 2222/13935, 13960, 14081.

[62] A law of the state of Washington provided that aliens who withdrew their declarations of intention in order to avoid military service had forfeited their homestead and fishing rights. *Ibid.,* 811. 2222/14667.

[63] The governments of those declarants and other aliens who were improperly drafted had grounds for bringing claims for damages against the United States. According to information provided by the Legal Adviser of the Department of State (January 3, 1942), such claims were not advanced, except by Mexico, which, pursuant to the convention of September 8, 1923, presented a few cases to the General Claims Commission on behalf of Mexican nondeclarants. In January, 1942, there had been no final determination of these cases.

less concerned about the national honor than the State Department, showed no enthusiasm for releasing the men in question; in fact, at times it revealed an unwillingness to co-operate at all.[64] Wilson sought and secured relief by Congressional amendment, characteristically placing his appeal to Congress on high moral as well as legal grounds. Basically, then, the situation was not the fault of the branch of the government that had to do with the conduct of foreign affairs. Wilson and the Department of State made every effort to correct an injustice, though in reality a great deal of injustice was done. But when we consider the immensity of the draft problem and the intensity of feeling against slackers, perhaps the surprising thing is that there were not more cases of duress and actual violence.[65]

viii

In the summer of 1917 the United States Shipping Board, under authority conferred by act of Congress and subsequently by executive order, requisitioned all ships (414 in number) over 2,500 dead-weight tons then being constructed in American yards. This included vessels being

[64] *Lansing Papers,* II, 197. Comment of Lester H. Woolsey (January, 1942): "Yes, at first. I worked for months to reconcile this difference." As an instance of inefficiency or non-co-operation, Ambassador Riaño told Chandler P. Anderson that several times he had sent his own secretary to Camp Meade to find a man who had been ordered released, after the commanding officer had reported that there was no such man in camp. "Diary of Chandler P. Anderson," May 3, 1918.

[65] In commenting on this part of the manuscript a former State Department official refers to the "hard-boiled attitude of the high draft officials," and adds that the situation was "Entirely the fault of the army. We [State Department] made constant protests."

built for both domestic and foreign registry, and it applied impartially to ships being constructed for cobelligerents and neutrals.[66] In this way the interests of certain Colombian, Argentinian, Swedish, and Norwegian concerns were affected, but the Norwegian shippers, who were the most heavily involved, were the only ones seriously to challenge the proposed American terms of indemnification.

At this time the United States had embarrassing treaties with Sweden (1783 and 1827) and Norway (1827), and under their terms these two nations could argue that Washington was estopped from requisitioning tonnage being built in American ports for Norwegian and Swedish subjects. In addition, these same treaties seemed to prohibit two other practices which the United States was finding essential to its war effort. First, forcing neutral shippers to sign bunkering agreements not to assist the enemy, even when the ships in question touched at American ports with an ample fuel supply for the entire voyage; and second, the commandeering of supplies held in the United States by Norwegian and Swedish subjects. Secretary Lansing regarded the Swedish and Norwegian treaties as archaic and entirely out of line with modern practices, and the Department of State seriously considered the desirability of abrogating them. But this would have taken a year, and in the meantime the United States was unwilling to refrain from what seemed to be the necessary war activity prohibited by these pacts. The problem of abrogation was so knotty that it appears to have been dropped altogether; and Washington

---

[66] The British, who had originally proposed requisitioning to the United States, were much irked when their ships were not given preferential treatment. See *For. Rel., 1917, Supp. 2*, I, pp. 12, 593 ff.; Hurley, *Bridge to France*, pp. 33 ff.

undertook to defend itself against the charges of treaty violations, although Solicitor Woolsey was of the opinion that in certain instances the Norwegian and Swedish governments would be upheld by fair tribunals.[67]

The United States contended that the requisitioning of the neutral ships was merely the exercise of an unquestioned belligerent right, and that such action violated neither international law nor existing treaties, provided proper indemnification was made. The chief question in dispute, therefore, was what constituted " just compensation." The cases involving fifteen Norwegian firms were finally lumped into one group, and Christiania made application for indemnity in the sum of $14,157,977.58.[68] The United States claimed that this figure was based on inflated wartime prices, and asserted that the correct estimate should be $2,679,220. The difference being irreconcilable, a special agreement was signed by the two governments on June 30, 1921, under the terms of which the dispute was submitted to the Permanent

[67] Lansing to Wilson, December 8, 1917, enclosing Woolsey memorandum of December 7, 1917, Wilson Papers, Library of Congress.

[68] Another case growing out of these seizures of Norwegian shipping involved the claims of one Christoffer Hannevig. After all other attempts at settlement had failed, a convention was signed on March 28, 1940, providing for an exchange of pleadings and evidence by the two governments, and then, failing a settlement, submission of the pleadings to the United States Court of Claims for adjudication. Following the German invasion of Norway, the Senate voted to return the convention to the State Department, on September 26, 1940. *Department of State Bulletin,* II, 351 (March 30, 1940); IV, 80 (January 11, 1941). See also Willard Bunce Cowles, " The Hannevig Case," *Amer. Jour. of Int. Law,* XXXII (1938), 142-148. This writer concludes that the exchange of briefs by the two governments constituted a new diplomatic method in the settlement of international disputes.

Court of Arbitration at The Hague. The case, which was one of the most important yet to come before that body, attracted widespread attention; and on October 13, 1922, the Court awarded $12,239,852.47 (including interest at six per cent) to the Norwegian shippers, or $1,918,125.11 less than they had sought, though $9,560,632.47 more than Washington had been willing to pay.[69]

The American member of the Court, Chandler P. Anderson, refused to be present at the award, and created a sensation when he resorted to the unusual step of filing a protest on the grounds that the tribunal had not followed the specific terms of the special agreement.[70] Despite rumors to the contrary, the United States promptly paid the sum assessed, as evidence of its adherence to the principle of arbitration.[71] But Secretary of State Hughes also filed a vigorous dissent on two grounds. First, the tribunal had not abided by the conditions of the special agreement under which it was operating, for, among other things, it had not

[69] The amount of the award is given as $11,995,000 in *For. Rel., 1923*, II, 617. For the text of the special agreement see supplement of *Amer. Jour. of Int. Law*, XVI (1922), 16-19; for texts of the award and the American protests, see *ibid.*, XVII (1923), 362-98. The correspondence leading up to the special agreement, as well as the text of the latter, appears in *For. Rel., 1921*, II, 571-99. For Norwegian assurances not to bring up in any way the question of treaty violation, see p. 594. The Norwegian counter case alleged that the purposes of the United States would have been fully served if (as in the case of the Dutch) only temporary possession had been taken of the vessels. *Norway-United States Arbitration Agreement of June 30, 1921: the Counter Case of the Kingdom of Norway against the United States of America* (n. p., 1922), p. 51.

[70] The protest was delivered by the American agent. *New York Times*, October 14, 1922.

[71] *Ibid.*, February 27, 1923.

given the reason for arriving at the final figures. Second, Hughes insisted that when belligerent states exercise the right to requisition they are under no obligation to favor neutrals above their own nationals, provided " just compensation " is made.[72] In brief, the Washington government, while discharging its solemnly contracted obligations, served notice on Norway in particular, and on the rest of the world in general, that it would not accept this decision as a precedent.

It would appear that the United States, in requisitioning ships being built for neutral flags, was not violating international law, but was merely exercising a well-recognized belligerent right. The treaty of 1827 with Norway was another matter; but, at the specific request of the State Department, Christiania agreed to exclude treaty considerations, and the issue finally became one of compensation. Although the Norwegian shippers on the whole were favored by the subsequent judgment, and although the United States protested against the award, Washington deserves some credit for its willingness to submit the issue to arbitration and abide by the somewhat unpalatable decision.[73]

[72] The text of Secretary Hughes' note of protest appears in *For. Rel., 1923*, II, 626-28. In a much more revealing letter to President Harding, Hughes pointed out that, despite the agreement with Norway to the contrary, the question of treaty violation had been brought up, though the Court had affirmed that this had not entered into its considerations. Hughes also noted that it would be well to pay the award, because failure to do so would not only place the United States in an unfortunate position but would reopen the embarrassing matter of treaty violation. *Ibid.*, pp. 617-25.

[73] A not dissimilar case involved the seizure by the United

ix

The detention of certain ships in American ports resulted in an interesting case involving the treaties of 1783 and 1827 with Sweden. In June, 1917, the Swedish motorship *Kronprins Gustaf Adolf* entered New York harbor, and during the following month the Swedish motorship *Pacific* put in at Newport News, Virginia. Both of these vessels brought considerable quantities of oil with them; and when they prepared to depart they were detained for a period of several months by having to secure export licenses for this fuel, even though it was not of American origin.[74] The Swedish minister in Washington made repeated representations to the Department of State on the grounds that these detentions were in violation of the Swedish-American treaties of 1783 and 1827. Secretary Lansing denied this contention and pointed out that by those treaties Sweden was not excused from complying with the general commercial regulations of the United States. When the ships were

---

States, in November, 1917, of certain munitions purchased by the Netherlands government. The Dutch claimed that they had not been paid enough; and on March 18, 1938, a convention was signed between the two governments providing for the submission of the issue to an arbitrator. The outbreak of war in 1939 suspended action on the case. See *Arbitration of a Difference Relating to Payment for Certain Military Supplies: Convention between the United States of America and the Netherlands,* Treaty Series, No. 935 (Washington, 1938). The Norwegian minister protested against the commandeering of a quantity of cotton duck which was needed by the Norwegian army, but the case appears not to have been pushed. Bryn to Lansing, June 21, 1918, State Dept., 657. 119/557.

[74] For regulations see War Trade Board, *Daily Record,* October 12, 1917.

eventually permitted to sail, the owners claimed that they had suffered damages in the sum of $3,000,000.[75]

The affair had an interesting and revealing postwar sequel. Responding to the importunities of Stockholm, the United States signed a special agreement in 1930 (ratified in 1931), under the terms of which the dispute was to be referred to a special arbitrator. He was to decide specifically whether the detentions had been in express violation of the treaties involved, and he was not to concern himself at all with general questions of international law. The man chosen was Eugène Borel, Honorary Professor of International Law at the University of Geneva, and, on July 18, 1932, he found in favor of the United States, largely because the owners had failed to make formal application for clearance papers and otherwise comply with official regulations. The argument of the shippers, which the arbitrator held to be unsound, was that they were sure of being denied such applications. Borel also declared that the American officials were unjustified in requiring a license for the cargo and fuel of the *Pacific*, and that they were also unjustified in refusing to grant a license; yet he concluded that it did not necessarily follow that the action of Washington was in violation of the two treaties in question.[76]

This case was perhaps the most important one in twenty-five years to be submitted to a sole arbitrator.[77] The wil-

---

[75] *For. Rel., 1918, Supp. 1*, II, pp. 1224-25, 1278-79; Polk (Acting Secretary) to Ekengren, January 24, 1918, State Dept., 658. 119/108.

[76] The texts of the special agreement and the decision may be found in the *Amer. Jour. of Int. Law*, XXVI (1932), 834-903. See also the accompanying commentary, Anna A. O'Neill, "United States-Sweden Arbitration," *ibid.*, pp. 720-34.

[77] *Ibid.*, p. 734.

lingness of Washington to settle this matter in a friendly and amicable fashion reveals a spirit of fair dealing that was commendable. But the final decision does not mean that the United States was totally without censure. Solicitor Woolsey believed that the treaties had been violated;[78] and it is clear that Washington won the case in part because the Swedish shippers had failed to comply with certain technicalities. On the question of fair play and international law there was much to be said against the United States; but on the question of a violation of the two treaties, the only question submitted to this arbitrator, the American position was sustained.

X

In another interesting case of a not dissimilar nature the United States fared less well. In October, 1917, the Dutch steamer *Zeelandia* put into New York harbor en route to the Netherlands with a cargo that had been taken on in Latin America. Although she had ample bunkers and ships' stores for the homeward trip, and although she desired to add no cargo in the United States, the War Trade Board denied her clearance papers. It later developed that she was detained primarily for the purpose of securing her services for the Associated Powers, and secondarily for the purpose of keeping her cargo from reaching the Netherlands. After having lain idle from October 22, 1917, to March 21, 1918, with mounting costs to her owners, she

---

[78] At the bottom of the note from Polk to Ekengren, January 24, 1918, Woolsey penned this comment: "Prepared by direction of the Secretary with approval of the President, but in my own view the case presents an infringement of the treaty." State Dept., 658. 119/108.

was finally seized in the general requisitioning of Dutch shipping that was authorized on March 21, 1918. The vessel was then put into the service of the Associated Powers, at adequate rates of compensation; but the owners naturally sought indemnification for the losses incurred by the involuntary five-month delay.

Under a special jurisdictional act of Congress approved on March 3, 1927, the *Zeelandia* case was referred to the United States Court of Claims, which handed down its decision on December 7, 1931. The tribunal found that the vessel had been detained contrary to the laws of the United States and the law of nations, and awarded the plaintiff damages in the sum of $446,826.22, with interest at five per cent from March 20, 1918, to December 7, 1931.[79]

The *Zeelandia* must not be confused with the other eighty-six ships requisitioned by the United States in March, 1918. To be sure, she was seized, and her seizure resulted from what the Court held to be an unjustifiable detention. In this case, at least, it is clear that the anger of the Dutch was well-founded. But the other ships that were requisitioned were loaded for the most part with cargoes of grain and feedstuffs produced in the United States for which export licenses had been denied; and this was quite another matter.

The *Zeelandia* case is of special interest to us because the claim of the plaintiff was based primarily on international law. This, in fact, was the only instance found in the present study where a competent tribunal held that the

[79] The decision is conveniently printed in the *Amer. Jour. of Int. Law*, XXVI (1932), 399-419. See also *For. Rel., 1918, Supp. 1*, II, pp. 1382, 1383, 1388, 1389, 1390, 1393, 1437, 1446.

Another issue of considerable importance had to do with the Panama Canal, which, under treaties with Great Britain (1901) and Panama (1903), the United States was bound to neutralize in time of war.[80] When the question arose of coaling British warships under certain circumstances, and of granting facilities to Australian troops passing through the Canal, the United States, if anything, interpreted its obligations to the advantage of its Associates. But when the British asked to use the dry dock and repair facilities at Balboa for their Pacific squadron, and also requested that these ships be supplied with coal, oil, and stores, Washington flatly refused, for Balboa was within the Canal Zone. As the Department of State declared in a memorandum to the British Embassy, such a concession would be "an infringement of the peculiar status of the Canal which the United States is under obligation to maintain."[81]

In other ways the Washington government sought to honor its treaty obligations. Early in the war it ruled that ships merely passing through the Canal, and not taking on

[80] For the relevant published documents see *ibid., 1917, Supp. 2,* II, pp. 1265-82.

[81] *Ibid.*, p. 1271. In January, 1919, while the United States was still technically at war, the Washington government ruled that men on transient British warships might be given shore leave in the Canal Zone, but not troops on transports. Norman J. Padelford, "Neutrality, Belligerency, and the Panama Canal," *Amer. Jour. of Int. Law*, XXXV (1941), 71.

provisions and bunkers, would not be required to secure export licenses for their cargoes.[82] This, it will be remembered, was not the same practice that was followed in the ports of the United States. After the general requisitioning of the Dutch ships, in March, 1918, it was discovered that two had been seized in the Canal Zone, and these were promptly released.[83] When the proposal came before the Department of State for rerouting Spanish ships so that they would have to pass through the Canal and thus become subject to American jurisdiction, this scheme was strongly objected to on the grounds that it would involve the neutralization treaties.[84]

We may conclude that the United States displayed an unusual degree of sensitiveness in attempting to discharge its treaty obligations regarding the Canal. In several instances, notably in the case of denying facilities to the British fleet, it made rulings that were adverse to its own interests. To be sure, the British were able to secure what they wanted less conveniently elsewhere; and this refusal had no bearing on the outcome of the war. Whether the United States would have done the same thing if there had been more at stake we cannot say. But this is the record; and, on the whole, it is distinctly to the credit of the Washington government.[85]

[82] "Minutes of Exports Council," pp. 13-14 (July 9, 1917); *For. Rel., 1917, Supp. 2*, II, p. 1282.

[83] *Ibid., 1918, Supp. 1*, II, p. 1433.

[84] *Ibid.*, p. 1011. There is some interesting correspondence on the status of the Panama Canal during the World War in Green H. Hackworth, *Digest of International Law* (Washington, 1941), II, 785-90.

[85] Professor Padelford points out that in 1917 Congress amended a statute so as to permit Allied subjects to enlist in the Canal

xii

Another interesting problem relating to neutral rights came to the fore in the summer of 1918. On April 7, 1917, the day after the war was declared, Acting Secretary of the Navy Franklin D. Roosevelt requested the Treasury Department to issue certain orders to the Division of Customs, the most significant passage of which read:

> That all incoming merchant vessels of whatever nationality be boarded and information requested concerning vessels of war which have been sighted, their nationality, approximate position, probable course, and other circumstances in regard to the vessels, and that the same information be obtained for vessels sighted which may be suspected of carrying supplies for Germany or for German vessels of war.

Put bluntly, this meant that neutral captains were to give information that would enable the United States to hunt down and destroy German submarines and other craft.

The remainder of the proposed order made provision for inducing the masters of all *outbound* merchantmen to send similar information to Washington as expeditiously as possible. In this connection, the utmost discretion and secrecy were to be used, and "only such ships officers approached as it is thought likely would be inclined to give such information." Further provision was made for remunerating those who proved co-operative, the extent of the remuneration to depend on the accuracy and value of

---

Zone, in probable contravention of the Hay-Pauncefote Treaty. But since the treaty was binding only upon the United States and Great Britain (the latter obviously would not raise objections), this matter is not relevant to our study of the neutrals. *Loc. cit.*, p. 76.

their observations. If the officer in question happened to be a neutral, "he should be assured that every precaution will be taken to safeguard his identity and activities." [86]

This striking order was adopted by the Treasury Department and sent to the various customs officials on April 10, 1917. On April 26, these instructions were significantly amended, at the request of the Secretary of the Navy. The provisions regarding the securing of information from *incoming* vessels remained as before, but those regarding *outgoing* vessels were thereafter to apply only to American ships. It may be presumed that the Navy Department, after more mature consideration, foresaw that this part of the program would involve it in serious difficulties with the neutrals.[87]

So far as the records examined for this study reveal, the soliciting of information from neutral captains did not become a diplomatic issue until a year later. On June 5, 1918, the Danish minister filed a note with the Department of State in which he indicated that shipmasters considered it "inconsistent with their duties as neutrals" to furnish information regarding German craft. The minister added that, as then advised, he was disposed to agree with this view.[88] The documents do not show that the matter was pushed further.

It doubtless was inconsistent with the spirit of true neutrality for Danish captains to give information that would help one belligerent to the disadvantage of the other. But it does not appear that the United States violated any

[86] Roosevelt to McAdoo, April 7, 1917, State Dept., 763. 72111/7071.
[87] McAdoo to Collectors of Customs, April 10, 26, 1917, *ibid*.
[88] Lansing to McAdoo, June 12, 1918, *ibid*., 763. 72111/7063.

INTERNATIONAL LAW AND TREATIES

well-established principle of international law in attempting to secure such information. The order read that foreign captains were merely to be "requested" to report certain observations; and there is no evidence that compulsion was used. If the officer in question did not wish to violate his neutrality, and if he did not wish to run the risk of offending American authorities and be denied bunker and other privileges, he could forswear himself like a gentleman and say that he had seen nothing on the trip across. In most cases such would doubtless have been the truth. But, at worst, this was a minor grievance against which only one of the neutrals appears to have complained, and that complaint was made without undue bitterness.[89]

xiii

The present study is not concerned to a primary degree with American propaganda in neutral countries. In the first place, this is a subject of such large proportions that it cannot be developed at length within the space available. In the second place, and more important, propaganda work in general did not provoke an open clash with treaty rights or international law.[90] This type of activity has come to be

[89] Comment of Lester H. Woolsey (January, 1942): "I never gave weight to her [Denmark's] argument that a private Danish subject in the U. S. could by such acts attaint the neutrality of the Danish government."

[90] As will be pointed out, the United States used the territory of the border neutrals to send propaganda into Germany for the purpose of weakening enemy morale. The principle is clearly established that neutral territory should not be employed by a belligerent as a base for military operations, such as dispatching radio messages to submarines operating at sea; but the present writer has found no evidence that this principle has been generally

a general and well-recognized weapon of warfare; both sets of belligerents employed it within the borders of the neutral countries. Far from being objectionable, the kind of propaganda that the United States disseminated was often welcomed; and in the case of literature and films there were instances of the people in the neutral countries actually clamoring for more. But some consideration of the general problem is necessary for a well-rounded discussion of America's policy toward the neutrals.[91]

As far as the United States was involved, there were two principal types of propaganda. The first was the campaign conducted from neutral soil, especially from Switzerland, Holland, and Denmark, for the purpose of breaking down the enemy's morale.[92] This, in a sense, was an invasion of the sovereign jurisdiction of the neutral concerned; but both

---

accepted as applying to propaganda work. With reference to propaganda within the neutral country itself for good will and other purposes, the neutral involved is at perfect liberty to restrict the activities of foreign agents, should it so desire, by municipal legislation. In 1915, for example, Denmark provided appropriate punishment for any one who "publicly in writing or orally endeavors to incite the population against a belligerent nation." Naval War College, *International Law Documents, 1917*, p. 84. On this general subject see Vernon Van Dyke, "Responsibility of States for International Propaganda," *Amer. Jour. of Int. Law*, XXXIV (1940), 58-73. The present writer is also personally indebted to Professor Van Dyke for additional information on this point.

[91] For the general story see George Creel, *How We Advertised America* (New York, 1920); James R. Mock and Cedric Larson, *Words that Won the War* (Princeton, 1939); *Report of Committee on Public Information*.

[92] See George G. Bruntz, *Allied Propaganda and the Collapse of the German Empire in 1918* (Stanford University, 1938), pp. 30 ff.

sets of belligerents resorted to such measures, apparently without serious protest from the neutral governments, including Washington when neutral. At worst, this practice seems to have been extralegal rather than illegal. The second type consisted of a propaganda campaign within the neutral countries themselves for the purpose of combating pro-German propaganda, winning public sentiment to the Allied cause, and correcting German-sponsored misconceptions regarding the United States. With this second type we are more particularly concerned.

The propaganda campaign in foreign lands was directed by George Creel's Committee on Public Information, the chief instruments of which were lectures, pictures, posters, books, pamphlets, newspaper information, and the cinema. The newspaper service sponsored by the Committee was quite popular, especially in the Northern Neutrals, Switzerland, and Mexico; and it proved very effective in counteracting German misrepresentations regarding the resources and war effort of the United States.[93] The cinema was also well-received, particularly in those countries, like Mexico, where there was a relatively high amount of illiteracy.

In pursuance of its objectives, the Committee on Public Information secured the effective co-operation of the Department of State, the War Trade Board, and other agencies in Washington. In Spain, the American minister subscribed

---

[93] A group of twenty Mexican journalists was taken on a tour of the United States. Mock and Larson, *op. cit.*, p. 330; *Report of Committee on Public Information*, p. 164. Six Swiss newspaper men made a similar tour. Bruntz, *op. cit.*, pp. 63-64. The representative of the Committee on Public Information in Denmark also arranged to have twelve Scandinavian journalists visit the United States. *Report of Committee on Public Information*, p. 209.

to a certain pro-Ally newspaper for all of the consulates in that country, because he felt that this journal, which needed support, would be helpful to the United States.[94] The Department of State also brought effective pressure on American concerns to dissuade them from placing advertising in offensively pro-German Spanish newspapers.[95] The War Trade Board adopted the policy of licensing paper and printer's ink only to those newspapers in neutral countries that were definitely pro-Ally.[96] Various restrictions were placed on the export of motion-picture film, and in particular the Board required the consignees to sign an agreement not to exhibit it in any theater where the enemy product was shown or where any kind of performance was given of a nature detrimental to the United States. This practice was very effective in driving out German competition.[97] Some of these methods raise again the question of pressure on the neutrals through export embargoes; but we must conclude, as before, that the ink, paper, and film

[94] Willard to Lansing, December 27, 1917, State Dept., 652. 119/473.

[95] See particularly *ibid.*, 763. 72112/5425.

[96] *For. Rel., 1918, Supp. 1,* p. 986; "Minutes of War Trade Board," I, 481 (March 11, 1918); II, 153-54 (April 12, 1918); Carr to Oliphant, December 5, 1917, State Dept., 600. 119/466. On occasion, the War Trade Board permitted the licensing of commodities to pro-Ally and not to pro-German firms in neutral countries. Lansing to Stockholm Legation, May 29, 1918, State Dept., 658. 119/360.

[97] *Report of War Trade Board,* p. 51; Creel, *op. cit.,* p. 276. As finally arranged, every consignment of United States film shipped abroad had to contain twenty per cent propaganda pictures, and foreign exhibitors had to arrange their programs so that twenty per cent of the films shown would consist of such propaganda. Will H. Irwin, *Propaganda and the News* (New York, 1936), p. 197.

belonged to the United States, and that the importers could either agree to American terms or go without.

American propaganda work in the neutral countries encountered many difficulties, among which we may note a lack of adequate funds, working at cross-purposes with the Allies, poor co-operation among inexperienced people, opposition by officials in the State Department to some of the agents in the field,[98] and particularly the head start that the Germans had over Allied propaganda in every, or practically every, neutral country in Europe.[99] But it must be strongly emphasized that the work of the United States was generally conducted on a high plane. An agent of the Committee on Public Information who was about to sail for Spain received a letter from President Wilson

---

[98] An outstanding case of working at cross-purposes was that of Mrs. Norman de R. Whitehouse, a prominent American women's suffrage leader, who was chosen by Creel, without consulting the Department of State, to go to Switzerland and conduct an educational campaign. When the press heralded her propaganda mission, the Swiss expressed resentment; and Creel then published a statement saying that Mrs. Whitehouse was going to inquire into the condition of women and children in Europe. This had a good effect on the Swiss, temporarily; but Mrs. Whitehouse openly repudiated any such denial. The American Legation in Berne showed strong hostility to her, yet she appears to have done much good work in spite of this opposition. Creel was indignant over her treatment by the professional diplomats, and President Wilson was inclined to agree with him. Phillips to Lansing, January 4, 1918; Creel to Wilson, March 26, 1918; Stovall to Wilson, March 27, 1918; Wilson to Creel, March 27, 1918, Wilson Papers, Library of Congress. See also Creel, *op. cit.*, pp. 317 ff., which pays a high tribute to Mrs. Whitehouse's work; and Mrs. Whitehouse's own story, *Year as Government Agent*.

[99] Seymour, *House Papers*, III, 141; Morris, *American Legation*, pp. 129 ff. Morris wrote that there were 800 German propagandists in Sweden by 1918 whose names were known to American agents.

warning him to refrain from intrigue and to carry on an honest campaign of education in a frank and open way.[100] Will Irwin, Chief of the Foreign Department of the Committee on Public Information, cabled a representative in Sweden: "Will allow you $20,000 for your work *with usual understanding* that none of it shall be spent for bribing officials, secretly influencing the press, buying space in newspapers, or for any other method which would not bear exposure." [101]

There can be no doubt that the American campaign of education was strikingly successful, particularly when combined with generous treatment (as in the case of the Swiss grain shipments) and the swelling tide of victory. Wilson's

---

[100] Mock and Larson, *Words that Won the War*, p. 264. The agent in question later wrote that he carried out these instructions literally. Irwin points out that the Wilsonian injunction against using corrupt methods helped strengthen the impression that the United States was a crusading nation. Irwin, *Propaganda and the News*, p. 194.

[101] Italics inserted. Mock and Larson, *op. cit.*, p. 280; also p. 329. Yet Mrs. Whitehouse wrote of spending money for "necessary but illegal work. . . ." *Ibid.*, p. 278. Dr. James R. Mock, of the National Archives, writes that the records of the Committee on Public Information show that a newspaper was subsidized in Switzerland. Letter to writer, January 27, 1942. For evidence as to the honest nature of the American campaign see Creel, *op. cit.*, pp. 242-43. Also George Creel, "The Truth Shall Make You Free," *Collier's*, November 1, 1941, pp. 17, 27-29, in which Wilson's personal injunctions are set forth at length. On May 23, 1918, Wilson wrote Mrs. Whitehouse: "I am glad to learn that your own convictions and investigations lead you to endorse the unreservedly American policy of absolute openness. We have nothing to conceal, no secret ambitions to further, and our activities in every foreign country are properly confined to a very frank exposition of America's war aims and national ideals." See also Wilson's letter to the commissioner for Spain. *Report of Committee on Public Information*, p. 195.

stirring speeches outlining America's war aims—perhaps the most potent weapon of all—did much to undermine pro-German sentiment and activity. Moving pictures were extremely effective in combating German allegations that the resources of the United States were negligible and that a great expeditionary force was not coming to insure victory. In fact, the task that had to be done in the neutral countries fitted in remarkably well with Wilson's insistence upon a genuine and honest campaign of education rather than propaganda. So Herculean were the American war efforts that to tell the truth was almost to tell a lie. The United States could ask for nothing better than to have the neutrals, to say nothing of the enemy, know what it was doing.[102] Possibly the Committee on Public Information would have lied if it had had to; but, unlike the Germans, it did not have to. (Mr. Creel disagrees with this judgment.)[103] The best propaganda was the truth.

[102] Creel, *How We Advertised America*, pp. 242-43, 258-59, 304, 306. Mrs. Whitehouse was so confident of the power of truth that in Switzerland she employed suspected German spies and hoped that they would send on information to Germany. Whitehouse, *Year as Government Agent*, pp. 119-23. For further evidence of candor see *Report of Committee on Public Information*, pp. 153, 183, 202, 204, 209.

[103] Comment of George Creel (November 25, 1941): "You are mistaken in saying that the Committee would have lied if it had had to. Not only did I myself hold that lies were always found out, smearing the whole campaign, but W. W. [ilson] himself kept a vigilant Presbyterian eye on all of our activities." Will Irwin recalls that there was "no need of lying—except for lies of suppression in spots. It was the sober truth. And truth is more easily maintained than untruth." Irwin, *Propaganda and the News*, p. 103. One interesting instance of suppression was the attempt to conceal the American shipbuilding program from the Danish press, lest the Danes become unduly concerned about postwar mercantile competition. Mock, *Censorship 1917*, pp. 82-83.

xiv

In the matters discussed in this chapter it would seem as though the United States did not appear to such good advantage as it did in connection with the problems relating to freedom of the seas.

As regards cable censorship, the Department of State clearly reversed the position it had taken as a neutral, although it must be emphasized that the early protests of the United States to London had been based on international comity rather than international law. In the matter of mail censorship, Washington also reversed itself, although not in all particulars, and its practice in general was less objectionable to the neutrals than that of Britain. Yet even here the American position could be defended with some plausibility on the grounds of international law. With reference to alienage, the United States unquestionably did much injustice to neutral aliens, and, from the international point of view, actually violated treaty guarantees. The best that can be said in regard to this controversy is that the Administration moved as rapidly as it could to correct inequities, but even this was far from satisfactory.

Where courts or arbitral tribunals actually rendered decisions we are treading on firmer ground. The United States was found to have violated international law in detaining the Dutch steamer *Zeelandia*. In the case of the Norwegian vessels that were requisitioned while under construction, the issue was not one of law but of just compensation; and here Washington had to pay more than it had been willing to. It is possible that the seizure was also a violation of the treaty of 1827; but this issue never came

INTERNATIONAL LAW AND TREATIES 467

up for adjudication. In the case of the two detained Swedish motorships, the court found that technically the United States had not violated the existing treaties. If the issue of international law had been involved, as it was not, the decision might possibly have been otherwise.

The Washington government was to some extent censurable in seeking unneutral information from neutral masters regarding submarines, although this attempt seems not to have been contrary to any specific rule of international law. On the other hand, the scrupulous regard of the United States for its obligations to neutralize the Panama Canal was highly commendable. And the American propaganda campaign in neutral lands, though possibly an invasion of their sovereignty, was kept on a high plane of truth and decency.

In brief, we may say that in connection with the problems discussed in this chapter the United States was actually convicted of only one violation of international law, the detention of the *Zeelandia*. There may have been other violations, but this was the only instance of an adverse decision on such grounds by a properly constituted tribunal. As regards treaty rights, the United States was not convicted of a single infraction. This does not mean that there were no such violations; but here we must take cognizance of actual decision, not unofficial opinion. In the case of alienage, the Department of State, which was not to be blamed for what happened, admitted that the Selective Service Act violated existing treaties. But even here the United States had a technical escape, for its own courts have held that acts of Congress take precedence over treaties. Such a technicality did not, of course, release Washington from its international responsibilities or assuage the bitterness of the neutrals. Nor does the fact that these small countries failed to present wholesale claims in connection with these and other grievances necessarily mean that the position of the United States would have been sustained at law. Yet when all this has been said, the fact nevertheless remains that in these matters the Administration made a determined and generally successful effort to pursue a policy of fair and honorable dealing.

Chapter XIV

THE BALANCE SHEET

i

We are now in a position to determine with some degree of finality how great a " criminal " the United States actually became. At the outset we may well review those things that Washington protested against as a neutral and later adopted as a belligerent. It must be constantly borne in mind, however, that a protest against a certain practice does not necessarily mean that the practice in question is a violation of international law.[1]

First, the blacklist. While America was neutral the Department of State protested vigorously against this instrument on the grounds of international morals—not international law. As a belligerent, the United States belatedly and reluctantly adopted the blacklist in a wholesale fashion. Nevertheless, the War Trade Board did not employ it as ruthlessly as it might have done, or as sweepingly as the British did. We may conclude, then, that the blacklist was not a violation of international law, but because of certain vicious by-products it proved to be highly offensive to the neutral nations affected.

Second, bunker control. While America was neutral the Department of State protested against this weapon on the

[1] Conversely, the absence of a protest does not mean that certain practices are necessarily in conformity with international law.

grounds of inconvenience and loss—not on the grounds of international law. As a belligerent, Washington adopted it in a thorough-going manner. This instrument was not, however, a violation of international law, because the fuel belonged to the United States, which was at perfect liberty to prescribe conditions for its use. But in actual practice certain aspects of bunker control came into sharp conflict with the equally sovereign rights of neutral states.

Third, postal censorship. While America was neutral the Department of State protested emphatically against this practice on legalistic grounds. As a belligerent, the United States adopted postal censorship on a widespread scale, and also induced several of its cobelligerents to follow suit. Although Washington refused to employ several restrictions to which it had earlier objected, notably the searching of pouches on the high seas, it did resort to certain practices against which it had earlier protested. Perhaps the most important of these was the examination of mail on neutral vessels which had only casually touched at American ports, or had been forced to stop there through bunker control regulations. But in general it may be said that, as far as the results were concerned, the postal control finally established by Washington was substantially the same as that employed by London. Yet, at worst, this kind of censorship was an arguable violation of international law; and even if it had been a clear violation of international law as of 1914, a good case could have been made out for it on the basis of the changed conditions of warfare. But as was true of the blacklist and bunker control, there were aspects of postal censorship which were extremely disagreeable from the neutral point of view.

Fourth, cable censorship. While America was neutral the Department of State repeatedly protested to London against this practice on the grounds of inconvenience and loss. As a belligerent, Washington instituted a practically airtight cable censorship. About the legality of such measures no reasonable question can be raised, for the United States owned the cables in question and was under no obligation to permit them to be used by the enemy. Nevertheless, neutral business suffered considerable hardship.

Fifth, hovering. While America was neutral the Department of State protested strongly to London against the practice of hovering off the three-mile limit in pursuance of visit and search. These representations were based upon the annoyance and unfriendliness of such an act, for no one could allege that the British did not have an undeniable legal right to visit and search on the high seas. As a belligerent, the United States employed hovering to a limited extent, the only instance uncovered by this study being off the Mexican port of Mazatlán. Upon representations from the Mexican government, orders were issued by the Navy Department to abandon this practice, not because it was illegal but because it was both offensive to Mexico and inconsistent with Washington's earlier stand.

In looking back over the five practices against which the United States had earlier protested but which it later adopted, we may conclude that none was clearly at variance with international law. Only postal censorship appears to have been arguable. The blacklist, bunker control, cable censorship, and hovering were all fundamentally legal, but it must be noted that in varying degrees all of these measures bore harshly upon the neutrals.

ii

Our second category consists of those practices against which the Washington government did not formally protest while a neutral—merely reserving its rights—but which it later adopted.

First, inclusive contraband lists. In general, the United States as a neutral took a tolerant view of British extensions of contraband, and merely reserved its rights when London abolished all distinctions between absolute and conditional contraband. As a belligerent, Washington adopted sweeping contraband lists which were virtually identical with those of the British. The United States also assimilated its theoretical position on continuous voyage with that of the Allies and with its own traditional policy. Yet the question of contraband and continuous voyage is largely academic, because the Americans took no prizes and left to the British the task of enforcing the blockade. Even so, we may conclude that the paper position of the United States was not demonstrably at variance with international law, nor seriously out of line with its pronouncements as a neutral.

Second, planting mines in the open seas. While America was neutral the Department of State did not protest against the Allied practice of mining large areas on the high seas, but merely entered a reservation of rights. As a belligerent, the United States took the leading role in laying the enormous North Sea mine barrage. But this was not a clear breach of the law of nations, and it worked little hardship on innocent neutral commerce.

We may therefore conclude that the extension of contraband lists and the laying of mines, matters concerning which the United States had entered reservations as a neutral, were not palpable violations of international law.[2]

iii

Our next category consists of clearly arguable violations of international law which did not involve earlier American reservations or protests.

First, the twenty-four hour and three-ship rules. The Navy Department was admittedly careless in permitting American warships to stay more than twenty-four hours in Mexican ports, and in allowing more than three vessels to remain at the same time in one harbor. The Mexican protests, based on the 13th Hague Convention of 1907, were rejected on the legally tenable grounds that this instrument, not having been ratified by all of the belligerents, was not binding. As a matter of fact, the twenty-four hour and three-ship rules were generally regarded as in the nature of municipal legislation, and should have been properly notified to Washington. Moreover, in most of these cases there were extenuating circumstances. But since the United States in its own naval regulations adopted both the twenty-four hour and the three-ship rules, the protests of Mexico necessarily had to be heeded and steps were taken to avoid further offense. At worst, the Navy seems to have been guilty of nothing more than carelessness in carrying out its own rules.

Second, the so-called law of angary. The commandeering

[2] It is to be noted that the Declaration of London made provision for reasonable extensions of contraband lists. Scott, *Declaration of London,* pp. 117-18.

of the eighty-seven Dutch ships in United States harbors was upheld by Department of State lawyers and by certain American publicists on the grounds of angary, though Washington later took its stand upon the right of a sovereign to requisition, provided just compensation was paid. The law of angary, though arguable, is supported by a strong majority of the writers on international law. That the compensation paid by the United States was satisfactory is indicated by the fact that the Dutch owners did not press any legal claims for indemnity.

Third, the requisitioning of partially constructed ships in American yards. It is a well-established principle of international law that a sovereign may commandeer property within its jurisdiction, provided just compensation is paid. After entering the war the United States seized a considerable number of vessels being built for neutral nations in American shipyards. The most important of these cases involved certain Norwegian interests; and when it proved impossible to agree on just compensation the dispute was submitted to the Hague Court, whose decision bound the United States to pay a considerably larger sum than Washington thought fair. But here the issue was not one of treaty or of law but of proper compensation. The requisitioning of certain Dutch munitions in the United States similarly created a dispute over compensation which the two nations agreed to submit to arbitration, but the outbreak of war in 1939 caused the discussions to be suspended.

We may conclude that in none of these instances of arguable violations of international law was the United States clearly in the wrong. In fact, a strong legal case was made out in support of each action.

iv

The next category consists of the various types of presures that were brought to bear upon the neutrals.

First, the embargo. This instrument was of undeniable legality, and when used by the Allies had not evoked official protests from Washington. As a belligerent, the United States effectively employed the embargo as a club for the purpose of extorting rationing and tonnage agreements from the neutrals.[3] These small countries naturally objected to negotiating while under duress, and they complained bitterly against the restrictions they were forced to place upon their sovereignty. But all of these pacts were entered into voluntarily, at least theoretically; some of them were quite generous; and all of them conferred substantial benefits upon the nations concerned. It should also be noted that the embargo was not used against the neutrals alone but in certain instances against cobelligerents as well.

Second, propaganda. The United States engaged in a propaganda campaign in all of the important neutral countries, primarily for the purpose of strengthening pro-Ally sentiment. Some of these small nations were also used as bases for carrying propaganda to enemy soil. Yet we should note that this type of thing was done by all of the principal belligerents; that America had tolerated such activity while a neutral; and that the propaganda campaigns directed from Washington seem not to have run counter to treaty stipulations or to well-recognized principles of

---

[3] The embargo was not looked upon solely or perhaps even primarily as a club, but as a means of conserving supplies and of keeping American products from flowing to the enemy.

international law.[4] We should also bear in mind that the propaganda of the United States was kept on a high plane, and that many of the neutral nations, far from resenting it, actually welcomed it as a means of increasing their information regarding America.

Third, inducing other nations to forsake their neutrality. Under this head we should recall that the United States sought to persuade a few of the lesser powers to enter the war on its side. Some slight effort was made in connection with China and Liberia; more as regards Honduras; and an actual threat of coercion in the case of Haiti. Yet such pressures and inducements were used by all of the belligerents, and there was nothing essentially illegal about them. Much less important, yet in somewhat the same category, were the efforts made by Washington to solicit from neutral shipmasters information about German submarine movements. This practice was objected to by Denmark as compromising her neutrality; but nothing more seems to have been done about it.

A far more serious matter was forcing the neutrals to make agreements for chartering their tonnage to the United States, particularly that which was required to ply in the danger zones. Since every ship used in behalf of the Allies weakened by that much the German submarine campaign, Berlin could argue that such service was a deviation from

---

[4] Another kind of propaganda is objectionable from the standpoint of international law; namely, that which is conducted within the borders of a friendly state by an outside power for the purpose of jeopardizing public order or effecting a revolutionary overthrow of the existing regime. Lawrence Preuss, "International Responsibility for Hostile Propaganda against Foreign States," *Amer. Jour. of Int. Law*, XXVIII (1934), 668.

the path of true neutrality.[5] This doubtless was true. But theoretically, at least, all of the neutrals entered into these tonnage agreements of their own free will. Actually, the coercive effects of the embargo had much to do with their final action.

Of a much different nature were purely voluntary steps taken by the neutrals to compromise their own neutrality. The United States, as we have noted, accepted the offer of port facilities in several of the Latin American nations, and took over from Uruguay and Peru the German ships which these two republics had requisitioned. But inasmuch as these favors were conferred by nations which had broken with Berlin, and inasmuch as such co-operation seems to have been offered without undue pressure from Washington, the United States cannot justly be condemned for having availed itself of these opportunities.

We may conclude, therefore, that the American government appears to have been guilty of no clear-cut or technical violation of international law in exercising these various pressures on the neutrals.

V

Turning now to the credit side of the balance sheet, we shall next consider those measures which America protested against as a neutral and later declined to adopt.

---

[5] The United States *Naval Instructions, 1917* (p. 19) stated that "A neutral vessel is guilty of direct unneutral service and may not only be captured but may be treated as an enemy merchant vessel" if she is "wholly chartered by or in the exclusive employment of the enemy Government. . . ." It will be noted, however, that under this definition the penalty was capture and forfeiture of the vessel, without guilt accruing to the neutral government for an unneutral act.

First, the blockade. As a neutral, the United States protested emphatically against British blockade methods; as a belligerent, it refused to have any direct part in the practices to which it had objected. There was, to be sure, a considerable amount of indirect American co-operation in the blockade, such as was brought about by the embargo, the blacklist, bunker control, postal censorship, and cable censorship—but all of these measures stood on an independent and different footing.

America has been accused of being a *particeps criminis* by tolerating or acquiescing in the British blockade, and by supplementing it with the embargo and other instruments. But one could not reasonably have expected the United States, as a cobelligerent, to have defeated the common cause by refusing to employ supplementary measures that were clearly legal.[6]

The unwillingness of Washington to participate in the blockade was due in part to the fact that Britain needed

---

[6] Professor Garner later wrote: "There is no reason to suppose that had the American embargo failed to accomplish its object, the American navy would not have co-operated with the British and French navies to the full extent of its power to maintain and enforce the blockade." Lord Eustace Percy testified that the United States "never admitted complicity with the action of the British navy against neutral trade, even after the American navy was patrolling the seas side by side with the British navy, but in the use of the economic resources of the Allied and Associated Powers . . . she not only eagerly accepted the position of an accomplice, but even took the lead in giving this kind of economic weapon a keener edge and in wielding it more effectively." Garner, "Violations of Maritime Law by the Allied Powers during the World War," *Amer. Jour. of Int. Law,* XXV (1931), 47-48. Nevertheless, the United States did not technically participate in the blockade.

little help, and in part to the fact that the State Department did not want to reverse itself and thus invalidate the numerous but largely ill-founded American claims which had grown out of British detentions and seizures during the neutrality period.[7] On May 9, 1927, a special executive agreement was drawn up between Great Britain and the United States under the terms of which each government agreed not to press claims for damages growing out of measures adopted during the war, although individual claimants might seek redress from the courts or from their own governments.[8] During the discussions leading up to this arrangement, the British strongly contended that the United States had vitiated its own case when it entered the war and became a beneficiary of, if not an active participant

---

[7] Frank L. Polk wrote to the author on January 31, 1941: "As a matter of fact, I always felt rather strongly on the subject, as we had a number of claims pending against the British and I thought we might be compromising our future negotiations on this subject if we went as far as they wanted us to go. It may have been a selfish point of view but it was my feeling that the British regulations were, in many instances, quite effective without our help and we could keep the principle so to speak on ice to be dealt with later."

[8] It was agreed that the nationals of both Great Britain and the United States might have free access to the proper courts, provided such courts were competent to pass on these matters; and it was expressly understood that the sum which Washington allegedly owed London would be used to satisfy American claimants who were unable to obtain redress in British courts. *Arrangement Effected by Exchange of Notes between the United States and Great Britain for the Disposal of Certain Pecuniary Claims Arising out of the Recent War,* Treaty Series, No. 756 (Washington, 1927). For negotiations leading up to the agreement, see *For. Rel., 1920,* II, pp. 601-48; *ibid., 1926,* II, pp. 214-308. See also E. M. Borchard, "The Neutrality Claims against Great Britain," *Amer. Jour. of Int. Law,* XXI (1927), 764-68.

in, British blockade methods.[9] Mr. Spencer Phenix, who as the assistant to the Assistant Secretary of State prepared an exhaustive report on this problem, conceded that " the right which the United States undoubtedly had prior to its entry into the war" had undergone "a considerable practical change as a result of our entry into the war, and the policies adopted . . . subsequent thereto." This report also noted that if Washington were to press Britain for claims arising out of the neutrality period, those neutrals which had been affected by American acts and pressures from 1917 to 1918 would have an encouraging precedent for similar action. Mr. Phenix concluded:

> The interests of belligerents and neutrals inevitably clash in any great conflict, and it may well be questioned whether the United States could successfully maintain before any international tribunal that its nationals are entitled to damages for losses suffered through belligerent interference with neutral commerce, without admitting at the same time liability on its own account for such losses as may have been occasioned to Scandinavian and Swiss nationals, for example, through its own belligerent operations.[10]

[9] *For. Rel., 1926*, II, pp. 217, 219, 220. The British ambassador in Washington pointed out that the British blockade had hastened the defeat of Germany, thus saving American lives and money; that the co-operation of the United States in rationing agreements and other measures had made the economic blockade of Germany more rigid than otherwise would have been possible; and that American officials had participated in the organizations that had directed the blockade, even though American warships had not actually seized vessels and cargoes on the high seas. He concluded, therefore, that the British government could see little merit in American protests against the blockade prior to April, 1917. *Ibid.*, pp. 222-23.

[10] *Ibid.*, p. 262. Mr. Phenix's concluding point was that if the United States, a great naval power, should again become involved in war, it would " unquestionably want to pursue very much the

It seems clear, therefore, that Washington's somewhat passive co-operation in the enforcement of the British blockade had a good deal to do with the decision not to press the claims of its own nationals.[11]

Our second item among those practices earlier protested against and later not adopted is the mandatory routing of neutral ships for the purpose of search under the blockade. As a neutral, the United States protested energetically against the forcing of American vessels into certain routes so as to facilitate their search by the British blockading authorities. As a belligerent, Washington pursued a consistent policy, at least technically. To be sure, neutral ships were forced into convoys for their own safety, or they were required to ply certain routes in return for bunkers. But all this was done primarily for conserving shipping and fuel in the interests of the Associated Powers, rather than for the

---

same procedure as that followed by the British. In these circumstances we should take no general position in our present discussions which might later hamper our freedom of action in case of emergency." *Ibid.*, p. 287. The Phenix memorandum appears on pp. 251-87.

[11] Another factor of importance was the discovery that the number of meritorious claims of American citizens could be reduced to a mere handful. Mr. Spencer Phenix carefully sifted 2,658 cases and concluded that only 11 were worthy of serious consideration. Many had already been satisfactorily settled by the British; others were vague and had not been followed up; others involved trifling amounts; and still others concerned property owned by aliens—in some cases enemy aliens—seeking American protection. See particularly *ibid.*, p. 286. Mr. Green H. Hackworth, Legal Adviser of the Department of State, reports that as yet there have been only three arbitrations in the United States of claims under the 1927 agreement. Letter to author, February 27, 1942. This in itself is strong evidence as to the fewness of meritorious claims.

enforcement of a blockade which the United States persisted in regarding as illegal.[12]

Third, removal of enemy nationals from neutral ships on the high seas. As a neutral, the United States had protested strenuously against this practice; as a belligerent, it flatly refused to reverse itself, despite pressure from the British that it do so. Here the record seems to have been kept impeccably clean.

In assessing the items in this category, we may note that the United States as a neutral protested sharply against the British blockade, against the mandatory routing of vessels for purposes of search, and against the removal of enemy nationals from neutral ships. As a belligerent the Washington government, technically at least, consistently refused to resort to any of these practices.

vi

We come now to certain unquestionable violations of treaty rights or international law by the United States.

First, conscription of neutral aliens in violation of treaty guarantees. Where such guarantees existed, as they did in the case of several nations, the drafting of aliens was clearly a violation of international obligations, even though one accepts the narrowly legalistic view that as municipal legislation the Selective Service Act took precedence over prior treaty commitments. The Wilson administration did what it

---

[12] Comment of Dr. Alonzo E. Taylor (November, 1941): "I suggest that in the summary you point out that we were green, the Allies experienced in the field of blockade and contracture of foreign trade. Thus, sometimes we were timid novices, at other times blundering novices. We were naïve, they were sated. We tried to be idealistic, they were realistic."

could to live up to its responsibilities, but even the specific exemption of such neutral aliens by an amendment of the original law did not put an end to injustices. The neutral nations affected had genuine and serious grievances, especially when their nationals were sent overseas and killed in action; and it is surprising that a large number of claims were not preferred against the Washington government.[13]

Second, violations of Mexican territorial waters. There was at least one well-authenticated instance of Mexico's territorial waters having been violated by the seizure of an American vessel by a United States warship. Washington took prompt punitive action and made what amends it could. This, however, was an isolated case of misunderstanding or insubordination rather than a deliberate attempt to violate Mexico's rights.

Third, the improper detention of neutral vessels. During the course of the war a number of neutral ships were quite properly detained through the refusal of Washington to grant export licenses for their cargoes. Others were held in port for reasons less sound, with a consequent loss through spoilage and demurrage charges. The first case of this kind pressed to the point of adjudication was that of the Dutch *Zeelandia*, and the United States Court of Claims held that the ship had been detained in violation of both domestic and international law. As a consequence, the American government was assessed approximately half a million dollars. In the case of two detained Swedish ships,

---

[13] As noted earlier (p. 445, n.) only Mexico presented a few claims involving alien nondeclarants. Comment of Lester H. Woolsey (January, 1942): "I never understood this apathy either, except on the theory that the neutral governments forsook the declarants as the latter did their countries."

the *Kronprins Gustaf Adolf* and the *Pacific*, a special arbitrator absolved the United States of a treaty violation, though considerations of international law were specifically excluded from the judgment. There were other instances of a not dissimilar nature, but these were the only ones upon which there were judicial decisions.

By way of summary we may say that the United States was plainly guilty of disregarding treaty engagements, at least in spirit, by conscripting certain aliens, and that it also ran counter to international law in violating Mexican territorial waters and in detaining the Dutch ship *Zeelandia*. This is the list; and considering the magnitude of the war it seems surprisingly short. There may have been other instances, whether minor or major, of violations of international law or treaty rights.[14] But in the present study we are primarily concerned with the legal record, not with what might have happened had certain actions been brought.

vii

In our next category we shall consider practices which the

[14] On March 20, 1941, Lester H. Woolsey told the present writer that during this period of confusion many things were done by other government branches which the State Department did not know about, and which in some cases later involved it in difficulties. In those days, he added, "there were times when the right hand hardly knew what the left hand was doing." On March 14, 1940, Dr. Alonzo E. Taylor wrote to the author: "There was too much to do and too much hurry. [John Foster] Dulles was supposed to watch out for this, but I can assure you from personal experience, that in cooperation with the Inter-Allied Blockade Board in Europe, on the occasion of my several trips there during the war, I took actions for our government which were not submitted to the State Department, and some of these actions I am quite sure were contrary both to the letter and spirit of international law."

United States refused to adopt but against which it had not specifically protested as a neutral.

The Washington government bluntly declined to close the North Sea mine barrage by laying mines in Norway's territorial waters. In this case uncompromising adherence to high principle interfered definitely but not seriously with the prosecution of the war.

The United States refused to violate the neutrality of the Panama Canal Zone by giving succor to British naval forces.[15] The American authorities also released two Dutch ships that were requisitioned in this area, and declined to exercise as rigid a control over cargoes in the Canal Zone as in the ports of the United States. All of these instances of self-abnegation hampered the common war effort to some extent, though certainly not to an important degree.

Washington did not accept the Allied suggestion that it join in a financial blockade of the neutral countries. We should observe, however, that essentially the same ends were accomplished by employment of the blacklist and other controls.

The United States flatly rejected a proposal for the reciprocal exchange of prizes with the Allies. This would have involved an objectionable recognition of British blockade practices.

The Wilson administration consistently avoided becoming a party to any multipartite pacts under which it would be regarded as giving direct or even indirect sanction to the

---

[15] In view of the general disregard of neutralized areas during this war, the action of the United States is particularly noteworthy. For the fate of other areas see Graham, "Neutrality and the World War," *Amer. Jour. of Int. Law,* XVII (1923), 720-21.

blockade and other devices against which it had protested. This was conspicuously true in the negotiation of the general agreement with the Netherlands.

The Department of State, despite considerable provocation, rejected a recommendation from the Food Administration that, if necessary, the United States take over Yucatán to control the production of sisal and keep the price within reasonable bounds. Practical as well as ethical considerations apparently entered into this decision.

Other incidents of less fundamental importance may be listed in summary form. The United States declined to exercise pressure with the object of forcing Spain into the war; to join in an Allied protest designed to secure the internment of German submarines in Spain; to press for similar action in Argentina; to hold a requisitioning club (at least actively) over Denmark for the purpose of securing tonnage; to back out of bunkering agreements with a Spanish steamship line;[16] and to evade its contractual obligations for providing Spain with ammonium sulphate. The United States also refused to enter upon a scheme with London to control neutral prices;[17] to adopt the British proposal for a trading white list with the neutrals; and to join with the French in a plan for postwar control of neutral trade.[18]

Most of these matters were of minor importance, and the decision in some instances was based on expediency rather than on law. But the total list is impressive. It indicates that the United States was determined not to reverse itself

[16] *For. Rel., 1918, Supp. 1,* II, p. 1741. The cases not here documented have been discussed earlier.
[17] *Ibid.*, pp. 973-74, 978.
[18] *Ibid.*, p. 995.

on certain of the principles it had stood for while a neutral, and that it was unwilling to become involved in unnecessary entanglements that ran counter to its traditional policies.

viii

The refusal of the United States to impose more drastic restrictions on the neutrals was in large measure due to the idealistic intervention of President Wilson. "He is not a belligerent among other belligerents," wrote Ambassador Spring Rice, "but something apart."[19] We have repeatedly had occasion to note that Wilson consistently opposed disagreeable measures, even when legal, and that when they had to be employed he reluctantly and belatedly gave in.[20] He fought the blacklist as long as he reasonably could; he opposed the requisitioning of the Dutch shipping until there seemed to be no other alternative; and then he deleted a paragraph from the note to the Netherlands chargé lest it be unnecessarily offensive. Wilson also revealed more than ordinary solicitude for the Swiss and the Norwegians.[21] In the case of Norway he vetoed the proposals for both joint representations and strong measures in connection with closing the mine-barrage gap. During the Swedish mail-pouch controversy with the British, Wilson took an active

---

[19] Stephen Gwynn, ed., *The Letters and Friendships of Sir Cecil Spring Rice* (Boston, 1929), II, 409.

[20] Vance C. McCormick later testified that the War Trade Board, in securing drastic but legal restrictions on the neutrals, repeatedly had to oppose and overcome Wilson's idealism. "We had to fight for everything we got," he said. Interview on March 23, 1941.

[21] Comment of Dr. Alonzo E. Taylor (November, 1941): "Wilson always admonished [the] War Trade Board to go easy on Switzerland and Norway."

interest in seeing that Sweden secured just treatment. With reference to Denmark, he vetoed the Hoover proposal for drastic restrictions on food supplies, and he opposed as unethical the policy of purposely delaying the Danish negotiations in the hope of securing better terms from the other neutrals.

In certain other matters the United States revealed a noteworthy generosity toward the neutral nations. Although Wilson's hand cannot be definitely found in all of these instances, it seems reasonable to assume that he had some share in them. At the outset—and this is of fundamental importance—the United States acknowledged an obligation to help feed the neutrals, provided they agreed to make proper provision against succoring the Central Powers.[22] The Administration also adopted the policy of Christmas concessions to the neutrals in the form of important cargoes; of convoying grain to Switzerland in order to carry out a solemn pact; of offering three cargoes of grain to the Dutch at a critical time; of intervening with Britain on behalf of Sweden in connection with both the mail-pouch controversy

---

[22] For the period ending December 31, 1917, the War Trade Board reported: " In several cases . . . exports have been offered to neutrals even where our own supplies and those of our co-belligerents have been very limited. In such cases the board has been actuated by a desire to prevent acute suffering in those neutrals and to prevent them from falling under the economic power of the enemy. It has been thought that even though such exports would entail an additional sacrifice on the part of our own people this burden should nevertheless be borne as a tangible evidence of the friendship of our people to those foreign peoples whose governments were endeavoring to maintain their neutrality on an equitable basis." *For. Rel., 1917, Supp. 2*, II, p. 1009. See also Jones to Wilson, November 24, 1917, Wilson Papers, Library of Congress.

and the rye transaction; of replacing oil for Spain that had been destroyed; and of securing the partial elimination of the annoying call at Halifax.

Not all of these gestures, to be sure, were motivated entirely or even primarily by altruistic motives. In some cases expediency and generosity merged. But this list of what the United States refrained from doing, or what it actually did when it might have taken a more rigorous course, is not unimpressive.

ix

Certain observations of a more general nature remain to be made, and in doing so we may refer, as we began, to Burton J. Hendrick's allegation that the United States, after entering the war, "immediately" became as great a "criminal" as England.[23]

Certainly enough has been said to prove that the adoption of American measures against the neutrals—as was also true of Britain—was anything but "immediate." For reasons that have already been presented in detail, the Administration moved with the utmost deliberation, refusing to be rushed into disagreeable decisions, and adopting as a free agent such policies as were finally established. This, of course, may have delayed the termination of the war by a matter of months; but so troubled was Washington by consistency and conscience that this price had to be paid.[24] The Administration's delay was very annoying to the British, but, like them, the Americans had to think of neutral good

[23] Hendrick, *Page Letters*, II, 265.
[24] Lansing later wrote: "While our conduct might be illegal, we would not be flagrantly inconsistent." Lansing, *Memoirs*, p. 128.

will and postwar trade. It should be added, however, that when Washington once adopted the embargo and other restrictions it in general adhered to them more steadfastly than London.

So much for the speed of movement; now for the degree of "criminality." Mr. Hendrick to the contrary, the United States did not become as great a "criminal" as Britain—even assuming that this is the proper word to use in reference to the latter. To be sure, Washington adopted a number of practices against which it had earlier protested on the grounds of expediency and, in a few instances, legality. But, as we have repeatedly observed, protests do not necessarily mean that international law has been violated. As a matter of fact, this study uncovered only two clear-cut and rather minor proved violations of international law; and only one rather serious violation of at least the spirit of treaty obligations. It is well to bear in mind that the embargo, bunker control, and the blacklist—the three most potent weapons wielded by Washington—were all undeniably legal.

Comparisons are often odious; but in this case we must note that Britain was situated differently. The United States, it now seems, was not in so favorable a position to take liberties with international law as the British. Matters of idealism, inconsistency, and pending claims were strong deterrents. But Britain had passed through no period of neutrality. She had been a belligerent—and hence a "sinner"—from the very beginning. In fact, the United States did not have to become as great a "criminal" as England. The British were doing effective work with their blockade when America came into the war, and Washington did not need to do more than acquiesce or passively cooperate. The United States might have become as great a "criminal" as Britain if it had been essential to do so in order to win the war. But this was not necessary; so America sinned no more than she had to.[25]

Even this last statement needs some qualification. The United States did at times, as we have noted, veer over to the side of generosity. But in no case was the war effort seriously hampered by such action. If losing the conflict had been the alternative, the result might well have been different. On the other hand, in the case of the trade and rationing agreements Washington drove about as hard bargains as the traffic would bear. Yet the United States on the whole was honest and aboveboard; and the neutrals did not suffer seriously, even from America's arguable violations of international law.[26] It is true that they complained; but this was the defense mechanism of the weak. And they presented relatively few protests or claims. Such failure to act, however, may not have been so much a measure of American right as of neutral weariness with lodging unheeded protests.

[25] Comment of John Foster Dulles (January 12, 1942): "My recollection corresponds generally to the impression which your chapter gives. We were able through our economic power and control of our own assets to put very strong pressure to bear on neutrals. In this way we were able to accomplish by 'legal' coercion what England had been able to accomplish by methods which we deemed improper. It is difficult for me to think of any situation where substantive gains were renounced when we had the power to achieve them, but feared that the use of power would be improper."

[26] We have repeatedly noted that the neutrals had important weapons with which to strike back, such as withholding tonnage and instituting retaliatory embargoes.

The crux of the problem is that neutrality and belligerency are diametrically opposite and fundamentally irreconcilable conceptions. Neither side fully appreciates the problems and point of view of the other. Certainly America did not—and she was successively in both camps.

The conclusion is inescapable that the Washington government did not violate international law in a sweeping and ruthless fashion, and that its record on the whole is creditable. There was, to be sure, considerable contrast between America's position as a neutral and her conduct as a belligerent. But when we remember that the stakes were desperately high, and that Germany almost won the war before American intervention could become effective, the wonder is that the United States showed such a surprising degree of deference to the weak neutral nations.

SELECT BIBLIOGRAPHY

(This bibliography includes only the more general or the more important references. Detailed citations appear in the footnotes.)

A. Archive Manuscript Materials

American Relief Administration Archives. Hoover Library on War, Revolution, and Peace. Stanford University.

    (An important body of material which contains little that bears directly upon the subject of this monograph.)

Department of State. Division of Communications and Records. Washington, D. C.

    (All the records of the Department of State for this period were made available to the writer without reservation. Fifty-six different files were examined, ranging in bulk from a few hundred items to twenty or thirty bound volumes containing between five and ten thousand manuscripts. These were an invaluable supplement to the records already published in *Foreign Relations*. In addition to the customary notes, dispatches, and instructions, all cablegrams from or to the War Trade Board were sent through the Department of State. Of particular value were memoranda prepared within the Department, interchanges of letters with other departments, and letters to and from President Wilson.)

Department of State. Records of the War Trade Board. Washington, D. C.

    (At the time these records were examined they were stored in a separate building, under the jurisdiction of the Department of State. They were arranged in approximately 800 standard-sized, four-drawer filing cases. The bulk of this material is of a routine nature, relating to such matters as license applications and enemy trading lists. The executive or policy files, with which the present study is more directly concerned, are far less voluminous and are adequately arranged and indexed; otherwise the task would have been staggering. This file contains the minutes of the Exports Council, of the Exports Administrative Board, and of the War Trade Board.)

Food Administration Archives. National Archives, Washington, D. C.

    (Herein referred to as F. A. A. Although indispensable for other studies, these records do not contain much on the policy of the United States toward the neutrals that could not be found in Herbert Hoover's files at Stanford University.)

Food Administration Records. Hoover Library on War, Revolution, and Peace. Stanford University.

(Herein referred to as F. A. R. This bulky collection proved to be of the highest importance, containing as it does the private files of Herbert Hoover and Dr. Alonzo E. Taylor. It supplements and to some extent duplicates the records of the War Trade Board and of the Department of State. There is a large amount of information on the food situation in the neutral countries, and on the activities of American agents abroad.)

United States Grain Corporation Archives. National Archives, Washington, D. C.

(This large collection yielded very little that was relevant to the problem under consideration.)

(*Note.* The records of the Navy Department were not investigated because Captain Dudley W. Knox, in charge of the Office of Naval Records and Library, informed the present writer that there was practically nothing there bearing upon this problem, and because the correspondence between the Department of State and the Navy Department with reference to the neutrals seems to have been fully preserved in the Department of State. The extensive records of the United States Shipping Board were not examined because all matters of policy affecting the neutrals were cleared through the Department of State. The bulky but incomplete records of the Committee on Public Information were not consulted because the subject of propaganda is somewhat incidental to the present study, and because general matters of policy may be determined through other sources. Dr. James R. Mock, of the National Archives, who has studied these records more completely than anyone else, has generously assisted the present writer in the formulation of his conclusions.)

B. Private Papers, Correspondence, and Reports

Conger, S. B. " Policy and Achievement of the War Trade Board."
(An eighteen-page typescript report, prepared by the Foreign Adviser of the War Trade Board, and made available through the generosity of Mr. Vance C. McCormick. It is now deposited with the Hoover Library, Stanford University.)

Herron, George D. Papers of George D. Herron. Hoover Library, Stanford University.
(Some light on the position of Switzerland.)

Long, Breckinridge. Papers of Breckinridge Long. Library of Congress.
>(Of little importance from the point of view of this study. Long was Third Assistant Secretary of State, January 22, 1917, to June 7, 1920.)

Wilson, Woodrow. Papers of Woodrow Wilson. Library of Congress.
>(Of considerable value; a number of items already published in R. S. Baker's *Wilson* and in *Foreign Relations*.)

Yale House Collection. Yale University, New Haven.
>(Some useful manuscripts on British-American co-ordination.)

C. Unpublished Diaries

Anderson, Chandler P. "Diary of Chandler P. Anderson." Library of Congress.
>(A full and gossipy diary by a distinguished international lawyer, then counsel for the War Industries Board, who was an intimate of Juan Riaño, the Spanish ambassador in Washington. Anderson's comments are not altogether objective and must be used with much caution.)

McCormick, Vance C. *Diaries of Vance C. McCormick, Member of the American War Mission to Inter-Allied Conference in London and Paris in 1917; and Adviser to President Wilson at the Peace Conference in Paris, in 1919.* N. p., n. d.
>(This account, which is printed but not published, gives some interesting background material. Mr. McCormick generously presented a copy to the Hoover Library, Stanford University.)

D. Unpublished Government Documents

(The following six booklets, which contain relevant official documents, are serially numbered and were printed, not published, for the use of government officials. Copies of those on Norway and Switzerland may be found in the Hoover Library; a complete set is in the War Trade Board files of the Department of State.)

War Trade Board, Bureau of Research and Statistics. *The Rationing Agreement with Norway.* Washington, 1919.
———. *The Rationing and Shipping Negotiations with Sweden.* Washington, 1919.
———. *The Rationing and Tonnage Negotiations with Switzerland.* Washington, 1919.

War Trade Board, Bureau of Research and Statistics. *The Requisitioning of the Dutch Shipping.* Washington, 1919.
———. *The Trade and Shipping Negotiations with Denmark.* Washington, 1919.
———. *The Trade and Shipping Negotiations with Spain.* Washington, 1919.
War Trade Board. *Daily Record.* September 19, 1917, to June 21, 1919.

(Mimeographed pages of news and announcements issued daily by the War Trade Board for the guidance and information of its employees. A complete file may be found in the Hoover Library.)

E. PUBLISHED GOVERNMENT DOCUMENTS

Complete Report of the Chairman of the Committee on Public Information. Washington, 1920.
Congressional Record. 65th Congress. Washington, 1917-18.
Instructions for the Navy of the United States Governing Maritime Warfare, June, 1917. Washington, 1924.
Papers Relating to the Foreign Relations of the United States, 1914, Supplement. Washington, 1928.
Papers Relating to the Foreign Relations of the United States, 1915, Supplement. Washington, 1928.
Papers Relating to the Foreign Relations of the United States, 1916, Supplement. Washington, 1929.
Papers Relating to the Foreign Relations of the United States, 1917, Supplement 1. Washington, 1931.
Papers Relating to the Foreign Relations of the United States, 1917, Supplement 2. 2 vols. Washington, 1932.
Papers Relating to the Foreign Relations of the United States, 1918, Supplement 1. 2 vols. Washington, 1933.
Papers Relating to the Foreign Relations of the United States, 1918, Supplement 2. Washington, 1933.
Papers Relating to the Foreign Relations of the United States, 1920. 3 vols. Washington, 1935-36.
Papers Relating to the Foreign Relations of the United States, 1921. 2 vols. Washington, 1936.
Papers Relating to the Foreign Relations of the United States, 1923. 2 vols. Washington, 1938.
Papers Relating to the Foreign Relations of the United States, 1926. 2 vols. Washington, 1941.
Papers Relating to the Foreign Relations of the United States, 1927. 3 vols. Washington, 1942.
Papers Relating to the Foreign Relations of the United States: The Lansing Papers, 1914-1920. 2 vols. Washington, 1939-40.
Report of the War Trade Board. Washington, 1920.

F. Collected Documents

Baker, Ray Stannard, and William E. Dodd, eds. *The New Democracy: Presidential Messages, Addresses, and Other Papers (1913-1917) by Woodrow Wilson.* 2 vols. New York, 1926.

Deák, Francis, and Philip C. Jessup, eds. *A Collection of Neutrality Laws, Regulations and Treaties of Various Countries.* 2 vols. Washington, 1939.

Gay, George I., and Harold Henry Fisher, eds. *Public Relations of the Commission for Relief in Belgium; Documents.* 2 vols. Stanford University, 1929.

Savage, Carlton. *Policy of the United States toward Maritime Commerce in War.* 2 vols. Washington, 1934-36.

    (Primarily a collection of official documents, most of which are published in *Foreign Relations,* with an introductory summary and abstract of 160 pages.)

Scott, James Brown, ed. *The Declaration of London, February 26, 1909.* New York, 1919.

United States Naval War College. *International Law Documents, 1917.* Washington, 1918.

―――. *International Law Documents, 1918.* Washington, 1919.

G. Published Diaries, Collected Letters, and Memoirs

Dawes, Charles Gates. *A Journal of the Great War.* 2 vols. Boston, 1921.

    (As general purchasing agent of the A. E. F., Colonel Dawes was intimately involved in the negotiations with Spain.)

Egan, Maurice Francis. *Ten Years near the German Frontier.* New York, 1919. (United States minister in Denmark.)

Grey, Sir Edward. *Twenty-Five Years, 1892-1916.* 2 vols. New York, 1925.

Gwynn, Stephen Lucius, ed. *The Letters and Friendships of Sir Cecil Spring Rice.* 2 vols. Boston, 1929. (Letters of British ambassador in Washington.)

Lansing, Robert. *War Memoirs of Robert Lansing.* Indianapolis, 1935.

Lloyd George, David. *War Memoirs of David Lloyd George.* 6 vols. Boston, 1933-37.

Morris, Ira Nelson. *From an American Legation.* New York, 1923. (United States minister in Sweden.)

Pershing, John J. *My Experiences in the World War.* 2 vols. New York, 1931.

Reinsch, Paul S. *An American Diplomat in China.* Garden City, N. Y., 1922.

Seymour, Charles, ed. *The Intimate Papers of Colonel House.* 4 vols. Boston, 1926-28.
Stimson, Frederic Jesup. *My United States.* New York, 1931. (United States ambassador in Argentina.)
Stovall, Pleasant A. *Switzerland and the World War.* Savannah, Ga., 1939. (United States minister in Switzerland.)
Whitehouse, Vira B. (Mrs. Norman de R. Whitehouse). *A Year as a Government Agent.* New York, 1920. (Representative of the Committee on Public Information in Switzerland.)
Wilson, Hugh R. *Diplomat between Wars.* New York, 1941. (Second secretary of the U. S. legation, Berne.)

H. Newspapers and Newspaper Digests

(As indicated in the introductory chapter, the present monograph is not primarily a study of public opinion, although enough was done with this aspect of this subject to provide a background. American opinion was analyzed through the debates in Congress, the New York *Times,* and various magazines, notably the *Literary Digest.* Opinion in the neutral countries was studied through the comprehensive press digests published in the belligerent countries and through the dispatches of American representatives abroad.)

Bulletin Périodique de la Presse Hollandaise. Paris, 1917-1918.
Bulletin Périodique de la Presse Espagnole. Paris, 1917-1918.
Bulletin Périodique de la Presse Scandinave. Paris, 1917-18.
Bulletin Périodique de la Presse Suisse. Paris, 1917-18.

> (These four French digests, prepared by the Ministères de la Guerre et des Affaires Étrangères for official use, were less satisfactory than those of the German or British, and tended to reproduce items that were favorable to the Allied cause.)

Daily Review of the Foreign Press: Neutral Press Supplement. London, 1917-18. Issued for official use by the General Staff, War Office.

> (This is the best balanced and most complete of the press digests. The accompanying economic section was of little value.)

Nachrichten der Auslandpresse, zusammengestellt bei der Auslandstelle des Kriegspresseamtes. Nachdruck oder Benutzung nach Massgabe der allgemeinen Vorschriften für die Presse, namentlich der Zensurbestimmungen, gestattet. Berlin, 1917-18.

> (Although full, this digest tended to select comment sympathetic with the German point of view. The accompanying economic section of this digest proved to be of little value.)

SELECT BIBLIOGRAPHY

New York *Times*. New York, 1917-1918.
Official Bulletin. Washington, 1917-18.
(Published by the Committee on Public Information and containing announcements, documents, and other information.)

I. MAGAZINES

American Journal of International Law, 1917-18. New York.
Annals of the American Academy, 1917-18. Philadelphia.
Atlantic Monthly, 1917-18. Boston.
Bellman, 1917-18. Minneapolis, Minn.
Century, 1917-18. New York.
Contemporary Review, 1917-18. London.
Current History Magazine, 1917-18. New York.
Current Opinion, 1917-18. New York.
Edinburgh Review, 1917-18. London.
Fortnightly Review, 1917-18. London.
Forum, 1917-18. New York.
Independent, 1917-18. New York.
Literary Digest, 1917-18. New York.
Living Age, 1917-18. Boston.
Nation, 1917-18. New York.
New Republic, 1917-18. New York.
North American Review, 1917-18. New York.
Outlook, 1917-18. New York.
Review of Reviews, 1917-18. New York.
Scientific American, 1917-18. New York.
Scribner's Magazine, 1917-18. New York.
Survey, 1917-18. New York.
World's Work, 1917-18. Garden City, N. Y.
Yale Review, 1917-18. New Haven, Conn.

J. BIOGRAPHIES

Baker, Ray Stannard. *Woodrow Wilson: Life and Letters*. 8 vols. Garden City, N. Y., and New York, 1927-39.
Hendrick, Burton J. *The Life and Letters of Walter H. Page*. 3 vols. Garden City, N. Y., 1922-25.

K. SPECIAL STUDIES

Bailey, Thomas A. "The United States and the Blacklist during the Great War." *Journal of Modern History*, VI (1934), 14-35.

Briggs, Mitchell P. *George D. Herron and the European Settlement.* Stanford University, 1932.

Brodnitz, Georg. *Das System des Wirtschaftskrieges.* Tübingen, 1920.

Bruntz, George G. *Allied Propaganda and the Collapse of the German Empire in 1918.* Stanford University, 1938.

Clarkson, Jesse D., and Thomas C. Cochran, eds. *War as a Social Institution.* New York, 1941.

Consett, M. W. W. P. *The Triumph of Unarmed Forces, 1914-1918.* London, 1928. (By British naval attaché in Scandinavia, 1912-1919.)

Creel, George. *How We Advertised America.* New York, 1920. (By Chairman of Committee on Public Information.)

Daniels, Josephus. *Our Navy at War.* New York, 1922. (By the Secretary of the Navy.)

Fayle, C. Ernest. *Seaborne Trade.* 3 vols. London, 1920-24.

―――. *The War and the Shipping Industry.* New Haven, 1927.

Flier, M. J. van der. *War Finances in the Netherlands up to 1918.* Oxford, 1923.

Garner, James W. *International Law and the World War.* 2 vols. London, 1920.

―――. "Violations of Maritime Law by the Allied Powers during the World War." *American Journal of International Law,* XXV (1931), 26-49.

Geering, Traugott. *Handel und Industrie der Schweiz unter dem Einfluss des Weltkrieges.* Basel, 1928.

Graham, Malbone W., Jr. "Neutrality and the World War." *American Journal of International Law,* XVII (1923), 704-23.

Grünfeld, Ernst. *Die deutsche Aussenhandelskontrolle vom Kriegsausbruch bis zum Inkrafttreten des Friedensvertrages.* Bonn and Leipzig, 1922.

Guichard, Louis. *The Naval Blockade, 1914-1918.* (Translated and edited by Christopher R. Turner.) New York, 1930.

Hackworth, Green H. *Digest of International Law.* Vols. I-II. Washington, 1940, 1941.

Heckscher, Eli F., *et al. Sweden, Norway, Denmark and Iceland in the World War.* New Haven, 1930. A translation and abridgement of monographs originally published in the Scandinavian languages. Sweden, by Eli F. Heckscher and Kurt Bergendal; Norway, by Wilhelm Keilhau; Denmark, by Einar Cohn; Iceland, by Thorsteinn Thorsteinsson. (Contributions based in considerable part on unpublished official records and of great value for background purposes.)

Hunter, Charles H. "Anglo-American Relations during the Period of American Belligerency, 1917-1918." Stanford University,

1935. Unpublished doctoral dissertation in Stanford University Library.

Hurley, Edward N. *The Bridge to France.* Philadelphia, 1927. (By Chairman of U. S. Shipping Board.)

Hyde, Charles C. *International Law Chiefly as Interpreted and Applied by the United States.* 2 vols. Boston, 1922.

Irwin, William Henry. *Propaganda and the News.* New York, 1936. (By Chief of the Foreign Department, Committee on Public Information.)

Japikse, Nicolaas. *Die Stellung Hollands im Weltkrieg politisch und wirtschaftlich.* (Translated from the Dutch by Dr. K. Schwendemann.) Gotha, 1921.

Jastrow, Ignaz. *Völkerrecht und Wirtschaftskrieg: Bemerkungen und Aktenstücke zur Methode der englischen Wirtschaftskriegführung.* Breslau, 1917.

Jessup, Philip C. *American Neutrality and International Police.* Boston, 1928.

Jöhlinger, Otto. *Der britische Wirtschaftskrieg und seine Methoden.* Berlin, 1918.

Keller, G. *N.O.T.: The Netherlands Oversea Trust.* (Translated from the Dutch by E. N. Cox.) London, 1917.

Kenworthy, J. M., and George Young. *Freedom of the Seas.* New York, 1928.

La Fargue, Thomas E. *China and the World War.* Stanford University, 1937.

Laurens, Adolphe. *Le blocus et la guerre sous-marine.* Paris, 1924.

McDiarmid, Alice Morrissey. "American Civil War Precedents: Their Nature, Application, and Extension." *American Journal of International Law,* XXXIV (1940), 220-37.

Martin, Percy A. *Latin America and the War.* Baltimore, 1925.

Mathieu, Beltran. "The Neutrality of Chile during the European War." *American Journal of International Law,* XIV (1920), 319-342.

Maury, Lucien. *Les problèmes scandinaves: le nationalisme suédois et la guerre, 1914-18.* Paris, 1918.

Mock, James R. *Censorship 1917.* Princeton, 1941.

———. "The Creel Committee in Latin America." *Hispanic American Historical Review,* XXII (1942), 262-79.

Mock, James R., and Cedric Larson. *Words that Won the War.* Princeton, 1939. (A monograph on the Work of the Committee on Public Information.)

Moore, Blaine Free. *Economic Aspects of the Commerce and Industry of the Netherlands, 1912-1918.* Washington, 1919.

Morrissey, Alice M. *The American Defense of Neutral Rights, 1914-1917.* Cambridge, Mass., 1939.

———. "The United States and the Rights of Neutrals, 1917-

1918." *American Journal of International Law,* XXXI (1937), 17-30.

Mullendore, William C. *History of the United States Food Administration, 1917-1919.* Stanford University, 1941. (A forty-page introduction written by Herbert Hoover in 1920.)

Obrecht, Max. *Die kriegswirtschaftlichen Überwachungsgesellschaften S. S. S. und S. T. S. und insbesondere ihre Syndikate.* Berne, 1920.

Padelford, Norman J. *The Panama Canal in Peace and War.* New York, 1942.

Parmelee, Maurice. *Blockade and Sea Power; the Blockade, 1914-1919, and Its Significance for a World State.* New York, 1924.

Paxson, Frederic L. *America at War, 1917-1918.* Boston, 1939.

Pfenninger, Rudolf. *Die Handelsbeziehungen zwischen der Schweiz und Deutschland während des Krieges, 1914-1918.* Zürich, 1928.

Phillips, Ethel C. "American Participation in Belligerent Commercial Controls, 1914-1917." *American Journal of International Law,* XXVII (1933), 675-93.

Ritchie, H. *The "Navicert" System during the World War.* Washington, 1938.

Ruchti, Jacob. *Geschichte der Schweiz während des Weltkrieges, 1914-1919.* 2 vols. Berne, 1928.

Rufener, Louis A. *The Economic Position of Switzerland during the War.* Washington, 1919.

Schmidt, Peter Heinrich. *Der Wirtschaftskrieg und die Neutralen.* Zürich, 1918.

Seymour, Charles. *American Diplomacy during the World War.* Baltimore, 1934.

Sims, Rear-Admiral William S. *The Victory at Sea.* Garden City, N. Y., 1921.

Surface, Frank M. *The Grain Trade during the World War.* New York, 1928.

Surface, Frank M., and Raymond L. Bland. *American Food in the World War and Reconstruction Period.* Stanford University, 1931.

Tansill, Charles C. *America Goes to War.* Boston, 1938.

Trimble, E. G. "Violations of Maritime Law by the Allied Powers during the World War." *American Journal of International Law,* XXIV (1930), 79-99. (James W. Garner's article, cited above, is a reply to this.)

Turlington, Edgar. *Neutrality: The World War Period.* New York, 1936. (Perhaps the most important of the comprehensive earlier works.)

Vandenbosch, Amry. *The Neutrality of the Netherlands during the World War*. Grand Rapids, Mich., 1927.

Vigness, Paul G. *The Neutrality of Norway in the World War*. Stanford University, 1932.

Warren, Charles. "Lawless Maritime Warfare." *Foreign Affairs*, XVIII (1940), 424-41.

Westergaard, Harald. *Economic Development in Denmark before and during the World War*. Oxford, 1922.

Zaalberg, C. J. P., *et al*. *The Netherlands and the World War*. Vols. II-IV. New Haven, 1928.

INDEX

A

Ackerman, Carl W. (journalist), on neutral trade, 107-3.

Adams, Charles Francis (Secretary of the Navy), on U. S. and blockade, 388-9.

Adams, John, and Dutch in American Revolution, 204,n.

A.E.F. *See* American Expeditionary Forces.

Albania, and war, 18.

Alienage, policy of U. S. on, 435-46, 466, 482-3.

Aliens, drafting of, 435-46.

Alliances, U. S. antipathy for, 3,n.

Allied and Associated Powers, defined, 3,n. *See also* Allies.

Allied Blockade Committee, 390.

Allies, defined, 3,n.; encourage China to enter war, 32; U. S. adopts independent attitude re, 62; seek to place odium on U. S., 91; oppose stringent embargo, 101,n.; favor embargo on Norway, 106; disturbed over Norway's delay, 111,n.; and Norway agreement, 115; seek complete cessation of Norway exports, 117; demands of, on Norway, 120-1; approve Norway agreement, 125; co-operate with U. S. re Norway agreement, 130; and Russian transit, 138; and pressure on Sweden, 140; and Swedish iron-ore problem, 149-51; negotiate with Sweden in London, 152-5; and Swedish ore deal, 157-8; sign Swedish agreement, 159; and Swedish agreement, 160-2; shift blame on U. S., 175-6; and Iceland agreement, 189,n.; and Dutch neutrality, 196-7; favor requisitioning of Dutch ships, 210; conclude *modus vivendi* with Dutch, 206-7; discussions with Dutch in London, 206; allegedly hold Dutch telegrams, 220; differ with U. S. on Dutch agreement, 232; and Dutch agreement, 234-5; and Swiss silk agreements, 251-2; urge leniency with Swiss, 252; and U. S. declaration re Swiss, 254; Swiss trade with, 240-3; sign commercial agreement with Swiss, 249,n.; and Swiss lumber agreement, 263,n.; oppose sale of tonnage in Spain, 269; Spanish antipathy for, 274; propaganda in Spain, 274; importance of Spain to, 275; need Spanish supplies, 276; and German interned merchantmen, 286; and German submarines in Spain, 281-4; oppose paper embargo on Spain, 287,n.; collaborate in Spanish negotiations, 288; seek internment of submarines in Argentina, 331; and Argentine grain agreement, 332-3; U. S. bunker control affects, 347; remove U. S. from blacklists, 357; blacklists of, in Europe, 366,n.; co-operate on blacklist, 368-70; and financial blockade, 372 ff.; establish more stringent blacklist than U. S., 377-8; convention of, re prizes, 389,n.; and A.B.C., 390; and safe-conduct system, 404-8; and Norway mine gap, 414, 417; and mail censorship, 422-5; and cable censorship, 433. *See also* Great Britain; France; Italy; Japan.

Alphonso XIII (King of Spain), regards self as leader of neutrals, 22; favors neutrality, 275; issues proclamation against submarines, 282; opposes U. S. coercion, 289; resents bunker pressure, 291.

American Expeditionary Forces, and Swiss supplies, 242, 263-4; and Spanish supplies, 276, 279, 289, 291-3, 297,n., 298-300.

American Revolution, and Dutch aid, 204,n.

American Textile Alliance, 75, 76.

Amsterdam, riots in, 200,n.

Anderson, Chandler P. (American jurist), on Spanish negotiations, 288,n.; on Chilean ship seizures, 335,n.; and alienage, 446,n.; dissents in Norway case, 449.

Angary, early suggestions of, by British, 54; applicable to Dutch ships, 208; Dutch deny validity of, 221; U. S. defends, 223; legal status of, 225-6; general U. S. position on, 473-4. *See also* Netherlands.

Argentina, preserves neutrality, 19; and U. S. invitation to sever relations, 26; and Luxburg affair, 145-6; neutral course of, 312; sells grain, 314; calls neutral conference, 315-7; and general U. S. relations, 331-4; and Allied grain agreement, 332-3; and *Bahia Blanca* controversy, 333-4; and U. S. armed merchantmen, 336; and requisitioned Dutch ships, 337; and U. S. bunker control, 347. *See also* Latin America.

Armed merchantmen, U. S. in Latin America, 336-7.

Asia, and U. S. mail censorship, 428.

Associated Powers, not joined by U. S., 3,n. *See also* Allies.

Azores, proposed censorship station on, 428,n.

B

B-23, German submarine in Spain, 282,n., 284.

Bahia Blanca, German steamer in Argentina, 333.

Bainbridge, U. S. warship, 397.

Balboa, U. S. denies British facilities at, 445.

Balfour, Arthur J. (British Foreign Secretary), and blacklist, 1-2; on Spanish trade, 277.

Balfour Mission, work of, 50-63; and British deference to U. S., 62-3; on Norway, 103; and Denmark, 168; and Netherlands, 198-9; and Swiss, 249; and Spain, 276-7; and bunker control, 341; urges blacklist, 357; and blockade, 385.

Banco Salvadoreño, on blacklist, 371.

Barcelona, and cotton problem, 272, 278.

Belgium, invasion of, and Dutch, 195,n.

Belgian relief, and neutral shipping, 81,n.; beneficiary of Norway grain deal, 109-10; and Swedish grain deal, 143-5; and Holland, 196; and Dutch grain negotiations, 200-2; and Dutch shipping, 206, 207, 211.

Belknap, Captain R. R. (U. S. Navy), lays mine barrage, 410,n.

Benson, Admiral W. S. (U. S. Navy), on closing mine barrage, 416.

Blacklist, early British overtures re, 1-2, 50, 51, 56-7; early U. S. policy re, 61; German, 207; U. S. refuses to be bound by Allied, 235; and Argentine coal, 331; and general problem re U. S., 349-79; categories of, 360-1; Allied, 366,n.; U. S. extends and relaxes, 368; general U. S. policy re, 376-9; and mail censorship, 429; and cable censorship, 434; and financial blockade, 485. *See also* Financial blockade.

Blockade (British), British seek U. S. co-operation in, 2,n., 50; U. S. protests against, 12; and navicerts, 42; tightened by U. S. entry, 55-6; and Sweden, 140; and bunker control, 339; and continuous voyage, 382,n.; nature of, 383; U. S. co-operates in, 385-92; strengthened by U. S. embargo, 391-2; general U. S. policy re, 478-9.

Blockade, financial. *See* Financial blockade.

Boeg, N. V. (Danish negotiator), on Danish conditions, 180,n.

Boers, and Dutch problems, 197,n.

Bolivia, responds to U. S. invitation to sever relations, 25-6; pro-Ally, 310. *See also* Latin America.

Bonillas, Ignatio Y. (Mexican ambassador), on Mexican neutrality, 314,n.

Borel, Eugène (Swiss arbitrator), arbitrates Swedish claims, 452-3.

Boston Swiss Society, opposes embargo, 245,n.

Brazil, declares war, 19, 28; favors U. S. call to sever relations, 25; and neutral conference, 316; and mandatory routing, 401. *See also* Latin America.

Brun, Constantin (Danish minister), on conditions in Denmark, 180; and Danish negotiations, 183-4; signs agreement, 187.

Bryan, William Jennings (U. S. Secretary of State), on neutral rights, 382-3,n.; on long-range blockade, 383; on contraband, 394,n.; and mining open seas, 408-9.

Bryn, H. H. (Norwegian minister), and embargo, 105-6; urges release of grain, 109.

Bullitt, William C., on Dutch, 231,n.

Bunkers, early British overtures re U. S. use of, 52, 54, 56; early U. S. policy re, 60-1; and U. S. differences with Sweden, 155,n.; War Trade Board and Spain, 290-1; pressure threatened re Spain, 295; and suggested pressure on Spain, 301-2; and British policy before 1917, 339-41; general U. S. relations with, 339-49, 469-70; and routing of neutrals, 398-9,n.; and mail censorship, 428, 430-1; and Norway, 447; and Spain, 486.

Bureau of Enemy Trade, and blacklist, 357.

Burleson, A. S. (Postmaster General), opposes postal censorship, 424-5.

INDEX 507

C

Cable censorship, of financial cables, 373; and U. S., 431-5; general position of U. S. on, 466, 471.
Camp Meade, and alienage, 446,n.
Canada, U. S. embargo on (1861), 76,n.
Canal Zone, bunker control at, 344; immunity of, 402-3; U. S. policy re, 455-6, 485.
Canary Islands, submarine activity near, 287.
Catalonia, cotton supply of, 278,n.
Catt, Mrs. Carrie Chapman, and Denmark's plight, 180.
Cecil, Lord Robert, on blockade, 42-3; delays Norway agreement, 125; favors Dutch requisitioning, 210.
Censorship, cable. *See* Cable censorship.
Censorship, postal. *See* Mail censorship.
Censorship, wireless. *See* Wireless censorship.
Censorship Board, 428.
Central Powers, defined, 3,n. *See also* Germany.
Chadbourne, Thomas L. (Legal Adviser, War Trade Board), on War Trade Board, 92,n.; and Dutch requisitioning, 209,n.
Chadbourne, W. A. (War Trade Board representative in Spain), urges denunciation of pact, 294; on tonnage negotiations with Spain, 296.
Chief Cable Censor, 433.
Chile, and U. S. call to sever relations, 26; remains neutral, 311-2; and raw materials, 314; and neutral conference, 316; seizes German ships, 334-5; and U. S. armed merchantmen, 336; and requisitioned Dutch ships, 337; and U. S. bunker control, 344,n.; and U. S. blacklist, 359,n. *See also* Latin America.
China, enters war, 18; and U. S. call to sever relations, 23-5; breaks with Germany, 25; and Allied pressure to enter war, 32; and U. S. blacklist, 353,n.
Christmas cargoes, 97-8.
Cleveland, Grover (U. S. President), and Venezuela, 311.
Colombia, and U. S. call to sever relations, 26; remains neutral, 311; bitter against U. S., 311,n.; rebuffs neutral conference, 316. *See also* Latin America.
Comisión Reguladora, and Yucatán sisal, 327-9.
Commission Internationale de Contingents, 391,n.

Committee on Public Information, work of, 461-5; and Mexico, 313,n. *See also* Creel, George.
Communists, in Holland, 233,n.
Confidential Cloaks List, 360-1.
Confidential Consignors' List, 361,n.
Confidential Enemy Trading List, 360.
Confidential Suspect List, 360. *See also* Blacklist.
Conger, S. B. (Foreign Adviser of War Trade Board), on effect of embargo, 4,n.; and strictness of Board, 101.
Congress (U. S.), fails to investigate War Trade Board, 6,n.; and establishment of export control, 64-9; passing Trading with Enemy Act, 95; retaliates against British blacklist, 353; amends Selective Service Act, 443-4; and *Zeelandia* case, 454; and Canal Zone, 456-7,n.
Continuous voyage, and Declaration of London, 381; and Britain, 382; U. S. uses against South, 382; and U. S. in 1917-18, 396-7; general U. S. position on, 472.
Contraband, and Declaration of London, 380-1; British extensions of, 382; U. S. position on, 392-6, 419, 472; and mails, 422.
Contraband Committee, 391,n.
Control stations, U. S. declines to be bound by, 236.
Costa Rica, enters war, 29,n. *See* Latin America.
Cotton, trade in, with neutrals, 35. *See also* Spain.
C.R.B. *See* Belgian Relief.
Creel, George (Chairman, Committee on Public Information), and Latin American bitterness, 311,n.; and U. S. propaganda, 461, 463, 465.
Crosby, Oscar T. (Assistant Secretary of the Treasury), and financial blockade, 374.
Cuba, declares war, 18, 27; favors U. S. call to sever relations, 25; U. S. pressure on, to enter war, 27,n.; U. S. bunker control in, 343,n.; and U. S. mail censorship, 429-30. *See also* Latin America.
Cummins, Albert B. (U. S. Senator), and exports control, 67,n.
Curaçao, U. S. bunker control at, 343.

D

Danger zone, early U. S. policy re service in, 61; Swedish tonnage chartered for, 154; and Danish tonnage, 179, 182-4, 190, 191; Dutch refuse

to send ships into, 202; U. S. policy re forcing ships into, 342, 348, 476-7.
Daniels, Josephus (Secretary of the Navy), on Mexican rights, 325, 326,n.; on U. S. navy and blockade, 388; proposes prize procedure, 389.
Danish Chamber of Commerce, and U. S. agreement, 187.
Danish Special Shipping Committee, 187.
Davis, Norman H. (U. S. Treasury Department agent), in Spain, 297.
Declaration of London, U. S. departs from, 396-7; and U. S. Navy instructions, 387; provisions of, 380-1; and contraband, 473,n.
Denmark, declines U. S. call to sever relations, 21-2; sells food to Germany, 36; trade with Allies, 44,n.; and possible invasion, 83; and Christmas cargoes, 98,n.; general relations with U. S., 165-93; and German aggression, 165-6; general position of, 165-9; trade with Germany, 166; employment of tonnage, 166-7; German threat to, 168; and Balfour Commission, 168-9; criticism of, in U. S., 169-70; resents U. S. criticism, 170-1; opens negotiations with U. S., 170-1; and U. S. detentions of ships, 171; continued negotiations with U. S., 173-5; petroleum shortage in, 174-5; British hold up negotiations with, 176-7; various proposals of, 178-82; and tonnage problem, 179, 182-5; and Christmas cargoes, 179-80; alleged suffering in, 180-1; critical stage in U. S. negotiations, 182-5; capitulates on danger zone, 184; concludes negotiations with U. S., 185-7; German threats to, 185-6; trade agreement with Germany, 186; and final U. S. agreement with, 187-90; general observations on agreement with, 191-3; press comments on agreement with, 192; and trade with Germany, 194-5; and U. S. bunker control, 346, 348; and U. S. blacklist, 377,n.; favors safe-conducts, 404,n.; protests U. S. soliciting of information, 458-9; legislates against propaganda, 460; U. S. conceals ship program from, 465,n. See also Neutrals.
Department of State, and neutral rights, 1-2; publication policy, 6-7; research policy, 6-7; and U. S. call to sever relations, 20-7; recognizes British agreements in U. S., 76; and War Trade Board, 92-3; and Luxburg telegrams, 146; and mail-pouch dispute, 147-8; and shift of Swedish negotiations, 152; and proposed seizure of Danish tonnage, 184; on angary, 209; defends Dutch ship seizures, 223-4; opposes Stovall, 247,n.; severity with Spain, 279; refuses to make joint protest to Spain, 281-2; and German sinkings of Spanish ships, 283; protests escape of U 293; joint action on Spanish unneutrality, 284, 286-7; and Spanish tonnage, 289; blocks neutral conference, 316; and Mexican munitions, 318,n.; and twenty-four hour rule, 320-1; and three-ship rule, 322; defends hovering, 323; defers to Mexico, 326; and Yucatán, 329; and the Bahia Blanca, 333-4; protests British bunkers, 340; policy re blacklist, 361-2, 371; and financial blockade, 373-5; protests British blacklist, 384; and blockade, 388; on contraband, 393-6; vetoes mandatory routing, 401-3; on safe-conducts, 405-6; and British mined areas, 408-9; protests submarine zone, 409; and closing Norwegian mine gap, 413-4; and mail censorship, 427,n., 430; and cable censorship, 431-2; and alienage, 439,n., 445-6, 446,n.; plans to abrogate Norwegian and Swedish treaties, 447; and Norway arbitration, 450; and U. S. propaganda, 461-3; and cross-purposes, 484,n. See also United States; War Trade Board; Lansing; Polk; Woolsey.
Detentions, U. S. policy re maritime, 483-4.
Dominican Republic. See Santo Domingo.
Dulles, John Foster (Assistant to War Trade Board Chairman), goes to Panama, 27,n.; on angary, 223-4,n.; and War Trade Board, 484; on neutral coercion, 491,n.
Dutch. See Netherlands.

E

Ecuador, and U. S. call to sever relations, 26; pro-Ally, 309; and neutral conference, 315,n. See Latin America.
Embargo, and U. S. public opinion, 72; U. S. attitude re as neutral, 74 legality of, 74-7; bolsters blockade, 85, 391; discussions over relaxation

INDEX

of, 99-101; Allied opposition to stringent, 101; forces Norway agreement, 132; and Swedish agreement, 161-2, 164; effect of, in Denmark, 181-2; relaxation on nonessentials to Denmark, 182,n.; clubs Denmark into agreement, 192-3; Dutch complain against, 229; reduces Dutch exports, 237; and U. S. opinion re Swiss, 245,n.; causes alarm in Switzerland, 247-8; forces Swiss to sign agreement, 249,n.; on Mexico, 318; general U. S. policy re, 475; of U. S. more rigid than British, 490.

Emergency Fleet Corporation, and requisitioned ships, 336.

Enemy trading list. *See* Blacklist.

England. *See* Great Britain.

Ensenada (Mexico), incident at, 324.

Entanglements, U. S. policy against, 159-60, 236.

Espionage Act, debate on, in Congress, 64-9.

Exports Administrative Board, created, 88-9; establishes restrictions, 90; replaced by War Trade Board, 91.

Exports control, early U. S. policy re, 59; debated by Congress, 64-9; effects of first proclamation, 72-3; second proclamation issued, 89-90; and Hoover's recommendations re Denmark, 171-3. *See also* Exports Council; Exports Administrative Board; War Trade Board; Embargo.

Exports Council, created, 69-70; outlines policy to neutrals, 77-8; new one created, 89.

F

Far East, and censorship, 433.

Federal Reserve System, and financial blockade, 373.

Financial blockade, British seek U. S. co-operation re, 51, 372-6; general U. S. policy re, 485.

Finland, and detention of ships, 16,n.

Food Administration, and sisal problem, 327-30, 486.

France, and Liberia's declaration of war, 32; supplements Balfour Commission, 63,n.; and U. S. delays, 81; praises U. S. embargo, 84-5; and Christmas cargoes, 97; and Swedish negotiations, 152; and coal shortage, 153; and proposed requisitioning of Swedish tonnage, 156; shifts onus to U. S., 175; and Swiss trade, 240,n.; and U. S. submarine at Las Palmas, 287,n.; and Spanish financial agreement, 294; and U. S. blacklist re Sweden, 366; and blacklist, 367; and Swiss censorship, 424; urges mail censorship, 424; plan for postwar trade control, 486. *See* Allies.

Freedom of the Seas, U. S. problems re, 380-420.

Freiland (Denmark), suffering in, 180.

Fullam, Admiral William F. (U. S. Navy), on Mexican rights, 322 3,n., 325.

Fuller, Paul, Jr. (of War Trade Board), on blacklist, 354, 359,n., 360,n., 362-3,n., 365,n., 368-9,n.

G

Garrett, John W. (U. S. minister in Holland), opposes requisitioning, 211; on Dutch reaction to requisitioning, 214; on brutality of requisitioning, 217.

Germany, morale hurt by neutral restrictions, 4,n.; emasculates submarines, 12; relies on U. S. food, 36; neutral trade with, 43-4; condemns embargo, 73-4; possible invasion of neutrals, 83; trade with neutrals essential, 84; increases trade following embargo, 99; propaganda in neutrals, 100, 440; trade with Norway, 102; sinks Norway ships, 103, 105; pressure on Norway, 113; agreement with Norway, 113,n.; influence in Norway, 113-4; threatens to delay Norway agreement, 125; threatens Norway, 131; attacks Swedish shipping, 137; and Swedish iron ore, 137-8, 149-51, 156,n.; ties with Sweden, 139; and Luxburg affair, 145-6; threats re *modus vivendi*, 153; threatens Sweden, 156,n.; and Swedish-Allied iron-ore deal, 157-8; Sweden restricts exports to, 161; reprisals against Sweden, 162; propaganda in Sweden, 163, 463,n.; aggressions on Denmark, 165-6; trade with Denmark, 166; threats to Denmark, 168, 185-6; loss of Danish exports, 182; and trade agreement with Denmark, 186; and Netherlands trade, 194-5; possible attack on Denmark, 196; trade negotiations with Dutch, 203; relaxes demands on Dutch, 205; opposes *modus vivendi* with Dutch, 207; and Dutch requisitioning, 219-20; and transport dispute with Dutch, 227; threatens Dutch, 228; and Swiss trade, 240-3; propaganda in Switzerland, 244; promises grain to Swiss, 263-4; sinks *Sardinero*, 265,n.; issues Swiss safe-conducts, 265, 268; and Swiss grain crisis, 267; and tonnage in Spain, 269; and Spanish wireless, 272,n.; U-boats in Spain, 273; attacks Spanish ships, 273, 283, 300; influence in Spain, 273-4; submarines in Spain, 275, 278, 281-4; merchantmen in Spain, 286-7; pressure on Spain, 294; and crisis with Spain, 303; influence in Latin America, 305, 425; influence in Chile, 311; propaganda in Mexico, 313, 317, 325-6, 429; seeks submarine bases in Mexico, 318,n.; and twenty-four hour rule, 321; and blacklist, 351, 368; proclaims submarine blockade, 383; decrees food control, 393; extends contraband, 395; and safe-conducts, 404; and Allied mine laying, 408; and North Sea mine barrage, 414-5; protests wireless censorship, 432,n.; and U. S. censorship, 434,n.

Great Britain, seeks U. S. support re neutrals, 1-2; and Liberia, 31-2; and neutral blockade, 42; and early U. S. co-ordination, 49-63; and early non-exportation agreements with U. S., 75-6; and U. S. embargo delay, 78-82, 489-90; and Norway purchases, 80; concern over rationing agreements, 82,n., 86-8; on forcing neutrals into enemy arms, 82-4; praises U. S. embargo, 84-5; desires strict embargo, 85; on sharing odium with U. S., 88; and U. S. embargo, 90,n.; and Christmas cargoes, 97-8; for embargo relaxation, 99-101; trade friction with U. S., 101; trade with Norway, 103; and treatment of Norway, 117,n.; interrupts Norway agreement, 125; and Norwegian tonnage, 128; denies Swedes bunkers, 137,n.; and Swedish iron ore, 140,n., 149-51; suggests courses re Sweden, 142-3; and Swedish grain deal, 144-5; and Swedish mail pouches, 145-9; and Luxburg affair, 146; and mails (1916), 148; and shift of Swedish negotiations, 152-5; opposes Swedish requisitioning, 157; trade with Denmark, 168-9; and Danish negotiations, 175-7, 185,n.; trade with Dutch, 196; recommendations re Dutch, 198-9; and Dutch transit, 202; seizes Dutch ships, 208,n.; seeks requisitioning of Dutch ships, 208; opposes generous Netherlands policy, 213,n.; demands Dutch ships for war zone, 220-1; un-co-operative on requisitioning, 222,n.; and Dutch grain, 227,n.; and Dutch convoy dispute, 229; displeases U. S. in Dutch negotiations, 230, 233, 237; seeks reopening of Dutch negotiations, 232; recommendations re Swiss, 248-9; and Italian fruit, 252; and Swiss grain, 260-4; and Spanish trade, 277; and German U-boats in Spain, 281-2; seeks U. S. support in Spain, 283-4; opposes Spanish agreement, 289-90,n.; and Argentine friction, 333-4; and Chile, 334; and bunkers, 339-41; and blacklist, 350-7, 368-9, 372,n., 377; proposes financial blockade, 372-6; opposes Declaration of London, 380; extends contraband lists, 382; begins blockade, 383; abandons letters of assurance, 385-6; and prizes, 386; and U. S. co-operation in blockade, 385-92; and contraband extension, 393-5, 396,n.; and U. S. visit of neutral ships, 398; and Halifax call, 399-401; instructs U. S. in search, 400; and mandatory routing, 401-3; establishes mined area, 408; and mine barrage, 410-1, 413-7; and mail censorship, 421-4, 426,n., 427; and cable censorship, 431-5; and U. S. requisition of ships, 447; denied Canal Zone facilities, 455-6; U. S. claims against, 479-81; proposes to control neutral prices, 486; status different from U. S., 490-1. *See also* Allies; Balfour Commission.

Greece, status of, 18; declines U. S. invitation to sever relations, 22.

Gregory, Thomas W. (U. S. Attorney General), on financial blockade, 374.

Grey, Sir Edward (British Foreign Secretary), and U. S. blacklist protest, 355-6; on U. S. and blockade, 392,n.

Guam, protests wireless censorship, 432.

Guatemala, favors U. S. call to sever relations, 25; declares war, 28-9. *See* Latin America.

H

Hackworth, Green H., on claims, 481,n.
Hague Convention (1907), on neutral passage, 416,n.; and Mexican rights, 320-2; and mails, 423, 427; and alienage, 438.

INDEX

Hague Court, and Norwegian claims, 448-50.
Haiti, and U. S. call to sever relations, 26; encouraged to enter war, 30. *See* Latin America.
Halifax, call at eliminated, 399-403.
Hannevig, Christoffer, and claims against U. S., 448,n.
Harding, W. P G. (of Federal Reserve Board), and financial blockade, 373.
Hart, Professor Albert B., on U. S. inconsistency, 41.
Hellner, Justice (Swedish Foreign Minister), 151.
Hendrick, Burton J., on U. S. inconsistency, 1, 489, 490.
Herron, George D. (U. S. writer), appeals to Wilson, 248, 250-1; and Swiss grain crisis, 267.
Holland. *See* Netherlands.
Honduras, and U. S. call to sever relations, 26; U. S. encourages to enter war, 30-1; warned by U. S. against neutral conference, 316-7. *See* Latin America.
Hoover, Herbert C. (U. S. Food Administrator), favors strictness with neutrals, 38-9; on feedstuffs shortage, 72,n.; and Norway grain deal, 109-10; and Swedish grain deal, 143-4; and drastic policy re Denmark, 171-3; drops Dutch grain deal, 200-1; opposes fruit deal with Italy, 252; and Swiss grain needs, 253; grants grain to Swiss, 255; treats Swiss leniently, 271,n.; and sisal problem, 328-9; recommends more marines for Santo Domingo, 329,n.; suggests financial pressure on Mexico, 330,n.; proposes Argentine grain scheme, 332; and cable censorship, 434,n.
House, Colonel Edward M., in London, 210, 212,n.
House of Representatives. *See* Congress.
Hovering, U. S., off Mexico, 323; general U. S. position on, 471.
Hughes, Charles E. (U. S. Secretary of State), dissents on Norway award, 449-50.
Hurley, Edward N. (Chairman, U. S. Shipping Board), on Dutch requisitioning, 209,n.; and Dutch crews, 214,n.; and Swiss trade, 240,n.
Hyphenates, 40.

I

Iceland, and Allied agreement with, 189,n.
Ihlen, Nils C. (Norwegian Foreign Minister), allegedly pro-German, 114; thanks U. S. for agreement, 133.
Import control, of U. S., 95-6.
Insurance, embargo on marine, 52.
Interallied Trade Committees, 391.
International law, violations of, 14-5; and U. S. embargo, 85; and Declaration of London, 380-1; and U. S. mail censorship, 431; and *Zeelandia*, 454-5; U. S. violations of, 467, 490.
Irigoyen, Hipólito (Argentine president), preserves neutrality, 19, 312; explains neutral conference, 315; and Latin American leadership, 317.
Iron ore. *See* Sweden.
Iroquois (U. S. warship), in Mexico, 324.
Irwin, William H. (of Committee on Public Information), on German propaganda in Spain, 275,n.; on honest propaganda, 464, 465,n.
Italy, and Swedish negotiations, 152; coal shortage, 153; and proposed Swedish requisitioning, 156; and silk trade, 251; and citrus fruit trade, 252; collapse of, 253-4; and contraband, 393,n. *See* Allies.

J

Japan, aggression in China, 23; and U. S. bunker control, 347; and blacklist, 369. *See* Allies.
Joint Subcommittee on Export Licenses, 55-7.
Jones, Thomas D. (of War Trade Board), and Norway negotiations, 115-9; and Danish negotiations, 177-8; and blacklist, 362,n.
Jones, Wesley L. (U. S. Senator), and alienage, 444.
Jusserand, J. J. (French ambassador), urges export control, 81; and Swiss trade, 240,n.

K

Kahn, Rep. Julius, on alienage, 443,n.
Kellogg-Briand Pact, 8.
Ketchikan, alienage case at, 445.
Key West, and bunker control, 344,n.
Kim, detained Norwegian ship, 124-5,n.
King, William H. (U. S. Senator), and neutral exports, 64.
Knox, Capt. Dudley W. (U. S. Navy), on Latin American ports, 29,n.; on naval records, 494; on U. S. blockade, 389-90,n.
Knox, Philander C. (U. S. Senator), on coercive embargo, 67.

INDEX

Kronprins Gustaf Adolf, detained Swedish ship, 451-3.

L

La Follette, Robert M. (U. S. Senator), opposes embargo, 67-8.

Lagercrantz, Herman, heads Swedish mission, 142-3.

La Guaira, U. S. bunkers at, 343.

Langhorne, Marshall (U. S. chargé), and Dutch reaction to requisitioning, 220,n.

Lansing, Robert, on U. S. championing of neutrals, 12; avoids inconsistencies, 13-4; appeals to sever relations, 20-7; urges Panama to enter war, 27; urges Guatemala to enter war, 28; wishes Honduras to enter war, 28,n.; wishes to checkmate Mexico, 28,n.; encourages Liberia to enter war, 31-2; and China's entry, 32; on neutral policy, 91, 93-4; and Norway's neutrality, 126; on onus for Norway agreement, 135; and Swedish grain deal, 144; and mail pouches, 147; opposes Swedish requisitioning, 156-7; and Currness out of Swedish agreement, 163; on requisitioning of Dutch shipping, 209-11; replies to Dutch protests, 222-4; and Dutch grain cargoes, 227; assurances on requisitioning, 227-8; displeased with Dutch, 229,n.; on Swiss policy, 246,n.; on Swiss needs, 250; declaration re Swiss neutrality, 254-5; requests grain for Swiss, 255; on Swiss relief, 256,n.; on grain deliveries to Swiss, 260; on Swiss grain crisis, 264; on Spanish coal trade, 277-8; on Spanish embargo, 280; on Spanish cotton, 280; on Spanish unneutrality, 285,n.; opposes U. S. submarine at Las Palmas, 287-8,n.; favors relaxing Spanish embargo, 290; on Spanish war crisis, 302-3; on Mexican neutrality, 314; blocks neutral conference, 316; on twenty-four hour rule, 320-1; on Mexican rights, 324,n.; on Mexican protests, 325; on U. S. rights in Mexico, 326,n.; opposes Allied conference in Argentina, 331; on *Bahia Blanca*, 333; on British bunker control, 340-1,n.; on British blacklist, 353, 355,n.; and financial blockade, 373,n., 374; protests British blockade, 484; inquires re prizes, 389,n.; on British contraband, 395; on British mining, 409; on closing Norway gap, 413-4; and mine barrage, 416; protests re mail censorship, 422-3; favors mail censorship, 425; and cable censorship, 434,n.; on alienage, 439, 441, 443; and Swedish and Norwegian treaties, 447; on U. S. illegal course, 489,n. *See* Department of State.

Larsen, Somner (Swedish merchant), and cable censorship, 434,n.

Las Palmas, German submarines near, 287,n.

Latin America, status of, 18-9; response to U. S. call to sever relations, 25-7; and U. S. nonrecognition policy, 61,n.; general relationship to war, 305-38; sympathies of, 305, 308; groupings in, 306-10; relative importance of, 314-5; moves toward neutral conference, 315-7; and U. S. armed merchantmen, 336; and Dutch requisitioned ships, 337; summary of relations with U. S., 337-8; and U. S. blacklist, 358, 363 ff., 370-2; and British blacklist, 363; German propaganda in, 425; and mail censorship, 425, 428; and U. S. postal censorship, 428; and cable censorship, 433, 434.

League of Nations, and universal peace, 8.

Legge, Alexander (of War Industries Board), and sisal problem, 327.

Letters of assurance. *See* Navicerts.

Liberia, accepts U. S. call to sever relations, 23; encouraged by U. S. to enter war, 31-2.

Licenses. *See* Exports Control.

Lodge, Henry Cabot (U. S. Senator), and alienage amendment, 444.

London Conference (1909), 380.

Loudon, John (Dutch Foreign Minister), on requisitioning, 216.

Luxburg, Count Karl von (German minister in Argentina), 146.

Luxemburg, status as neutral, 16.

M

McCormick, Vance C. (Chairman, War Trade Board), on nonpublicity of Board, 6,n.; heads Board, 91-2; on Board's work, 92,n.; and Norway negotiations, 116-9; on delayed Denmark negotiations, 177; signs Danish agreement, 187; on House Mission, 205, 212,n.; on Wilson's reluctance to requisition Dutch

INDEX 513

ships, 212,n.; on Swiss negotiations, 253; signs Swiss agreement, 256; on Wilson's opposition to blacklist, 358; on Wilson's dislike of censorship, 425,n.; favors continued censorship, 426; on Wilson's idealism, 487,n.

McFadden, George (War Trade Board representative), on Swiss neutrality, 245-6,n.; on Spanish sentiment, 274,n.

Mail censorship, and controversy with British (1916), 148; and U. S. (1916-18), 421-31; U. S. position on, 466, 470.

Mandatory routing. *See* Routing, mandatory.

Maracaibo, U. S. bunker control at, 343.

Mazatlán, U. S. hovers off, 323.

Merchant marine, of world, 104.

Merchants' Guild of Copenhagen, 187.

Mexico, unfriendly to U. S., 19; U. S. tries to checkmate, 28,n.; sends editors to U. S., 313,n., 461,n.; hostility to U. S., 313-4; sells oil, 314; sends delegates to conference, 317; minor friction with U. S., 318; trouble over U. S. ships, 319-26; and twenty-four hour rule, 319-22; and U. S. violations of three-ship rule, 322; protests hovering, 323; U. S. ships violate rights, 324-5; summary of grievances against U. S., 325-6; and sisal problem, 326-30; German propaganda in, 429; and Cuban mail censorship, 430; and alienage, 444,n.; and U. S. propaganda in, 461; and general problem of U. S. violation of rights, 473, 483. *See* Latin America.

Milner, Lord Alfred M. (of British War Cabinet), on blockade, 42.

Mine barrage. *See* North Sea mine barrage.

Mines, general U. S. position on, 408-12, 472; U. S. policy on, re Norway, 485. *See* North Sea mine barrage.

Mock, Dr. James R. (of National Archives), on propaganda in Switzerland, 464,n.; on records of Committee on Public Information, 494.

Modus vivendi. See Sweden; Netherlands.

Morris, Ira N. (U. S. minister in Sweden), and British censorship of Sweden, 147,n.; and Swedish situation, 151; opposes requisitioning, 156; on blacklist, 379; on German propaganda in Sweden, 463,n.

Munro, Dana G., on Latin American neutrality, 312-3,n.

N

Nansen, Dr. Fridtjof (Norwegian negotiator), arrives in U. S., 107-8; makes grain agreement, 109-10; seriously begins negotiations, 119; independent attitude, 127; signs agreement, 127; and political factors, 131,n.; praised for agreement, 132,n. *See* Nansen Commission.

Nansen Commission, reaches U. S., 107-8; concessions of, 121-2; publishes proposals, 123-4. *See* Nansen, Dr. Fridtjof.

Navicerts, issued in U. S., 42; British delay, 81; licenses substituted for, 385-6.

Navy Department (U. S.), concern over raiders, 318; and twenty-four hour rule, 320; and visiting Mexican ships, 324-5; defers to Mexico, 326; and British blockade, 386-9; and Halifax search, 400; pushes mine barrage, 410; seeks to close mine gap, 415-6; exercises cable censorship, 433; solicits information from neutrals, 457-8; general policy re Mexico, 473.

Netherlands, declines Wilson's invitation to sever relations, 22; purchases U. S. grain, 34; sells food to Germany, 36; coal problem, 39; trade with England, 44,n.; humanitarian work, 44; and Belgian relief, 48; alarmed by embargo, 48-9; ships detained, 72-3; general position of, 194-8; value of tonnage, 197-8; and Balfour Commission, 198-9; tonnage in U. S., 200-1; commission to U. S., 210; sand-and-gravel dispute, 202; coal famine, 203; slaughters cattle, 204; negotiations transferred to London, 205; concludes *modus vivendi*, 206; *modus vivendi* breaks down, 207; beginnings of requisitioning talk, 208-10; disturbed by requisitioning rumors, 209-10; and U. S. desire to requisition, 210-2; tonnage seized, 212; outraged by seizure, 214-20; compensation for seizure, 214,n.; and U. S. reaction to seizure, 215,n.; ships in German employ, 217; benefited by seizure, 218-9; sincere in protesting seizure, 219-20; official protests against seizure, 220-2; protests to British, 222,n.; U. S. replies to protests, 222-4; legality of seizure, 224-6; post-requisitioning negotiations,

226-31; and difficulties with Germany, 227-9; and U. S. grain, 228; and British convoy dispute, 229-30; cabinet organized, 231; U. S. relaxes embargo on colonies, 231; concluding negotiations with, 231-3; Communists in, 233; summary of agreement with, 234-6; observations on agreement, 236-8; and U. S. armed merchantmen, 336; requisitioned ships in Latin America, 337; and U. S. bunker control, 346; U. S. seizes munitions, 451,n.; and *Zeelandia* case, 453-5; requisitioned ships released in Canal Zone, 456; and U. S. policy re angary, 473-4. *See* Netherlands East Indies; Netherlands Oversea Trust; Neutrals.

Netherlands East Indies, and Dutch embargo, 195-6; vulnerable to attack, 198; and blacklist, 371,n.

Netherlands Oversea Trust, function of, 230; U. S. agreement with, 234-5.

Neutrals, U. S. policy re shortens war, 3-4; U. S. treatment and press, 5; to be abolished by League, 8; U. S. champions while neutral, 10-3; condemn U. S. abandonment of, 14; listed, 15-9; area and population of Europeans, 16; trade with Central Powers, 34-5; purchase U. S. grain, 34-5; transship products to Germany, 35-6; and normal trade with Germany, 39-40; and U. S. hyphenates, 40; and U. S. censure, 41-2; defense of position, 42-9; dislocation of food supplies, 44-5; charge U. S. with inconsistency, 45-7; and U. S. entrance into war, 47; defensive weapons of, against embargo, 48; and Congressional action, 64-9; embargoed, 73; U. S. outlines policy re, 77-8, 93-4; division of opinion in, 82-3,n.; allegedly forced into enemy arms, 82-4; licenses to withheld, 90; fail to provide information, 94; effect of U. S. import control on, 96; decline of exports to Germany, 96-7; and Christmas cargoes, 97; relaxation of embargo on, 99-101; and mandatory routing, 398-9, 403; U. S. solicits information from, 457-9; and U. S. propaganda, 459-65; U. S. pressure to forsake neutrality, 476; general complaints against U. S., 491. *See also names of neutral countries.*

New York City, and bunker control, 344,n.

Nicaragua, and U. S. call to sever relations, 26; declares war, 29. *See* Latin America.

Nonrecognition policy, and export control, 61,n.

North Sea mine barrage, U. S. lays, 410-2; U. S. policy re, 420.

Northern mine barrage. *See* North Sea mine barrage.

Northern neutrals, defined, 16. *See* Neutrals.

Norway, declines U. S. call to sever relations, 21-2; sells products to Germany, 36, 39-40; alarm over embargo, 63,n., 105-7; forces British purchases, 80; general position of, 102-5; merchant marine, 103-5; sends Nansen Commission, 107-8; makes grain agreement, 108-10; delays negotiations, 111-4; Scandinavian program, 112; food situation, 112, 130-1; prosperity, 112; politics, 112-3, 114,n., 131; and German pressure, 113, 125, 131; agreement with Germany, 113,n.; German influence in, 113-4; U. S. delays negotiations with, 114-9; fails to provide information, 115; confusion in early U. S. policy re, 115-9; Wilson seeks leniency for, 115-9, 487,n.; discussion of complete exports stoppage, 115-9; demands of Associated Powers, 120-1; objectives in negotiations, 121; reaction to War Trade Board publicity, 122; final stages of negotiations with, 124-7; reaffirms neutrality, 125-6; U. S. agreement signed, 127; terms of agreement, 127-30; tonnage arrangements with, 128,n.; general observations on agreement, 130-5; and blacklist, 132,n., 377,n.; reaction to agreement, 133; U. S. drives hard bargain, 133-5; agreement with compared with Swedish, 164; and U. S. bunker control, 344, 346; invites U. S. to protest mined areas, 408; and closing of mine gap, 412-9; and alienage, 438, 440,n., 444; and U. S. seizure of ships, 447-50, 466-7; protests seizure of goods, 451,n. *See* Neutrals.

O

Orders in Council. *See* Great Britain.

P

Pacific, Swedish motorship, 451.
Page, W. H. (U. S. ambassador in

Index

London), and Swedish grain deal, 144.

Panama, declares war, 18, 27; response to U. S. call to sever relations, 25; U. S. pressure on, to enter war, 27-8,n.; declares war on Austria, 28,n.; U. S. warns against entering conference, 316; and U. S. mail censorship, 429; and U. S. policy re Canal Zone, 455-7. See Latin America.

Panama Canal. See Canal Zone.

Paraguay, and U. S. call to sever relations, 26; remains neutral, 311; and neutral conference, 315,n.; U. S. opposes participation in conference, 316. See Latin America.

Parcel post. See Mail censorship.

Percy, Lord Eustace (of Balfour Commission), and U. S. delays, 79-81; and Danish embargo, 174,n.; on Allied shifting of odium to U. S., 175-6; on embargo, 478,n.

Permanent Court of Arbitration at The Hague, and Norwegian claims, 448-50.

Pershing, General John J., and Swiss supplies, 242,n.; on Swiss grain crisis, 263,n.; on Spain succoring Germany, 275,n.; on Spain as an ally, 301,n.

Persia, and U. S. blacklist policy, 366.

Peru, and U. S. call to sever relations, 26; pro-Ally, 309; seizes German ships, 336; and U. S. bunker control, 344,n. See Latin America.

Phenix, Spencer (of U. S. State Department), and British claims, 480-1.

Phifer, T. M., on Halifax call, 403-4,n.

Philips, August (Dutch minister in U. S.), and requisitioning, 212,n.

Phillips, William (Assistant Secretary of State), on Swiss grain shipments, 266-7; on prizes, 389.

Polk, Frank L. (Counselor for State Department), on violations of neutral rights, 1-2; encourages Haiti to enter war, 30; and Woolsey memorandum, 58,n.; on U. S. coercive policy, 67,n.; questions British on practices, 86-7; on effectiveness of embargo, 90,n.; on War Trade Board, 93,n.; and Norway negotiations, 116,n.; and Wilson's desires re Norway, 117,n.; and British censorship of Sweden, 147,n.; and U. S. policy re Denmark, 172-3; on Allied shifting of odium to U. S., 175,n.; and purposeful delay of Danish negotiations, 177; on Dutch requisitioning, 209,n., 219,n.; on Swiss grain crisis, 262; and Spanish unneutrality, 285; and hovering off Mexico, 323; objects to violent measures in Yucatán, 329; on Chilean ship seizures, 335,n.; protests British blacklist, 354-6; and financial blockade, 375; on British blockade, 385,n.; on Cuban censorship, 429-30; on alienage, 444,n.; on claims against Britain, 479,n.

Postal censorship. See Mail censorship.

Postwar trade, U. S. concern for, 48, 490; British concern for, 269, 490.

Pratt, E. E. (of Department of Commerce), on value of embargo, 72.

Prizes, U. S. refuses reciprocal exchange of, 386, 485; U. S. takes none, 388, 389,n.; general U. S. position on, 472.

Propaganda, German in neutrals, 100; Danish in U. S., 171; German in Denmark, 181; German in Holland, 205; U. S. in Holland, 231; German in Switzerland, 244, 256, 265; U. S. in Switzerland, 246, 268-9; German in Spain, 273-5; German in Mexico, 313, 317-8; U. S. in Mexico, 313-4; German in Latin America, 425; German in neutrals, 440; U. S. and neutrals, 459-65; German in Sweden, 463,n.; nature of U. S., 467; general U. S. policy re, 475-6.

Puerto Cabello, U. S. bunker control at, 343.

R

Rappard, W. E. (Swiss commissioner to U. S.), 243,n.

Rationing agreements, suggested by British, 55-6; British with neutrals, 82,n.; Allied attitude toward those extant, 86-7. See Norway; Sweden; Denmark; Netherlands; Switzerland; Spain.

Red Cross, in Switzerland, 258.

Redfield, William C. (Secretary of Commerce), and Norway, 117,n.; and financial blockade, 374.

Reinsch, Paul S. (U. S. minister in China), and pressure to sever relations, 21,n., 23-5.

Requa, Mark (of Food Administration), on sisal, 327-30.

Requisitioning, proposed for Swedish tonnage, 156-7; threatened re Denmark, 184-5; of unfinished shipping in U. S., 446-50, 474; of neutral materials in U. S., 474. *See also* Angary; Netherlands.

Reservists, U. S. refuses to remove from neutral ships, 397-8.

Riaño, Juan (Spanish ambassador in U. S.), on Franco-Spanish deal, 289; on Halifax search, 400,n.; on alienage, 439.

Roosevelt, Franklin D. (Assistant Secretary of the Navy), solicits information from neutrals, 457-8; favors mine barrage, 410,n.

Routing, mandatory, U. S. avoids, 236; of neutral ships, 398-9, 403; general U. S. policy re, 481-2.

Russia, and Swedish transit route, 138, 141-2, 161; Swedish fear of, 139; and shipments to Sweden, 149,n.; and Swedish negotiations in London, 152,n.

S

Safe-conducts, and Danish ships, 186; and Swiss ships, 265, 268; U. S. attitude on, 404-8, 419.

Salvador, offers U. S. harbors, 19; and U.S. call to sever relations, 26; benevolent neutrality of, 310-11; protests blacklist, 371. *See* Latin America.

San Francisco Park Commission, and Danish incident, 169.

San Juan (Puerto Rico), and bunker control, 344,n.

Santo Domingo, U. S. influence over, 19, 309; marines in, 329,n. *See* Latin America.

Sardinero, torpedoed, 265,n.

Scandinavia, protests to Germany, 21; division of opinion in, 82-3,n.; proposed program for, 112, 187; newsmen tour U. S., 461,n. *See* Norway; Sweden; Denmark.

Schmedeman, A. G. (U. S. minister in Norway), on Norway trade, 106; urges publicity, 122; on Norway's satisfaction with agreement, 133.

Schoenfeld, H. F. A. (U. S. chargé in Norway), and closing of mine gap, 413-5, 417.

Schulthess, Edmund (President, Swiss Confederation), on Swiss situation, 49, 247-8.

Selective Service Act, and alienage, 436, 439,n., 442-4.

Senate (U. S.), not consulted in agreements, 160; offense to avoided in agreements, 188; and treaty-making power, 257; returns Hannevig convention, 448,n.

Sheldon, L. P. (of War Trade Board), and Swedish agreement, 159.

Siam, enters war, 18; responds to U. S. call to sever relations, 23.

Sims, Admiral William S. (U. S. Navy), on Spanish situation, 275,n.

Sisal, problem of, in Yucatán, 326-30, 486.

Skinner, R. P. (U. S. consul general in London), and British co-ordination, 49-50.

Smith, Alfred G., and Spanish tonnage, 296-7.

Smith, Hoke (U. S. Senator), and export control, 65-6.

Société Suisse de Surveillance Economique, and Swiss imports, 241-2, 249, 257-9, 366.

South (U. S.), and cotton for Spain, 280; aroused by British contraband list, 393-4.

Southworth, W. B., on Swiss embargo, 245,n.

Spain, declines U. S. invitation to sever relations, 22; general position in war, 272-304; general conditions in, 272-6; foreign propaganda in, 273-5; neutral policy of, 22, 275; importance to Central Powers, 275-6; and British trade, 277; and pyrites problem, 279; and embargo, 279-81; opens negotiations with U. S., 280-1; and German submarines, 281-4; and unneutrality problem, 284-7; and financial agreement with France, 288-9, 294; negotiates commercial agreement, 288-9; resents bunker pressure, 291; context of agreement with U. S., 291-3; reacts favorably to agreement, 293; and nonexecution of U. S. agreement, 294-5; U. S. seeks tonnage agreement with, 295-7; financial agreement with U. S., 297-8; and A. E. F. supplies, 298-300; threatens reprisals against Germany, 300; and war crisis, 300-3; summary of U. S. relations with, 304; and U. S. bunker control, 343,n., 346,n., 347, 348; on U. S. blacklist, 367; protests Allied blacklists, 372; and mandatory routing of ships, 401-3; and U. S. protest on safe-conducts, 407,n.; and Allied censorship, 425; and mail censorship, 428, 431,n.; and alienage, 441,n.; and routing through Panama, 456; and miscellaneous problems re U. S., 486. *See* Neutrals.

INDEX 517

Spanish-American War, and Spanish feeling, 274.

Spring Rice, Sir Cecil (British ambassador in U. S.), and U. S. delays, 80-1; provides information, 87-8; on Wilson, 487.

Standard Oil Company of New Jersey, in Iceland, 189,n.

Stimson, F. J. (U. S. ambassador in Argentina), and Argentine conference, 331.

Stovall, Pleasant (U. S. minister in Switzerland), on Swiss neutrality, 243,n., 251,n.; and Wilson, 246-7,n.; on Swiss humanitarianism, 249-50; on grain crisis, 266, 268-9,n.

Subcommittee on Statistics and Sources of Information, 57.

Submarines. *See* Germany.

Sulzer, Hans (Swiss minister in U. S.), appeals to U. S., 266.

Supreme Court, on alienage, 437.

Supreme Economic Council, abolishes blacklists, 368.

Swartz, C., ministry of resigns in Sweden, 151.

Sweden, and U. S. invitation to sever relations, 20,n., 21; and iron trade with Germany, 36; influences Norway, 112; general status, 136-41; food problem, 136-7, 139-40; merchant marine, 137; iron-ore traffic, 137,140,n.; defensive weapons, 138; pro-German bias, 139; weakness of position, 139-41; alarm over U. S. embargo, 141; and Russian transit, 141-2,n.; sends mission to U. S., 142; British policy re, 142-3; negotiations in U. S. deadlocked, 143; and U. S. grain deal, 143-5; and Luxburg affair, 145-6; and mail-pouch dispute, 145-9; growing impasse in discussions, 149-53; and iron-ore discussions, 149-51; change of ministry, 151; shift of negotiations to London, 151-2; and negotiation of *modus vivendi*, 152, 154-5; and bunker dispute with U. S., 155,n.; and grain ships for Argentine, 155,n.; reopens negotiations, 155-7; seeks consent of Berlin to negotiations, 156; proposed seizure of tonnage of, 156-7; and Allied iron-ore deal, 157-8; concludes agreement, 159-60; text of agreement with, 160-2; reaction to agreement, 162; and carrying out of agreement, 162-3; more friendly pro-Ally feeling in, 163; strict neutrality of, 163; general observations on agreement, 164; food situation critical, 164; and U. S. bunker control, 348; favors safe-conducts, 404,n.; and U. S. protest against safe-conducts, 407,n.; and British mine fields, 408; and U. S. censorship, 435; and alienage, 437,n., 438,n., 439, 440,n.; and U. S. seizure of ships, 447; and detained ships, 451-3, 467; German propaganda in, 463,n. *See* Neutrals.

Switzerland, and U. S. call to sever relations, 22; disturbed by embargo, 41-2,n.; humanitarian work of, 44; announces mission to U. S., 49, 249; division of opinion in, 82,n.; continued U. S. shipments to, 90,n.; and general position in war, 239-71; an ideological battleground, 243-6; U. S. sympathy for, 244-6; importance to Allies, 245-6; U. S. propaganda in, 246; alarm over U. S. embargo, 247-8; signs commercial agreement with Allies, 249,n.; misrepresentation of, 250; and silk agreements, 251-2, 259,n.; negotiations shifted to Paris, 252-3; food problem, 253; fears German invasion, 243-4; and U. S. declaration re neutrality of, 255; agreement with U. S. signed, 256; context of agreement, 256-9; reaction to agreement, 259; and dispute over grain shipments, 260-4; and Allied lumber agreement, 263,n.; and U. S. grain shipments to, 264-8; and Spanish tonnage, 268-70; further delay in grain shipments, 270; agreement with extended, 270; U. S. lenient with, 270-1, 450-7; and safe-conduct ships, 345,n.; exempted from blacklist, 366; objects to blacklist, 371; and French mail censorship, 424; and alienage, 439, 440,n.; journalists tour U. S., 461. *See* Neutrals.

T

Taft, William H. (ex-President of U.S.), on angary, 225,n.

Tampico, U. S. ships at, 321-2.

Taylor, Dr. Alonzo E. (of War Trade Board), on work of Board, 93,n.; and conditions in Denmark, 180-1; on Denmark agreement, 190,n.; on Dutch negotiations, 202,n.; on House Mission, 205; on Dutch requisitioning, 217; on Swiss negotiations, 253; favors grain for Swiss, 255; on Swiss needs, 256,n.; on Swiss grain dispute, 261-2,n.; on Spanish situation, 275; on blockade, 482,n.; on U. S. agencies at cross-purposes, 484,n.

Three-ship rule, U. S. conflict with, in Mexico, 322, 473.

Tinoco government (of Costa Rica), U. S. relations with, 29,n.

Tonnage, British seeks U. S. control of, 52, 53-4; early U. S. policy on, 59, 60-1. *See* Netherlands; Sweden; Norway; Spain.

Townsend, Charles E. (U. S. Senator), on exports control, 66-7.

Trading with the Enemy Act, passed, 95; British, 353; authorizes blacklist, 358-9; and blacklist operations, 371; establishes censorship, 426.

Treasury Department (U. S.), and financial blockade, 374-5; solicits information from neutrals, 457-8.

Twenty-four hour rule, and Mexico, 319-22, 473.

U

U 293, German submarine in Spain, 283-4.

UC 52, German submarine in Spain, 281-2.

United States, leader of neutrals, 10-3; adopts belligerent viewpoint, 14; appeals to neutrals to sever relations, 20-7; exerts pressure on other countries to enter war, 29-33; public opinion demands embargo, 37-9; minority condemns inconsistency, 40-1; inconsistencies, 45-7; early attempts at co-ordination with British, 49-63; general policy at outset, 58-62; seeks to avoid inconsistencies, 63; attitude toward embargo while neutral, 74-7; slowness in co-operation with Allies, 78-82, 86-7; general policy re neutrals, 91, 93-4; food situation serious, 94; and Christmas cargoes, 97-8; favors strict embargo, 99-101; trade friction with British, 101; and negotiations with Norway, 102 ff.; and negotiations with Sweden, 136 ff.; and mail-pouch dispute, 145-9; protests Russian shipments to Sweden, 149,n.; forces Swedish ships to stop at ports, 155,n.; and negotiations with Denmark, 165 ff.; and negotiations with Holland, 194 ff.; and requisitioning of Dutch shipping, 209-14; and negotiations with Switzerland, 239 ff.; and negotiations with Spain, 272 ff.; and German submarines in Spain, 281-4; and relations with Latin America, 305 ff.; and bunkers, 339-49; and blacklists, 349-79; and blockade, 380-92; and contraband and continuous voyage, 392-7; and visit and search, 397-8; and mandatory routing, 398-403; and safe-conducts, 404-8; and mining seas, 408-12; and closing the Norwegian mine gap, 412-19; and postal censorship, 421-31; and cable censorship, 431-5; and drafting of aliens, 435-46; requisitions ships being built, 446-50; detains neutral ships, 451-5; and Panama Canal, 455-6; solicits information from neutrals, 457-9; engages in propaganda, 459-65; summary of policy re neutrals, 469-92. *See also* Department of State; War Trade Board; Wilson; Lansing; Polk; Woolsey.

United States Court of Claims, rules on *Zeelandia*, 454.

United States District Court, rules on alienage, 441,n.

United States Emergency Fleet Corporation, and requisitioned ships, 336.

United States Food Administration. *See* Food Administration.

United States Navy. *See* Navy Department.

United States Shipping Board, and agreement with Norway, 128,n.; seeks requisitioning of Dutch ships, 209; requisitions ships, 446-7. *See* Hurley, Edward N.

Uruguay, and U. S. call to sever relations, 26; pro-Ally, 308-9. *See* Latin America.

V

Van Aalst, Mynheer, letter to Wilson, 203-4.

Van Loon, Hendrik W., favors embargo, 70,n.

Van Tyne, Claude H., on Dutch in American revolution, 204,n.

Venezuela, and U. S. call to sever relations, 26; remains neutral, 311; bitter against U. S., 311,n.; rebuffs neutral conference, 316. *See* Latin America.

Venizelos, Eleutherios, and Greek neutrality, 18,n.

Visit and search, War Trade Board declines to, except in U. S. ports, 235; U. S. engages in, on high seas, 389, 397.

INDEX 519

W

Walsh, Thomas J. (U. S. Senator), on embargo, 65,n.
War Department, and alienage question, 436, 439, 440-2, 445-6.
War Industries Board, and blacklist, 359,n.
War Trade Board, shuns publicity, 6,n.; complicated machinery of, 9; created, 91; nature of organization and work, 92-3; and Christmas cargoes, 97; opposes embargo relaxation, 99-100,n.; opens negotiations with Nansen, 119; publishes proposals to Norway, 122; issues ultimatum to Nansen, 126-7; fairness with Norway, 134; and shift of Swedish negotiations, 152; opposes relaxation of Swedish embargo, 153-5; objects to terms of Swedish pact, 158-9; explains nature of adherence to Swedish pact, 160; accepts lenient terms for Sweden, 164; against purposeful delay of Danish negotiations, 177; and Danish negotiations re food exports, 179; approves ink for Denmark, 180,n.; relaxes embargo on Denmark, 182; ultimatum on Danish tonnage, 183; licenses iron tubing to Denmark, 186,n.; and Iceland, 189,n.; lifts embargo on nonessentials to Holland and Sweden, 206; votes for Dutch requisitioning, 210; and Dutch grain ships, 228,n.; refuses bunkers to Dutch, 229; relaxes embargo on Dutch East Indies, 231; and Dutch negotiations, 233; adheres qualifiedly to Dutch agreement, 235-6; and Swiss obligations, 257; and Swiss grain shipments, 260-1; licenses goods to Spain, 278, 290, 294; considers paper embargo for Spain, 287,n.; puts bunker pressure on Spain, 290-1; threatens bunker pressure on Spain, 295; seeks Spanish tonnage agreement, 295; lenient re Spain, 297; and A. E. F. supplies, 299-300; and bunker control, 343-5, 347-8; and blacklist, 360-2, 364-9, 376-7; and British instruction in search, 400,n.; and mandatory routing scheme, 401-3; and safe-conducts, 406; detains *Zeelandia*, 453; and propaganda, 461-2; on obligation to feed neutrals, 488,n.; records of, 493.
War Trade Intelligence Department, 391,n.
War Trade Statistical Department, 391,n.
Warren, Charles (Assistant Attorney General), on blockade, 391; on mine laying, 411,n.
Washington (State), and alienage, 445.
White list, early British suggestions re, 56; early U. S. policy on, 61; U. S. opposes, 100; U. S. uses, 361.
Whitehouse, Mrs. Norman de R. (agent of Committee on Public Information in Switzerland), on Swiss neutrality, 243-4; propaganda work in Switzerland, 268-9,n., 463-4,n.
Whittall, Commander Hugh (British officer), on Swiss neutrality, 244,n.
Willard, Joseph E. (U. S. ambassador in Spain), recommends leniency on embargo, 279; on cotton deal, 280; negotiates commercial agreement, 288; opposes tonnage demands, 289; favors stringent embargo, 290; opposes abrogating pact, 294; opposes bunker pressure, 295; favors stronger policy, 296; on encouraging Spain to enter war, 301-3. *See* Spain.
Williams, Pierce C. (U. S. commercial attaché), on Swiss importance, 246,n.
Wilson, Charles S. (U. S. chargé in Spain), recommends co-operation with Allies, 285; on interned German ships, 286-7.
Wilson, Hugh R. (U. S. chargé in Switzerland), on German threat to Swiss, 254.
Wilson, Woodrow (U. S. President), on abolition of neutrality by League, 8; leader for neutral rights, 11-3; appeals to neutrals to sever relations, 20-7; favors checkmating Mexico, 28,n.; policy of nonrecognition re Costa Rica, 29,n.; promises leniency to Holland, 49; signs Espionage Act, 69; creates and explains Exports Council, 69-70; issues first exports proclamation, 70-2; explains U. S. control policy re neutrals, 71; Germany condemns, 73; creates Exports Administrative Board and new Exports Council, 88-9; issues second exports control proclamation, 89-90; restricts monetary exports, 90,n.; creates War Trade Board, 91-2; confers with McCormick, 93,n.; signs Trading with Enemy Act, 95; establishes import control, 95-6; issues third exports control proclamation, 96; proclaims all imports and exports subject to licensing, 96; dele-

gates authority to subordinates, 110; favors food shipments for Norway, 110,n.; urges leniency in Swedish mail-pouch controversy, 147-8; favors Swedish ore purchase, 158,n.; lenient policy re Denmark, 173; opposes purposeful delay of Danish negotiations, 177-8; temporizes on Dutch requisitioning issue, 209; approves requisitioning, 211-2; defends requisitioning, 212-4; explains concessions to Dutch, 213; interested in problem of Dutch crews, 214,n.; condemned by Dutch for requisitioning, 215-6; tones down U. S. reply to Dutch, 222; edits note to Dutch, 223,n.; displeased with Dutch attitude, 229; patient with Dutch, 238; declines to remove Stovall, 247,n.; favors joint action re Spain, 285-6; addresses Mexican editors, 313,n.; favors leniency for Mexico, 318,n.; opposes Allied conference in Argentina, 331; opposes adoption of blacklist, 354,n., 358-9; objects to Lansing's draft of blacklist note, 355,n.; belatedly approves blacklist, 362-3; revises protest against British blockade, 384,n.; favors North Sea mine barrage, 410; vetoes joint representations to Norway on mine gap, 413; vetoes forcible closing of gap, 416; idealistic position on treatment of Norway, 418; dislikes postal censorship, 425; sets up Censorship Board, 426; favors continuance of censorship, 426,n.; authorizes cable censorship, 433; orders aliens released, 441-2; presses alienage issue, 443; favors justice in alienage matter, 446; supports Creel in Switzerland, 463,n.; demands honest propaganda, 463-4; administration of avoids multipartite pacts, 485-6; summary of idealistic interventions, 487-9.

Wireless censorship, 432.

Woolley, Clarence M. (of War Trade Board), acts as vice-chairman, 6,n.

Woolsey, Lester H. (Solicitor, Department of State), policy memorandum of, 58-62; on confusion in Administration, 93,n., 484,n.; on bunker control, 341-2; memorandum on blacklist, 358; on Lansing's protest against British blockade, 384,n.; memorandum on British blockade, 385-6,n.; drafts naval instructions, 387,n.; opposes mandatory routing scheme, 402-3; on safe-conducts, 405; on cable censorship, 434,n.; on alienage, 439,n., 483,n.; on requisitioning of ships, 448; on detention of Swedish motorships, 453; on soliciting information from Danish masters, 459,n.

Y

Yucatán, and sisal problem, 326-30, 486.

Z

Zeelandia, detained Dutch ship, 226,n., 453-5, 466.